S0-ACF-428

Laura Mader
Homeroom 308

GREGG SPEED BUILDING

Diamond Jubilee Series

GREGG SPEED BUILDING

JOHN R. GREGG

LOUIS A. LESLIE

CHARLES E. ZOUBEK

Shorthand written by Charles Rader

Diamond Jubilee Series

GREGG DIVISION

McGraw-Hill Book Company

New York Chicago San Francisco Dallas
Toronto London

GREGG SPEED BUILDING, DIAMOND JUBILEE SERIES

 Library of Congress Catalog Card Number 64-16290.

3 4 5 6 7 8 9 RRD-64 2 1 0 9 8 7 6 5

24600

Preface

Gregg Speed Building, Diamond Jubilee Series, is an advanced shorthand textbook that has for its major objectives the further development of the student's shorthand skill and of his ability to produce letters that are rapidly and accurately transcribed on the typewriter, correctly spelled and punctuated, and attractively placed on letterheads.

Gregg Speed Building, like the other volumes of the Diamond Jubilee Series, is lesson planned. It contains 4 parts, divided into 16 chapters, which in turn are divided into 80 lessons. *Gregg Speed Building, Diamond Jubilee Series,* contains the following features that are designed to help the student achieve the objectives stated above:

SHORTHAND SKILL DEVELOPMENT

The student's ability to construct outlines under the stress of dictation is developed through the following features:

Cycle of Review Drills. Each of the 16 chapters contains a five-drill review cycle as follows:

LESSON 1: *Outline Construction.* These drills enable the student to take greater advantage of the principle of analogy in outline construction.

LESSON 2: *Recall Drill.* These drills review all the situations in which the letters of the shorthand alphabet are used.

LESSON 3: *Word Families.* The words in each family contain a common word-building problem. By practicing these words as a group, the student is able to make further use of the principle of analogy.
Frequent Names. These drills teach the student fluent outlines for common last names and for common first names of men and women.

LESSON 4: *Frequent Phrases.* These drills review the most frequently used business-letter phrases.
Geographical Expressions. These drills teach the student fluent outlines for many geographical expressions.

LESSON 5: *Word Beginnings and Endings.* These drills review all the word beginnings and endings of Gregg Shorthand.

Charts. At the end of each of the first four chapters, there is a chart of brief-form derivatives. On the inside back cover, there is a complete list of the brief forms given in alphabetic order.

Connected Practice Material. *Gregg Speed Building* contains 68,538 words of practice material – 39,686 in shorthand and 28,852 in type. The practice material consists of modern, representative business letters and articles that have been chosen not only for their shorthand values but for their informative and inspirational content as well. The practice material in each chapter is devoted to a specific line of business or a specific industry.

Reading and Writing Practice. Each lesson contains a Reading and Writing Practice in shorthand containing from 300 to 600 words.

Writing Practice. Each second, third, and fourth lesson contains a Writing Practice consisting of several letters in type. The letters are counted in such a way that the teacher may dictate them either separately, to develop speed by short spurts, or consecutively, to develop endurance. Each Writing Practice is preceded by a preview.

Progressive Speed Builder. The fifth lesson of each chapter contains a Progressive Speed Builder designed to force the student's speed. Each Progressive Speed Builder contains five one-minute letters (preceded by a shorthand preview) counted at progressively increasing speeds.

The speeds of the Progressive Speed Builders increase after each four chapters, until in Chapters 13 through 16 the student is writing at the rates of 120, 125, 130, 135, and 140 words a minute.

The letters in each Progressive Speed Builder are related to the same transaction and contain substantially the same vocabulary. Consequently, after the student has taken from dictation the first letter in the Progressive Speed Builder, his problem in taking the succeeding, faster letters is simplified.

TRANSCRIPTION SKILL DEVELOPMENT

Gregg Speed Building, Diamond Jubilee Series, continues to develop the student's mastery of the nonshorthand factors of transcription through the following features:

Punctuation. In Chapters 1 through 4 the punctuation pointers presented earlier in the student's stenographic course are reviewed. In Chapter 5 more advanced points of punctuation are presented. In every Reading and Writing Practice punctuation marks are encircled in color, and a brief explanation of the reason for the use of each mark is indicated directly above the encircled mark.

Spelling. Words that often cause transcription difficulty have been selected from the Reading and Writing Practice exercises and appear in type in the left margins of the shorthand.

Typing Style. All the Typing Style suggestions that the student has previously studied are reviewed. In addition, several new, more advanced Typing Style suggestions are provided.

Vocabulary Building. Many of the lessons contain words or expressions, selected from the Reading and Writing Practice, that may be unfamiliar to the student. These words and expressions are defined briefly.

The first lesson of each chapter, beginning with Chapter Six, contains a Similar-Words Drill that alerts the student to pairs of words that stenographers often mistranscribe because of their similarity of sound.

Accuracy Practice. The second lesson in each chapter, beginning with Chapter Six, contains an Accuracy Practice that stresses the importance of proper proportion.

Secretarial Tips. Throughout the book the student will find secretarial tips that provide information that will be helpful to him when he becomes a transcriber on the job.

OTHER FEATURES

Model Letters. The student is supplied with several letter models that show the commonest letter setups used in business.

Part Openings. Each of the four parts opens with a discussion of some phase of shorthand speed development or transcription and gives the student helpful suggestions on such topics as self-dictation, devising shortcuts, etc.

Photographs That Teach. Many photographs of "office workers in action" appear throughout the book. The photographs not only brighten the appearance of the book but also teach the student something as well.

Appendix. The Appendix contains a complete review, in list form, of all the word beginnings, word endings, and phrasing principles of Gregg Shorthand. In addition, the Appendix contains a list of addresses that are to be used by the student in transcription.

SUPPLEMENTARY LETTERS

In the *Instructor's Handbook to Gregg Speed Building, Diamond Jubilee Series,* there are two counted supplementary letters for each of the eighty lessons in the text – 160 letters in all, containing approximately 20,000 words of dictation. The letters for each lesson in the *Handbook* are answers to, or are related to, the letters in the corresponding lessons in *Gregg Speed Building.* Addresses to be used by the students when transcribing these letters are provided on pages 504-509 of the text.

The authors are confident that *Gregg Speed Building, Diamond Jubilee Series,* will enable teachers to do an even more effective job of developing rapid and efficient transcribers.

Louis A. Leslie
Charles E. Zoubek

Contents

PART ONE

Sales Promotion
Insurance
Finance
Food

SELF-DICTATION

As you have no doubt discovered, a major factor in your shorthand speed development is large quantities of the right kind of dictation. The more dictation practice you get, the more rapidly will your shorthand speed increase.

Of course, you will receive a great deal of dictation practice in class, and it is there that your greatest growth will take place.

However, if you can supplement that class dictation with additional practice at home, your progress will be even more rapid.

There are a number of ways in which you can obtain this additional dictation practice:

1. Appoint a member of the family as a dictator. This, however, has some disadvantages: first, a member of the family may not be available when you want to practice; and, second, his inexperience as a dictator may retard rather than increase your shorthand speed.

2. Use the television or the radio. In general, people on television and radio speak too rapidly, with the result that your efforts in trying to "take" them may be discouraging. However, you may occasionally be able to tune in on someone who speaks approximately at your dictation speed.

3. Use records and tapes. This is by far the most satisfactory way to obtain home dictation practice. There is available today a large selection of records and tapes. Their use has two definite advantages: first, you can choose records and tapes that contain dictation within the range of speed that you are writing;

and second, the material on them is dictated by experienced dictators. Ask your teacher about the dictation records and tapes that are on the market.

4. Use the "self-dictation" method that will enable you to practice by yourself. Here are the steps you should follow:

(a) Select a magazine or other reading matter that is printed in a fairly large-size type. (Full-page advertisements in some of the leading national magazines are ideal for this purpose.) Select material that deals with many different types of subject matter — automobiles, radios, books, airplanes, etc. — so that you will encounter the widest possible vocabulary.

(b) Read through the material quickly to be sure that you can write the outlines for each word. If you find you do not know the outlines for some of the vocabulary, look up those words in the Gregg Shorthand Dictionary or construct an outline of your own. By thus eliminating all the stumbling blocks, you will be able to write continuously as you dictate to yourself.

(c) Read the material aloud at the fastest rate that you can write fairly good notes, and write slightly below the words that you read. The exact point at which you write each outline is not important.

This type of self-dictation may seem a little strange to you during the first few attempts, but you will soon be able to adjust your self-dictation to the speed that you can write.

(d) After you have self-dictated the material once, redictate it a second time, faster. Write over the outlines that you originally wrote.

(e) Occasionally dictate a piece of material slowly, striving for perfection of outline rather than for increase of speed.

On page 12 you will find an illustration of how your "self-dictation" will look.

Whenever you have the urge to practice at home, try this method of self-dictation; you will be pleased with the effect it will have on your shorthand writing speed.

The daily newspaper and the weekly or monthly magazine are so often taken for granted. Many people have no idea of all the work that must go into any printed page.

The first job in getting together a printed page belongs to the editorial staff. The editor and his assistants must decide what articles and pictures they want to go into their particular magazine and go about getting the articles written and the pictures taken. Then the typist must prepare the manuscript, keeping careful count of the length of each typescript or copy, as it is often called in the printing world. Then an array of editors, artists and layout men consult over the way each article is to be presented and the sequence the articles will take.

When the copy has been marked up and the pictures engraved, the next phase of the job is the printer's. A printer is extremely proud of his job and carefully checks all the markings the editor has made for him on the copy. He then sets his typesetting machine accordingly. Most type is set by a Linotype machine, which is operated almost like a typewriter. The printer sits at his machine and types the copy while metal letters fall into place in the machine. When one line has been typed, the printer presses a long lever and molten lead falls into each mold and casts what is known as a slug. Each line of type appears on a slug, which is next placed into a long metal tray, known as the galley tray.

After the copy has been set in this way, the printer hands this galley tray to a young apprentice who rolls ink over the type and "pulls" a proof of the galley. The proof is carefully

Illustration of Self-Dictation

CHAPTER 1

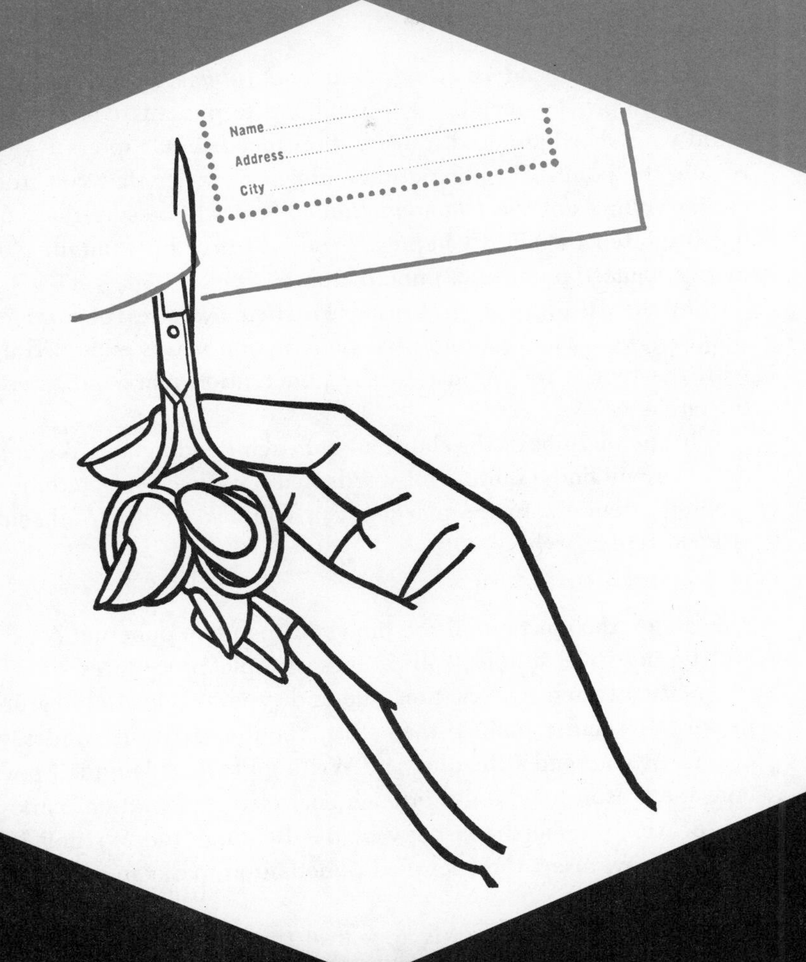

Sales Promotion

Punctuation Brushup

In *Gregg Speed Building, Diamond Jubilee Series,* you will continue to improve your ability to spell and to punctuate as you strive to build your shorthand and transcription speed. In Chapters 1-4 you will review the points of punctuation and typing styles that you studied in earlier volumes of the *Diamond Jubilee Series* to be sure that you have not forgotten them. In Chapter 5 you will take up a number of new, more advanced pointers of punctuation.

In the Reading and Writing Practice exercises in *Gregg Speed Building,* you will again find the punctuation marks encircled in color, with the reason for the use of the punctuation mark indicated above the circle.

In the margins of the shorthand of each Reading and Writing Practice, you will find a number of words that have been selected for special spelling attention. In the margins you will also find helpful reminders of good typing style.

How to Practice

To get the most out of the time you spend on punctuation, spelling, and typing-style studies, follow these simple procedures:

1. Read each punctuation rule and typing-style study carefully to be sure you understand it; then study the illustrative examples.

2. As you read a Reading and Writing Practice (aloud, if possible), note the reason for the use of each encircled punctuation mark.

3. Make a shorthand copy of the Reading and Writing Practice. As you copy, insert the encircled punctuation marks in your shorthand notes.

4. When spelling words appear at the left of the shorthand pages of your textbook, spell them aloud, if possible, pausing slightly after each syllable. Spelling aloud helps to impress the correct spelling on your mind.

5. When typing-style pointers appear at the left of the shorthand pages under the heading "Transcribe," be sure you understand them so that you can apply them when you transcribe.

In the lessons of Chapter 1 you will review the following ten very common uses of the comma:

, parenthetical

par
(,)

A word, phrase, or clause that is not necessary to the grammatical completeness of the thought of the sentence should be set off by commas. If the expression occurs at the beginning or end of a sentence, only one comma is needed.

> I cannot, however, make you any promises.
> I think we can please you, too.

, apposition

ap
(,)

Expressions that identify or explain other expressions should be set off by commas. If the expression occurs at the end of a sentence, only one comma is needed.

> Mr. Green, the treasurer of the company, is home ill.
> I will see you on Friday, March 14.

, series

ser
(,)

When the last member of a series of three or more items is preceded by a conjunction, place a comma before the conjunction as well as between the other items.

> Harry sells books, supplies, and stationery.
> I talked to him on January 1, on March 11, and on May 16.

, conjunction

conj
(,)

A comma is used to separate two independent clauses that are joined by a conjunction.

> He purchased the television set on March 18, and our serviceman installed it on March 20.
> I think I can be with you for the opening of the exhibit, but I will not be sure until I hear from the president.

, and omitted and o

When two or more adjectives modify the same noun, they are separated by commas.

He is a quiet, efficient man.

The comma is not used, however, if the first adjective modifies the combined idea of the second adjective plus the noun.

The book was bound in an attractive blue cloth.

, nonrestrictive nonr

A nonrestrictive clause or phrase — one that can be omitted without changing the meaning of a sentence — should be set off by commas.

Mr. Green, who has been with the firm since 1950, will retire soon.

, when clause when **, as clause** as **, if clause** if **, introductory** intro

A comma is used to separate a dependent clause from a following main clause. A comma is also used after such introductory expressions as *frankly, consequently, on the contrary*.

When I have more information, I will write you.
As you know, John was elected president.
If ten o'clock is not a convenient time, please let me know.
Before I leave on Friday, I will sign the papers.
Frankly, I cannot agree with you.
On the contrary, he is the one who is wrong.

Developing Shorthand Writing Power

1. OUTLINE CONSTRUCTION

The first lesson in each chapter contains a number of principles of outline construction. Your ability to apply these principles will play an important part in developing your power to construct outlines for new words that you encounter during dictation.

In practicing the lists of words that follow, as well as the lists of words in succeeding lessons, use this procedure:

1. Cover the type key and read the shorthand outlines.
2. When you come to an outline you cannot read, spell it.
3. If the spelling does not immediately give you the meaning of the outline, refer to the type key. Don't spend more than a few seconds trying to decipher an outline.

At this stage of your shorthand study, you should be able to read any word or phrase list in *Gregg Speed Building* in a minute or two.

Omission of vowel from -er, -ar, -or. When the endings *-er, -ar, -or* are not stressed or accented, the vowel is omitted from those endings.

-er

a

-ar

b

-or

c

a. Binder, folder, retailer, cover, manner, printer.
b. Similar, sugar, grammar, popular, dollar.
c. Factor, supervisor, humor, operator, error, honor.

Inclusion of vowel in -er. When the ending *-er* is stressed or accented, the vowel is written. It is also written in derivatives of words ending in accented *er,* even though the *e* may no longer be accented in the derivatives.

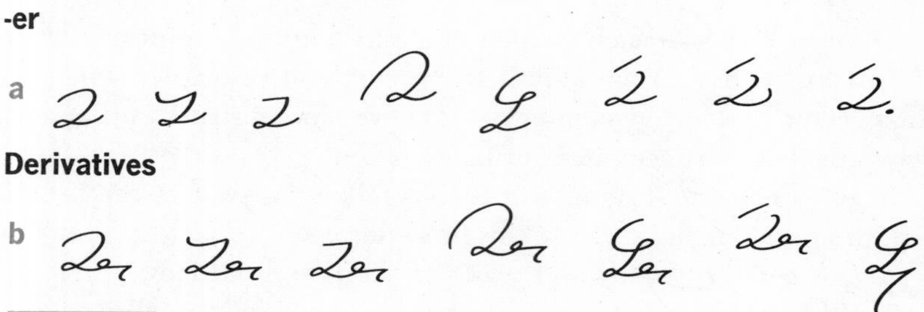

a. Confer, refer, infer, defer, prefer, transfer, transferred, transferring.
b. Conference, reference, inference, deference, preference, transference, preferable.

Building Transcription Skills

2. BUSINESS VOCABULARY BUILDER

The Business Vocabulary Builders are intended to improve your command of business terminology. Be sure you study each Business Vocabulary Builder before you begin your work on the Reading and Writing Practice.

centralized heating The heating of several units, such as rooms, floors, or even buildings, from one source, such as a boiler or a power station.

managerial caliber The capacity or ability to lead people or to run a business.

vocation Occupation; profession.

Reading and Writing Practice

Reading and copying a great deal of well-written shorthand, such as that in the Reading and Writing Practice exercises, will help your skill grow rapidly. Be sure you read each Reading and Writing Practice before you make a shorthand copy of it.

3. Advertising

1880

Bathroom facilities

30%

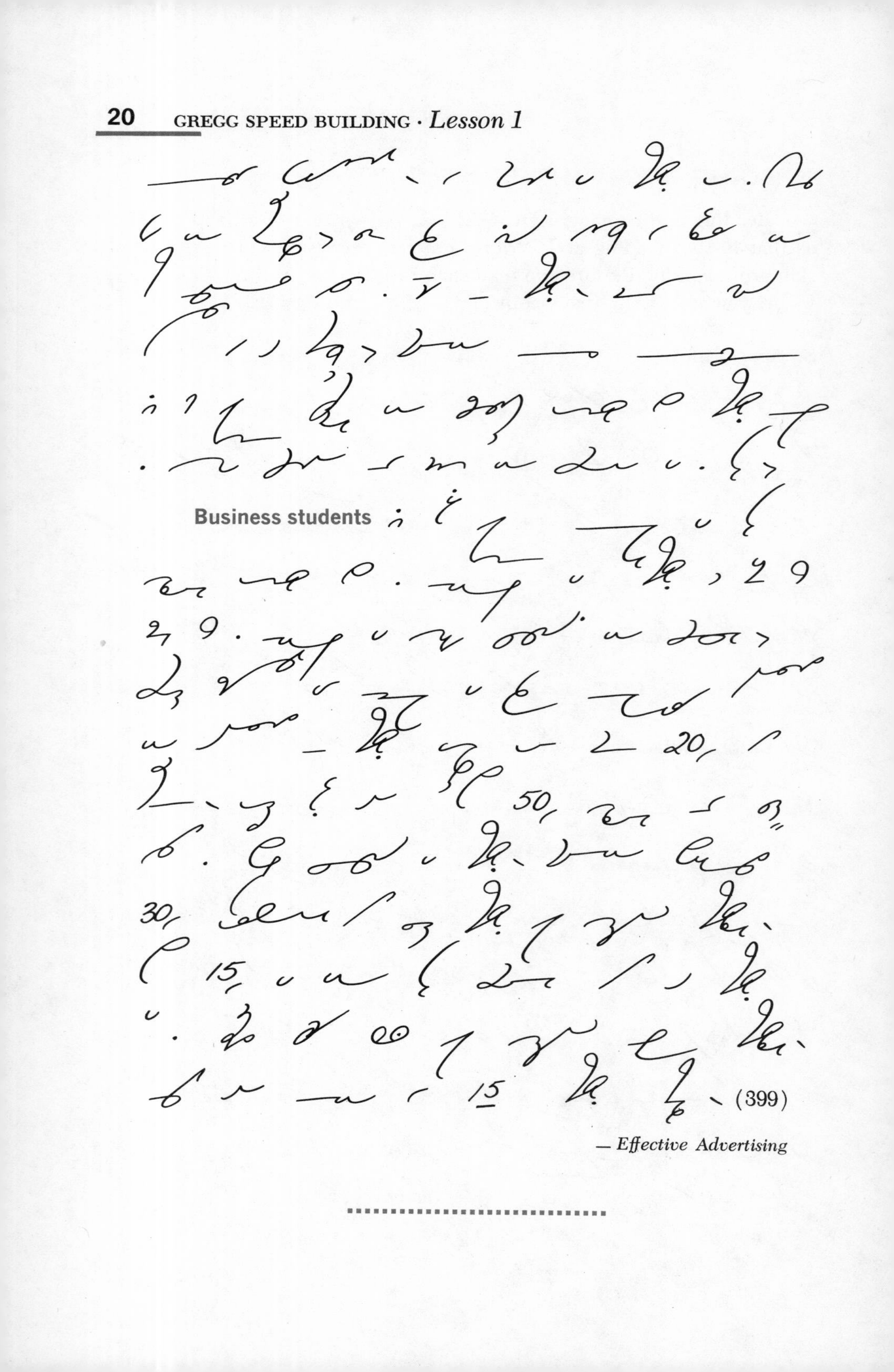

Business students

(399)

— *Effective Advertising*

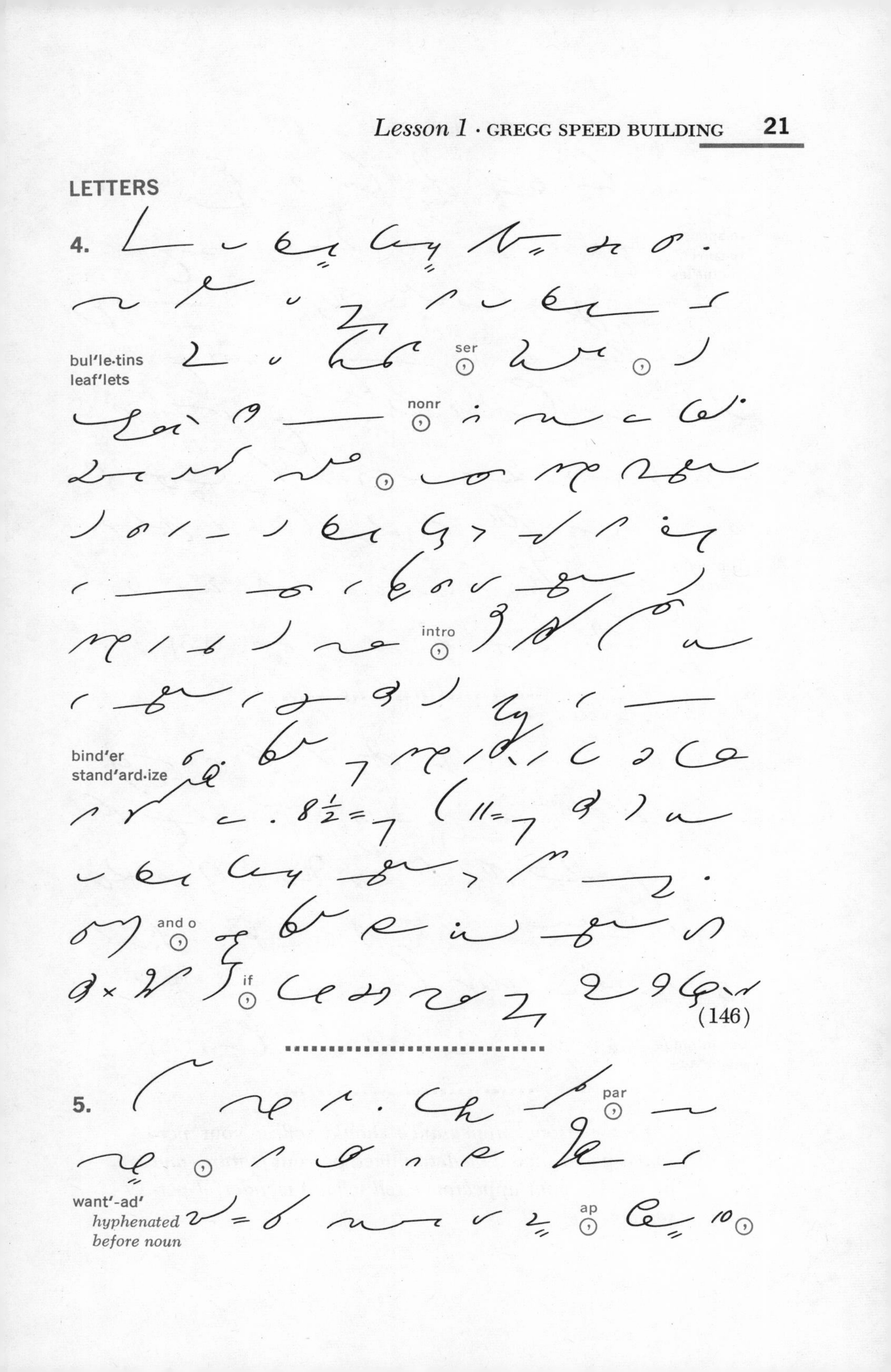

LETTERS

4.

bul'le·tins
leaf'lets

ser

nonr

intro

bind'er
stand'ard·ize

$8\frac{1}{2}$ 11

and o

if

(146)

5.

par

want'-ad'
hyphenated before noun

ap

10

re·sponse′
re·ceived′
in·quir′ies

conj

Trib′une's
source

(123)

6.

ap

as

par

and o

be·gin′ning
en·joy′a·ble

(78)

Your personal appearance should reflect your *personality and should be determined by your features and figure. Let your appearance tell what a wonderful person you are!*

LESSON 2

Developing Shorthand Writing Power

7. RECALL DRILL — SH

This drill illustrates the different situations in which the *sh* stroke is used in Gregg Shorthand. Read from the shorthand, referring to the key whenever you cannot immediately read an outline.

Sh

a

-ish

b

-tion, etc.

c

-tial, -cial

d

-ship

e

a. Show, sharp, shield, shares, shirt, shoe, appreciate, rush, shake.
b. Furnish, finish, abolish, vanish, blemish, Spanish, accomplish.
c. Conditions, addition, instruction, national, illustration, production.
d. Special, commercial, substantial, official, social, initialed, credential, partial.
e. Relationship, hardship, friendship, workmanship, partnership, authorship.

Building Transcription Skills

8. BUSINESS VOCABULARY BUILDER

copy *(in advertising)* Reading matter, usually typewritten, that is to be set in type.

allocate To distribute as a share.

appropriation An amount of money set aside for a special purpose.

Writing Practice

The second, third, and fourth lessons of each chapter contain business letters in type, preceded by a preview in shorthand of the more difficult words and phrases that occur in those letters. If you practice this preview before you take the letters from dictation, you should be able to take the letters without difficulty.

Follow the suggestions for practice given in paragraph 1 of Lesson 1. In addition, make one copy of the entire list.

9. PREVIEW

Note: The numbers in the preview refer to the letters from which the words and phrases have been selected.

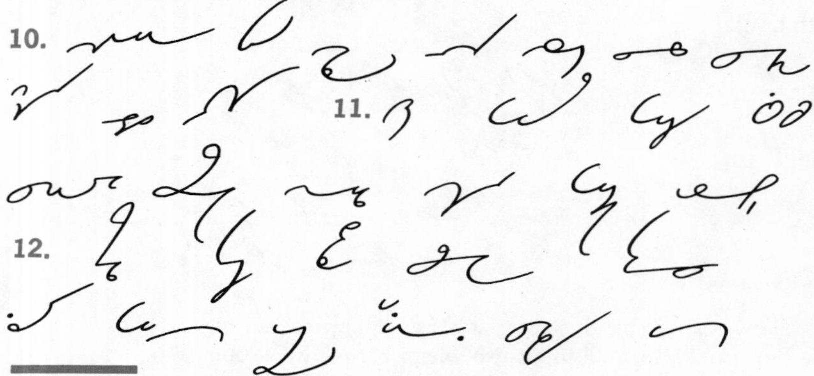

10. Control, beyond, compelled, enclosed, careful, immediately, I am sure, understand, necessity, at this time.

11. Thank you for, promptly, proceed, highway, accordance, available, closely, confident, profitable, relationship.
12. Agency, benefit, experience, example, businessman, he wanted, program, revealed, overhauling, accepted, organization.

LETTERS

Note: Each small raised number represents 20 standard words.

10. Mr. Shields: Conditions beyond our control have compelled us to raise our commercial advertising rates sharply.[1] Please give the enclosed rate card your careful attention. The new rates are going into effect immediately.[2]

I am sure that our customers will understand the necessity for raising rates at this time. Harry P. Green.[3]

---

11. Dear Mr. Sharp: Thank you for sending us your contract so promptly. We will proceed with the building of the special[4] highway signs advertising your cars.

In accordance with the contract, we will do the following:

1. We will erect[5] the signs in the best available spots.
2. We will keep them in good condition for five years.
3. In preparing[6] the copy for the advertising on the signs, we will follow closely the instructions in the contract.

We[7] are confident that this will be the start of a long, profitable relationship for both of us. Sincerely,[8]

---

12. Dear Mr. Price: Our advertising agency does more than write copy to sell your products. It gives you the[9] benefit of the experience of its large staff.

For example, a short time ago a businessman came to[10] us with a new product that he planned to put on the market. He wanted to start an immediate national[11] advertising program. Our Research Department revealed that his product was overpriced and poorly designed, and[12] we pointed out ways in which it could be improved. We suggested a complete overhauling of the product itself[13] before releasing a program of advertising. Our client accepted our suggestions and saved himself[14] a good deal of hardship and money.

This is just one illustration of the type of service you will receive if[15] you entrust our organization with the advertising of your products. Very cordially yours,[16] (320)

Reading and Writing Practice

13.

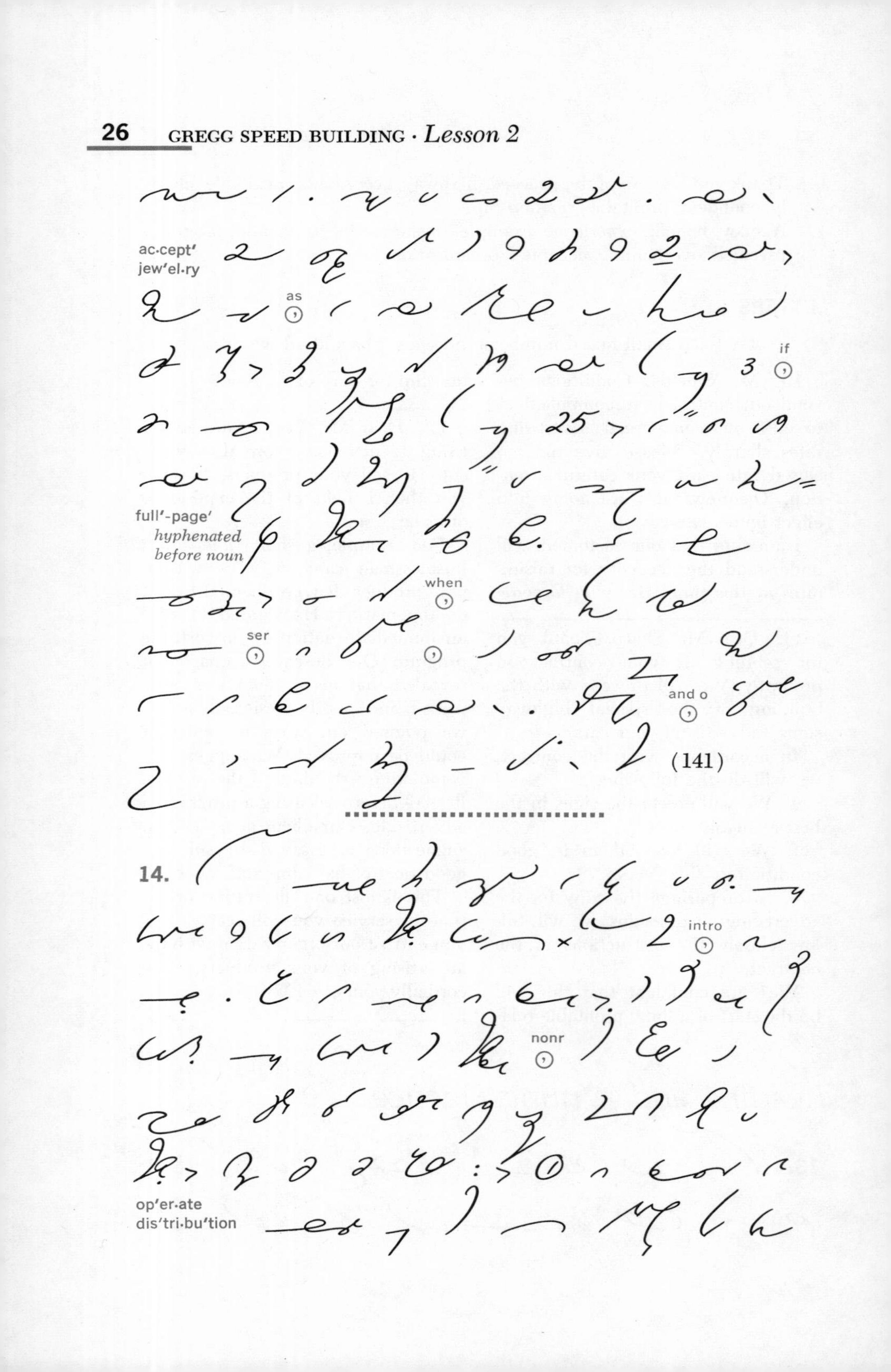

ac·cept'
jew'el·ry

as

if

full'-page'
hyphenated before noun

when

ser

and o

(141)

14.

intro

nonr

op'er·ate
dis'tri·bu'tion

conj

films
a'rea

intro

(144)

15.

past
a·nal'y·sis
in·quir'y

intro

ap

al'lo·cate
sub·stan'tial

(128)

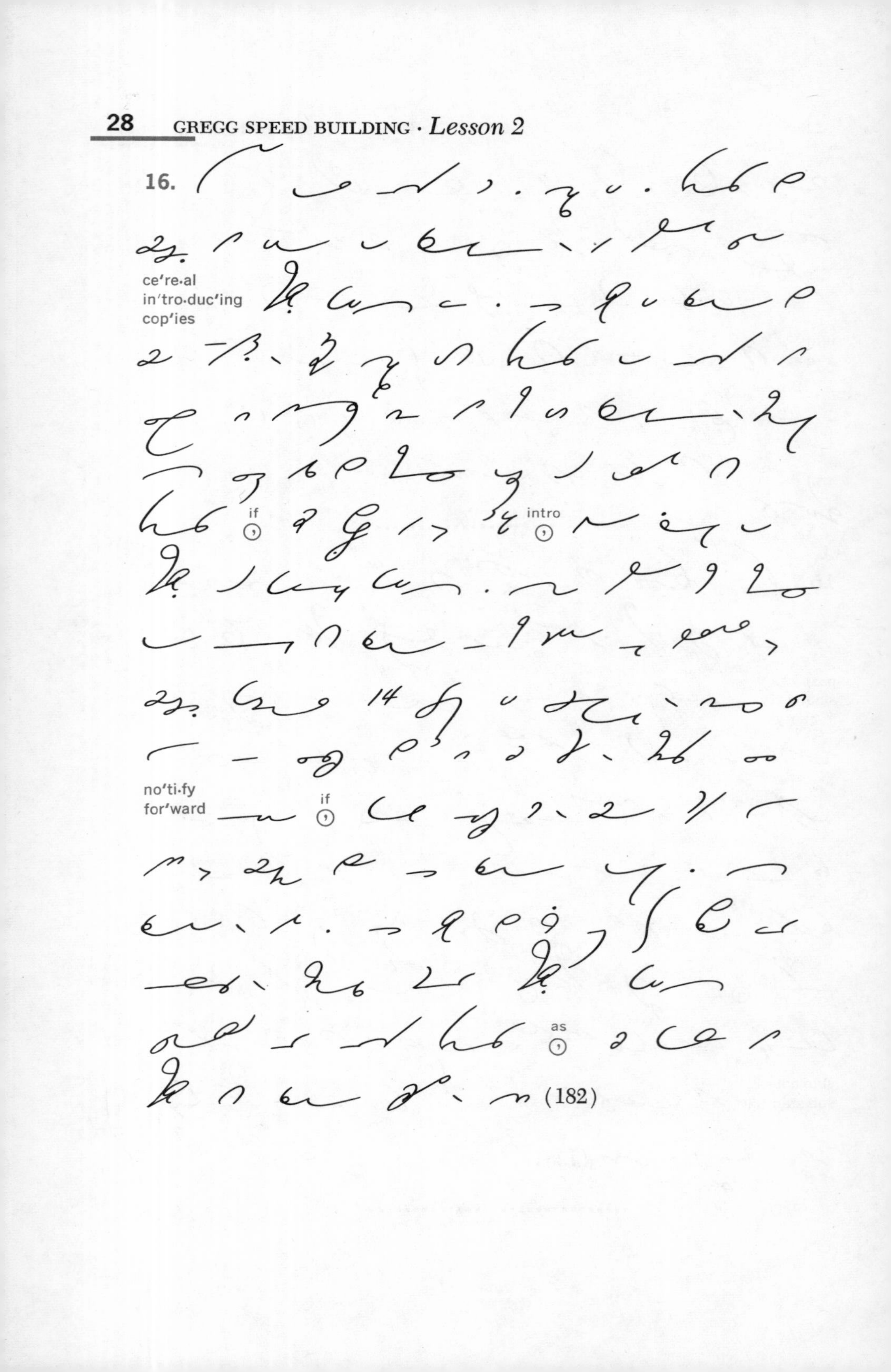

16.

ce′re·al
in′tro·duc′ing
cop′ies

if

intro

no′ti·fy
for′ward

if

as

(182)

Developing Shorthand Writing Power

17. WORD FAMILIES

Word families enable you to take advantage of analogy in the construction of shorthand outlines for new words. You will find a number of word families in the third lesson of each chapter. Read the shorthand words in each family. Refer to the key whenever you cannot immediately read an outline.

-tified

a

-sive

b

a. Gratified, notified, fortified, justified, identified, testified.
b. Extensive, impressive, inexpensive, expensive, intensive, defensive, offensive.

18. FREQUENT NAMES

In the third lesson of each chapter you will also find (1) a number of frequently used last names and (2) a number of frequently used women's names or frequently used men's names.

Simply read through the list, referring to the key whenever you cannot immediately read a name.

Last Names

a

Women's First Names

b

a. Adams, Anderson, Baker, Barry, Becker, Bennett, Brennan, Brown.
b. Adeline, Agnes, Amelia, Annabell, Barbara.

Building Transcription Skills

19. BUSINESS VOCABULARY BUILDER

extensive Broad; wide

prospect file List of potential customers.

justified Proved to be just.

Writing Practice

20. PREVIEW

21.

22.

23.

21. As you know, manufacturers, extensive, equipment, gratified, during the past, handle, qualifications, interested, interview, grateful.
22. I wish, to thank you for the, completeness, accuracy, requirements, program, efficient, relationship.
23. Effective, persuade, assembled, successful, many of these.

LETTERS

21. Dear Mr. Baker: As you know, we are manufacturers of an extensive line of farm equipment. We have[1] been extremely gratified with the increase in our business during the past few years, and we have decided to[2] open a branch in the Middle West. To handle the sales promotion of our line, we shall need a man to fill the[3] position of sales manager.

If you know of a man who seems to have the qualifications and who is[4] interested, please ask him to submit his application. I will then arrange an interview for him.

Needless[5] to say, Mr. Baker, we shall be extremely grateful for any help you can give us. Yours very truly,[6]

---

22. Dear Mr. Barry: I wish to take this opportunity to thank you for the completeness and accuracy[7] with which you have taken care of our requirements. We are especially gratified with the fine manner in[8] which you have kept our prospect file. As you know, this file represents our most important source of new business.

The success[9] of our advertising and promotion program depends in a large measure on your efficient service.

It[10] is our hope that we may continue our pleasant business relationship for many years. Very cordially yours,[11]

---

23. Dear Mr. Anderson: Are you looking for effective sales letters that you can use to get direct orders, obtain[12] leads for your salesmen, or persuade dealers to purchase your line?

We have carefully assembled a binder of[13] more than 300 of the most successful sales letters submitted to us in recent years. Every one of[14] these letters is a winner. With minor changes you can use many of these sales letters in your own business.

The[15] binder costs $10.50. A single letter selected and used by you will more than repay the cost.[16] If you will return the attached postal card, we shall gladly send you the binder on approval. Cordially yours,[17] (340)

Reading and Writing Practice

24.

per·mis'sion
tes'ti·mo'ni·al

as

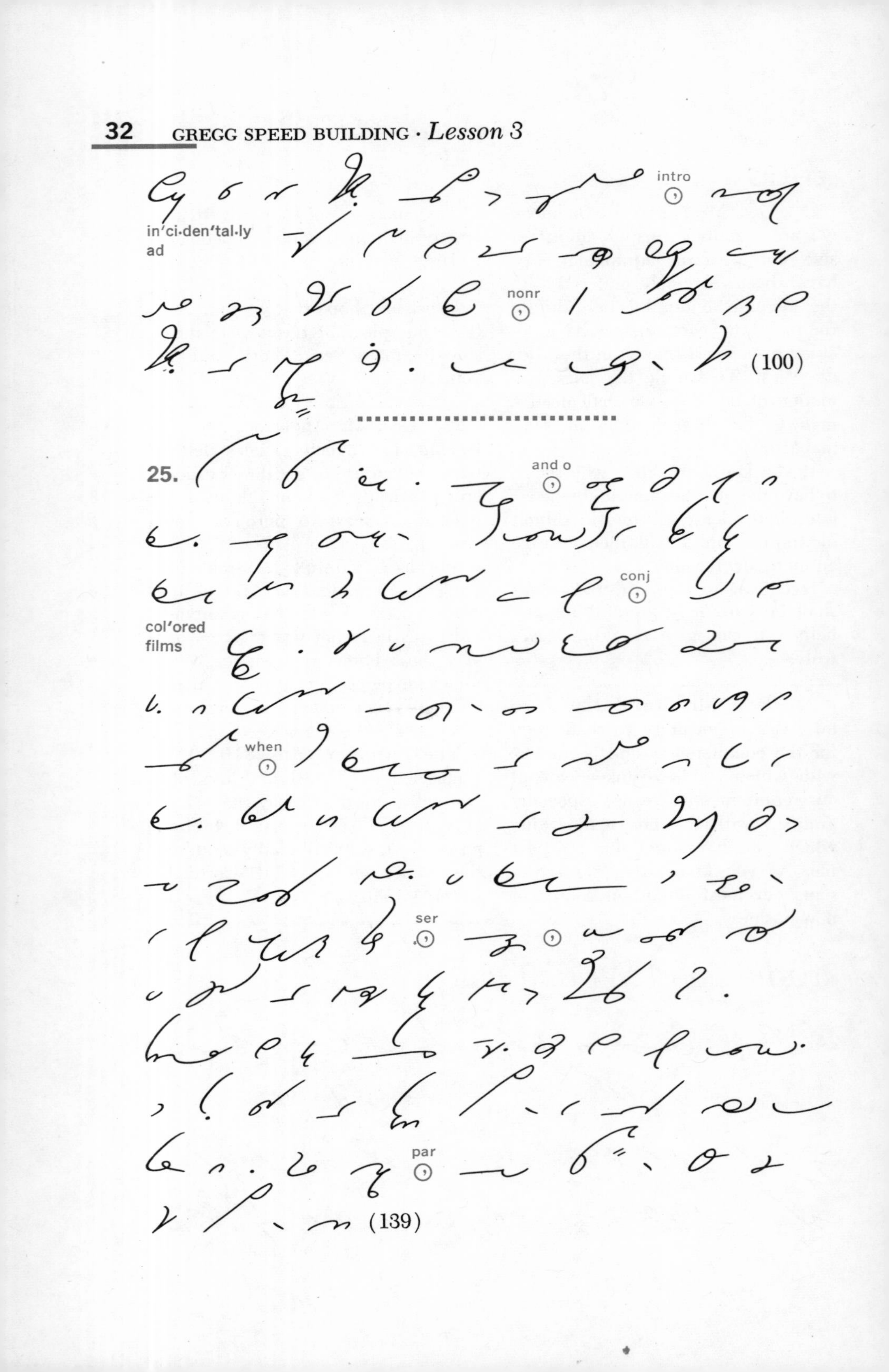

intro

in′ci·den′tal·ly

ad

nonr

(100)

25.

and o

conj

col′ored films

when

ser

par

(139)

26.

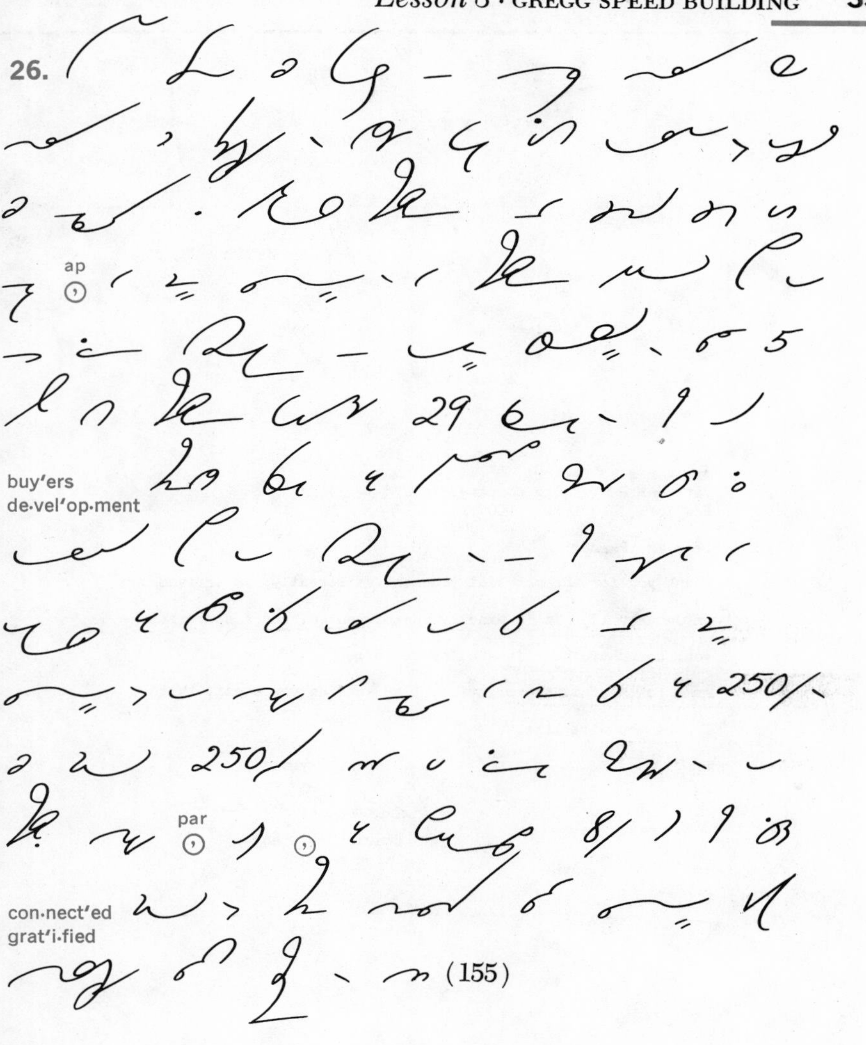

When your boss or the person who is training you explains the work, do not be afraid to ask questions. No one expects you to absorb all the details of a job immediately. Asking pertinent questions is a sign of intelligence.

SPLANE & GARDNER, INC.

SPECIALISTS IN INVESTMENTS

1238 CAPITOL AVENUE • LITTLE ROCK, ARKANSAS • FRANKLIN 2-4201

January 28, 19--

Mr. James R. Parker
National Publishing Company, Inc.
New York, New York 10077

Dear Mr. Parker:

Thank you for the material you sent me recently; it arrived on January 12. It is exactly what I wanted, and I appreciate your thoughtfulness in sending it to me.

As a token of my appreciation, I am sending you a gift that I hope you will like.

Sincerely yours,

Charles R. Grant

Charles R. Grant
Sales Manager

CRG:LEA

Short Letter—Double Spaced
Blocked Style
Standard Punctuation

Developing Shorthand Writing Power

27. FREQUENT PHRASES

The fourth lesson in each chapter contains illustrations of a number of useful phrasing principles. As you are already familiar with these phrases, they are given here for a quick review. You should be able to read these phrases in half a minute or less.

Been

a. Who have been, you have been, I have been, have not been, would have been, could have been, he might have been, has been, it has been.
b. Week ago, some time ago, months ago, years ago, days ago.

28. GEOGRAPHICAL EXPRESSIONS

The fourth lesson in each chapter also contains a list of geographical expressions, divided into three parts—names of: (1) cities containing a common beginning or ending; (2) states; and (3) foreign countries or foreign cities.

Read through the list quickly. You will find several of these geographical expressions in the practice material of this lesson and of the following lessons.

-field

a

States

b

Foreign Countries

c

a. Springfield, Plainfield, Greenfield, Fairfield, Winfield, Westfield.
b. South Dakota, North Carolina, Missouri, Kentucky, Delaware, Connecticut, Massachusetts.
c. Argentina, Australia, Belgium, Bolivia, Brazil, Canada.

Building Transcription Skills

29. BUSINESS VOCABULARY BUILDER

organization chart A chart showing the structure of a business or department and indicating the person to whom each employee reports.

creative Having the power to originate.

fundamentally Basically; essentially.

Writing Practice

30. PREVIEW

31.

32.

33.

31. Include, bulletin, sketch, who have been, understand, experience, essential, picture.
32. Considerable, progress, $1,000,000, next year, required, continued, strengthening, duplication, personnel, I shall be glad.
33. In time, part, 10 a.m., helpful, previous, meetings, editorial, forward.

LETTERS

31. Mr. Davis: As you know, we try to include in the monthly company bulletin a brief sketch of the salesmen[1] who have been added to the staff recently. I understand that about a week ago you added two men[2] to your department and that they will represent your department in Bolivia and Brazil.

Would you please let[3] me have a few lines about each man. I should like to have some information about the experience of each[4] and the type of work he will do. Even though it is not essential, please include a recent picture of each if you[5] have one conveniently available.

Can you let me have this material by April 1? Agnes Trees[6]

---

32. To the Staff: As you know, considerable progress has been made toward the achievement of the $1,000,000[7] sales goal we have set for ourselves for next year. Much planning and building and hard work will be required to reach this goal;[8] but with the continued strengthening of our sales efforts, we should be able to realize it.

At the last meeting[9] of the Planning Committee, several decisions were made that should strengthen our staff further and help us avoid[10] duplication. These changes, which will be effective on September 1, are indicated in the enclosed[11] organization chart.

If any of the changes described on the chart are not clear to any of the personnel[12] affected by them, I shall be glad to hear from these persons and answer any questions they may have. John A. Smith[13]

---

33. To the Sales Staff. Our annual sales conference will be held this year in Springfield, Massachusetts, from August 4[14] to 15. Please arrange your travel plans so that you will be in Springfield in time to take part in the first session[15] at 10 a.m. on Monday, August 4. It is our hope that this sales meeting will be even more helpful than our [16] previous meetings.

Before you come to Springfield, be prepared to discuss three things:

1. Your most important sales problems.[17]

2. Your most important editorial needs.

3. Your most important general problems.

Our meetings will be[18] held at the Hotel Westfield.

I am looking forward to seeing you all at the sales conference. James R. Ramsey[19] (380)

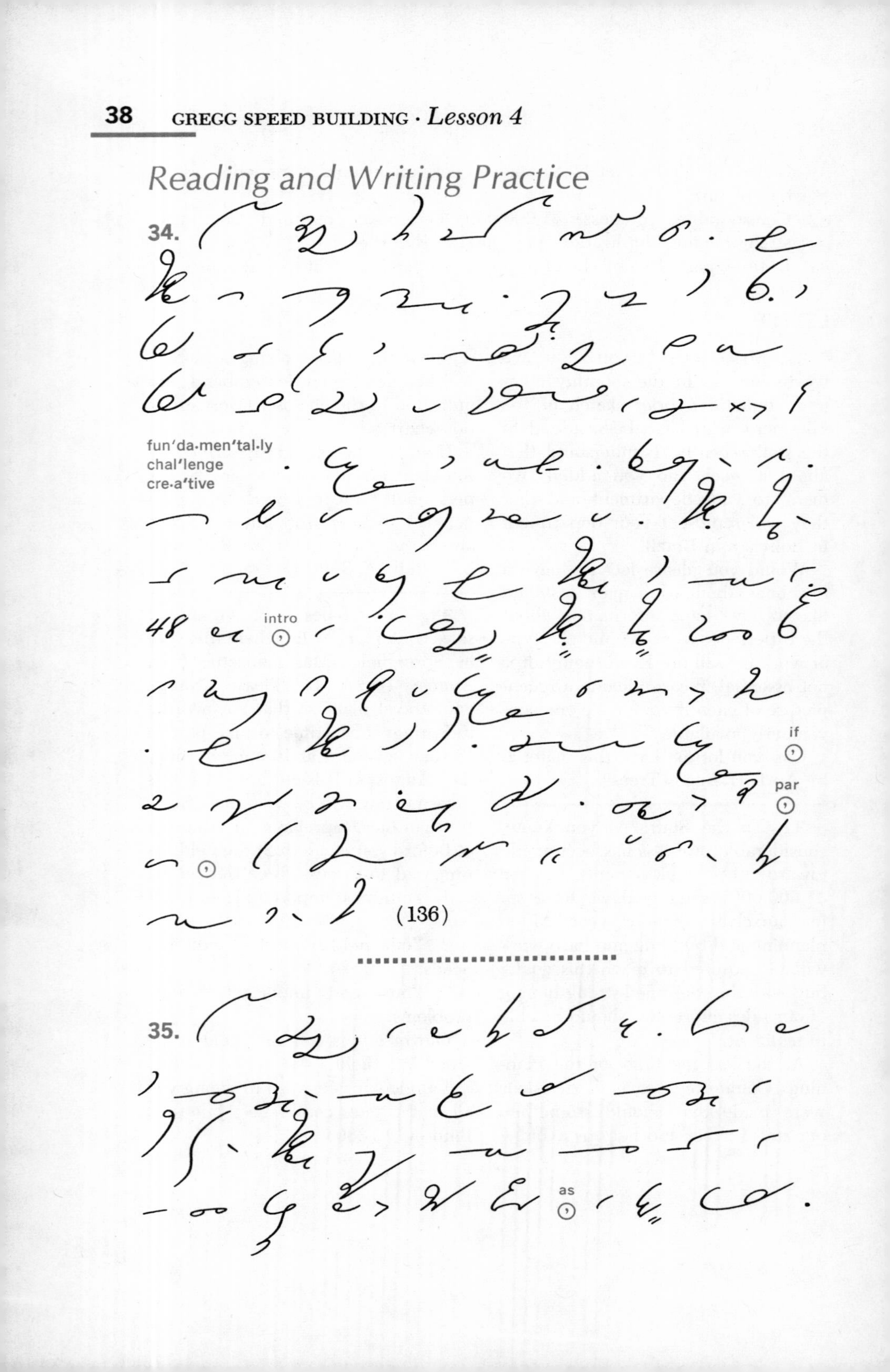

Reading and Writing Practice

34.

fun'da·men'tal·ly
chal'lenge
cre·a'tive

48

intro

if

par

(136)

35.

as

its
me'di·um
par'tial·ly

if

when

(126)

36.

as

and o

de·pend'a·ble
clas'si·fied

as

cov'er·age
in'flu·ence
es·pe'cial·ly

intro

par

ad·vice′
their

par

(197)

37.

ap

par

as

well′-known′
hyphenated before noun

and o

(116)

LESSON 5

Developing Shorthand Writing Power

38. WORD BEGINNINGS AND ENDINGS

The fifth lesson in each chapter contains a number of word beginnings and endings for quick review. You should be able to read all the words in the following list in thirty seconds or less.

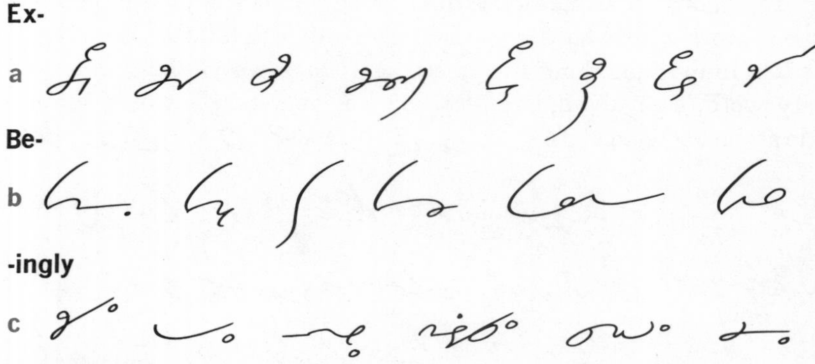

a. Expansion, exact, excise, executive, expenses, excessive, expresses, extent.
b. Becoming, because, before, begin, belittle, betray.
c. Exceedingly, willingly, increasingly, unhesitatingly, accordingly, seemingly.

Building Transcription Skills

39. BUSINESS VOCABULARY BUILDER

acute Critical; grave.

excise tax A duty levied upon the manufacture, sale, or use of commodities within the country.

excessive Too much.

Progressive Speed Builder (50-90)

In each fifth lesson there is a Progressive Speed Builder, the purpose of which is to force you to write faster. Each Progressive Speed Builder consists of five letters or memoranda, all related to the same transaction. Each letter or memorandum is counted at a slightly higher speed. In this lesson the letters are counted progressively at 50, 60, 70, 80, and 90 words a minute.

Your first step always should be to practice the preview for the Progressive Speed Builder by reading it, with the help of the key when necessary, and making a shorthand copy of it. The numbers within the preview refer to the letters to which each group of outlines applies.

You should find the first two or three letters quite easy; you will have to work a little harder on the fourth and fifth letters.

The important thing to remember is *to get something down* for every word, even though the legibility of your outlines may suffer a little at the higher speeds.

40. PREVIEW

41.
42.
43.
44.
45.

41. I told, advertising, exceedingly, acute, weeks ago, hired, to put.
42. I realize, however, along, best, available, before, action.
43. News, contract, building, enough, sufficient, as soon as, definite.
44. Complete, located, third, private, sometime, disturb.
45. Opportunity, quarters, pleased, provided, I think, during, week or two, conveniently.

LETTERS

Note: One diagonal indicates the end of a quarter minute's dictation; two diagonals, the end of a half minute's dictation; three diagonals, the end of three-quarter minute's dictation; the number after each letter, the end of a minute's dictation.

(1 Minute at 50)

41. Mr. Davis: As I told you, the problem of space in our advertising/agency is becoming exceedingly acute. Two weeks ago//we hired two new girls. When they report, we shall have no place to put them.///

May I suggest that we have a meeting to discuss this matter. Harry Lee (1)

(1 Minute at 60)

42. Mr. Lee: I realize that the space problem in our advertising agency/is becoming exceedingly acute. For the present, however, I am afraid you//will have to get along as best you can with the space you have available. It will///be a few weeks before we can take any action on the matter of space. James Davis (2)

(1 Minute at 70)

43. Mr. Lee: I have good news for you. We have just signed a contract for the purchase of a new building./The building is large enough so that each department will have sufficient space. We shall have a great//deal of room for expansion. The building is now vacant and we can move in at once. I will write///you as soon as we have made definite plans for the location of each department. James Davis (3)

(1 Minute at 80)

44. Mr. Lee: Our plans for moving to our new building are now complete. Your department will be located on the/third floor. You will have a private office.

I do not know the exact date on which you will move, but it will be sometime//during the week of July 12. In the meantime, please make whatever preparations you feel are necessary///so that the moving will disturb the operation of your department as little as possible. James Davis (4)

(1 Minute at 90)

45. Mr. Davis: I had an opportunity today to look over our quarters in the new building. For the first time in/more than 10 years, our advertising agency will have all the space it needs. I was pleased with the office that you have provided//for me.

I think, too, that the staff will be happy because there is plenty of light.

We have started packing those things that we shall///not have to use during the next week or two. By Friday, we shall finish all the packing we can conveniently do. Harry Lee (5) (350)

Reading and Writing Practice

46.

as

intro

ex′cise
billed

al·read′y
re·ceived′

(138)

47.

as

past
un·for′tu·nate·ly

intro

ris′ing
be·com′ing
ex·pense′

intro

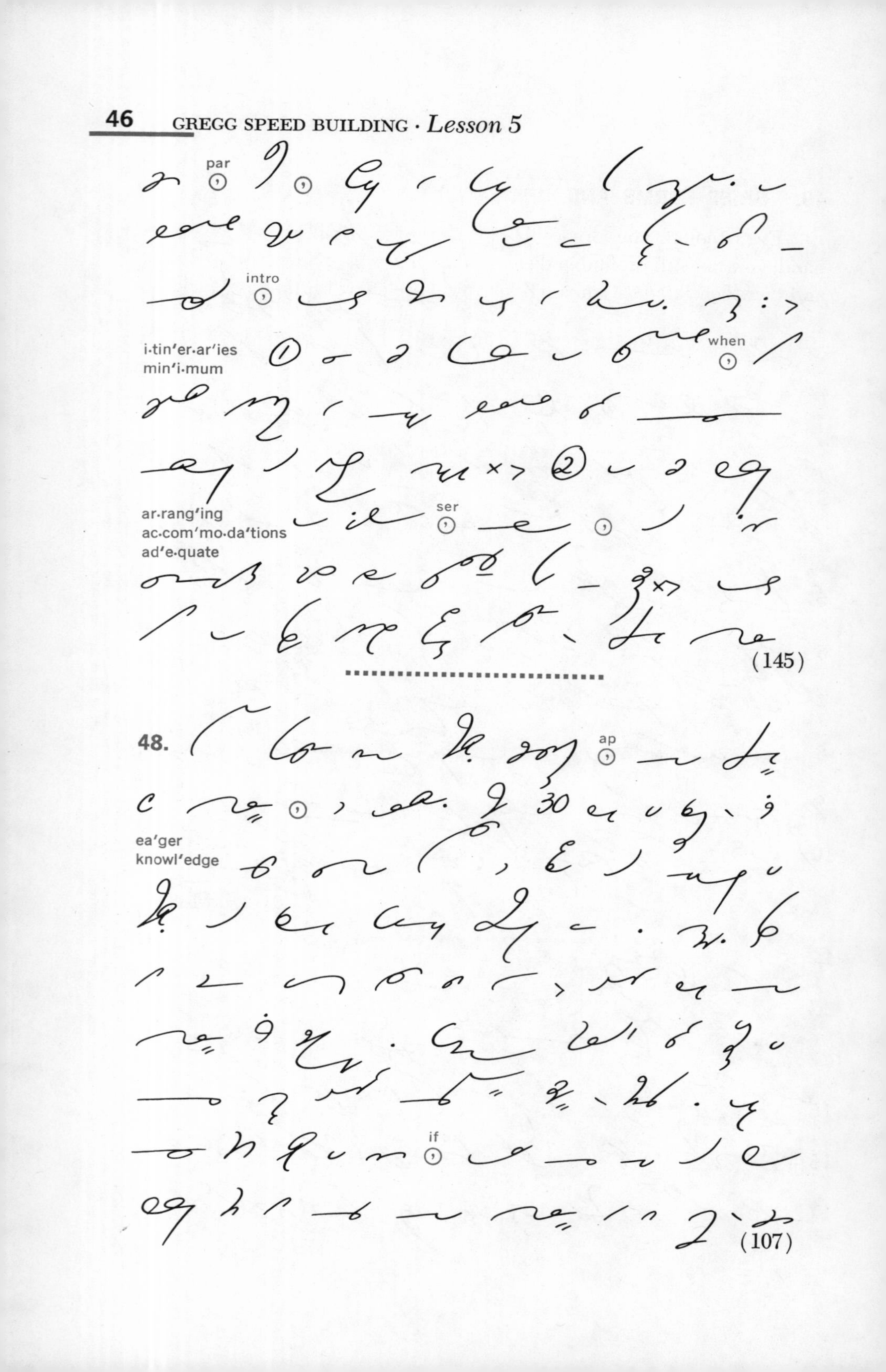

par

intro

i·tin′er·ar′ies
min′i·mum

when

ar·rang′ing
ac·com′mo·da′tions
ad′e·quate

ser

(145)

48.

ap

ea′ger
knowl′edge

if

(107)

49. BRIEF FORMS AND DERIVATIVES

Even though you already have considerable skill in writing shorthand, you can still profitably devote some time to a review of brief forms and their derivatives. Can you read this entire chart in 7 minutes or less?

	a	b	c	d	e	f
1						
2						
3						
4						
5						
6						
7						
8						
9						
10						
11						
12						
13						
14						
15						
16						
17						

CHAPTER 2

Insurance

Punctuation Brushup

In the lessons of Chapter 2 you will review:

; because of comma **bc** (;)

A comma is used to separate two independent clauses that are joined by a conjunction. However, when a comma occurs within one or both of the independent clauses, a semicolon is used to separate the two clauses.

> Our records indicate, Mr. Green, that we filled six orders for you last year; and every one of them was delivered within three days.

; no conjunction **nc** (;)

A semicolon is used to separate two independent, but closely related, clauses when no conjunction connects them.

> John received an increase in salary; Harry did not.

The above sentence could be written as two sentences, with a period after *salary*. Because the two thoughts are closely related, however, the use of the semicolon is preferred.

; illustrative **il** (;)

When an illustration is introduced by an expression such as *namely, that is,* or *for example,* the expression should be preceded by a semicolon and followed by a comma.

> We render what we believe you want; namely, dependable service.

: enumeration **enu** (:)

A colon is used after an expression that introduces some following material, such as an explanation of a general statement, a list, or an enumeration.

> We wrote you on the following days: April 10, May 15, and July 6.
>
> At our meeting we will discuss the following topics:
> 1. How to increase sales.
> 2. How to win good will.
> 3. How to improve our advertising.

. courteous request cr ⊙

When a request for definite action is put in the form of a question, a period is used at the end of the sentence.

> Won't you please send us your check today.

The Apostrophe

1. A noun that ends in an *s* sound and is followed by another noun is usually a possessive, calling for an apostrophe before the *s* when the word is singular.

> This company's advertising is designed for three colors.

2. A plural noun ending in *s* calls for an apostrophe *after* the *s* to form the possessive.

> Their employees' wages have been raised.

3. An irregular plural calls for an apostrophe *before* the *s* to form the possessive.

> We sell children's toys.

4. The possessive forms of pronouns do not require an apostrophe.

> These papers are *theirs*, not *ours*.

Developing Shorthand Writing Power

50. OUTLINE CONSTRUCTION

Vowel written in -er, -ar, -or. When the word endings *-er, -ar,* or *-or* follow *ī,* left *s,* or *sh, ch, j,* more legible outlines result if the vowel is written in those word endings.

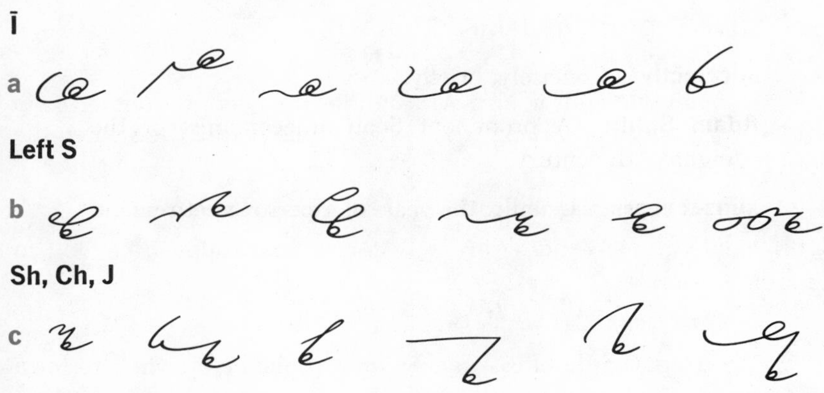

a. Prior, drier, crier, flyer, liar, buyer.
b. Eraser, condenser, appraiser, closer, nicer, announcer.
c. Washer, polisher, teacher, manager, danger, larger.

Omission of vowels in -el, -al, -ial, -eal. When the endings *-el, -al, -ial, -eal* are not accented, the vowels are omitted from those endings.

-el

a

-al

b

-ial, -eal

c

a. Model, channel, panel, level, tunnel.
b. Central, total, original, renewal.
c. Material, editorial, testimonial, cereal.

Building Transcription Skills

51. BUSINESS VOCABULARY BUILDER

succinctly Concisely, briefly.

Adam Smith A prominent Scottish economist of the eighteenth century.

sunset years Usually, the years of a person's retirement.

Reading and Writing Practice

52. Insurance

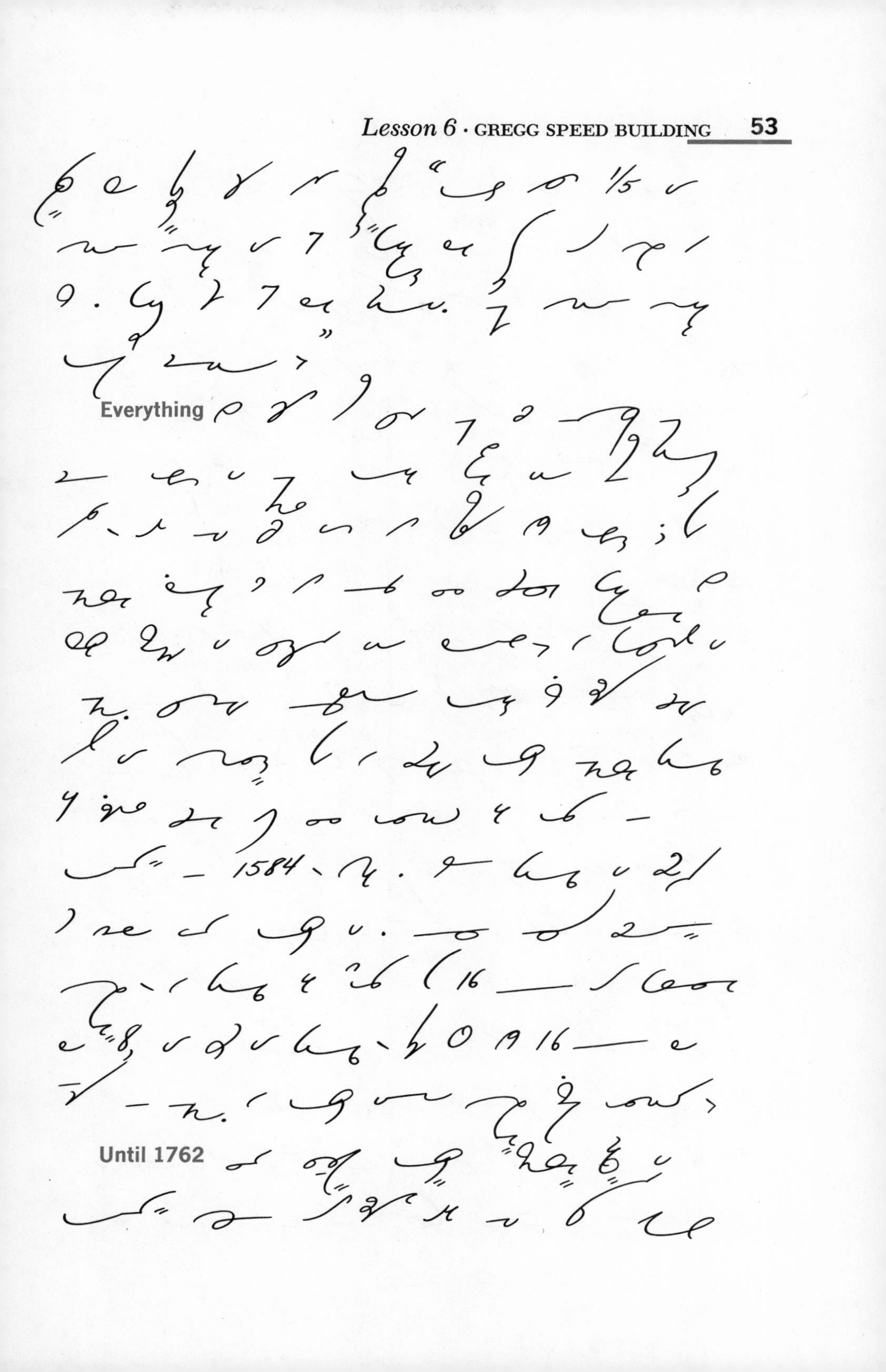

Everything

Until 1762

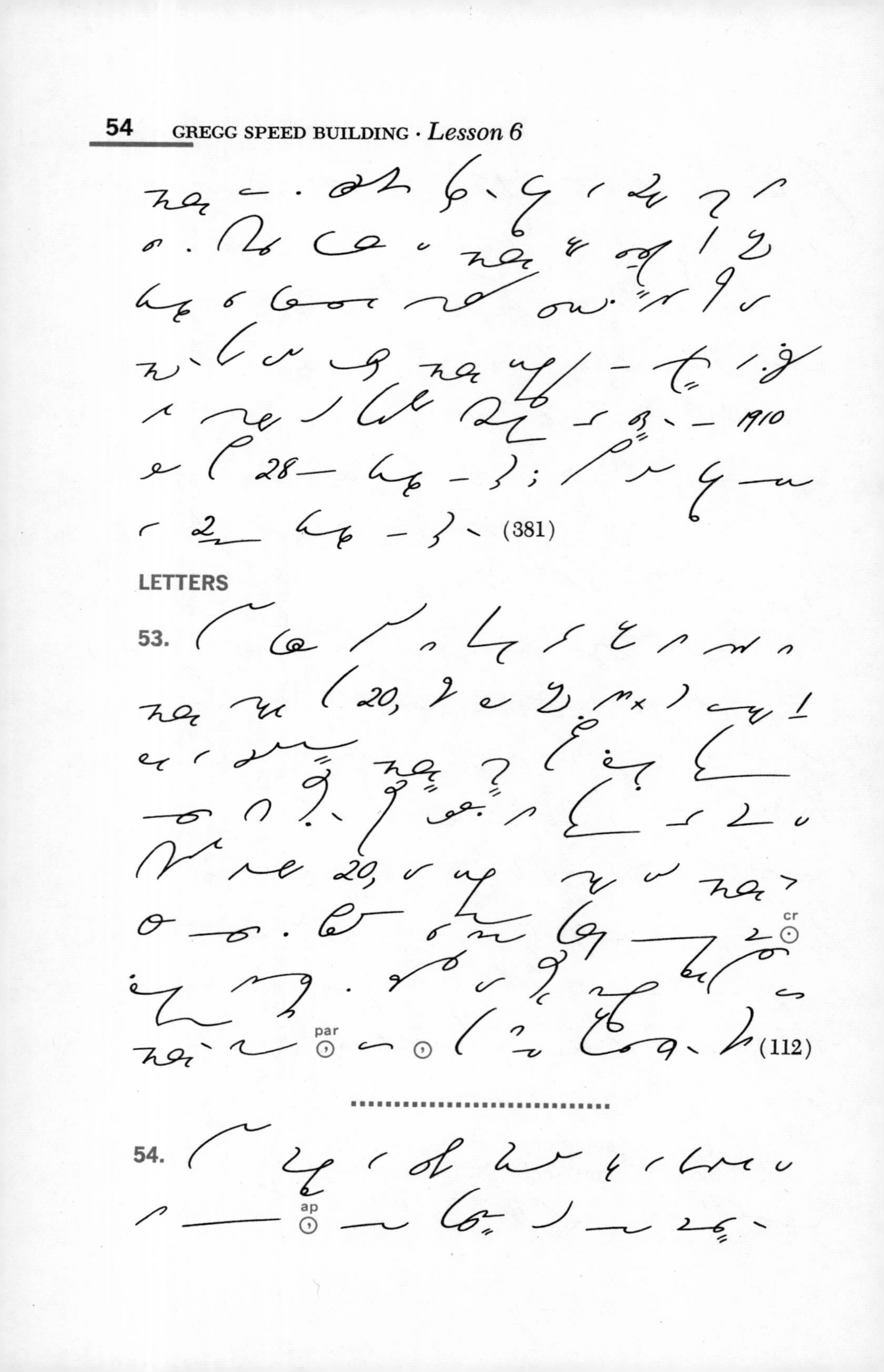

(381)

LETTERS

53. (112)

54.

In almost any group of people—offices being no exception—you will find petty annoyances. The idea is to make sure they remain just that—petty.

LESSON 7

Developing Shorthand Writing Power

55. RECALL DRILL — K

This drill reviews all the different situations in which the shorthand stroke *k* is used in Gregg Shorthand.

K

a

Com-

b

Con-

c

-ical, -cle

d

-ic

e

a. Occur, cover, careful, because, actual, checked, keep.
b. Compare, complete, complex, comfort, complicated, combine.
c. Continue, discontinue, reconsider, congratulate, control.
d. Medical, technical, critical, surgical, article, particle.
e. Tragic, basic, logic, magic, specific, scientific.

Building Transcription Skills

56. BUSINESS VOCABULARY BUILDER

reinstated Placed in its former position.

portfolio A portable case for keeping loose papers, prints, etc.

Writing Practice

57. PREVIEW

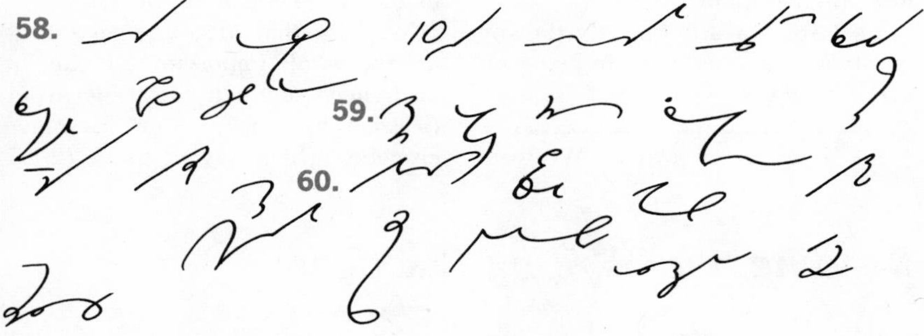

58. Enclosed, liability, $10,000, includes, medical, period, servants, we hope that, satisfactory.
59. Thank you for your, representative, suggest, he will be glad, advantages, interested, decision, questions.
60. Discontinue, expires, to place, do so, investigate, dividends, we have been able, during the last, reconsider, transfer.

LETTERS

58. Dear Mr. Stern: Enclosed is personal liability policy No. 17415. This[1] policy is made out for $10,000. It includes medical payments up to $350[2] for a period of three years.

This policy covers your liability for any injury to the[3] public or to any servants in your house.

We hope that you find the enclosed policy entirely satisfactory,[4] and we wish to thank you sincerely for the privilege of handling your insurance. Cordially yours,[5]

59. Dear Mr. Brown: Thank you for your letter of June 19 in which you ask us to send a representative to[6] discuss our policies with you.

We shall be very glad to have our representative, Mr. Martin, call to[7] talk with you next Friday evening as you suggest. He will be glad to tell you about the advantages of dealing[8] with an organization like ours when you are in the market for insurance.

You will be interested[9] in the figures that Mr. Martin will show you. We hope that you will compare them with those of other companies[10] before you make a decision.

Feel free to ask Mr. Martin any questions that may occur to you. Sincerely yours,[11]

---

60. Dear Mr. Crowder: We were sorry to receive your letter of January 8, informing us that you[12] plan to discontinue your insurance with us when your present policy expires on February 3. We assume[13] that you are planning to place your insurance with some other company.

Before you do so, be sure to investigate[14] the dividends paid by that company. Because of the careful way in which we select the persons whom[15] we insure, we have been able to pay a high dividend each year. The actual rates that we have paid during[16] the last 20 years are given on the enclosed folder.

We hope that, after you have studied the whole important[17] matter of insurance, you will reconsider your decision to transfer your insurance elsewhere. Sincerely yours,[18] (360)

Reading and Writing Practice

61.

nonr

as

par

com·plet'ing
urge
in·duce'

bc

par

conj

(149)

62.

intro

par

trag′ic
lapsed

il

two′-page′
hyphenated before noun

re′in·stat′ed
Can′cel

if

nc

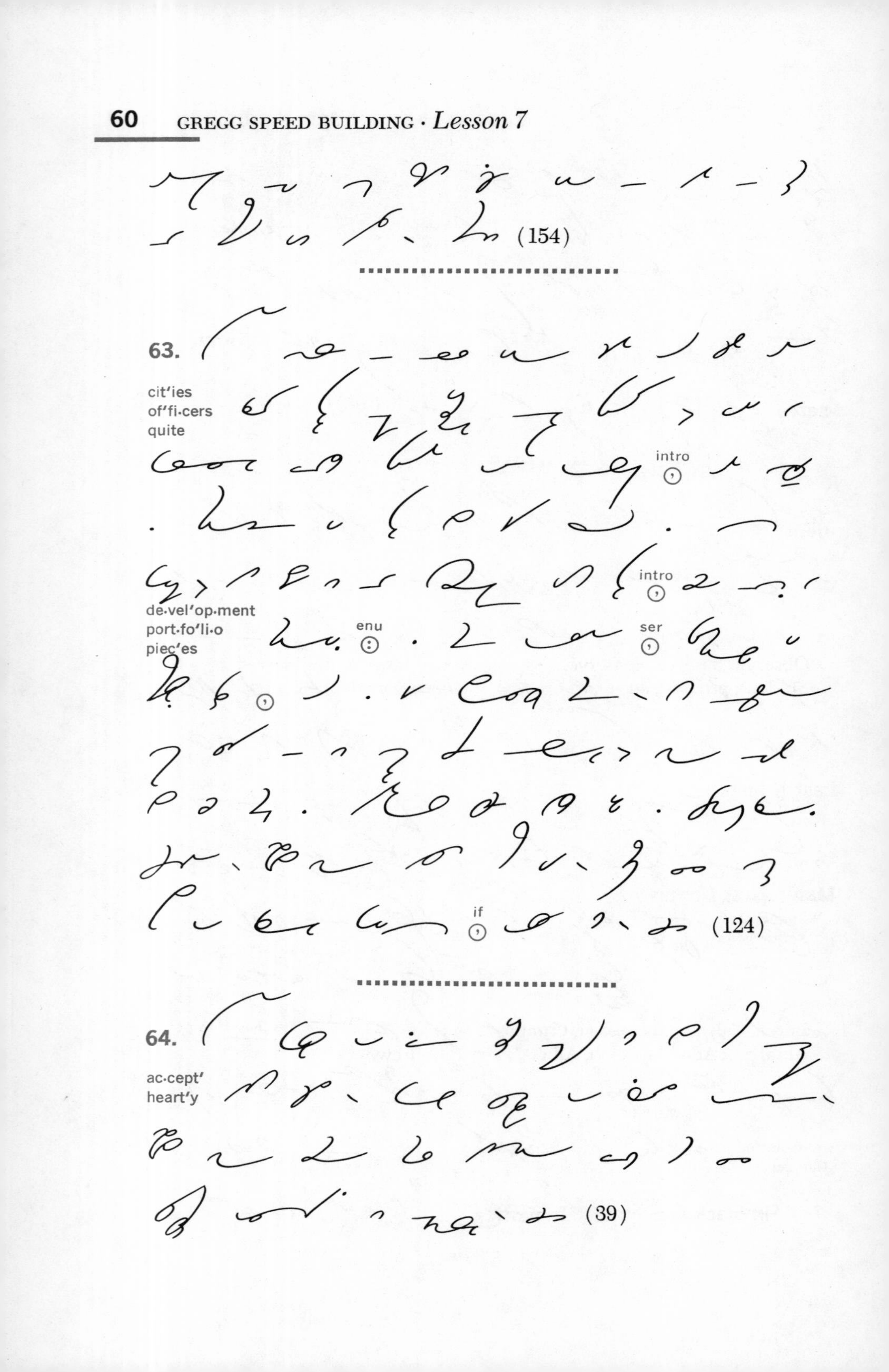

(154)

63.

cit'ies
of'fi·cers
quite

intro

intro

de·vel'op·ment
port·fo'li·o
piec'es

enu

ser

if

(124)

64.

ac·cept'
heart'y

(39)

Developing Shorthand Writing Power

65. WORD FAMILIES

-serve

a

-dent

b

a. Observe, deserve, conserve, serve, preserve, reserve, undeserved.
b. Student, prudent, accident, resident, incident, confident.

66. FREQUENT NAMES

Last Names

a

Men's First Names

b

a. Burke, Callahan, Cameron, Campbell, Carroll.
b. Abraham, Adam, Adolph, Albert, Alfred, Andrew.

Building Transcription Skills

67. BUSINESS VOCABULARY BUILDER

in black and white In writing.

cardiogram A record made on a cardiograph of the duration and character of the heart's movements.

Writing Practice

68. PREVIEW

69.

70.

71.

69. Accordance, conversation, afternoon, dwelling, garage, period, $18,000, riots, confidence.
70. Superstitious, mirror, accidents, precaution, themselves, wouldn't, mishap, I shall be glad.
71. Pleasant, discovery, inventory, furnishings, many times, inasmuch, policies, hazards.

LETTERS

69. Dear Mrs. Callahan: In accordance with our telephone conversation this afternoon, I am enclosing[1] a fire insurance policy, written by the Mutual Insurance Company, covering your dwelling and[2] garage in the amount of $18,000 for a period of three years beginning April 27.[3]

This policy also contains a provision that protects you up to $18,000 for any loss[4] or damage by explosions, riots, and airplanes.

Thank you for your confidence in us. Very cordially yours,[5]

70. Dear Mr. Cameron: Today is Friday, the 13th. Perhaps you are one of those people who are not superstitious.[6] Perhaps you pay no attention to black cats walking across your path or to walking under a ladder or to breaking[7] a mirror. Perhaps Friday, the 13th, is just like any other day for you.

Accidents happen on Friday,[8] the 13th, however, and on every other day. Wise people take the precaution to insure themselves against[9] expenses resulting from accidents.

Wouldn't you like to see a plan that, for only a few cents a day,[10] would pay all your bills if you had a mishap?

If you would, I shall be glad to give you all the facts. Cordially yours,[11]

---

71. Dear Mr. Albert: Would you like to make a pleasant discovery? Then write for our inventory booklet; it[12] is free. In this booklet list all your home furnishings at their value today. You will probably be amazed when[13] you see in black and white exactly how much they are worth. Your home furnishings are now worth many times the amount[14] you paid for them.

This means that it will take more insurance to protect these goods, inasmuch as their replacement value[15] is so much higher now than it was on the day you bought them.

Our representative can take care of this for you.[16] Let him tell you about the policies that we offer, policies that cover your home and its contents against[17] fire and many other hazards.

Don't wait until your present policy expires; act now. Very sincerely yours,[18] (360)

Reading and Writing Practice

72.

phys'i·cal
e·lapse'

nc

par

bc

as

pol′i·cy·hold′ers
high′-qual′i·ty
hyphenated before noun

intro

il

20/ (176)

73.

ex·pens′es
a·rise′
ac′ci·dent

5/

9[50] 11[50]

if

ser

cr

(143)

74.

ap

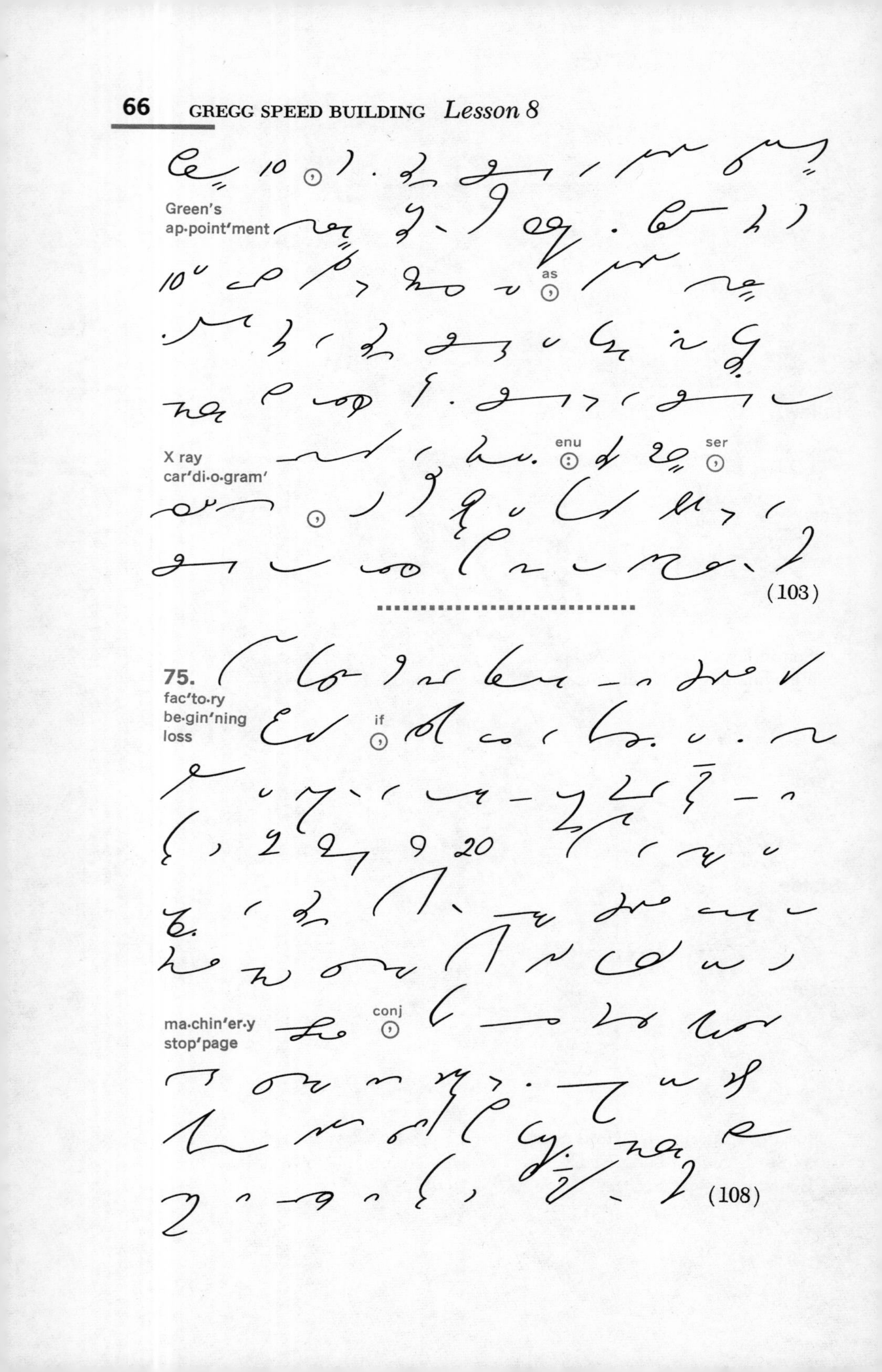

10

Green's
ap·point'ment

10

as

X ray
car'di·o·gram'

enu

ser

(103)

75.
fac'to·ry
be·gin'ning
loss

if

20

ma·chin'er·y
stop'page

conj

(108)

Developing Shorthand Writing Power

76. FREQUENT PHRASES

In-law

a

Few

b

a. Son-in-law, brother-in-law, mother-in-law, father-in-law, sister-in-law.
b. Few minutes, few moments, few days, few months, few times.

77. GEOGRAPHICAL EXPRESSIONS

-ford

a 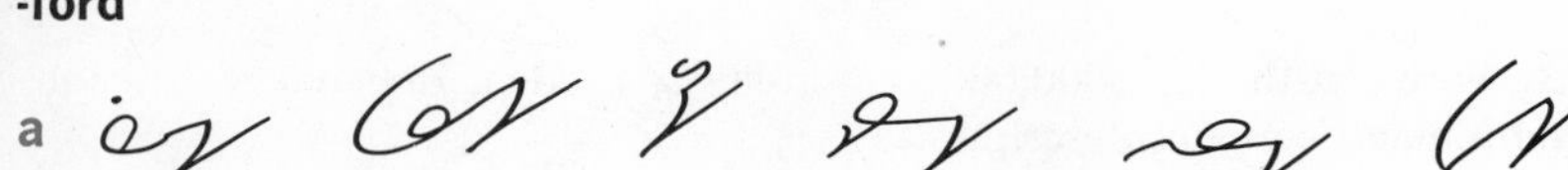

States

b

Foreign Countries

c 

a. Hartford, Bradford, Oxford, Stamford, Cranford, Bedford.
b. West Virginia, Rhode Island, New Mexico, Minnesota, Iowa, Colorado.
c. Ecuador, Egypt, France, Greece, India, Iran, Iraq.

Building Transcription Skills

78. BUSINESS VOCABULARY BUILDERS

pathetic Pitiful, sad.

heirs Those who inherit assets from one who has died.

incredible Unbelievable.

Writing Practice

79. PREVIEW

80. [shorthand]

81. [shorthand]

82. [shorthand]

80. Recently, pathetic, $300,000, son-in-law's, burden, dependent, anyone, retirement, coupon, description.

81. Understanding, successful, continue, anything, to purchase, be able, preservation, situation, worthwhile.

82. Interested, immediately, arithmetic, New Mexico, figures, few months, protection, transaction.

LETTERS

80. Dear Mr. Trees: We recently heard of the pathetic case of a man who earned $300,000 in[1] his day but who is now just his son-in-law's burden. He is a man without a home of his own.

Perhaps you have[2] seen men like him, dependent on a son or a daughter.

Thousands of young men today are making sure that they will[3] never become burdens to anyone; they are investing in retirement insurance.

Under our plan, you,[4] too, can assure yourself of an old-age income.

Send the attached coupon for a

description of this plan. Yours truly,[5]

---

81. Dear Mr. Norris: It is our understanding that your partnership has been very successful in the past few[6] years. It is our hope that it will continue to be successful for many years to come.

It is good business, however,[7] for you to give some thought to the time when your partner's share will pass to his heirs, who may not know anything about[8] business. When your partner passes away, you will, no doubt, wish to purchase his share of the business. Will you be[9] able to do this? You will if you hold our business-preservation policy.

No matter what your present[10] situation may be, you will find it well worthwhile to learn just what this new policy will do for you. Yours truly,[11]

---

82. Dear Mr. Perry: Would you be interested in a plan that for only $5 a week will give you[12] $1,300 at the end of five years, as well as $1,000 worth of insurance starting[13] immediately. Of course, simple arithmetic will tell you that when you save $5 a week for five years, you will[14] have $1,300. But when you place that amount with the New Mexico Bank each week, you will not only have the[15] $1,300 at the end of that time, but you will have a $1,000 life insurance policy[16] as well.

These figures are based on your present age—thirty. If you act within the next few months, you can take[17] advantage of the present low rate. If you delay too long, you will have to pay more to get this same protection.[18]

You can handle the entire transaction by mail if you wish. Send for our free booklet. Cordially yours,[19] (380)

Reading and Writing Practice

83.

lose its

enu

and o

low'-cost'

hyphenated before noun

min'utes'

nc ;

(142)

84.

in'de·pend'ent

coun'tries

ser ,

,

,

intro ,

ful·fill'

in·ten'tions

par ,

intro ,

in·cred'i·ble

rep're·sent'a·tives

5 ser 10

cr (140)

85.

com'pa·ny's
due

nc

par

cus'tom·ar'y
e·con'o·my

31

intro

intro

(144)

People are judged to a large degree by their ability to work with other people.—Robert F. Black

LESSON 10

Developing Shorthand Writing Power

86. WORD BEGINNINGS AND ENDINGS

For-, Fore-

a

-rity

b

-lity

c

a. Fortunate, unfortunate, afforded, forward, forget, foreman, foremost.
b. Security, sincerity, popularity, minority, majorities.
c. Responsibility, possibility, ability, locality, facilities.

Building Transcription Skills

87. BUSINESS VOCABULARY BUILDER

home office The office from which an organization having more than one branch is managed.

comprehensive Including much.

legislation Laws that have been enacted.

Progressive Speed Builder (50-90)

The letters in this Progressive Speed Builder range in speed from 50 to 90 words a minute. Be sure to:

1. Practice the preview before taking the letters from dictation.
2. Get something down during dictation for every word, even though your outlines may be "shaky." Do not stop writing!

88. PREVIEW

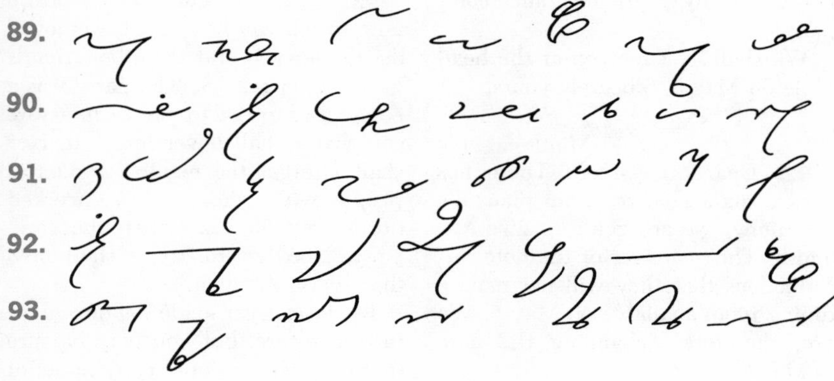

89. You will be, insurance, dinner, honor, I hope that, you will be able, return.
90. Glad to hear, it has been, pleasure, some years, to see, of course, contribute.
91. Thank you for, promptly, possible, complete, without, toward, watch, table.
92. There has been, manager, informed, available, prevent, meant, surprise.
93. How much, enjoyed, wonderful, worked, I have not yet, definite, include.

LETTERS

(1 Minute at 50)

89. Dear Mr. Green: You will be happy to learn that on May 5 our/insurance company will hold a dinner in honor of Mr. Smith. He//is retiring on June 1.

I hope that you will be able to be///present. If you can come, please return the enclosed card. Cordially yours, (1)

(1 Minute at 60)

90. Dear Mr. Jones: I was glad to hear that your insurance company is planning a/dinner for Mr. Smith. It has been my pleasure to work with him for some years, and I//shall be sorry to see him go.

I shall, of course, be present. My card is enclosed. If///you are planning to buy him a gift, I shall be glad to contribute. Sincerely yours, (2)

(1 Minute at 70)

91. Dear Mr. Green: Thank you for returning your card so promptly.

I am glad that you will find it/possible to be with us. The dinner would not be complete without you.

Thank you also for your offer//to contribute toward a gift. We are planning to give him a watch, but it will be paid for by///the insurance company.

We shall look for you at the head table on May 5. Sincerely yours, (3)

(1 Minute at 80)

92. Dear Mr. Green: There has been a slight change in our plans for the dinner we are going to give Mr. Smith. The/manager of the hotel informed us that they will not have a dining room available on May 5. We are, therefore,//changing the date to May 8.

I hope that this change in plans will not prevent you from being with us. As this dinner///is meant to be a surprise party, please do not say anything about it to Mr. Smith. Cordially yours, (4)

(1 Minute at 90)

93. Dear Mr. Jones: This is just a note to tell you how much I enjoyed the dinner you and my other friends gave me on May 8./The party was a complete surprise to me. I can assure you that I shall never forget it. Nor shall I forget the many//wonderful people with whom I have worked during my 30 years with the company. Needless to say, I shall miss them very///much.

I have not yet made definite plans for the future, but you may be sure that they will include many hours of fishing. Sincerely, (5) (350)

Reading and Writing Practice

94. par

is′su·ing
ap·pre′ci·ate

bc

ceas′es
wor′ry

when

long′-last′ing
hyphenated before noun

if

up to date
no noun,
no hyphen

(151)

95.

in′di·vid′u·als
cel′lar

if

par

intro

cov′ered
com′pre·hen′sive

Smith's
ex·am′ple

il

nc

(129)

96.

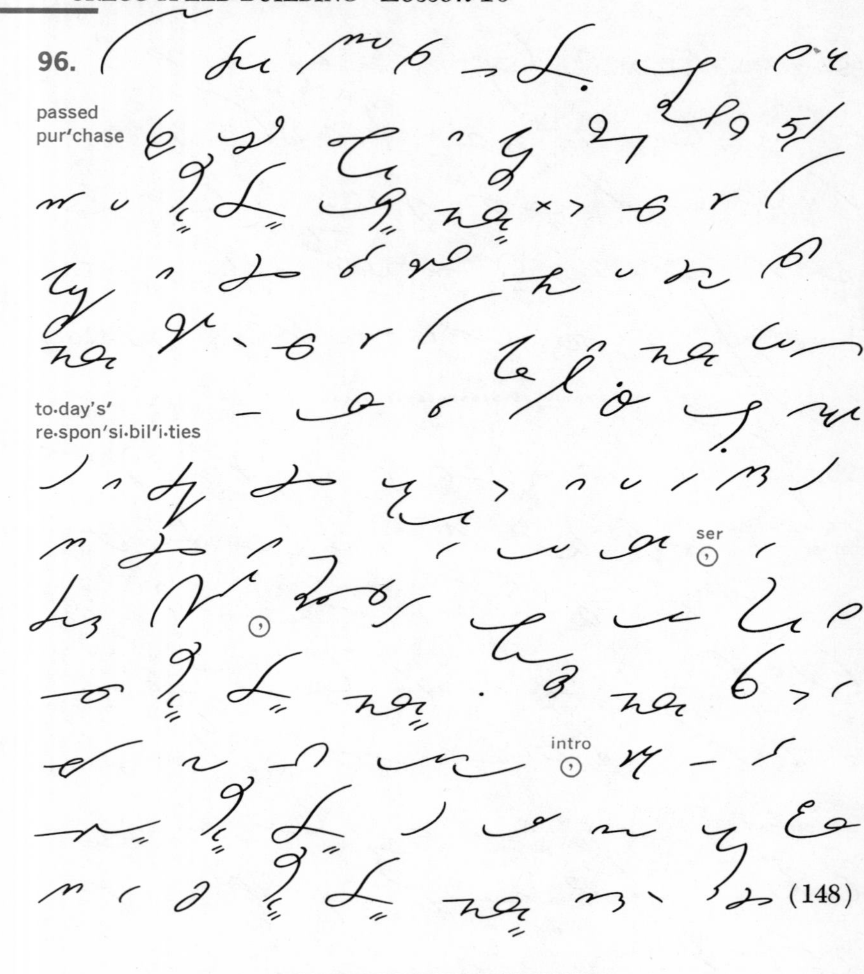

Secretaries who "chitchat" on the telephone are a distracting element in any business office. Whether the boss is in his office alone or in conference with his associates, he appreciates his secretary's maintaining "phone silence" unless her personal phone calls are absolutely *necessary.*—Catherine R. Ready

97. BRIEF FORMS AND DERIVATIVES

The following chart contains 102 brief forms and derivatives. First read the brief forms from left to right. Then read the chart *down* each column.

Reading goal: 7 minutes or less.

	a	b	c	d	e	f
1						
2						
3						
4						
5						
6						
7						
8						
9						
10						
11						
12						
13						
14						
15						
16						
17						

CHAPTER 3

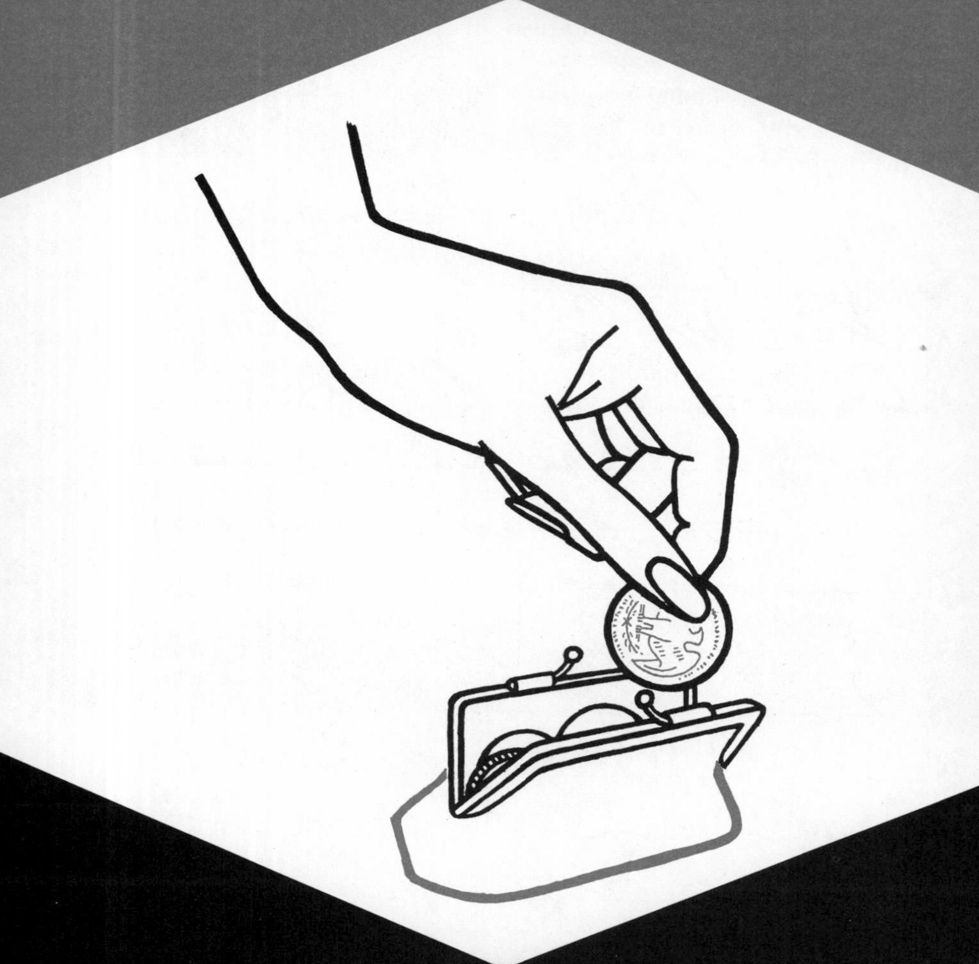

Finance

Typing-Style Brushup

In the lessons of Chapter 3 you will review the correct method of typing addresses, amounts, dates, and expressions of time. You will also review the correct use of commas in numbers and the correct use of the hyphen.

Commas in Numbers

1. Numbers that contain four or more digits require a comma to separate thousands, millions, billions.

$5,000 (not *$5000*)   314,168   1,451,316   4,000,000,000

2. No comma is used, however, in large serial numbers, house or street numbers, telephone numbers, page numbers, and dates.

No. 14511	3515 First Street	LOngacre 4-3000
Page 1414	1967	971-2173

Addresses

1. Always use figures in house numbers.

   He lived at 600 (not *six hundred*) Market Street.

2. Spell out numbered street names from one through ten.

   He worked at 330 Fourth Avenue.

3. Use numbers in street names over ten.

   His address is 18 East 67 Street.

Amounts of Money

1. When transcribing even amounts of dollars in business letters, do not use a decimal point or zeros.

   His check for $152 (not *$152.00*) was lost.

2. In business letters, use the word *cents* for amounts under $1.

   The book cost only 39 cents (not *$.39*).

Time

1. Spell out the time of the day when it is accompanied by *o'clock.* (Remember the apostrophe!)

He came at ten o'clock (not *10 o'clock*).

2. Use numbers in expressing time with *a.m.* and *p.m.*

He left at 9:15 a.m. and returned at 9:30 p.m.

Dates

1. If the name of the month precedes the day, do not use *th, st,* or *d* after the number. This is the most frequent way that dates are expressed in business letters.

On June 16, 1968, he must retire.

2. If the day precedes the month, *th, st,* or *d* should be included.

On the 25th of May he will be able to vote.

Illustrations of these typing-style pointers will occasionally be called to your attention in the left margin of the shorthand in the Reading and Writing Practice exercise under the heading "Transcribe."

Hyphens

You can quickly decide whether to use a hyphen in compound expressions like *past due* or *well trained* by observing these rules:

1. If a noun follows the expression, use a hyphen.

We are concerned about your *past-due* account (*noun*).

2. If *no* noun follows the compound expression, do *not* use a hyphen.

Your account is past due.

3. No hyphen is used in a compound modifier where the first part of the expression is an adverb that ends in *ly*.

He was editor of a widely read magazine.

Occasionally, illustrations of these three hyphen rules will be called to your attention in the left margin of the shorthand in the Reading and Writing Practice exercises thus:

past-due	**well trained**	**widely read**
hyphenated before noun	*no noun, no hyphen*	*no hyphen after ly*

Developing Shorthand Writing Power

98. OUTLINE CONSTRUCTION

Vowel written in -ance, -ence. The vowel is written in the word endings *-ance, -ence* when those endings follow *ī, n, r,* or *l.*

Ī

a

N

b

R

c

L

d

a. Compliance, alliance, appliance, defiance, reliance, self-reliance.
b. Maintenance, dominance, eminence, prominence.
c. Recurrence, reference, conference, endurance, appearance, assurance.
d. Balance, brilliance, resemblance, violence, silence.

Vowel omitted in -ance, -ence. The vowel in the word endings *-ance, -ence* is omitted in the following words because its omission gives much more fluent, and at the same time legible, outlines.

-ance

a

-ence

b 

a. Accordance, issuance, nuisance, annoyance, acquaintance, disturbance.
b. Negligence, essence, independence, diligence, absence, influence.

Building Transcription Skills

99. BUSINESS VOCABULARY BUILDER

synonym One of two or more words having essentially the same meaning.

rectify To correct.

Reading and Writing Practice

100. Money

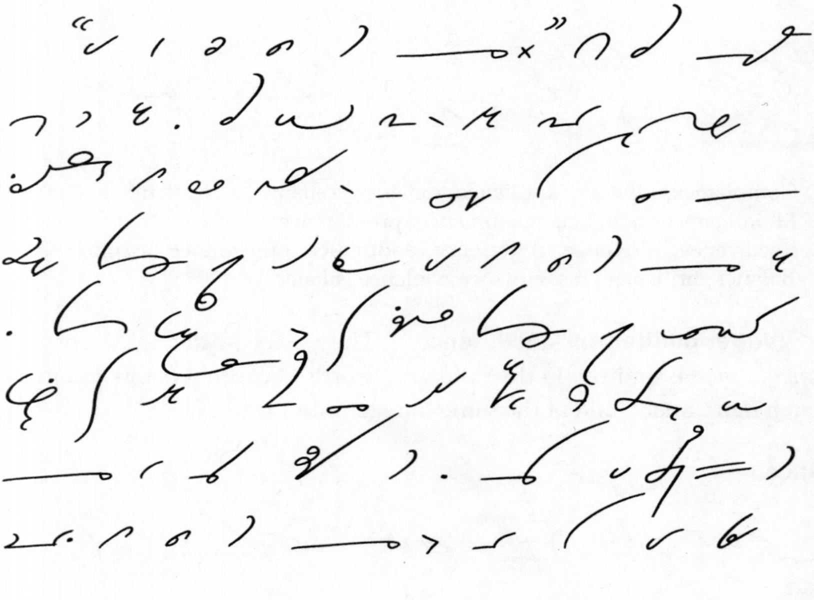

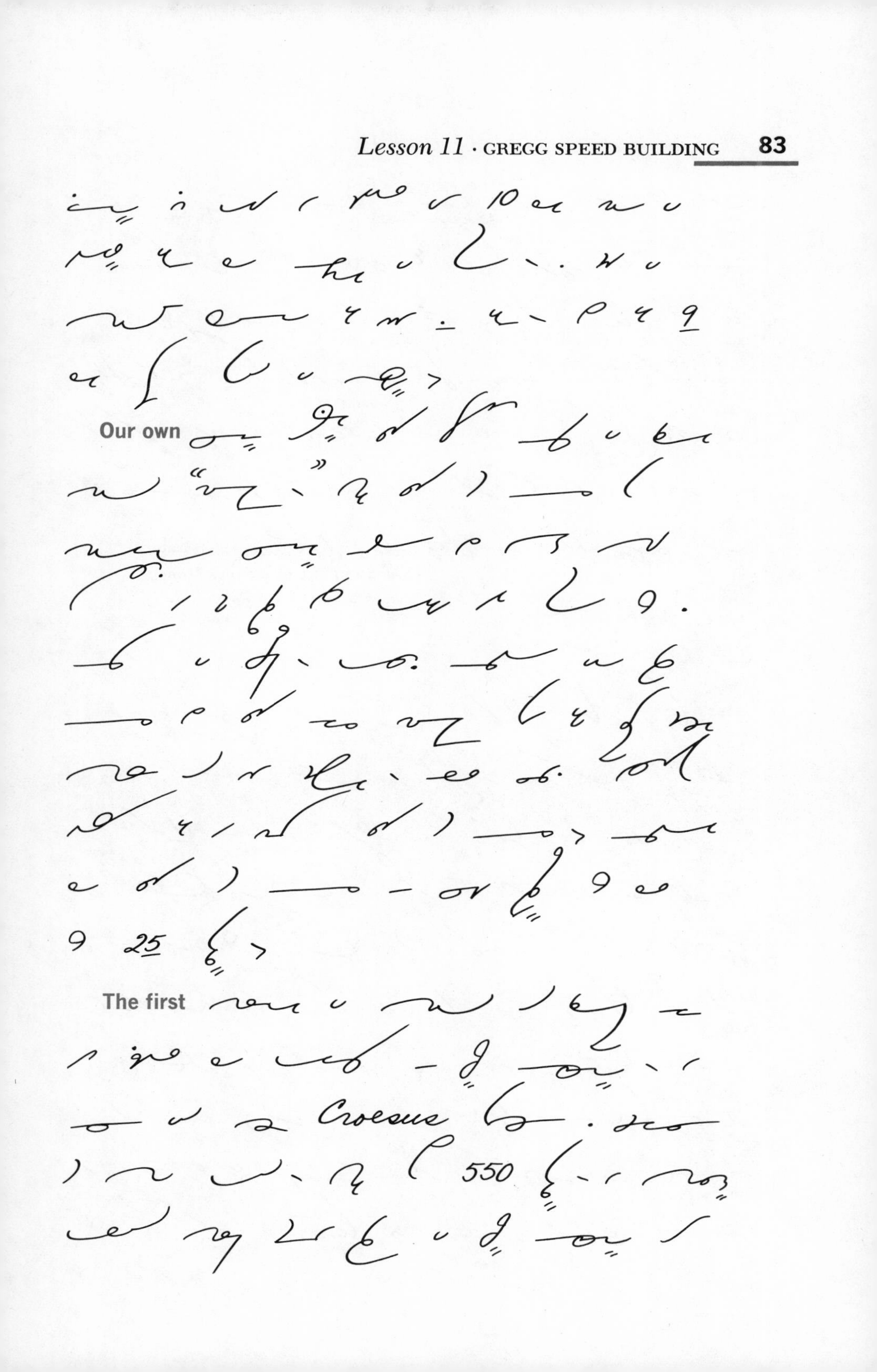

Our own

The first

(329)

—The Story of Uncle Sam's Money

LETTERS

101.

if

Transcribe:
$1,000
$10,000
$100,000

ser

conj

intro

in'ter·fere'
de·duct'i·ble

if

Transcribe:
Fifth Avenue
New York 10062
9 a.m.
4 p.m.

416

10062

961–1723 9 4

(186)

102. 50

Transcribe:
$50

par

Transcribe:
15th

15

(68)

103.

Transcribe:
June 5

5

(98)

ZIP CODE

The Post Office Department's ZIP Code (ZIP stands for "Zoning Improvement Program") is designed to speed up the sorting and distribution of mail. This code consists of five digits.

How the ZIP Code is typed in business correspondence is illustrated on page 87. If you will refer to that page, you will see how it is typed:

1. *On the envelope and in the inside address.* The ZIP Code is typed on the same line as the city and state. There are three spaces between the state and the ZIP number (this extra space makes it stand out). There is no punctuation before or after the ZIP number. The ZIP number is typed solid, with no spaces between the digits.
2. *In the body of a sentence.* When an address is given in running form in the body of a sentence, there is only *one* space between the state and the ZIP number. (There is no need to make it stand out, as there is in the address on the envelope.)

Appropriate punctuation follows the ZIP number when it appears within a sentence. (In the letter on page 87 a comma follows the ZIP number because the number is part of the expression in apposition, "Philadelphia 19104.")

McGRAW-HILL BOOK COMPANY

330 WEST 42ND STREET, NEW YORK, N.Y. 10036

A DIVISION OF McGRAW-HILL INC.

GREGG DIVISION

May 18, 19--

Mr. James R. Green
The Harrington Publishing Company
415 West 42 Street
New York, New York 10036

Dear Mr. Green:

Your letter asking for information about Mr. Harry Barnes, a former employee of this company, has been referred to me.

Mr. Barnes was with us for more than fifteen years but left us last June to accept another position. He was a loyal, efficient employee; and we were sorry to lose him.

If you wish to get in touch with Mr. Barnes, you can write him in care of the Philadelphia Supply Company, 181 Broad Street, Philadelphia 19104, where he is presently employed.

Sincerely yours,

GREGG DIVISION

McGRAW-HILL BOOK COMPANY

330 WEST 42ND STREET, NEW YORK, N.Y. 10036

Mr. James R. Green
The Harrington Publishing Company
415 West 42 Street
New York, New York 10036

Illustration of ZIP Code typed in business correspondence

LESSON 12

Developing Shorthand Writing Power

104. RECALL DRILL — S

In this drill you will review the different situations in which the two forms of *s* are used.

Self-, Circum-

a

Super-

b

Sub-

c

-ings

d

Per Cent

e

---

a. Self-supporting, self-confident, self-satisfied, self-educated, circumstance, circumstances.
b. Superior, supervise, supervision, supervisory, superhuman, supernatural.
c. Substantial, sublease, suburb, suburban, subway, submit, subnormal.
d. Savings, feelings, findings, sayings, hearings, helpings, clippings.
e. 7 per cent, 100 per cent.

Building Transcription Skills

105. BUSINESS VOCABULARY BUILDER

blithely Merrily; cheerfully.

paramount Of greatest importance.

denominations Series of related units, as denominations of United States currency.

Writing Practice

106. PREVIEW

107.

108.

109.

107. You have been, courage, county, one of the, useful, perform, welcome, sensible, repayment, include, suburban.
108. Blithely, millions, however, profit, commercial, savings, substantial, practice, advantage, discounts, exceeds.
109. Convenience, account, certain, departments, opened, first, 9 a.m., 4 p.m.

LETTERS

107. Dear Mr. March: If you have been longing for a car but have not had the courage to buy one, let the County Trust[1] Company finance it for you. It is one of the many useful banking services that we perform every[2] day. You will welcome the lack of red tape as well as our sensible monthly repayment plan.

In your monthly[3] payments we include a small charge to cover insurance. If you prefer, you can place this insurance through your own[4] broker. For further details phone 451-6633, or visit our suburban office on Lake Drive. Yours truly,[5]

108. Dear Mr. Smith: There are times when people talk blithely about millions of dollars. The wise businessman and his banker,[6] however, know that attention to small amounts makes the difference between profit and loss.

The commercial[7] bank is constantly helping its customers to make small savings as well as substantial ones, to avoid small losses[8] as well as great losses, to reap small profits as well as large profits.

It is good business practice to borrow[9] in order to take advantage of cash discounts when the saving exceeds the interest on a bank loan.

You are[10] invited to come in and discuss with us ways in which you can make use of our services and save. Sincerely yours,[11]

109. Dear Mr. Fisher: Would it be a convenience to you if you did not have to come to the bank to make payments[12] on your real estate loan? If so, you can do just that by opening a checking account with us.

As a service[13] to our real estate customers, we are happy to arrange to charge your monthly payments against your checking account[14] and mail you a copy of the charge.

We have two types of checking accounts, one of which is certain to fit your[15] needs.

We wish you to feel that this is your bank, Mr. Fisher; and we sincerely hope that you will make full use of[16] all our departments. A checking account can be opened for you by mail or by a personal visit to this[17] bank. Our offices at 15 First Avenue are open from 9 a.m. to 4 p.m. on weekdays. Yours truly,[18] (360)

Reading and Writing Practice

110.

il

Transcribe:
July 15

par

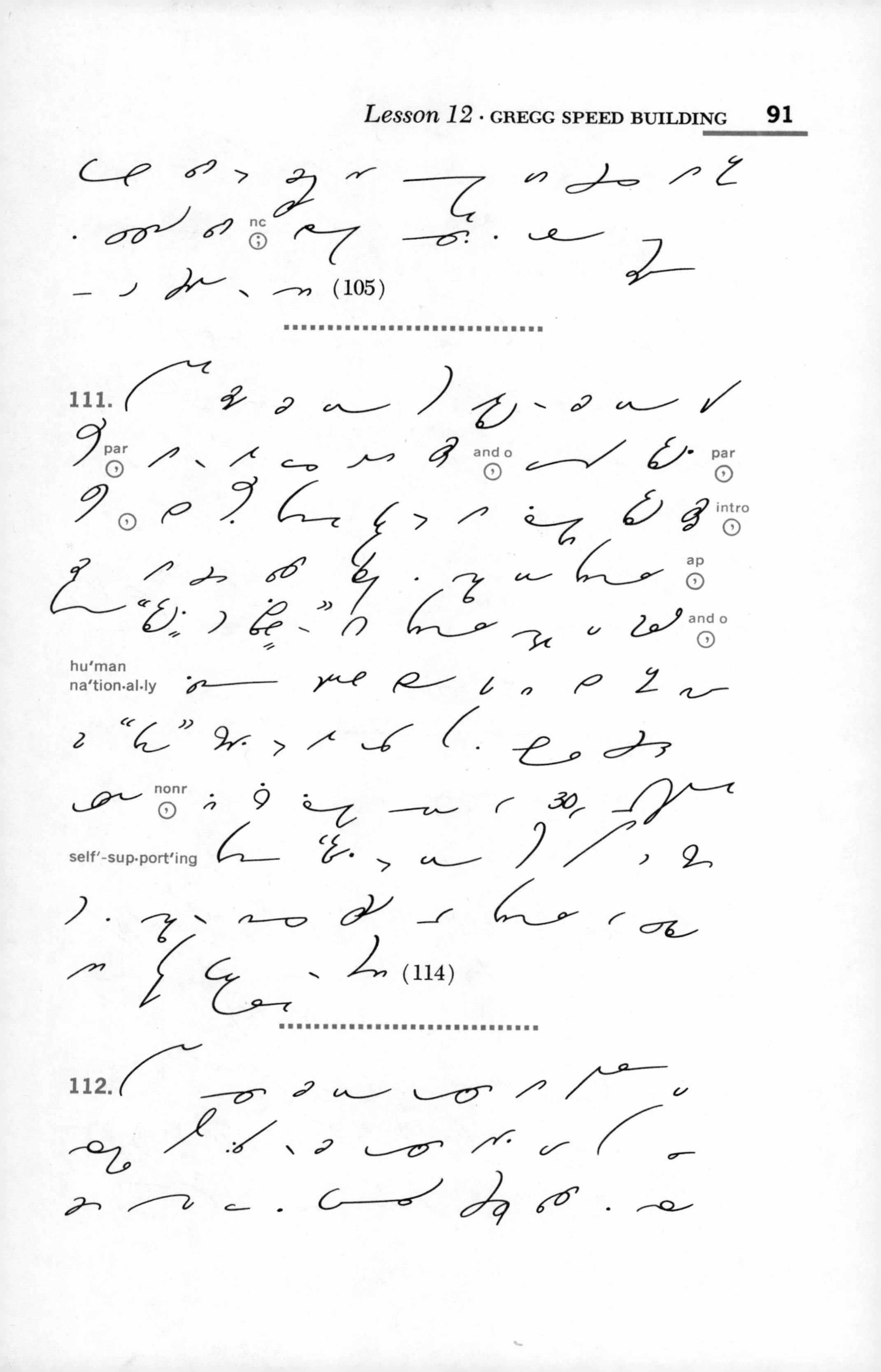

nc

(105)

111.

par

and o

par

intro

ap

and o

hu'man

na'tion·al·ly

nonr

30,

self'-sup·port'ing

(114)

112.

par

par

ex·am′ple
de·vel′op
de·pos′it

(125)

113.

intro

nc

nc

spend′a·ble
ac·cept′ed

ser

if

de·stroyed′
re·fund′

(86)

114.

intro

(70)

115.

yours
sur·prised′
col′lege

un·less′
em·bar′rass·ing

intro

par

conj

(93)

THURS.

LESSON 13

Developing Shorthand Writing Power

116. WORD FAMILIES

-ount

a

-ure

b

a. Count, account, discount, recount, amount, county.
b. Pleasure, assure, measure, treasure, pressure, insure, injure.

117. FREQUENT NAMES

Last Names

a

Women's First Names

b

a. Clarke, Cohen, Cohn, Collins, Connell, Cooper.
b. Beatrice, Belle, Bertha, Bridget, Caroline, Catherine, Celia.

Building Transcription Skills

118. BUSINESS VOCABULARY BUILDER

sizable Large.

perplexing Baffling; confusing.

significant Important.

Writing Practice

119. PREVIEW

120. **121.** **122.**

120. Financial, condition, handle, organization, completed, interesting, approximately, 30 per cent, I hope that, privilege.
121. Obligations, to make, county, combine, debts, convenient, nearest, telephone, simply, prepared.
122. Up-to-the-minute, benefits, security, available, anything, meantime, perplexing, details.

LETTERS

120. Dear Mr. Cooper: We are pleased to enclose our latest financial statement showing the condition of our[1] bank as of December 31. This statement should assure you that you will be taking the right step by letting us[2] handle your banking business.

We might add that our organization has just completed fifty years of[3] operation in this state. It is interesting to note that approximately 30 per cent of our business comes[4] from out of the state.

I sincerely hope that you will give us an opportunity to look after your banking[5] business and that we shall shortly have the privilege of opening an account for you. Very cordially yours,[6]

---

121. Dear Mr. Cohen: Many of us have doctors' bills and other obligations to pay, but some months we just cannot[7] seem to make our pay check cover them all. With a personal loan from the County Trust Company at low[8] interest rates, you can combine several debts into one that you can repay in convenient monthly installments.[9]

Most business organizations combine their debts in this way. You will find it good business, too.

Visit our nearest[10] office. If it is more convenient, arrange a loan entirely by telephone. Simply call 415-3456.[11]

Whatever your banking needs may be, our bank is prepared to take care of them. Very cordially yours,[12]

---

122. Dear Mr. Connell: Would you be interested in receiving the latest, up-to-the-minute information[13] about your benefits under the Social Security Act? Would you like to know what amount of money will[14] be available to you when you retire in March, 1978? Would you like to know what benefits[15] your wife would receive before reaching the age of sixty-five if anything should happen to you in the meantime?[16]

We shall be glad to answer these as well as any other perplexing questions you may have about the Social[17] Security Act. This service is rendered by our bank without cost or obligation to you.

For full details[18] on the Social Security Act and how it affects you, fill in and mail the enclosed slip. Sincerely yours, (380)

Reading and Writing Practice

25 par

proud
Rock'ville's
de·vel'op·ment

(122)

124.

par

wheth'er
priv'i·lege

205

intro

intro

bc

if

(139)

125.
per'son·al-loan'
hyphenated before noun

per'son·al loan
no noun, no hyphen

il

5

12

Transcribe:
$100
$5

5

9 3

Transcribe:
9 a.m.
3 p.m.

9 12

if

4:30

if

(127)

Boyd

126.

when

conj

car'ried
prompt'ly

nc

915-4321

(96)

LESSON 14

Developing Shorthand Writing Power

127. FREQUENT PHRASES

Want

a 

To

b 

a. I want, he wants, he wanted, you wanted, who wanted, if you want, do you want.
b. To pay, to buy, to plan, to spend, to form, to supply, to ship, to judge.

128. GEOGRAPHICAL EXPRESSIONS

-ington

a 

States

b 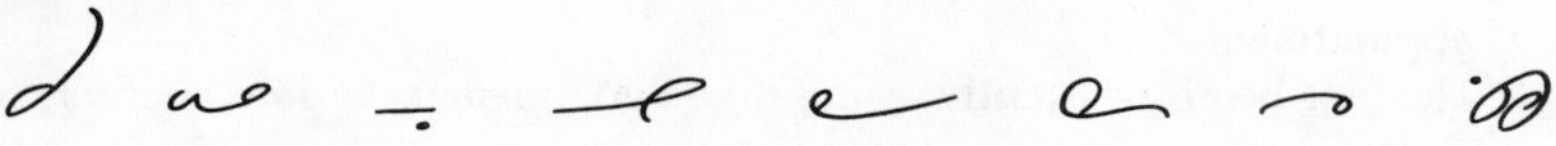

Foreign Countries

c 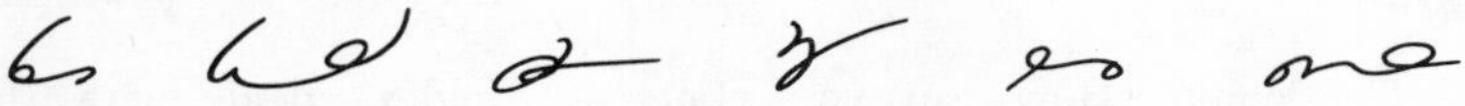

a. Arlington, Bennington, Bloomington, Irvington, Burlington.
b. Virginia, Oregon, New Hampshire, Massachusetts, Illinois, Arkansas, Kentucky, Hawaii.
c. Peru, Poland, Siam, Sweden, Turkey, Ukraine.

Building Transcription Skills

129. BUSINESS VOCABULARY BUILDER

infallible Incapable of error.

incur To bring down on oneself.

diversified Distributed, as investments among different types of securities.

Writing Practice

130. PREVIEW

131.

132.

133.

131. Gentlemen, successfully, infallible, accurately, strength, enable, to judge, program, analysis, improvement, facilities.
132. Apparently, mind, firmly, particular, period, fixed, undue, explanation, appointment.
133. Has not been, constantly, some time ago, opened, within, another, possible.

LETTERS

131. Gentlemen: How can you tell whether a business is operating successfully or not?

There is no infallible[1] way, but there are means of testing accurately the strength of an organization. The enclosed folder[2] deals with three services that we render that enable you to judge the success of a business; namely,[3] a carefully planned financial program, an analysis of methods of operation, and suggestions for[4] improvement.

May we discuss with you how the facilities of the Arkansas National Bank can be put to[5] work for you. Just return the post card that is enclosed, and an agent will call at your convenience. Very truly yours,[6]

---

132. Dear Mr. Fox: Apparently you have not had an opportunity to give much thought to our letter of May 6.[7] I am writing you again just in case the contents of that letter have slipped your mind.

I am firmly convinced that our[8] financing plan is the best one for your particular needs. It is the best one because you can arrange[9] to pay back your loan over a long period of time. It does not require any fixed payment dates; therefore,[10] it does not place an undue strain on the funds of your organization.

There is no obligation in asking[11] for an explanation. Why not call us at 415-6113 and arrange an appointment. Cordially yours,[12]

---

133. Dear Mr. Adams: Up to the present time your name has not been listed among our constantly increasing number[13] of new friends, although we sent you one of our steel banks some time ago.

As you will recall, we explained that we would[14] charge your account with the purchase price of the bank; but we promised to cancel the charge of $2 if you opened[15] an account within ninety days. This time has elapsed, but you have not yet opened an account. We want[16] to keep our part of the agreement; therefore, we are extending the time for opening your account for[17] another ten days.

We hope that you will find it possible to call soon and open an account. Cordially yours,[18] (360)

Reading and Writing Practice

134.

ser

Transcribe:
$10,000
di·ver'si·fied

(156)

135.

de·pos'it
sim'ple

sim'ply
re·ceipt'

conj

par

intro

(179)

136.

re·ceive'
com'pli·men'ta·ry

ser

intro

par

par

var'y·ing
match
right

intro

613-4156

(123)

Developing Shorthand Writing Power

137. WORD ENDINGS

-ment

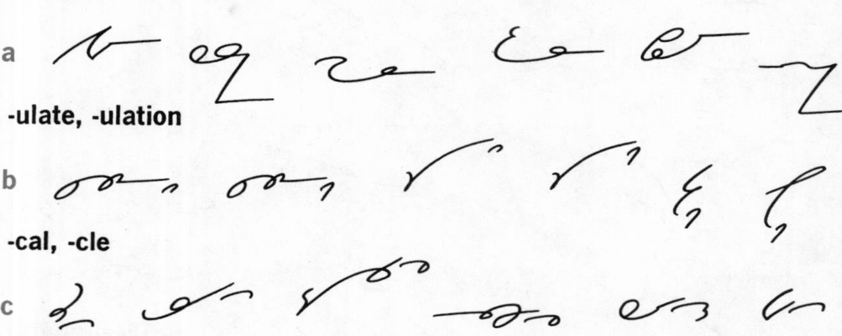

-ulate, -ulation

-cal, -cle

a. Department, arrangement, compliment, supplement, appointment, encouragement.
b. Accumulate, accumulation, stimulate, stimulation, population, tabulation.
c. Physical, radical, systematically, mechanically, articles, particle.

Building Transcription Skills

138. BUSINESS VOCABULARY BUILDER

systematically According to a definite plan.

unstinted Without limit.

crisis A crucial time.

Progressive Speed Builder (60-100)

139. PREVIEW

140.

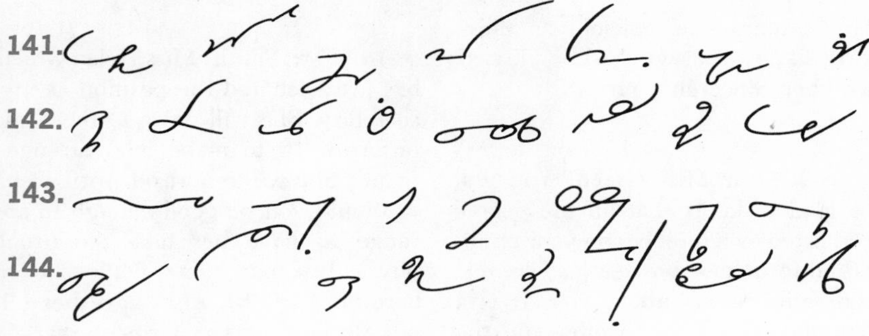

140. This morning, application, reference, shorthand, whether, opinion, envelope.
141. Pleasure, students, in fact, one time, becoming, reporter, hesitation.
142. Thank you for your, bank, written, highly, I might say, trained, efficient, pleased.
143. Glad to know, encouraging, therefore, convenient, arrangements, enjoy, anxious.
144. Accepted, to make, enough, usual, physical, judging, excellent, should be able.

LETTERS

(1 Minute at 60)

140. Dear Miss Lee: This morning I received a letter of application from Miss Helen/Green. She is applying for a position as my secretary and gave your name//as a reference. She tells me that you were her shorthand teacher.

I wonder whether///you would write us your opinion of Miss Green. A stamped envelope is enclosed. Yours sincerely, (1)

(1 Minute at 70)

141. Dear Mr. Gates: It is a pleasure to give you my opinion of Miss Helen Green, who is/applying for a position as your secretary. Miss Green is one of the best students I have ever//had. In fact, at one time she was thinking of becoming a shorthand reporter. In addition,///she is a fast typist.

I have no hesitation in recommending her to you. Cordially yours, (2)

(1 Minute at 80)

142. Dear Miss Lee: Thank you for your letter telling us that you have no hesitation in recommending Miss Green for/a position with our bank. All the people to whom we have written about her speak highly of her, and I plan//to offer the position to her.

I might say that we have in our department of the bank several of the///girls you have trained; and if

Miss Green is as efficient as these girls, I know that we shall be pleased with her. Sincerely yours, (3)

(1 Minute at 90)

143. Dear Miss Green: You will be glad to know that all the people you listed as references on your application form have written/us very encouraging letters about you. It is a pleasure, therefore, to offer you the position as my//secretary.

If it is convenient for you, please come to my office on Monday, April 10, so that we may make final///arrangements.

I am sure you will enjoy being with us. You will find all your fellow workers anxious to help you succeed. Cordially yours, (4)

(1 Minute at 100)

144. Mr. Smith: Miss Helen Green has just accepted the position as my secretary. She will come to the bank on April 10 to make final/arrangements. She will report on April 15.

Would you be good enough to arrange to have her take the usual physical examination//while she is here on April 10. Also, have her fill out all the necessary forms so that all these details will have been disposed of///when she reports.

Judging by the excellent reports I have received about Miss Green, she should be able to handle the job nicely. A. C. Gates (5) (400)

Reading and Writing Practice

145.

re·sponse'
cus'tom·ers
sys'tem·at'i·cal·ly

intro

par

ex·pens'es
de·pos'i·tor

enu

a·vail′
at·tached′

if ser

(152)

146.

nc

prac′ti·cal
thrift′y

and o

conj

if

cr

nc

conj

(132)

147. de·pos'i·tors un·stint'ed es·pe'cial·ly

40

par

30's

(55)

148. af·fect' read'i·est

ac·quaint'ed cus'toms

(132)

149. BRIEF FORMS AND DERIVATIVES

The following chart contains 102 brief forms and derivatives. Can you read the brief forms as rapidly going up and down each column as you can read them going from left to right?

Reading goal: 7 minutes or less.

	a	b	c	d	e	f
1						
2						
3						
4						
5						
6						
7						
8						
9						
10						
11						
12						
13						
14						
15						
16						
17						

CHAPTER 4

Food

Typing-Style Brushup

In the lessons of Chapter 4 you will review the punctuation with quotation marks and the correct methods of typing titles.

Titles

Books, booklets, and pamphlets. In letters, titles of books, booklets, and pamphlets are enclosed in quotation marks.

> Our book, "Modern Business English," just came off the press.
>
> "Bookkeeping and Accounting Practice" is the book we use.
>
> A copy of our booklet, "Punctuation in a Nutshell," is enclosed.
>
> Your pamphlet, "Economy and Oil Heating," was interesting and informative.

Magazines, newspapers, and bulletins. In letters, titles of magazines, newspapers, and bulletins are not quoted; they are simply capitalized.

> I subscribe to a magazine called Today's Secretary.
>
> Did you read today's New York Times?
>
> Our weekly bulletin, The Pipe Line, will be discontinued in July.

The first word and all the other main words in a title are capitalized. Words such as *in, the, and* in the body of the title are not capitalized.

Caution: These styles are recommended for general business letters; they are the ones followed in your textbook.

However, some publishers prefer to have the titles of their publications typed in all caps; others prefer to have them underscored.

, introducing short quote

isq

(,)

Short quotations are introduced by a comma.

> The businessman said, "I am leaving town tomorrow."
>
> He replied, "I cannot accept the position."
>
> Mr. Arnold declared, "We shall tolerate no further interruptions."

: introducing long quote

ilq

(:)

Long quotations are introduced by a colon.

The author said: "I am writing the first chapter of my book; and I expect to finish it by Friday, April 16. If all goes well, I should have the entire manuscript in your hands by May 20."

John said: "I cannot attend the conference in Toledo. I have several previously scheduled appointments that will necessitate my remaining here. I am sending James Brown in my place."

. inside quote　　, inside quote　　? inside quote

iq (.)　　iq (,)　　iq (?)

1. The comma and period are *always* typed inside the final quotation mark.

Harry said, "The book is very interesting."

The man remarked, "There should be two chairs in this office."

Our booklet, "How to Plan an Investment Program," is enclosed.

Her complaint, "I have been waiting for three hours," was ignored.

2. Question marks are placed inside or outside the final quotation mark according to the sense of the sentence.

She asked, "Have you read your mail?"

Why did she say, "I am not happy here"?

3. Semicolons and colons are *always* placed outside the final quotation mark.

Be sure to mark the letter "Confidential"; then place the carbon on my desk.

Shipments of the following goods should be marked "Fragile": China, glassware, and ceramics.

LESSON 16

Developing Shorthand Writing Power

150. OUTLINE CONSTRUCTION

Vowel written in -ant, -ent. The vowel is written in the endings *-ant, -ent* when those endings follow *ī, n, r,* or *l.*

a. Giant, reliant, self-reliant, defiant, client.
b. Prominent, permanent, component, dominant, indignant.
c. Current, transparent, tolerant, warrant, ignorant.
d. Excellent, silent, talent, transplant, implant.

Building Transcription Skills

151. BUSINESS VOCABULARY BUILDER

artificial Not real.

anecdote A brief, interesting story.

scores Large numbers.

Reading and Writing Practice

152. Courtesy — The Oil of Business

Do not

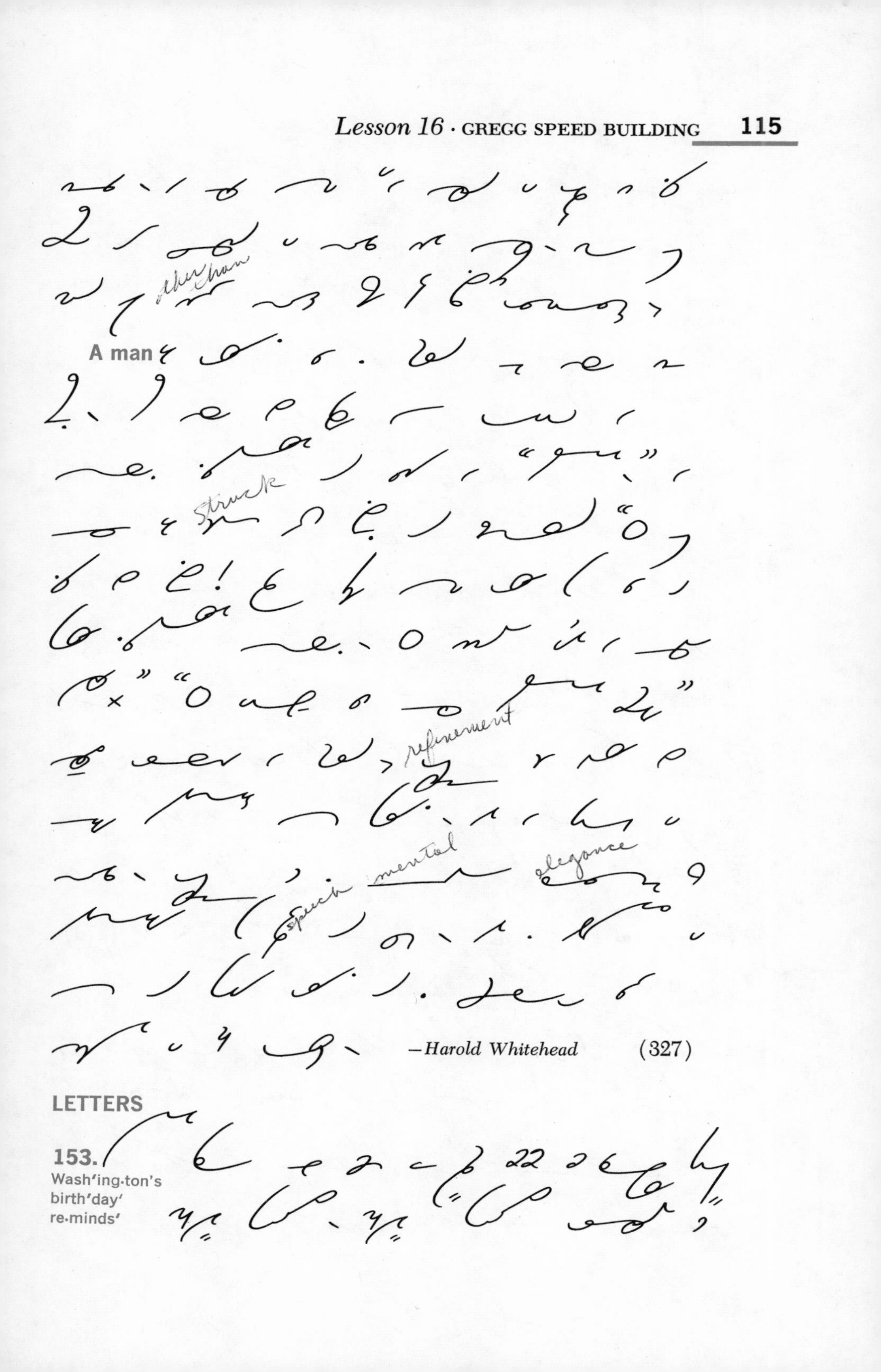

A man

—*Harold Whitehead* (327)

LETTERS

153.

Wash'ing·ton's
birth'day'
re·minds'

caught
wheth'er

isq iq intro par isq iq isq iq

guid'ed
pol'i·cies

conj if par

(176)

154.

max'i·mum
ris'ing

intro

intro

intro

ques'tion
prom'i·nent·ly

if

(103)

155.

ap

iq

(36)

156.

re·quire'ments
sea'sons

stocked

if

ex'cel·lent
suit'a·ble

(114)

157. intro enu ser if (86)

158. pur'chase gro'cer·y enu intro (53)

A substantial reserve of speed is essential for any secretary who is eager to move ahead.

Developing Shorthand Writing Power

159. RECALL DRILL — F

In this drill you will review the various situations in which the shorthand *f* is used.

F

a

-ful

b

Fur-

c

For- Fore-

d

-ification

e

Feet

f

a. Free, friend, frame, fleet, flame, flap.
b. Helpful, wonderful, thoughtful, dreadful, beautiful, tactful, harmful.
c. Furnace, furnaces, furniture, furnish, furnishings, further, furthermore, furlough.

d. Forgot, forgotten, forget, fortunate, foreclose, forfeit, foresight.
e. Notification, modification, fortification, classification, ratification, specifications.
f. 4 feet, 100 feet, several hundred feet.

Building Transcription Skills

160. BUSINESS VOCABULARY BUILDER

disbursements Payments; expenditures.

renovating Making new.

cuisine Style of cooking.

Writing Practice

161. PREVIEW

162.

163.

164.

165.

162. One of the most, helpful, you should have, representative, you want, listen, criticism.
163. Cancellation, supplied, products, rendered, fortunate, responsible, during the past.
164. Complimentary, men and women, daily, indeed, furnishes, ideas.
165. Football, won't, beaten, because, loyal.

LETTERS

162. Dear Mrs. Parks: One of the most important men in each of our stores is the manager. He is trained to give you[1] the kind of helpful service that we think you should have. He is our representative and is charged with the duty[2] of satisfying you.

He is in the store to see that you

get what you want—and he is there to listen when you[3] have something on your mind.

If you have a question or a suggestion or a criticism, he is there to hear[4] it.

The next time you are in one of our stores, make it a point to meet the manager; he is your friend. Cordially yours[5]

---

163. Mr. Green: A few days ago we received a cancellation notification from Mrs. E. H. Brown, of[6] 10 Main Street, Trenton, in which she tells that for more than twenty-five years you have supplied her with our milk and dairy[7] products. She says that during that time the service you rendered to her was so satisfactory that she almost[8] regrets moving.

This surely speaks well for you as one of our salesmen. Needless to say, we feel we are fortunate[9] to have you as a member of our organization.

It is the co-operation of men like you that has[10] been responsible for the wonderful growth of our company during the past thirty years. Henry H. Abbey[11]

---

164. Dear Mrs. Burns: During the past year, we received more than 5,000 complimentary comments about the men[12] and women who serve you daily in our stores—almost three times as many favorable comments about our[13] employees as there were the year before.

That makes all of us very happy indeed, as it furnishes proof that[14] we are giving you the kind of service you want.

If you have any ideas as to how we can make your shopping[15] even more satisfying, please write to our Customer Relations Department at 14 West Broadway. Yours truly,[16]

---

165. Dear Mr. Day: There is an old football saying that a team that won't be beaten can't be beaten. The same thing applies[17] to food stores.

Your local Johnson Store is a better place to shop because the loyal employees who make up[18] our team are striving always to give you better food, better service, and better values.

Once you have visited[19] our store, we think you will agree that for satisfying shopping our store cannot be beaten. Cordially yours,[20] (400)

Reading and Writing Practice

166.

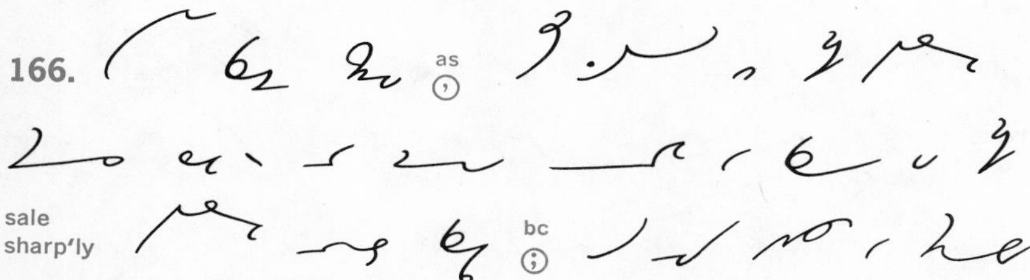

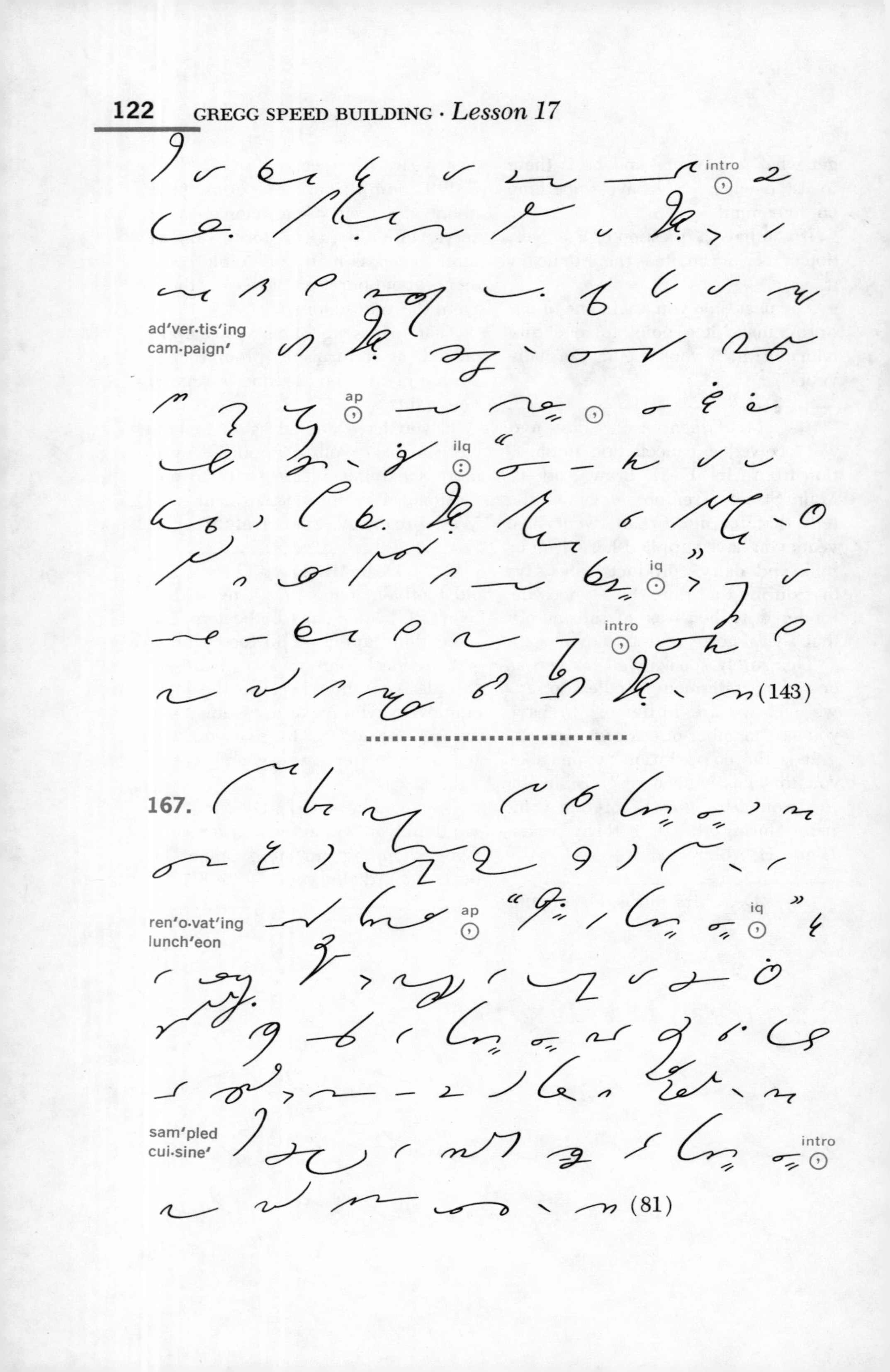

intro

ad'ver·tis'ing
cam·paign'

ap ilq iq intro

(143)

167.

ren'o·vat'ing
lunch'eon

ap iq

sam'pled
cui·sine'

intro

(81)

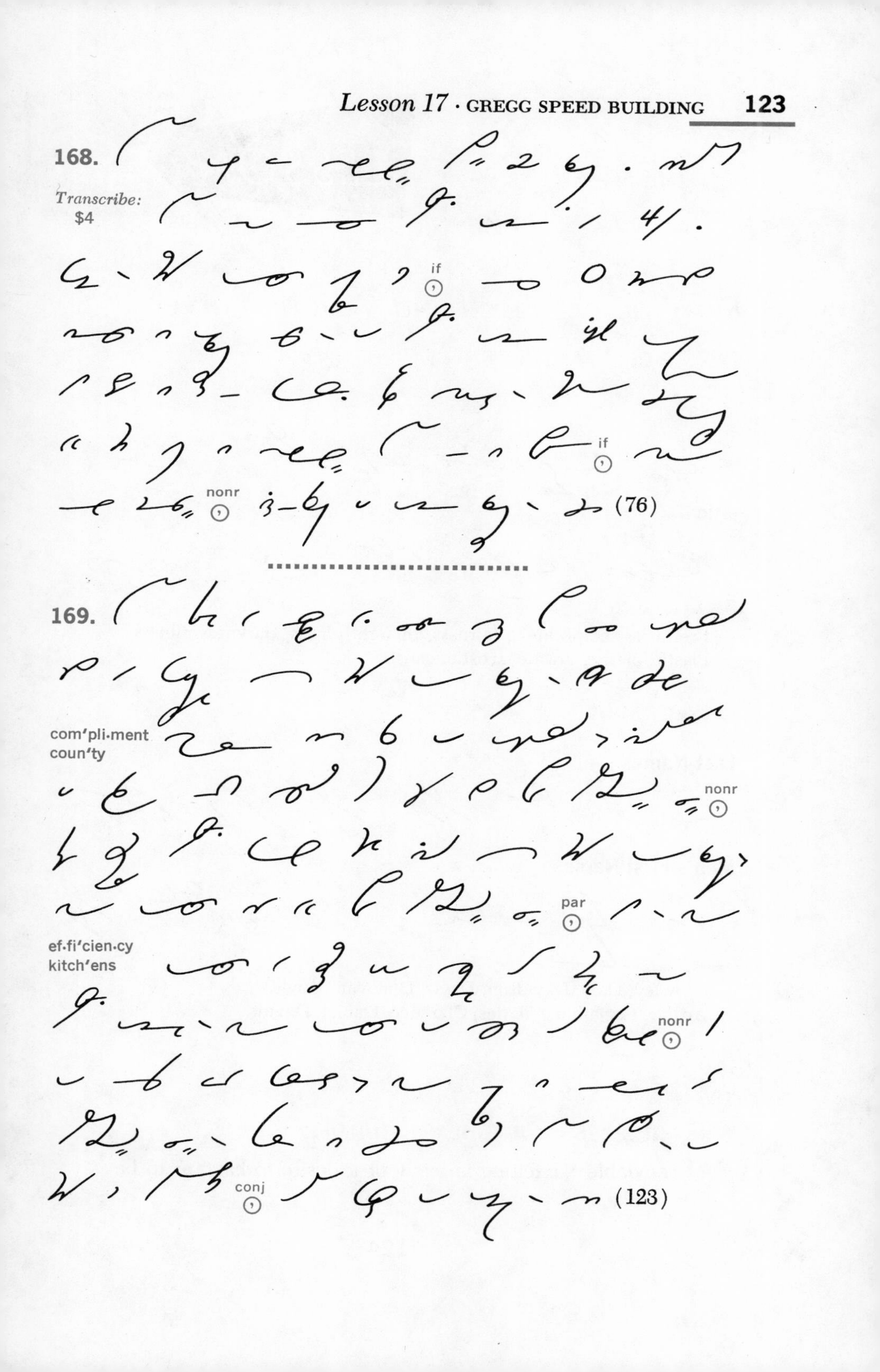

168.

Transcribe: $4

(76)

169.

com′pli·ment
coun′ty

ef·fi′cien·cy
kitch′ens

(123)

LESSON 18

Developing Shorthand Writing Power

170. WORD FAMILIES

-ness

a

-stic

b

a. Freshness, helpfulness, fairness, thoughtfulness, darkness, illness.
b. Plastic, elastic, drastic, artistic, caustic.

171. FREQUENT NAMES

Last Names

a

Men's First Names

b

a. Crowley, Daly, Davidson, Davis, Donovan, Doyle.
b. Arthur, Benjamin, Charles, Clarence, Daniel, David.

Building Transcription Skills

172. BUSINESS VOCABULARY BUILDER

enviable Exciting an envy or a desire to have or to be like.

inferior Of less value; of poorer quality.

concession A grant or lease of a portion of premises for some specific purpose; for example, a vegetable concession in a supermarket.

Writing Practice

173. PREVIEW

174.

175.

176.

174. I am sure, you want, family, one of the, Connecticut, enclosed, quality, interested, to know.
175. Description, manager, I want, helpfulness, attempt, neighborhood, profitable, quantity, sampled, scheduled, efforts, determine.
176. Reputation, itself, however, corner, attractive, buyers, in addition, procedures.

LETTERS

174. Dear Mrs. Arthur: I am sure you want the best when it comes to dairy products for your family. If you should like[1] these products delivered fresh from one of the finest farms of Connecticut, return the enclosed card telling us what[2] we can deliver to you as a trial order. I am sure you and your family will be so delighted with the[3] freshness and quality of the products you receive that you will want us to take care of all your dairy needs.

You[4] will be interested to know that we serve many of your neighbors.

Won't you give our products a trial? Sincerely yours,[5]

175. Dear Mr. Charles: Enclosed with this letter is a complete description of Daniel's Soup Sale that will start on Monday,[6] May 6.

As sales manager of the Charles Soup Company, I want to thank you for your helpfulness in our attempt[7] to get a sample of Daniel's Soup into the homes of as many families in your neighborhood as possible.[8]

We have tried to make our plan profitable to you as the dealer. We realize, of course, that the quantity[9] of soup sold and the number of families sampled depend on you. The advertising scheduled for May in the[10] Denver Times will help; but the displays in your store and the efforts of your clerks will help determine the amount of[11] Daniel's Soup you sell and the profit you make.

Many thanks for your wonderful co-operation. Cordially yours,[12]

176. Dear Mrs. Daniels: As you no doubt know, our store has made an enviable reputation for itself as a[13] meat market. For years we have been supplying local families with the finest cuts of meat.

We wonder, however,[14] whether you have had an opportunity to visit our fruit corner recently. You will find it more[15] attractive than ever before.

Our fruit buyers make every effort to buy only the finest of fruits. Our clerks[16] keep the fruit displays neat and fresh. In addition, we have improved our packing procedures to ensure freshness and[17] shopping convenience.

On your next visit, stop at the fruit corner. You will be pleased with what you find there. Cordially yours,[18] (360)

Reading and Writing Practice

177.

isq

iq

veg'e·ta·ble
con·ces'sion

nonr

par

nonr

rea'son
com·plaint'

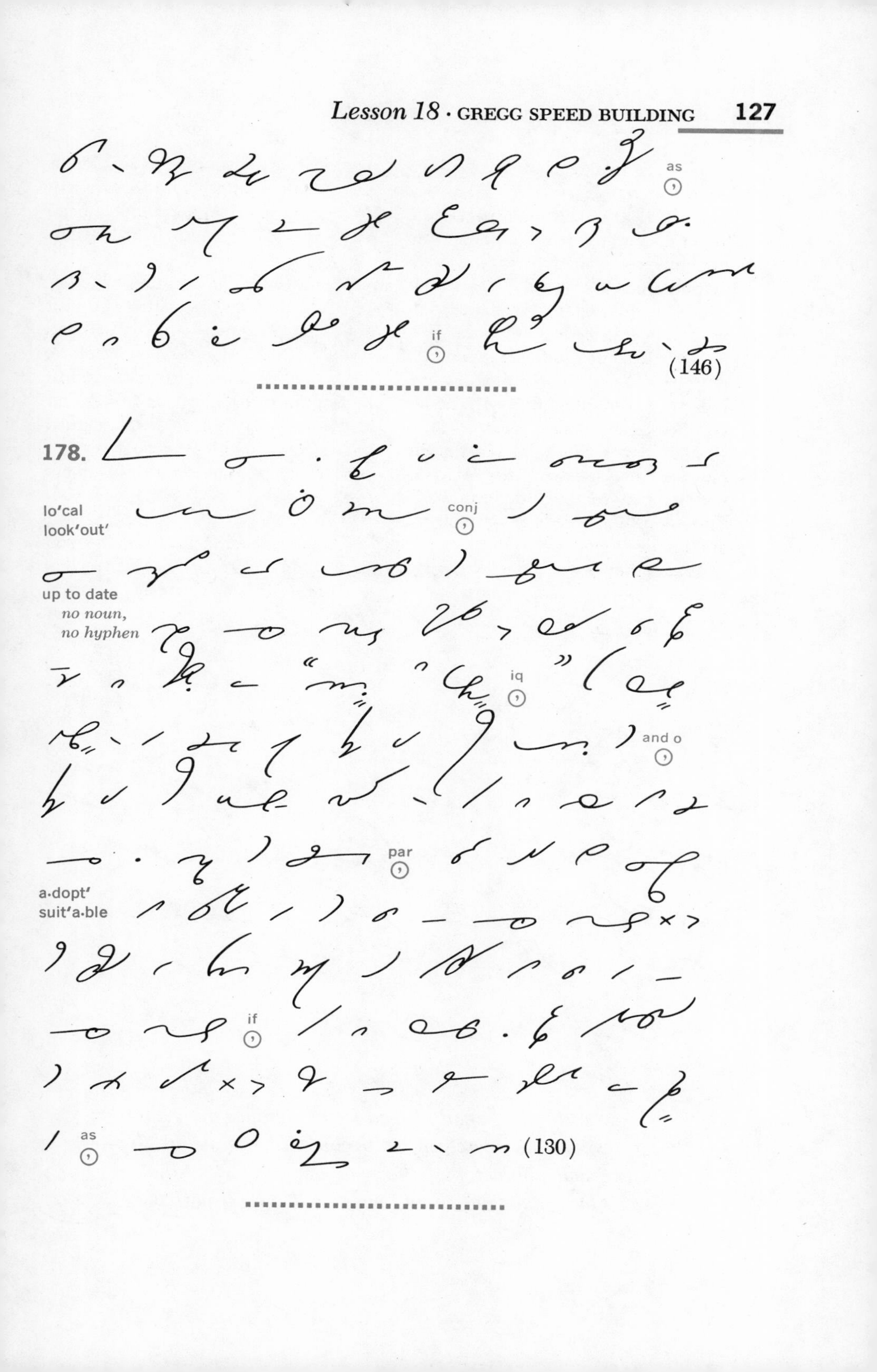

as

if

(146)

178.

lo'cal
look'out'

conj

up to date
no noun,
no hyphen

iq

and o

par

a·dopt'
suit'a·ble

if

as

(130)

179.

rise
work'ers'
mid'day'

intro

intro

nc

em·ploy'ees
mo·rale'

16 45

intro

ap

iq

(145)

An attractive, neatly typed letter signifies more than a responsible secretary; it becomes a sample of the taste and character of the company. No letter that a secretary mails out should ever be less than perfect.

LESSON 19

Developing Shorthand Writing Power

180. FREQUENT PHRASES

Time

a

As

b

a. Next time, same time, any time, one time, at a time, few times, several times.
b. As well, as good, as many, as much, as low, as little.

181. GEOGRAPHICAL EXPRESSIONS

-ingham

a

States

b

Foreign Countries

c

a. Birmingham, Framingham, Nottingham, Effingham, Cunningham.
b. Utah, Oklahoma, Nevada, Maryland, Idaho, Arizona, Alaska.
c. U.S.S.R., Uruguay, Venezuela, Albania.

Building Transcription Skills

182. BUSINESS VOCABULARY BUILDER

judiciously Wisely.

gratifying Pleasing.

recipes Formulas for cooking dishes.

Writing Practice

183. PREVIEW

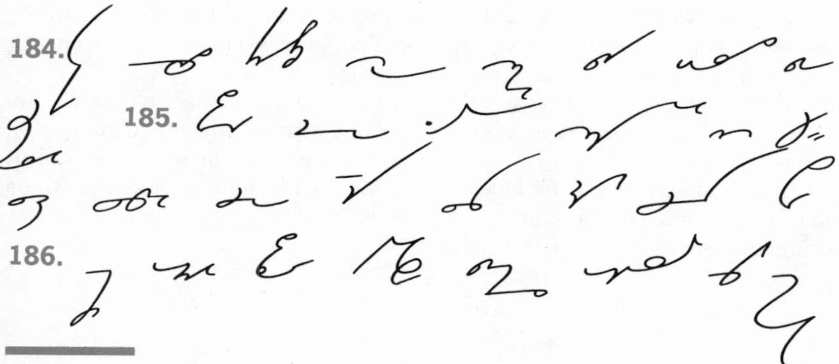

184. Budget, mighty, judiciously, quality, coupons, used, already, user, favorites.
185. Expect, summer, handle, customers, work, Saturday, enough, announce, senior, interested, any time, substantial, same time, about the.
186. In view, results, experienced, during the past, uniformly, restaurants, in addition, invaluable.

LETTERS

184. Dear Mrs. Knight: Your food budget is a mighty important item to both of us. It is important to you[1] because it is your job to use it judiciously; it is important to us because we strive to bring you the[2] very finest quality for your money.

We are enclosing several coupons in this letter to help you[3] stretch your food dollar. The coupons may be used for the purchase of a number of new Smith products that we know you[4] will want to try.

If you already are a user of these

products, you will be happy to save in the purchase[5] of them. If you are not, we know you will be delighted to add these products to your list of favorites. Yours truly,[6]

---

185. Dear Mr. Gray: Because of the increased business that we expect during the summer months, we shall need four boys to[7] handle stock and to work with customers. Two of the boys would work from nine to one; the other two, from one to five.[8] All four would work a full eight hours on Saturday, which is our busiest day.

I wonder whether you would be good[9] enough to announce these jobs to your class of senior boys and invite any who are interested to come in[10] to see me at any time that is convenient to them.

By doing this, you will be helping some boys to earn a[11] substantial sum during the summer and at the same time to learn a good deal about the food business. Cordially yours,[12]

---

186. Dear Mr. Murphy: In view of the fact that we were one of the first users of the Alaska Ice-Maker,[13] I thought you might be interested in the results we experienced.

During the past year we have installed one[14] of your units in every Smith Hotel. Our results with them have been uniformly good. The satisfaction[15] of our guests with the ice now supplied in our restaurants and in our hotel rooms is most gratifying.

Since[16] these machines were installed, our savings have been encouraging.

In addition to the savings we are making, the[17] advantage of having all the ice we want when we want it is invaluable in our business. Yours truly,[18] (360)

Reading and Writing Practice

187. intro

whetĥ'er
lunch'eon
shop'ping

nonr

par

bc

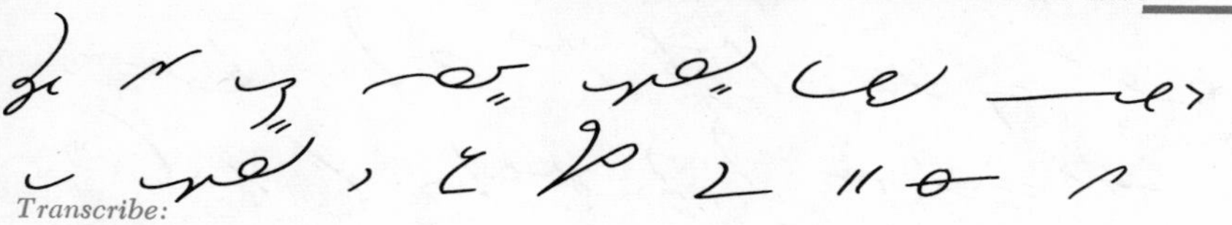

Transcribe:
11 a.m.
11 p.m.

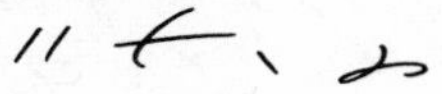

(103)

188.

intro ,

enu :

pleas′ant
rep′u·ta′tion

and o ,

low′-price′
hyphenated before noun

il ;

,

(129)

189.

es·pe′cial·ly
veg′e·ta·ble

par ,

rec'i·pe
week

conj

guests
yours

if

nc

(107)

190.

intro

de·signed'
in'di·vid'u·al

if

intro

conj

(119)

LESSON 20

Developing Shorthand Writing Power

191. WORD BEGINNINGS AND ENDINGS

-ble

a

De-, Dĭ-

b

Self-

c

a. Dependable, available, profitable, vegetable, considerably, honorable, reliable.
b. Delighted, delivery, delaying, depart, direct, direction.
c. Self-addressed, self-imposed, self-made, self-satisfied, self-supporting, self-respect.

Building Transcription Skills

192. BUSINESS VOCABULARY BUILDER

swapped Exchanged.

nutrition The process of nourishing, feeding.

meticulous Extremely careful.

asset Something of value.

Progressive Speed Builder (60-100)

193. PREVIEW

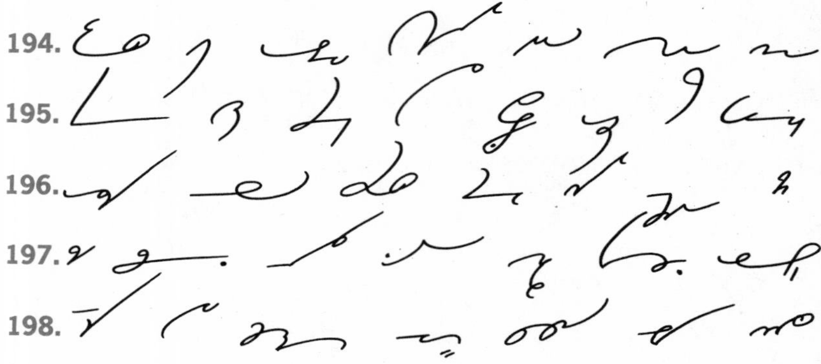

194. Supply, to have, let us know, dividends, toward, greater, one of our.
195 Gentlemen, thank you for, very much, to me, appreciate, receive, advantage, promotion.
196. Requested, mailed, variety, forms, your orders, in the future, issue.
197. Yesterday, examining, indeed, handle, copies, beginning, relationship.
198. Interested, to know, weeks ago, New York, account, next time, worthwhile.

LETTERS

(1 Minute at 60)

194. Dear Mr. Gray: Our new supply of catalogues just arrived. If you would like to have/a copy, please let us know.

It will pay you big dividends to place your food business//with us. You can take the first step toward greater profits by sending for one of our catalogues///now. A self-addressed envelope is enclosed for your convenience. Sincerely yours, (1)

(1 Minute at 70)

195. Gentlemen: Thank you for writing me about your catalogue. I should like very much to have a/ copy. Please send it to me personally, so that I shall be sure to see it.

I should also//appreciate it if you would place my name on your mailing list to receive all the sales helps that you///issue to food stores. We can use these helps to good advantage in our promotion work. Sincerely yours, (2)

(1 Minute at 80)

196. Dear Mr. Gray: As you requested, we have mailed you today a copy of our new catalogue. I think you will/be pleased with the large variety of food products it lists. In the back of the catalogue you will find a number//of forms that you can use in placing your orders. These forms will save you a great deal of time.

Your name has been placed/// on our mailing list, and in the future you will receive all sales helps that we issue to food stores. Sincerely yours, (3)

(1 Minute at 90)

197. Gentlemen: The catalogue you sent me arrived yesterday, and I have spent several hours examining it. I was indeed/impressed with your large variety of food products. I found many items that I am sure we can handle with profit to// you as well as to us.

I wonder whether you would be good enough to send me two more copies of the catalogue. I have/// the feeling that this is the beginning of a profitable business relationship for both of us. Very cordially yours, (4)

(1 Minute at 100)

198. Mr. Ames: You will be interested to know that some weeks ago we received a request for one of our catalogues from Mr. E. H./ Gray, of the New York Food Stores. We sent him a copy, and today we received an order from him amounting to $355.//If we give him the right kind of service, we can build this into a very profitable account.

May I suggest that the next time you///are in New York you stop in to see Mr. Gray. In fact, it might even be worthwhile for you to make a special trip to see him. Charles H. West. (5) (400)

Reading and Writing Practice

199.

iq

par

by'gone' swapped

to·day's'
sea'son
sim'ply

bc

par

mir'a·cle
mil'lions

intro

de·pend'a·ble
na'tion's
wel'fare'

(219)

200.

nonr

for'mer·ly
ap·ply'ing

rec'om·men·da'tion
tes'ti·fy·ing

ser

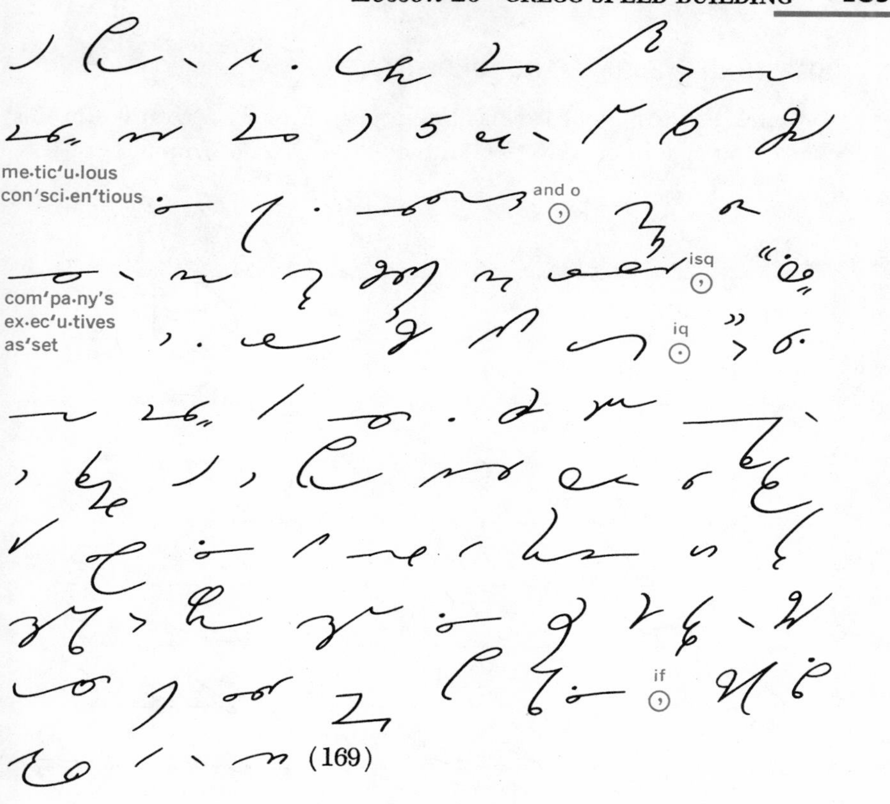

In keeping with the increased pace of business, the executive finds that he no longer has time to attend to much of his own detail work. He must now depend on his secretary to take care of many important matters that he formerly handled. He wants a truly competent and responsible assistant. If you can meet these requirements, many a harried executive will be eager and ready to roll out the red carpet for you—wall to wall!

201. BRIEF FORMS AND DERIVATIVES

How fast can you read the 102 brief forms and derivatives in this chart? You should be able to read the entire chart in 7 minutes or less.

	a	b	c	d	e	f
1						
2						
3						
4						
5						
6						
7						
8						
9						
10						
11						
12						
13						
14						
15						
16						
17						

PART TWO

Office Equipment
Merchandising
Home Equipment and Maintenance
Radio and Television

DICTATION PROBLEMS

Every shorthand writer, while he is in the process of developing his shorthand speed, at one time or another encounters three problems that he must learn to handle if he is to make progress:

1. What to do when he falls behind;
2. What to do when the dictator uses an unfamiliar word;
3. What to do when he does not hear (or mis-hears) some part of the dictation.

No doubt you have already encountered these problems in your speed-development practice.

Here are some suggestions that will help you cope with these problems.

1. You fall behind. It should not be a source of distress to you when you occasionally fall behind your dictator in your practice. It is only natural for you to fall behind sometimes when you are striving to reach a higher speed than the one at which you are writing. If you were always able to get all the dictation easily, it would be a sign that the dictation rate was not rapid enough and that consequently your speed was not increasing. (Of course, falling behind consistently is a different and more serious matter!) When you find yourself falling behind:

(a) Hang on as long as you can. Very often the dictator may pause to take a breath or to clear his throat, and the few seconds that it takes him to do this may be sufficient for you to catch up.

(b) When you can hold on no longer, skip the words that you have not written and leave a line or two blank. (When you transcribe, this blank space will indicate the point at which you have a break.)

(c) Pick up the dictation at the new point. (Never stop writing during a speed take. If you do, you will never become a really rapid writer.)

(d) When you transcribe, try, with the help of context, to supply some of the words that you had to leave out.

2. You meet an unfamiliar word. The most expert writer will occasionally have to write a shorthand outline for a word that is unfamiliar to him. When this happens to you, follow these suggestions:

(a) Try to write the word in full, alphabetically.

(b) If you cannot write it in full, try to get at least the beginning of the word. This beginning may help you locate the correct word in the dictionary when you transcribe.

(c) If the word completely escapes you, leave a space or even skip a line (so that you can readily locate the spot at which the word occurs) and keep on writing. The important consideration is that you do not become flustered and lose precious time worrying about the word as the dictation runs on ahead of you.

When you transcribe, you may be able to substitute a synonym for the word you missed that will not impair the meaning of the dictation.

The larger your English vocabulary, the less frequently will this problem confront you. Consequently, do all you can to increase your vocabulary through extensive reading.

3. You do not hear a word (or you mis-hear it). Even a writer with the most acute hearing will occasionally fail to hear (or will mis-hear) a word, either because the dictator did not enunciate clearly or because some noise interfered with hearing. These suggestions will help you to handle this problem:

(a) Leave a space or even skip a line when you do not hear a word. Once again, context may help you to supply the word — or at least a satisfactory substitute — when you are transcribing. Do not stop writing with the hope that the context of the next few words may suggest the word you missed. If you stop writing, you may fall hopelessly behind the dictator.

(b) If you think you hear a word but the context tells you that it could not possibly be the correct one, write what you think you hear anyway and, if you can, encircle the outline quickly. If you are pressed for time, leave a space or skip a line. By writing what you think you hear, your outline will often suggest the actual word that was dictated.

For example, if you think you hear, "There was a large increase in the building industry's reduction rate," write just that; when you transcribe, your outline for reduction will suggest to you that the correct transcription of the sentence is, "There was a large increase in the building industry's production rate."

(c) There will be occasions when a word that you mis-heard or did not hear it all, will occur to you words or even sentences later. When this happens, resist the temptation to go back and insert it. The dictator will not wait while you do so, and you may lose more than you gain. It is better to hope that you will still remember the word when you transcribe — and the chances are that you will.

Of course, the above suggestions are intended to apply only to your speed-development work. When you fall behind, encounter an unfamiliar word, or do not hear a word while you are taking dictation from your employer in the business office, you will interrupt the dictation, for you must not risk the possibility of turning in an imperfect transcript.

CHAPTER 5

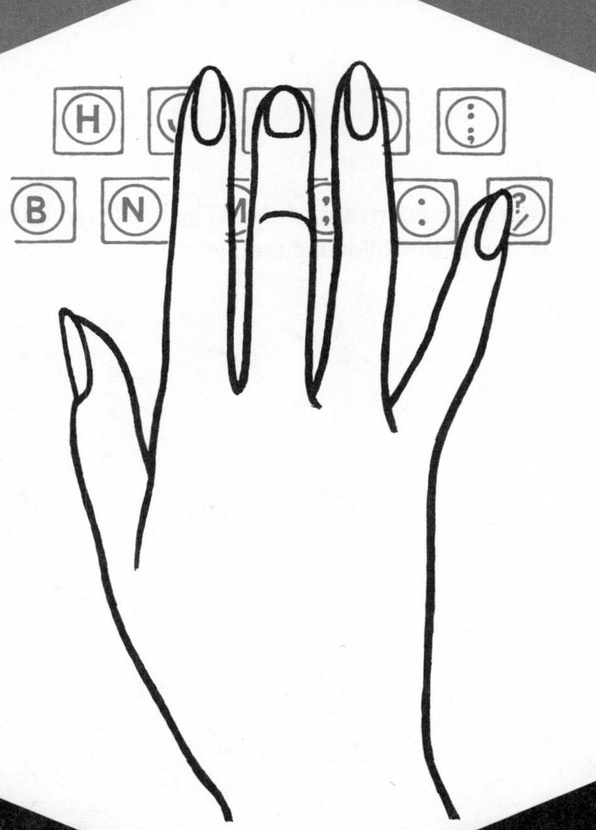

Office Equipment

LESSON 21

Developing Shorthand Writing Power

202. OUTLINE CONSTRUCTION

Omission of vowel in -ant, -ent. The vowel is omitted in the word endings *-ant, -ent* in the following families:

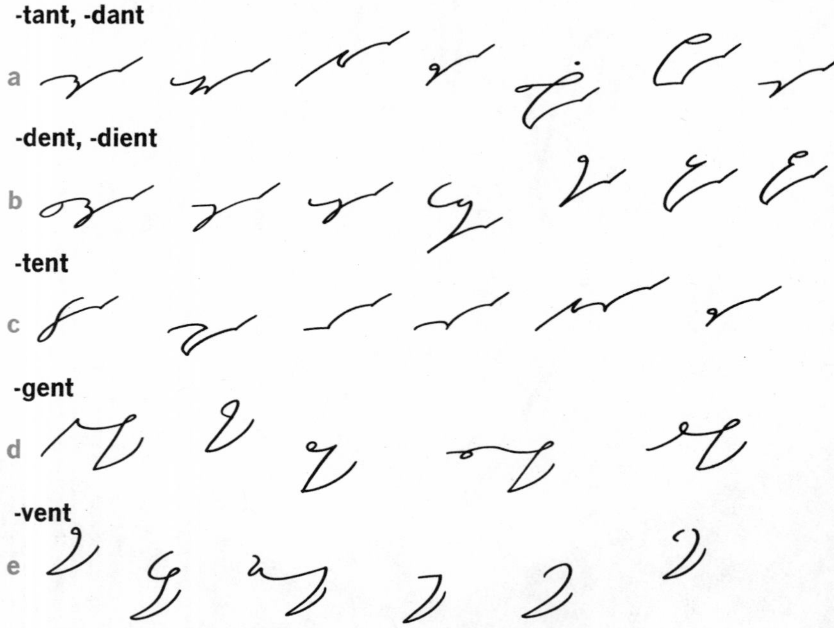

a. Constant, resultant, distant, extant, inhabitant, abundant, instant.
b. Accident, incident, resident, provident, evident, obedient, expedient.
c. Patent, competent, intent, content, discontent, extent.
d. Diligent, agent, urgent, negligent, intelligent.
e. Event, prevent, solvent, invent, convent, circumvent.

Building Transcription Skills

203. PUNCTUATION PRACTICE

, contrast

Contrasting expressions are set off by commas.

He wanted help, not advice.
I am going to the meeting, not because I want to, but because it is my duty.
The harder you work, the more you will earn.

Whenever one of these uses of the comma occurs in the Reading and Writing Practice exercises, it will be indicated in the shorthand thus:

cont

Reading and Writing Practice

204. Proofreading the Transcript

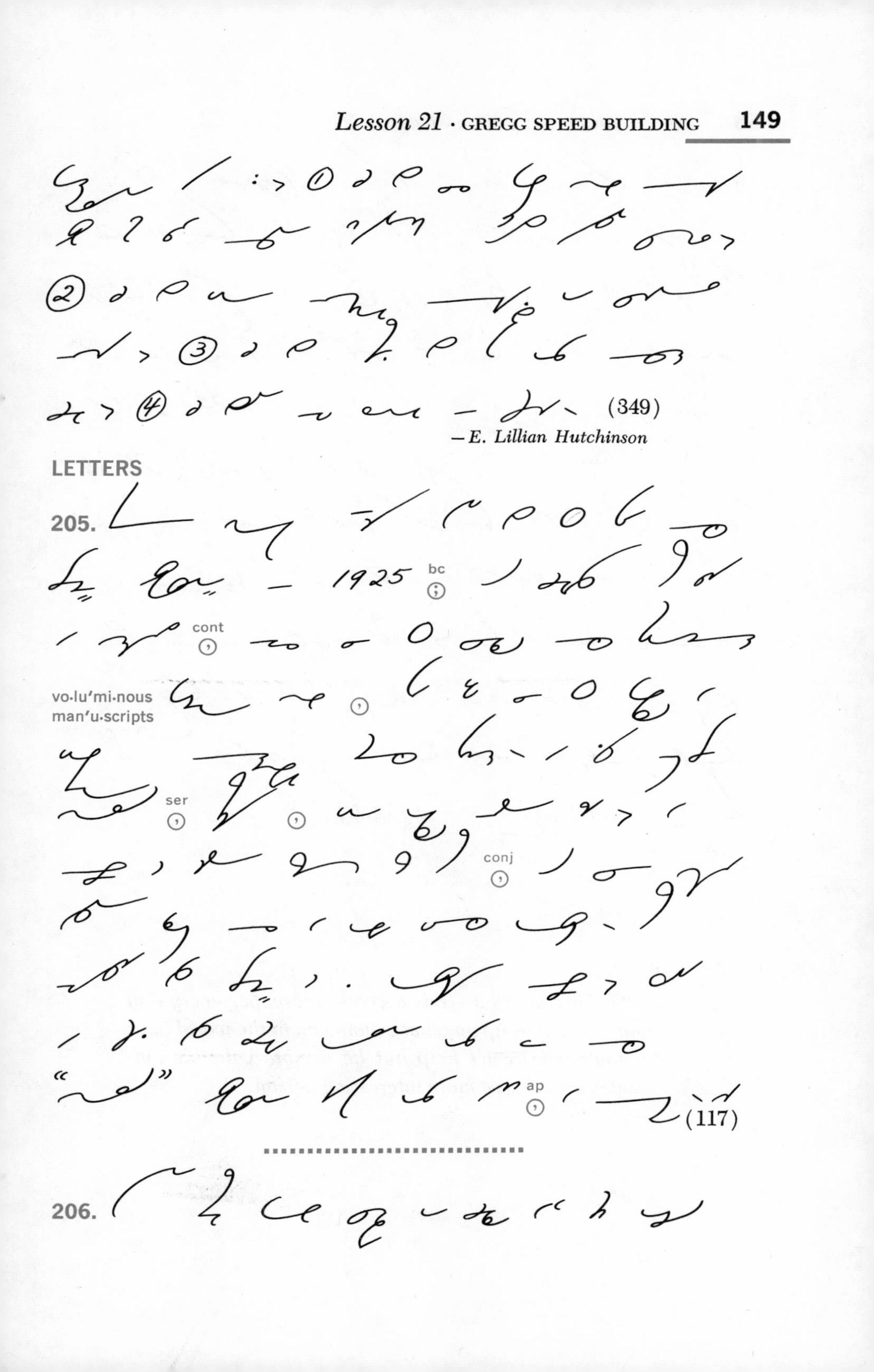

(349)

—E. Lillian Hutchinson

LETTERS

205. 1925 bc cont

vo·lu′mi·nous
man′u·scripts

ser conj ap (117)

206.

The person who reads a good newspaper every day and who keeps up on what is going on in the world (and in town, too) can't help but be a more valuable employee as well as a more interesting person.

LESSON 22

Developing Shorthand Writing Power

207. RECALL DRILL — N

In this drill you will review the several uses of the alphabetic stroke *n*.

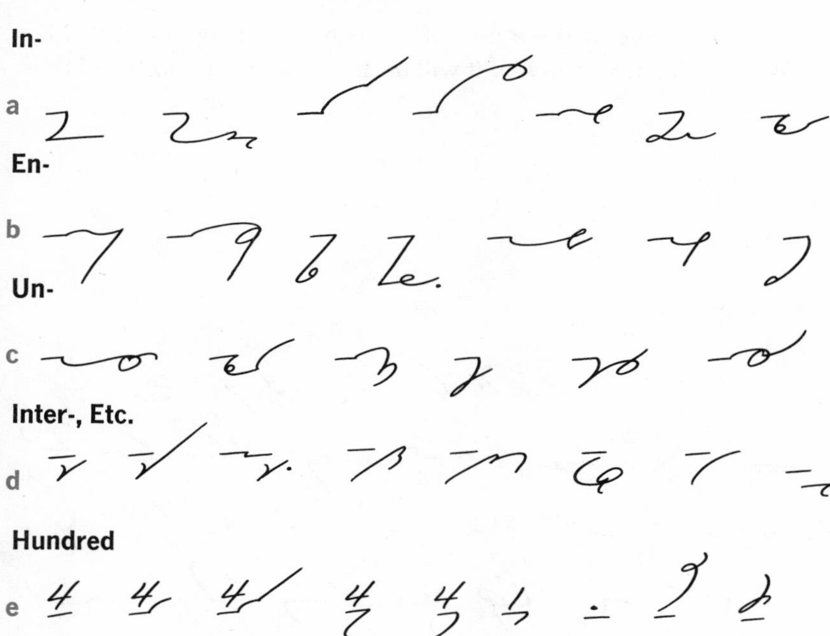

a. Inform, influence, intend, intimate, increase, inferior, insert.
b. Encourage, engage, enjoy, engineering, enlist, enrich, envy.
c. Unlike, uncertain, unconscious, unfit, unfortunate, unkind.
d. Interest, interested, uninteresting; introduce, introduction; enterprise, entertain, entrance.
e. 400, 400,000, $400,000, 400 pounds, 400 feet, 100 per cent, a hundred, several hundred, few hundred.

Building Transcription Skills

208. PUNCTUATION PRACTICE

, words omitted

A comma is used to indicate the omission of a word or several words that are completely understood from the meaning.

> One model sells for $35; the other, for $45.
> The first job is easy; the second, difficult.
> In June our volume was up 20 per cent; in July, 15 per cent.

Whenever one of these uses of the comma occurs in the Reading and Writing Practice exercises, it will be indicated in the shorthand thus:

wo

(,)

Writing Practice

209. PREVIEW

210.

211.

212.

213.

210. Considerable, engineering, discussing, possibility, expense, assembling, necessary, prohibitive, coming.
211. Someone, actually, emergencies, expedients, permanent, solution, reduced, return.

212. Result, efficiency, seldom, businesses, interested, procedure, consequently, private.
213. Manufacturing, difficulty, installed, months ago, will you please, investigate, organization, satisfied.

LETTERS

210. Dear Mr. Fairview: I have spent considerable time with our Engineering Department at the factory[1] discussing the possibility of making a timer of the type that you have in mind. Our engineers tell[2] me that the expense of assembling the necessary machinery would be prohibitive.

We do manufacture[3] a timer that is not automatic, and we might be able to adapt it to your needs.

If you will[4] be in your office during the coming week, I should like to see you to discuss the matter. Cordially yours,[5]

---

211. Dear Mr. Miles: Is there someone in your organization who thinks he is saving money for you but is[6] actually losing money? Is there someone who meets the emergencies that arise each month with such expedients[7] as having the staff work overtime and hiring temporary help instead of seeking a permanent[8] solution to your problems?

Our agent will be glad to call and explain how our machines will enable you to do[9] your accounting work more rapidly and at reduced cost. Simply return the card that is enclosed. Sincerely yours,[10]

---

212. Dear Mr. Harrison: As we all know, profits result from business efficiency. A business that is not run[11] efficiently seldom makes a profit.

For the past one hundred years our organization has been helping[12] businessmen run their businesses more efficiently. It has done this through its complete line of business machines.

We are[13] sure that you are interested in seeing the latest models of our machines and in learning how they will fit[14] into your office procedure. Consequently, we are inviting you to attend our private business show during[15] the week of October 27. I am enclosing four complimentary tickets. Sincerely yours,[16]

---

213. Dear Mr Jackson: Mr. A. J. Palmer, who is head of the Service Department of the Wells Manufacturing[17] Company, was in my office yesterday. He tells me that they are still having difficulty with the time[18] clock that we installed some months ago.

Will you please visit Wells as soon as possible to investigate the[19] situation. This organization has been a fine customer, and we should like to see them satisfied. Sincerely yours,[20] (400)

Reading and Writing Practice

214.

intro

nonr

loss glance

intro

conj

Transcribe: $85 de luxe

85/ nc

wo 120/ (114)

215.

prac'ti·cal fac'tors

nc wo nc

wo

smooth'ly run *no hyphen after ly*

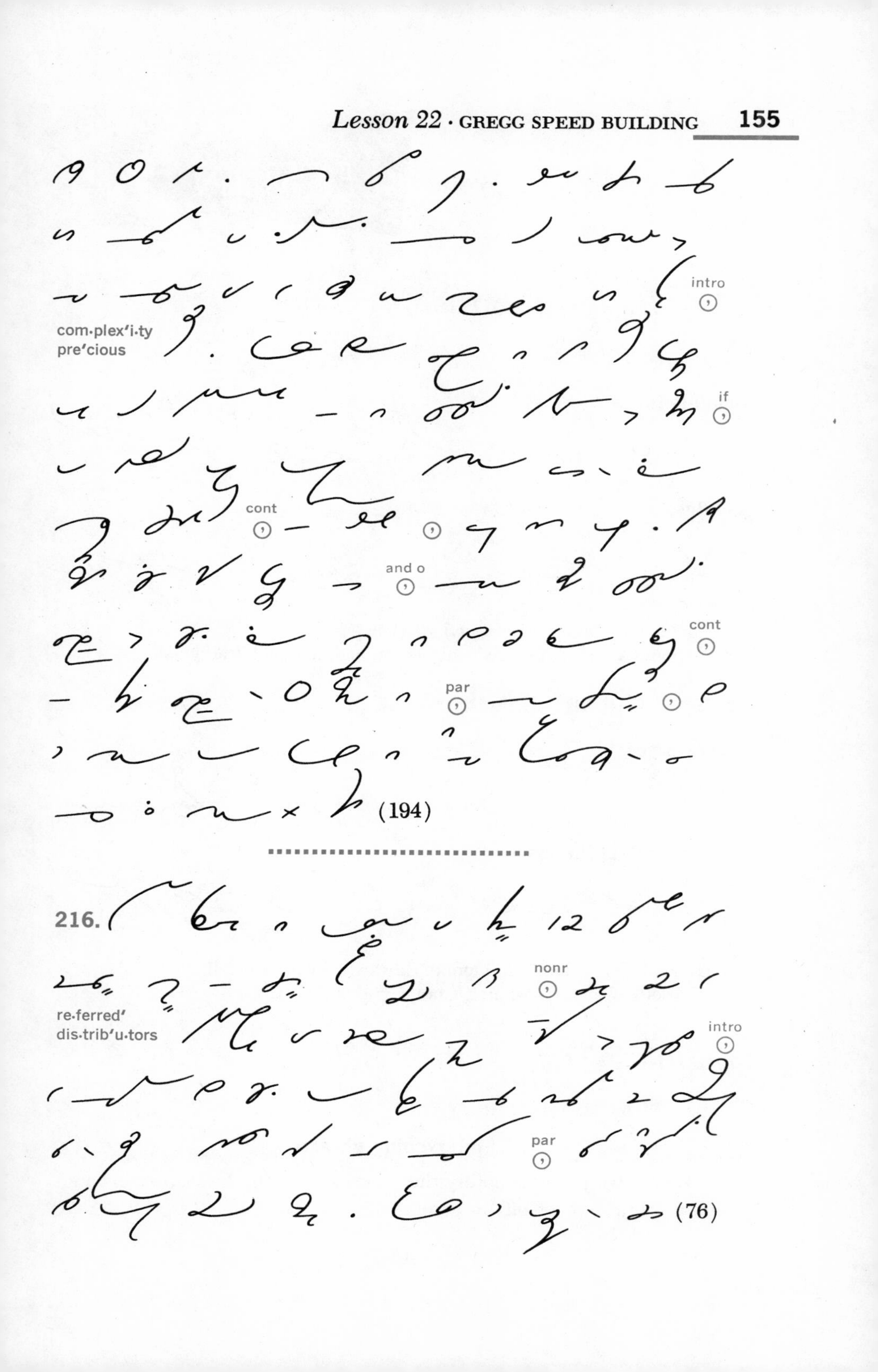

intro

com·plex′i·ty
pre′cious

if

cont

and o

cont

par

(194)

216.

nonr

re·ferred′
dis·trib′u·tors

intro

par

(76)

FRIDAY

LESSON 23

Developing Shorthand Writing Power

217. WORD FAMILIES

-claimed

a

-tional

b

a. Claimed, acclaimed, reclaimed, disclaimed.
b. National, rational, professional, sensational, fictional, fractional.

218. FREQUENT NAMES

Last Names

a

Women's First Names

b

a. Driscoll, Duffy, Duncan, Dunne, Edwards, Evans, Farrell.
b. Charlotte, Clara, Constance, Cora, Cynthia, Delia.

Building Transcription Skills

219. PUNCTUATION PRACTICE

, intervening phrase

When two phrases modify the same expression, the second, or intervening, phrase is set off by commas.

His last book is as interesting as, if not more interesting than, his other books.
He has no time for, nor interest in, any kind of sports.

Caution: Be sure to enclose the complete intervening expression, not just part of it.

No: Our business is as large as, if not larger, than it was a year ago.
Yes: Our business is as large as, if not larger than, it was a year ago.

Each time one of these uses of the comma occurs in the Reading and Writing Practice exercises, it will be indicated in the shorthand thus:

iph

Writing Practice

220. PREVIEW

221. Special, preview, furniture, among the, beautiful, practical, exhibit, in addition, decorating, reserve.
222. Comfort, very important, reflects, employees, adjustable, constructed, encourages, posture, rubber, obtain, neighborhood.
223. Edwards, two thousand, reduced, adjustments, permit, invest.

224. Have been, developed, acclaimed, users, scientifically, health, efficiency, physically.

LETTERS

221. Dear Mrs. Dunne: On May 27 we are having a special preview of National Office Furniture[1] products.

We should like you to be among the first to see what we consider the most beautiful and practical[2] office furniture available today. Here, in our new, air-conditioned building, you will find a complete[3] exhibit of our latest models. In addition, you will have an opportunity to discuss your decorating[4] problems with our experts, all of whom will be present.

Reserve May 27 to visit us. Sincerely yours,[5]

---

222. Dear Mr. Evans: Comfort is very important to people in business. Their work reflects this fact. The employer[6] who knows it and acts on his knowledge has the most efficient employees. National Posture Chairs provide comfort[7] throughout the day. Every model is adjustable; the occupant himself can adjust his chair to the most[8] comfortable position for him.

The chair is so constructed that it encourages good posture, with the result[9] that it eliminates many of the causes of fatigue. It has rubber cushions that stay cool and clean.

We[10] make posture chairs for all types of office workers. Visit our showroom to see our chairs and obtain posture advice[11] from one of our experts. Our dealer in your neighborhood is located on West 89 Street. Cordially yours,[12]

---

223. Dear Mr. Edwards: An office employee sits in a chair nearly two thousand hours a year. I am sure that you will[13] agree that his chair should be comfortable. Fatigue will be reduced and production increased.

There are five adjustments[14] on a Harris Aluminum Chair. These five adjustments permit each individual to set the chair in[15] the position most comfortable for him.

It is good business sense to invest in good furniture. Yours truly, [16]

---

224. Dear Mr. Farrell: Johnson Comfort Chairs have been developed to combat the poor posture developed by many[17] people who work in offices. Business and professional men have acclaimed these comfortable chairs, which have many[18] distinct features.

Johnson Comfort Chair users are enthusiastic about these scientifically designed[19] chairs that contribute to your comfort, health, and greater efficiency.

Write today for our free booklet, "How to[20] Keep Physically Fit." With the booklet we will send you the name of the nearest Johnson dealer. Cordially yours,[21] (420)

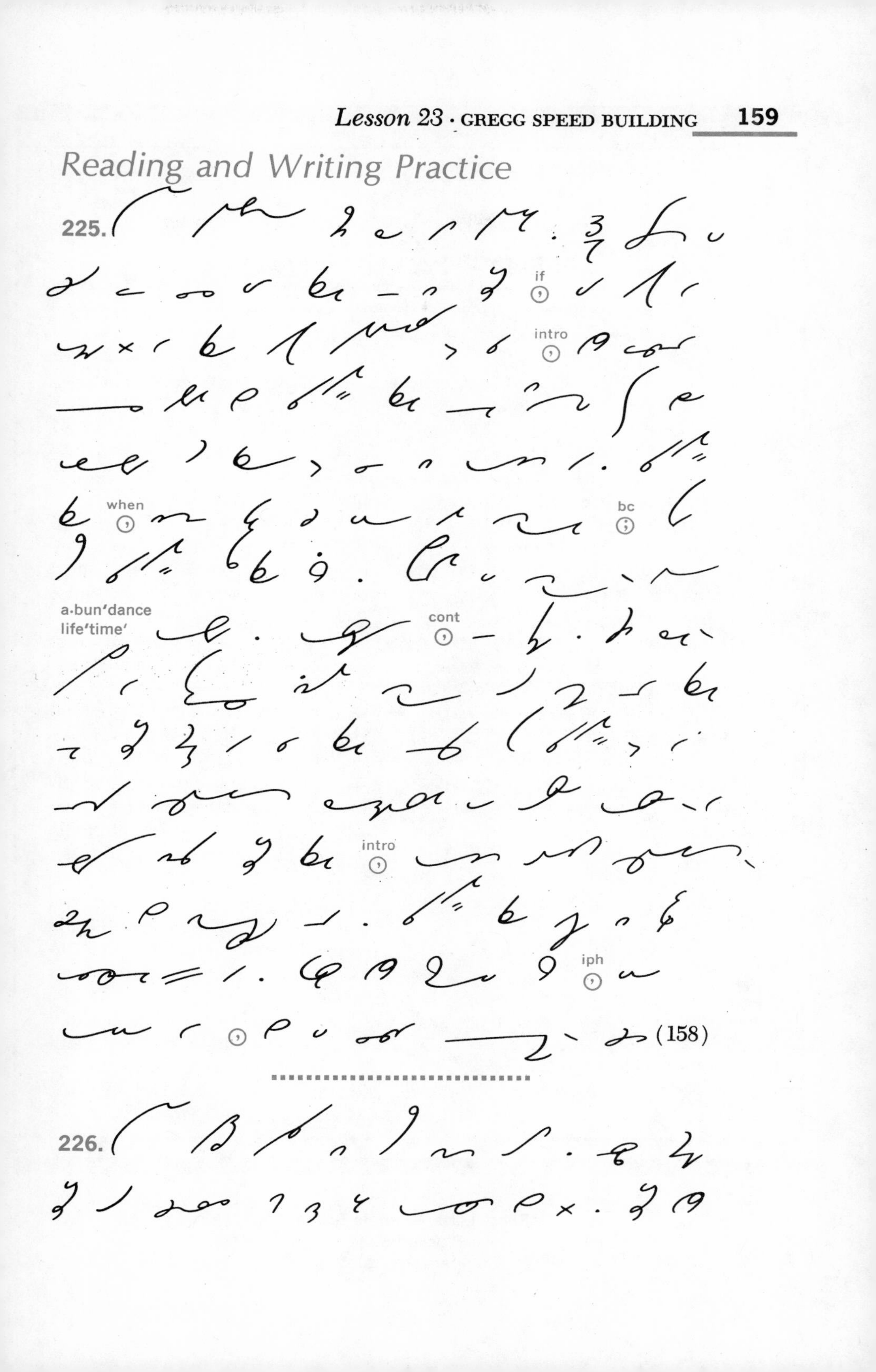

Reading and Writing Practice

225.

if

intro

when

bc

a·bun′dance
life′time′

cont

intro

iph

(158)

226.

JUDD-KANE, INC.

CABLE ADDRESS: JUDKANDEN

1410 GLENARM STREET • DENVER, COLORADO 80202 • TABOR 5-7500

October 13, 19--

Mr. Edward H. James
316 West Broadway
Milwaukee, Wisconsin 53202

Dear Mr. James:

As I am sure you know, your resignation came as quite a blow to me. I knew, of course, that your health was not the best. I had hoped that a long vacation would be the answer to your problems.

Under the circumstances, I think you are wise to take your doctor's advice to move to a warmer climate.

I do not have to tell you, Mr. James, that I appreciate your years of service and the part you played in building up our organization to its position of leadership in its field.

If you should later decide to return to us, there will always be a place for you on my staff.

Cordially yours,

John H. Moore

John H. Moore
Sales Manager

JHM:LEA

Short Letter—Single Spaced
Blocked Style
Standard Punctuation

isq

vis'i·tor
ex·pense'

iq

intro

cont

if

cr

nonr

and o

Transcribe:
9 a.m.
5 p.m.

nc

wo

(163)

227.

if

hun'dreds
ex·am'ple
ad'e·quate

il

ser

ap

iq

if

(71)

LESSON 24

Developing Shorthand Writing Power

228. FREQUENT PHRASES

Done

a

One

b

a. Be done, to be done, can be done, should be done, could be done, will be done.
b. One of these, one of the, one of those, one of them, one of our, one time, one year.

Building Transcription Skills

229. PUNCTUATION PRACTICE

Additional Expressions in Apposition

The following expressions, when they are used in context, are considered explanatory or appositive and should be set off by commas:

Inc. (abbreviation for *Incorporated*) in a company name.

Sr., Jr. (abbreviations for *Senior, Junior*) after proper names.

State name when it immediately follows the name of the city.

Year date when it immediately follows the name of the month.

Examples:

The Georgetown Lumber Company, Inc., is located on Elm Street.

John J. Brown, Jr., and James R. Wilson, Sr., are members of the Board of Directors.
I will visit Seattle, Washington, in March.
In June, 1978, I shall have to retire.

These expressions in apposition will be occasionally called to your attention in the Reading and Writing Practice exercises and will be indicated in the shorthand thus:

ap

Writing Practice

230. PREVIEW

231. Diminish, morale, overtime, reasonable, things, analyze, recommend, quickly, minimum, inconvenience, guarantee, workmanship, return.
232. Exhausted, controlled, efficiency, unnecessary, eliminates, moderate, problem.
233. Difficult, permanently, distracting, sturdily, moreover.

LETTERS

231. Dear Mr. Day: Do not allow noise to diminish your profits. Noise can undermine employee morale. It can[1] slow up work, cause errors, and result in needless hours of overtime.

You can dispose of your noise problem by[2] installing Morse tiles. The cost of installation is very reasonable and the savings in time and money are[3] great.

Here are three things that we will do for you:

1. We will analyze your noise problem and recommend the proper[4] type

of tile for your needs.

2. We will install the tiles quickly and with a minimum of inconvenience to you[5] and your staff.

3. We will guarantee our materials and workmanship.

If you would like us to send you a copy[6] of our booklet, "Questions and Answers on How to Eliminate Noise," return the enclosed card. Cordially yours,[7]

---

232. Dear Mr. Platt: Do you find that many of your employees leave the office exhausted and strained? They are probably[8] suffering from "noise" fatigue. In offices where noise is not controlled, efficiency is often diminished.[9]

Loss of time and efficiency resulting from noise represent unnecessary waste because noise can be[10] effectively controlled. Georgetown Sound Conditioning eliminates noise so that the entire office staff can work more[11] efficiently, with fewer errors and less overtime.

Georgetown Sound Conditioning can be installed at a[12] moderate cost. In a year's time it will more than pay for itself by increasing your employee's production.

Now that[13] you know the facts, shouldn't you act today?

Write for our free booklet, "How to Solve the Noise Problem." Yours sincerely,[14]

---

233. Dear Mr. Jones: Would you like to increase the efficiency of your office? You can do it by eliminating[15] noise.

This is not difficult to do. Install our special tile, and your noise problem will be permanently solved.[16] Once you have disposed of the distracting sounds that accompany the routine activities of most business[17] offices, you will find that everyone in the office feels better and works more efficiently.

Our tile is[18] sturdily built, but it is not expensive to install. Its surface can be painted without lowering its efficiency.[19] The tile is attractive, moreover, and will improve the general appearance of your office.

If you[20] would like to have our free booklet, "What to Do About Noise," return the enclosed postal card today. Cordially yours,[21] (420)

Reading and Writing Practice

234. intro intro

and o

ser

dis·tract′ing
nois′es

ap ap

nonr ap

ap 1959

(149)

235.

re′cent
weath′er

iph

if

intro

cont

ap

ap

(149)

236.

conj

(49)

237.

year's
di·min'ished
ef·fi'cien·cy

and o

drafts
qui'et

par

(100)

LESSON 25

Developing Shorthand Writing Power

238. WORD BEGINNINGS

Re-

a

Con-

b

Un-, En-, In-

c

a. Repairman, refund, received, reference, reports, reason, reliable.
b. Confirms, condition, constantly, conform, unconditional, reconsider.
c. Unless, unsatisfactory, unpaid, engineering, enforce, incident, instruction, installed.

Building Transcription Skills

239. PUNCTUATION PRACTICE

Connecting Words Repeated

When a connecting word such as *and, or, nor* is repeated in a series, the items are not separated by commas. Example:

> The papers were not stained or discolored or mutilated in any way.

BUT

> He purchased a desk, a chair, and a file.

Progressive Speed Builder (70-110)

Once again, the speed range of the letters in this Progressive Speed Builder has been increased. The letters begin at 70 words a minute and run to 110 words a minute.

If you practice the preview before you take the letters from dictation and pay close attention to the vocabulary of the early letters in this Progressive Speed Builder, the 110-word-a-minute letter will be easy for you.

240. PREVIEW

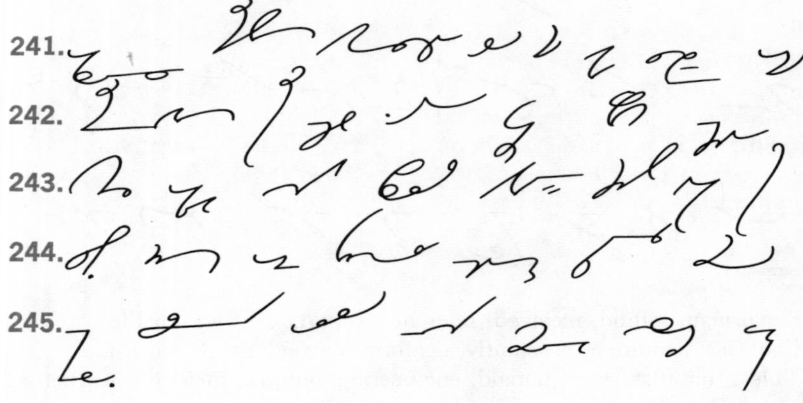

241. Repairman, several days ago, duplicator, third, further, to part, equipment, refund.
242. Several months ago, we have been, unsatisfactory, handle, purchase, I hope this, in the future.
243. Difficulty, reports, condition, apparently, Department, few days, trouble, you have been.
244. Attaching, suggestion, reason, booklet, instructions, admit, filled.
245. Engineering, examined, returned, enclosed, confirms, carefully, on the subject.

LETTERS

(1 Minute at 70)

241. Gentlemen: Your repairman was here several days ago to see what was wrong with my duplicator./He was the third man to look at it in the last two months. When he left, he said I would have no//further trouble. However, the duplicator broke down again today, and I am ready to ///part with it.

Please have your truck pick up this piece of equipment and send me a refund. Very truly yours, (1)

(1 Minute at 80)

242. Mr. Tracy: I am attaching a letter that we received from Mr. Fox with reference to the duplicator/that we sold to him several months ago. We have been asked to take back this equipment because it is//unsatisfactory.

Perhaps the best way to handle this matter is to take back the unit and refund the///purchase price to Mr. Fox.

I hope this incident will not lose business for us in the future. John H. Baker (2)

(1 Minute at 90)

243. Dear Mr. Fox: We are sorry that you have been having difficulty with the duplicator that you purchased from us several/months ago. Our repairman reports that the unit was in good working condition after his last visit, but apparently//something has again gone wrong.

We are, therefore, asking our Shipping Department to pick up the unit; and they will get in///touch with you soon. You should receive our check within a few days.

We sincerely regret the trouble you have been caused. Sincerely yours, (3)

(1 Minute at 100)

244. Mr. Baker: I am attaching a copy of the letter I wrote to Mr. Fox. I have followed your suggestion to take back the unit/and issue him a refund.

I have a feeling that the difficulty is not entirely with our equipment. I think that the real//reason why this unit broke down is that Mr. Fox has not followed the suggestions given in our booklet of instructions. Mr. Fox, of///course, will not admit this.

I have checked on Mr. Fox's orders, and I find that this was the first order we filled for him. John B. Tracy (4)

(1 Minute at 110)

245. Mr. Baker: Our Engineering Department examined the duplicator that Mr. Fox returned. A copy of the report is enclosed. You will/notice that the report confirms my feeling that Mr. Fox did not follow the suggestions given in our instruction book.

I think that in the future our//salesmen should stress the importance of reading the instruction book carefully before starting to operate the duplicator. Unless the users of///our equipment do this, we shall constantly have complaints.

Would you care to have me write a memorandum to our salesmen on the subject? John B. Tracy (5) (450)

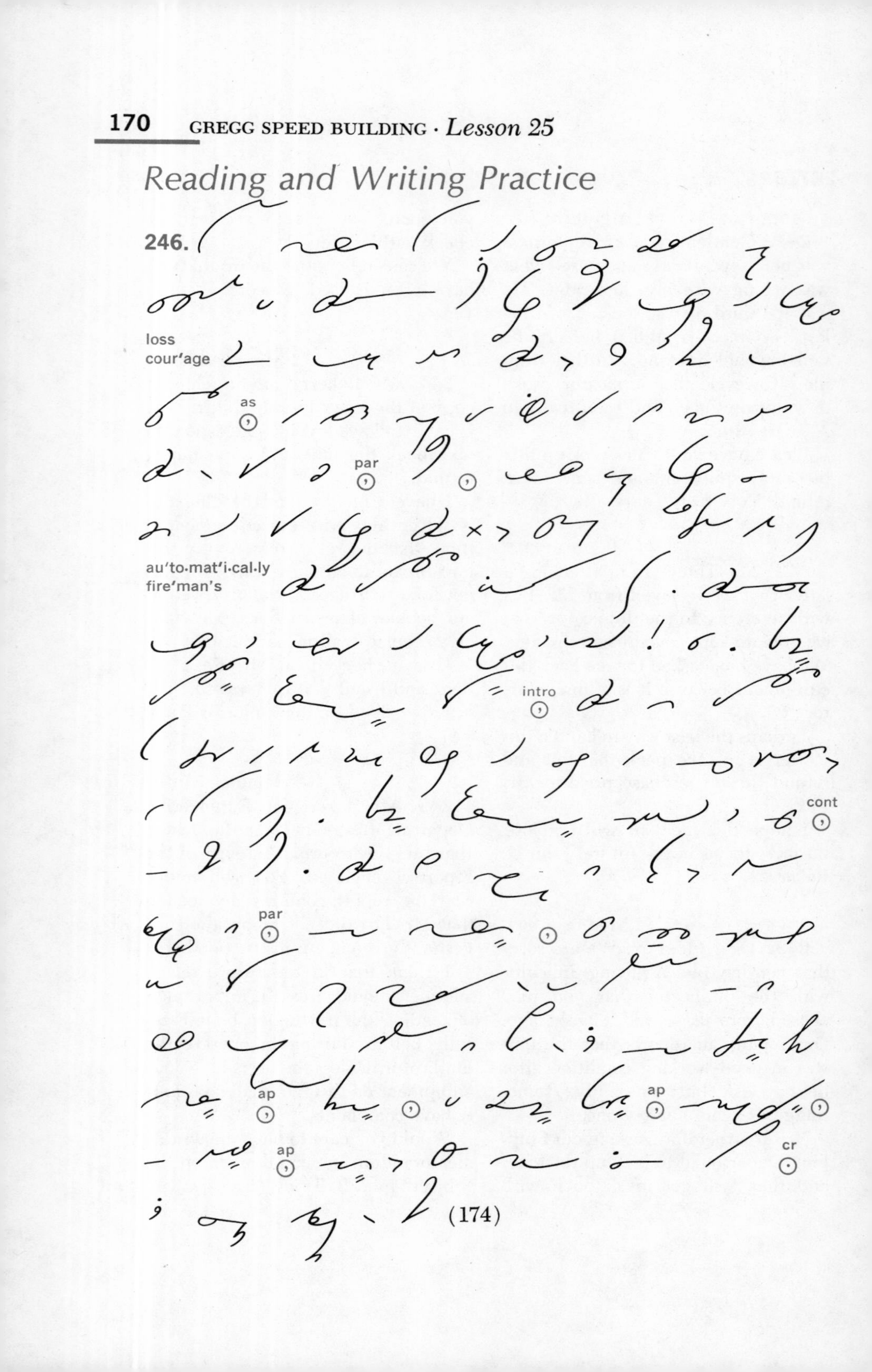

Reading and Writing Practice

246.

loss
cour'age

as

par

au'to·mat'i·cal·ly
fire'man's

intro

cont

par

ap

ap

ap

cr

(174)

247.

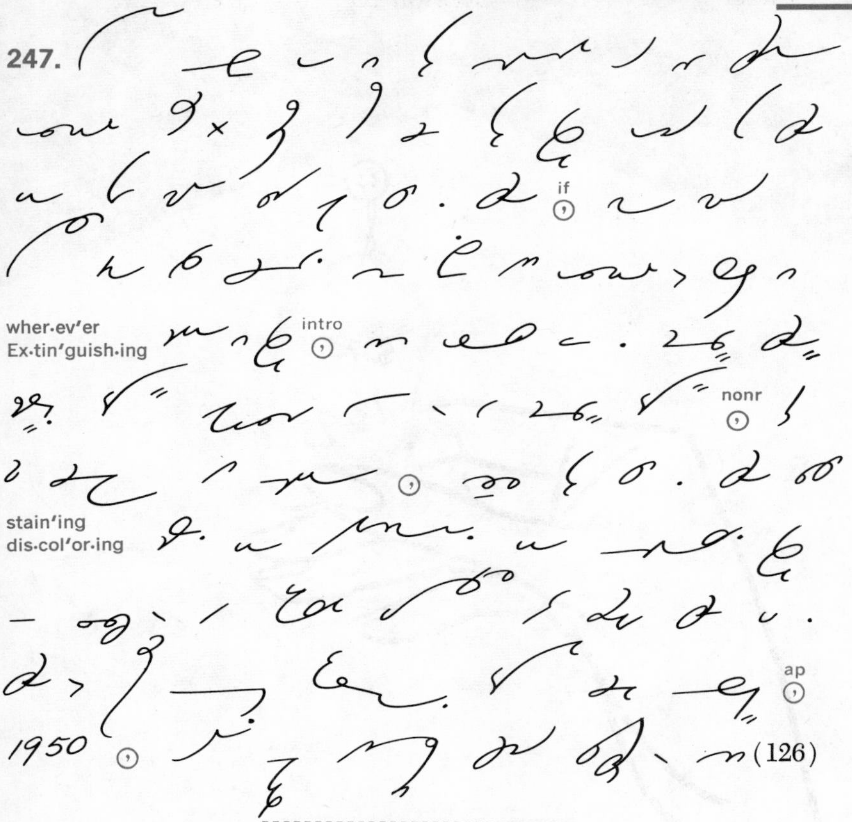

if
wher·ev′er
Ex·tin′guish·ing
intro
nonr
stain′ing
dis·col′or·ing
ap
1950
(126)

248.

intro
ser
ser
(75)

CHAPTER 6

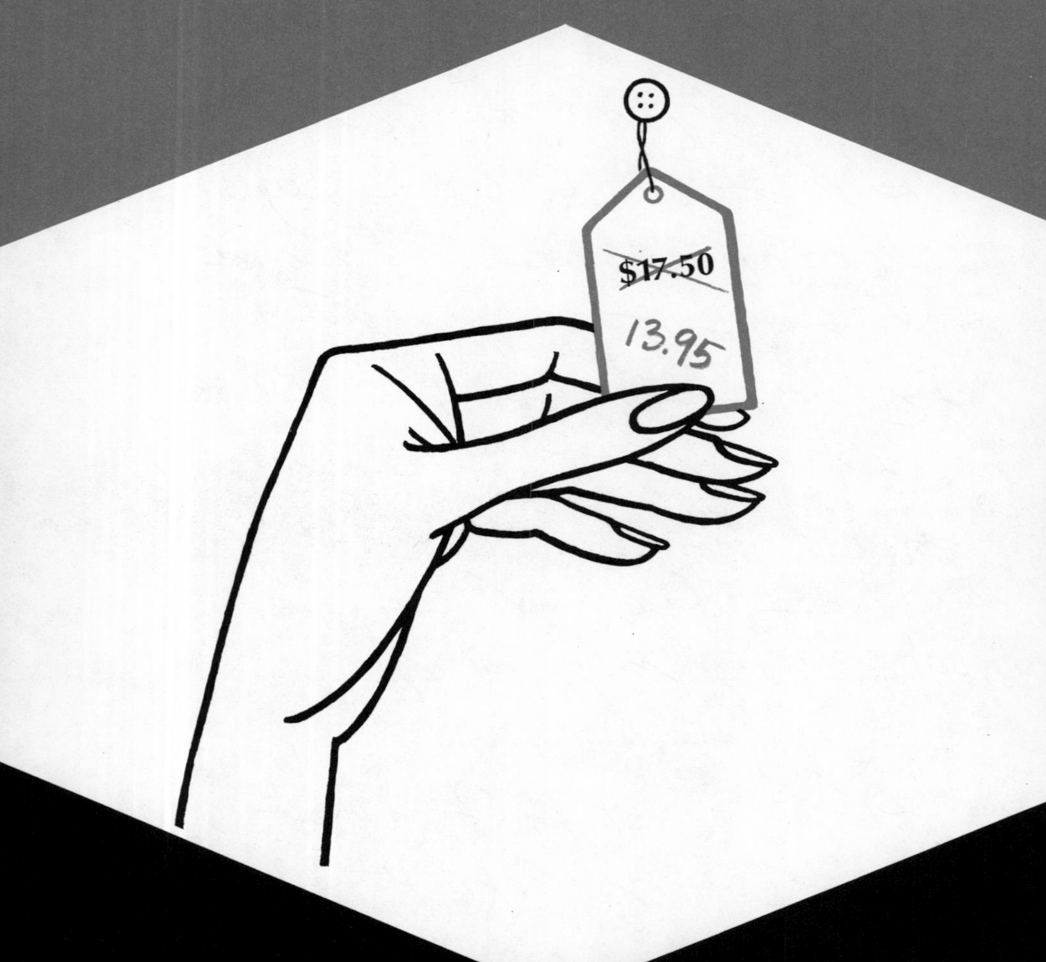

Merchandising

LESSON 26

Developing Shorthand Writing Power

249. OUTLINE CONSTRUCTION

Omission of vowel in syllables cur, ker. Omitting the slightly sounded vowel in the syllables *cur, ker* results in a very fluent joining.

a

b

a. Concur, occur, recur, incur, current, curve, courage.
b. Courteous, courtesy, excursion, skirmish, curtail, curtain.

The unaccented circle vowel is omitted between:

K and R

a

G and R

b

K and L, G and L

c

a. Baker, brokerage, career, maker, locker, thicker.
b. Eager, tiger, bigger, stagger, sugar.
c. Local, focal, vocal, legal, frugal.

Building Transcription Skills

250. SIMILAR-WORDS DRILL

You are already familiar with the Similar-Words Drill through your work with previous volumes of Gregg Shorthand, Diamond Jubilee Series. You will recall that these drills call to your attention groups of words that sound or look alike or *almost* alike, so that you will be on the alert to choose the correct member of a group when you transcribe.

Study the definition of each word and read the illustrative examples.

Personal, personnel

personal Individual; private; direct from one person to another.

He is careful of his personal appearance.
John is a personal friend of mine.

personnel *(noun)* The people who work for a business or department.

He is in charge of all sales personnel.

Reading and Writing Practice

251. Wanted!

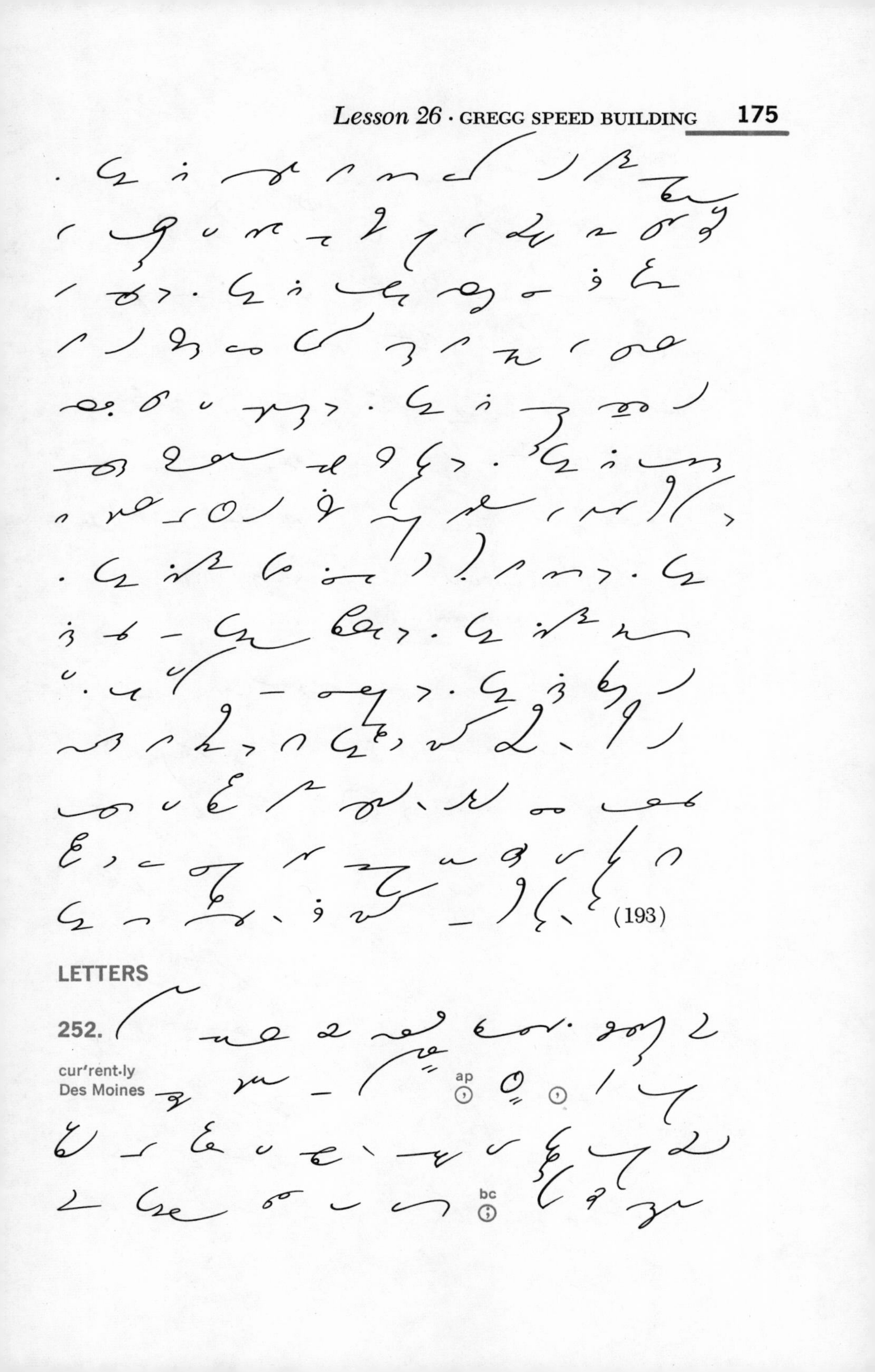

(193)

LETTERS

252.

cur'rent·ly
Des Moines

ap

bc

well'-qual'i·fied
hyphenated before noun

and o

as·sist'ant
ex·pe'ri·ence
buy'ing

25 35

if

(141)

253.

ea'ger
cour'te·ous·ly

25

com'pe·tent
e·nough'

par

if

ours
Per'son·nel'

ser

10

nc wo

5 9 11

(169)

254.

if

its
po·ten'tial

conj

40

if

par

(113)

The girl who stands out head and shoulders above the drones is the one who shows that she can assume responsibility—that she can think for herself and that she possesses the initiative to work out problems on her own.

LESSON 27

Developing Shorthand Writing Power

255. RECALL DRILL — OO

In this lesson you will review the various uses of the *oo* hook.

Diphthong U

a

Diphthong Ow

b

Ul

c

-ulate

d

Under-

e

a. Few, unit, unite, human, view, huge, rescue, pure.
b. Ounce, bow, proud, crowd, loud, blouse, outfit.
c. Ultimate, cultivate, adult, ulterior, insult, result, consult, consultant.
d. Congratulate, circulate, tabulate, speculate, speculation, speculator, speculates.
e. Understand, undergo, underestimate, undercurrent, undertaking, understaffed, understatement.

Building Transcription Skills

256. ACCURACY PRACTICE

The speed and the accuracy with which you can read your shorthand notes depend to a large extent on how well you write them. Your notes do not have to be as beautiful as those in this book, but they should be readable. They will be readable if you will be careful about one important thing—proportion.

The Accuracy Drills in this book are designed to help you develop correct proportion as well as to point out to you the correct joinings of the various strokes in Gregg Shorthand.

The drills in this lesson deal with groups of outlines that tend to look alike when they are written under the pressure of rapid dictation.

Suggestions for Practice

In practicing this and the other accuracy drills in this book, here is the procedure you should follow:

1. Read through the entire drill to be sure that you know the meaning of each outline.

2. The outlines in each drill are written in groups. Write each group once, striving to see how accurately, rather than how rapidly, you can write each outline.

3. Make another copy of the entire list.

The secret of writing the following outlines legibly is to keep the straight lines straight and the curves deep.

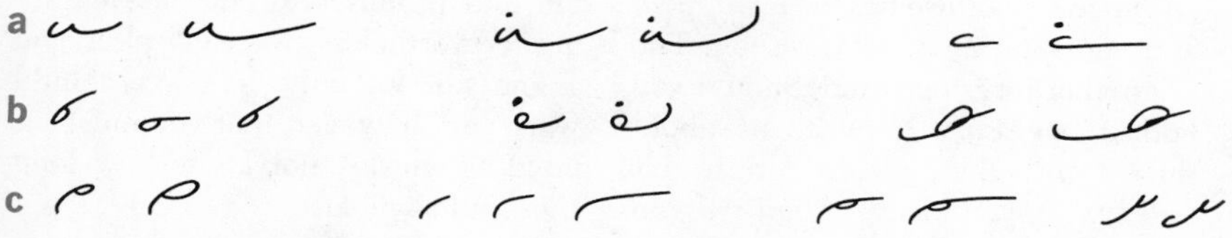

a. Or, all; whole, hold; on, home.
b. With, when, yet; hear, heard; write-right, light.
c. They, that; the, than, them; then, theme; though, although.

Writing Practice

257. PREVIEW

258.

259.

260.

258. Thank you for your order, shirts, also, merchandise, original, enclosed, transaction, return, expeditious.
259. Invitation, one of our, attend, continue, nevertheless, suits, choose, personally, requirements.
260. We have done, appreciation, presenting, toward, overcoat, 6 per cent, discount, comfort.

LETTERS

258. Dear Sir: Thank you for your order for a dozen shirts and also for your check.

The merchandise has been shipped, and you should[1] receive it soon. The original order is enclosed. Should you find it necessary to write us about this[2] transaction, please return this order with your letter; then we can take immediate action on it.

We hope that[3] you will like this method of handling orders. It will enable us to give you more expeditious service. Yours truly,[4]

---

259. Dear Friend: This is a personal invitation to you, one of our valued customers, to attend our fall showing[5] of clothes.

The price of clothing is still climbing and promises to continue climbing. Nevertheless, we can[6] offer you a fine suit for only $60. We should warn you, however, that you must act now, as we do[7] not know how long these suits will last.

If you choose your suits now, they will be available to you this winter. We will have[8] them ready for you on May 1.

I shall be here to attend personally to your requirements. Sincerely yours,[9]

---

260. Dear Mr. Day: As we have done for many years past, we are showing our appreciation of the business of[10] our friends by presenting them with a Christmas Gift Bond. The attached Bond, which has a value of $5, may be[11] applied toward the purchase of any suit or overcoat. In addition, it entitles you to a 6 per[12] cent discount on all cash purchases you make in any department of our store from now until December[13] 24.

Arrange to do your Christmas shopping now, while you can still do it in complete comfort. Yours sincerely,[14] (280)

Reading and Writing Practice

261.

when

men's cloth'ing

cont

when

enu

intro

bc

intro

(129)

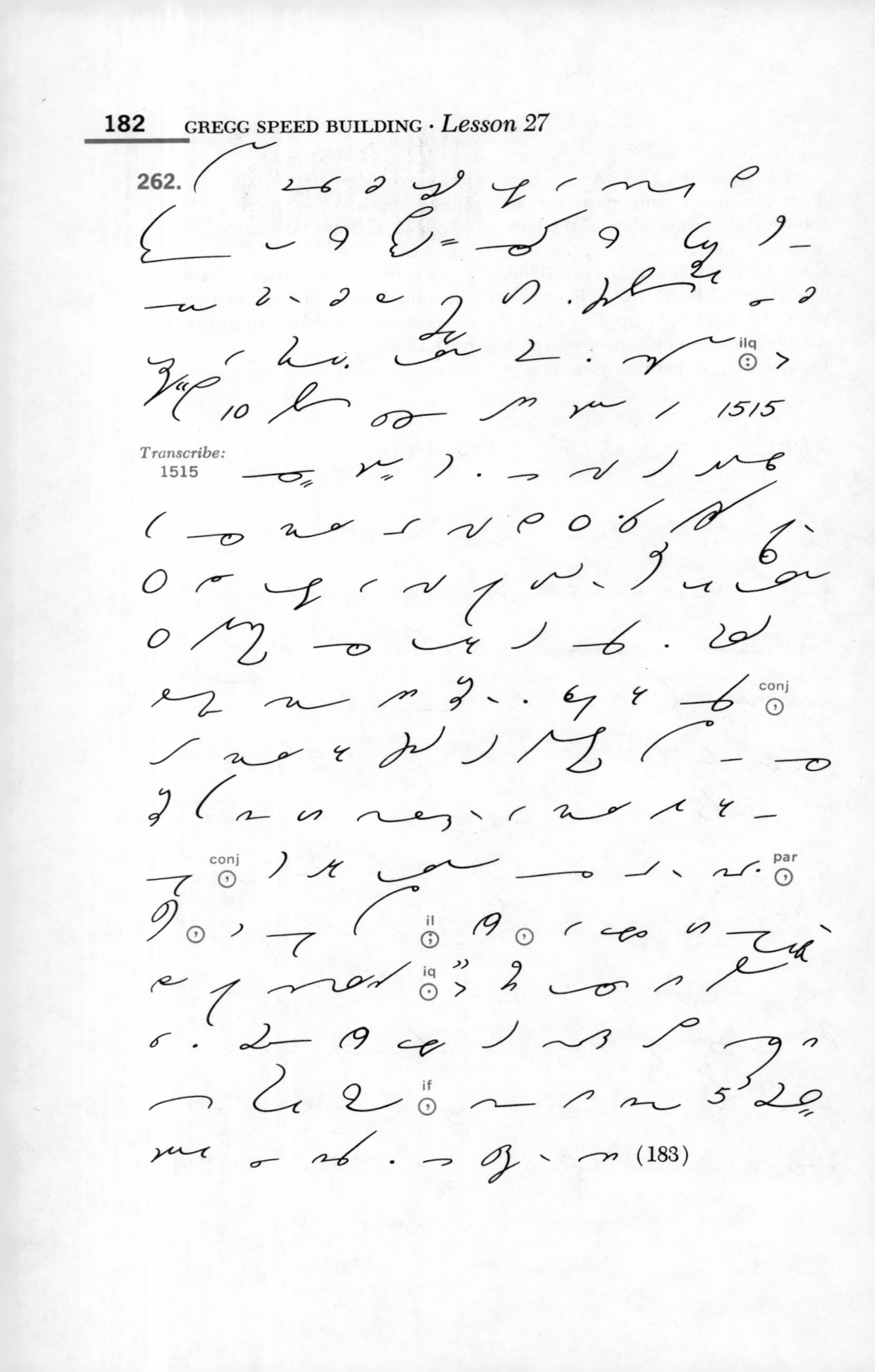

262.

ilq

10 1515

Transcribe:
1515

conj

conj par

il

iq

if

5

(183)

Developing Shorthand Writing Power

263. WORD FAMILIES

-cation

a [shorthand outlines]

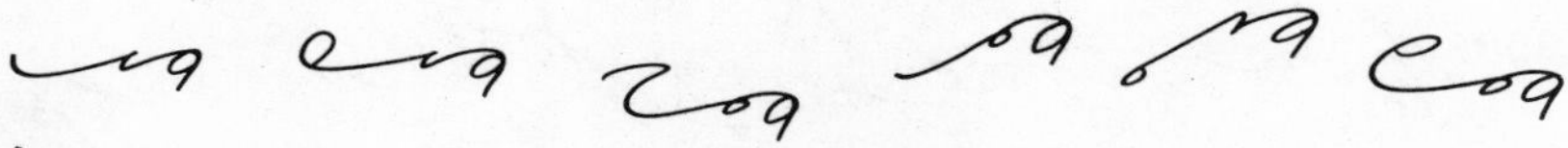

Out-

b [shorthand outlines]

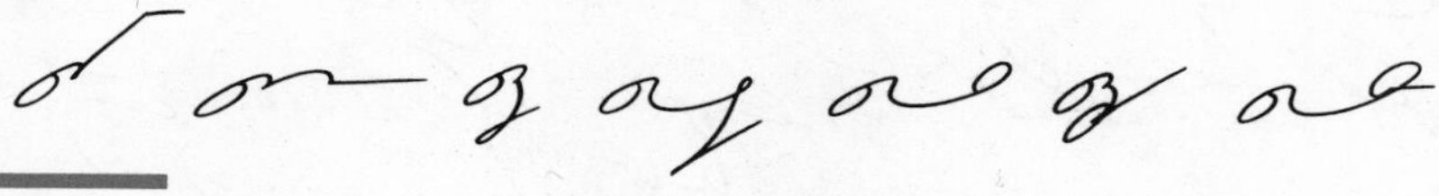

a. Location, allocation, complication, indication, education, application.
b. Outdone, outcome, outfit, outlived, outlay, outside, outline.

264. FREQUENT NAMES

Last Names

a [shorthand outlines]

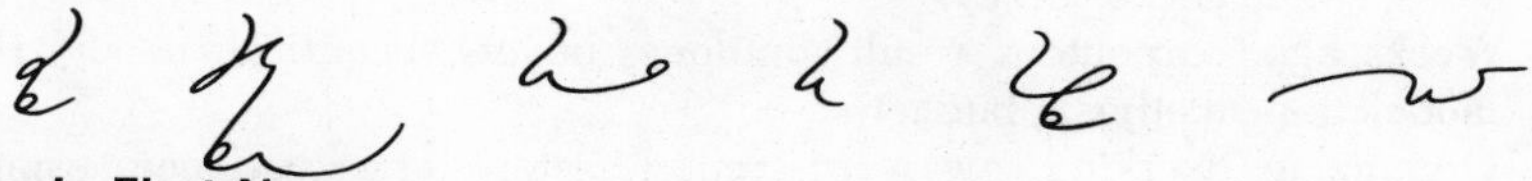

Men's First Names

b [shorthand outlines]

a. Fisher, Fitzgerald, Foley, Fox, Fraser, Gordon.
b. Duncan, Edgar, Edmond, Edward, Ernest, Eugene.

Building Transcription Skills

265. BUSINESS VOCABULARY BUILDER

laden Loaded.

extensive Broad; wide.

consolidation A combining into a single unit.

Writing Practice

266. PREVIEW

267.

268.

269.

270.

267. Notify, payments, properly, remittances, enable, we shall be able.
268. Busiest, warm, employees, convenience, features, atmosphere, comfort, let us, engineers, to survey.
269. Weeks ago, carpenters, result, outdone, buyers, beautiful, newly, remodeled, pocketbook, budget.
270. Organizing, working, awkward, report, astonishing, patience, using, credit, pamphlet.

LETTERS

267. Dear Madam: This is to notify you that on and after September 10 our office will be located at[1] 16 Main Street.

So that your payments will be properly charged to your account, please mail all remittances to the[2] new address.

It is our belief that our new location will enable us to provide even finer and more[3] efficient service. We shall be able to display an even greater variety of goods. Yours sincerely,[4]

268. Dear Mr. Fisher: The busiest store in town is the store that is cool in the summer and warm in the winter—and[5] that is the store that gives its customers and employees the convenience and comfort of Taylor Air

Conditioning.6

Walk into any drug or department store that features air conditioning, and you will find a refreshing7 atmosphere that is just right for comfort. The installation of air conditioning results in more customers8 and in more sales.

There is a Taylor Air Conditioning unit to fit the needs of your business. Let us send9 one of our engineers to survey your needs and suggest the unit that will be best for your store. Cordially yours,10

---

269. Dear Mr. Foley: Several weeks ago things started to happen at our store. Carpenters and painters moved in and11 gave our store a completely "new look." We hope that you will like the result and that you will be able to shop in12 greater comfort.

Not to be outdone, our buyers set out for the markets of the world to seek rare and beautiful13 merchandise. They found some of the finest gifts that it has ever been our pleasure to offer our customers.14 Our newly remodeled shelves are now laden with merchandise that will suit every shopper and every15 pocketbook.

If you cannot pay cash for your purchases, you can open a special budget plan. Sincerely yours,16

---

270. Dear Mrs. Fox: Organizing and completing our new store has been a little like raising a child. We knew that17 it would need "dressing up" and "working over" to get it through the "awkward stage."

We are happy to report now that18 the work is about completed. The results are really astonishing.

These and many other improvements in19 the store have taken time and have perhaps tried your patience, but the end result will, we feel confident, be a store20 that will be a joy to shop in.

Speaking of shopping joys, have you discovered the pleasure of using one of our three21 credit plans? If not, look through the enclosed pamphlet, which gives complete information about these plans. Cordially yours,22 (440)

Reading and Writing Practice

271.

re·mod'el·ing
un'der·tak'ing

intro

store's
mer'chan·dise

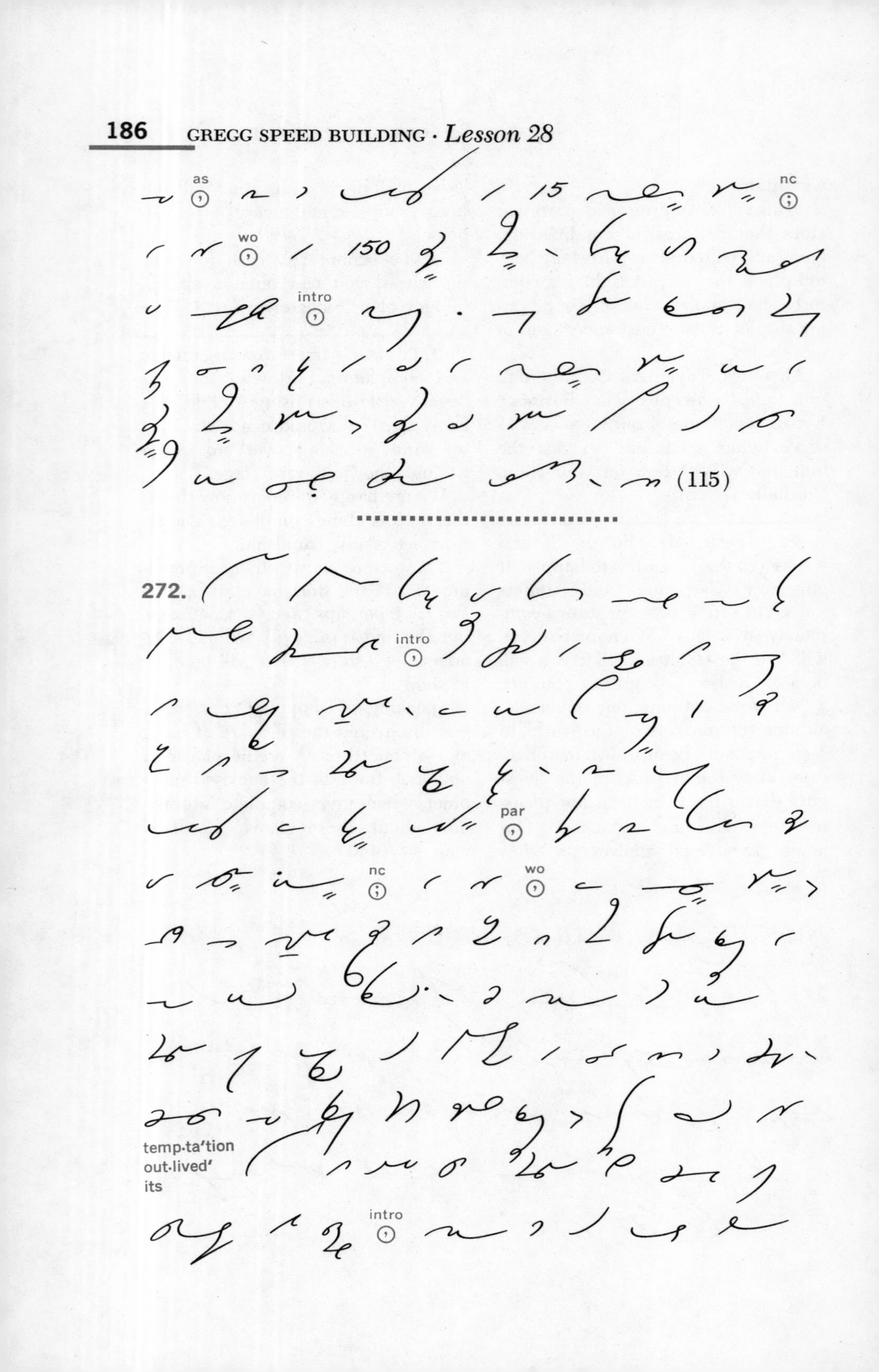

as nc wo intro (115)

272. intro par nc wo intro

temp·ta'tion
out·lived'
its

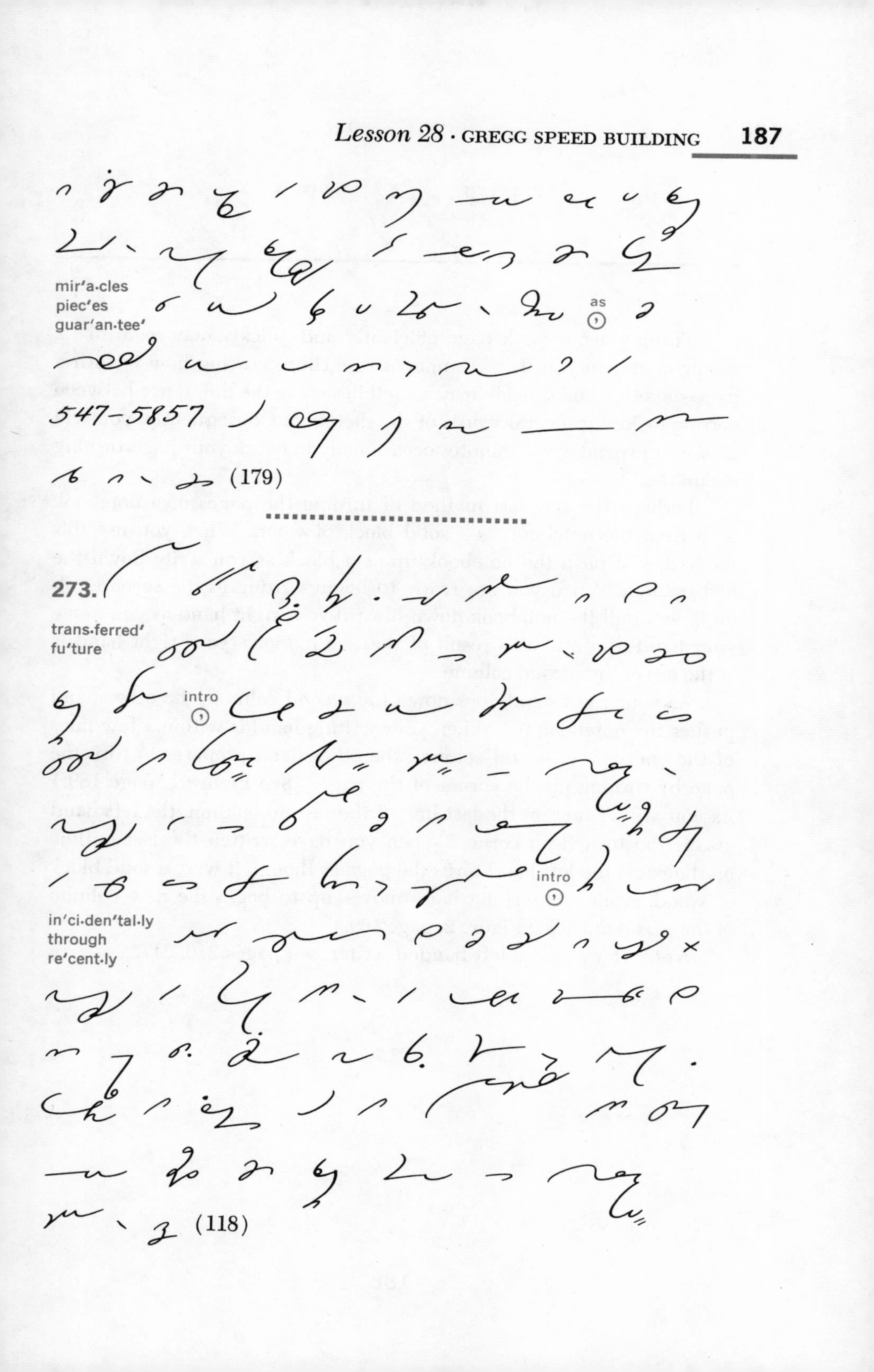

mir'a·cles
piec'es
guar'an·tee'

as

547-5857

(179)

273.

trans·ferred'
fu'ture

intro

intro

in'ci·den'tal·ly
through
re'cent·ly

(118)

SECRETARIAL TIP

Turning Pages

Turning a notebook page efficiently and quickly may seem like a minor matter to you. It is a minor matter, but knowing how to turn a page smoothly and quickly may sometimes make the difference between getting or losing several words of the dictation. Consequently, you will be wise to spend a few minutes occasionally to check your page-turning technique.

Perhaps the simplest method of turning the pages of a notebook is to treat the notebook as a solid block of wood. When you use this method, you push the notebook up as a block as you write down the first column. When you are ready to begin writing in the second column, you pull the notebook down toward your right hand as you move your hand up until, as a result of the two motions, your right hand is at the top of the second column.

As your right hand goes down the second column, the other hand pushes the notebook up. When your writing hand is within a few lines of the end of the second column, the other hand prepares to turn the page by turning up the corner of the page. (See Figure 1, page 189.) As you are writing on the last line of the second column, the left hand grasps the turned-up corner. When you have written the last outline on the page, the left hand turns the page as though it were a solid block of wood, while the writing hand moves up to begin the new column of the next page. (See Figure 2, page 189.)

Note: If you are a left-handed writer, see pages 216, 217.

As the writer nears the bottom of the second column, his left hand turns up the corner of the page.

Figure 1

After the writer has written the last outline in the second column, he grasps the turned-up corner of the page and turns the page as though it were a solid block.

Figure 2

LESSON 29

Developing Shorthand Writing Power

274. FREQUENT PHRASES

To

a

Hope

b

a. To be, to see, to have, to form, to fill, to follow, to ship, to charge.
b. We hope, we hope that, we hope that the, we hope you will; I hope, I hope that, I hope that the, I hope you are, I hope you will.

275. GEOGRAPHICAL EXPRESSIONS

-ton

a

States

b

Foreign Countries

c

a. Brockton, Charleston, Cranston, Evanston, Galveston.
b. Tennessee, North Dakota, Montana, Louisiana, Florida, Vermont, Delaware.
c. Italy, Japan, Portugal, Romania, Spain, Switzerland, Siam.

Building Transcription Skills

276. BUSINESS VOCABULARY BUILDER

podiatrist One who treats disorders of the feet.

phenomenal Extraordinary; unusual.

Writing Practice

277. PREVIEW

278. **279.** **280.** **281.**

278. Walked, district, diversified, Chamber of Commerce, community, I hope that, apart, evenings, attractively, interests.
279. Actually, away, profits, installing, conditioner, comfortable, authorities, consumer, consequently.
280. Anniversaries, today, appreciate, to thank you for this, occasions, any time, suggestions, pleasant, always.
281. Frequently, interested, to know, established, daily, request, whenever.

LETTERS

278. Dear Mr. Thomas: Yesterday I walked through the Evanston business district, visiting all the stores. Never before[1] had I seen them display such a diversified line of merchandise. I am proud to be a member of the[2] Chamber of Commerce of such a business community.

I hope that you will set apart one or two evenings between[3] now and the end of the year to go downtown for dinner and then visit as many of the stores as possible,[4] to see for yourself how attractively they are decorated and how completely they are stocked.

I know that[5] you, too, will be proud that you live in a city where the stores look after your shopping interests. Cordially yours,[6]

---

279. Dear Mr. Brockton: Do you realize how much summer heat actually costs you? It costs you more than you think, because[7] it keeps many customers away.

You can stop this drain on your profits by installing a Vermont Air Conditioner.[8] Not only will this air conditioner stop the drain on your profits, but it will actually make your[9] profits in hot weather greater than those during the comfortable months of the year.

Authorities say that during[10] this coming summer the consumer will be more careful than ever with his money. Consequently, that provides[11] an even more important reason why your business should install a Vermont Air Conditioner. Yours sincerely,[12]

---

280. Dear Mrs. Warner: Do you like anniversaries? We do. Just a year ago today we had the pleasure of[13] adding your name to our list of charge customers.

We appreciate the fine business you have given us during[14] this past year. We wish to thank you for this business, and we hope that during the coming year you will visit us on[15] many occasions.

If at any time you have suggestions that will enable us to make your shopping at our[16] store more pleasant, I hope you will let us know. We are always happy to hear from our customers. Sincerely yours,[17]

---

281. Dear Mrs. Ford: We are pleased to open a charge account for you at Tracy's. We appreciate your business and[18] hope that we may serve you frequently.

You will be interested to know that we have established a daily[19] delivery service. All purchases over $5 will be delivered on request. You are invited to[20] use this service whenever you can.

I hope you will find your account a real convenience. Yours very truly,[21] (420)

Reading and Writing Practice

282.

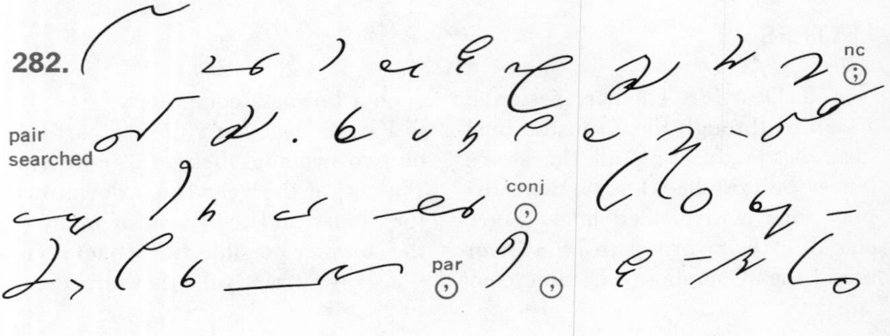

nc

pair searched

conj

par

po·di′a·trist
coun′se·lor

ap

wear′ing intro

(123)

283.

and o

nonr

for′ward
be·gin′ning

15 intro

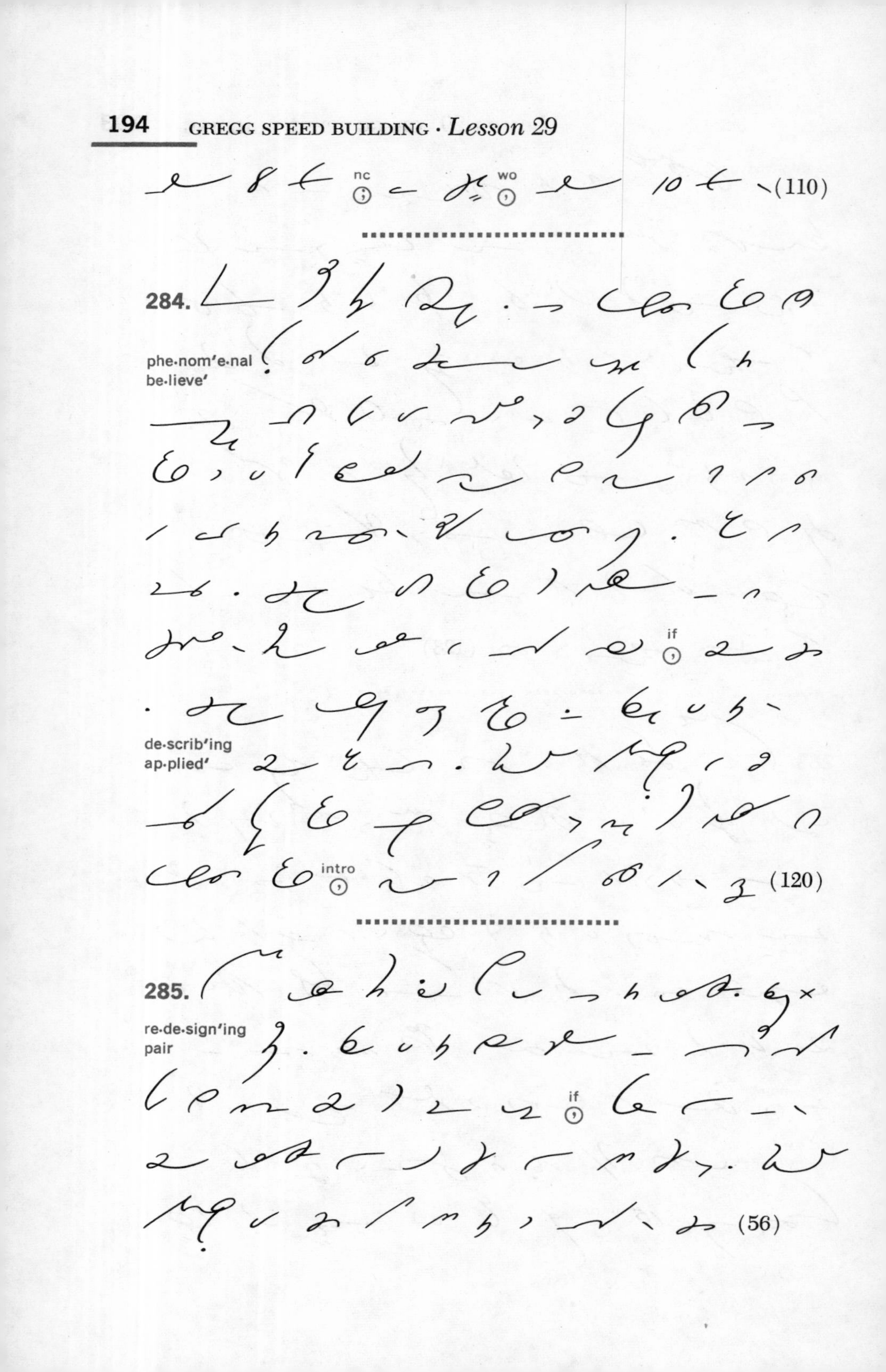

nc wo (110)

284.

phe·nom′e·nal
be·lieve′

if

de·scrib′ing
ap·plied′

intro (120)

285.

re·de·sign′ing
pair

if

(56)

Developing Shorthand Writing Power

286. WORD BEGINNINGS AND ENDINGS

-ther

a [shorthand outlines]

Al-

b [shorthand outlines]

-gram

c [shorthand outlines]

a. Bother, whether, neither, mother, father, either, further, brother-in-law.
b. Although, almost, also, altogether, alternate, alternative, alteration.
c. Diagram, program, monogram, radiogram.

Building Transcription Skills

287. BUSINESS VOCABULARY BUILDER

delinquent Behind.

authorize Permit; empower.

litigation A suit at law.

instituting Starting.

Progressive Speed Builder (70-110)

288. PREVIEW

289. Account, gold, person, to forget, bother, remittance, afford.
290. Perhaps, first, around, available, almost, to be, necessary, next.
291. You must have, anything, confident, arrangement, part, enclose, wrong, let us.
292. Suggested, delinquent, authorize, inclined, correspondence, realize.
293. Heard, I do not, neither, profit, credit, unnecessary, prevent, standing.

LETTERS

(1 Minute at 70)

289. Dear Mr. James: We know that your account with us is as good as gold. We know, too, how easy it/is for a person to forget to pay a bill.

If yours were the only account we had, we should never//bother to remind you about a remittance. Having many accounts such as yours, however,///we cannot afford to do this.

Won't you please send us a check to balance your account. Sincerely yours, (1)

(1 Minute at 80)

290. Dear Mr. James: Perhaps the reason why we did not receive an answer to our first letter is that you meant to/send us a check but did not get around to it. Perhaps at the time the money was not available. We can//understand that, for it happens in almost any business.

Although we wish to be fair, it is also necessary///that we collect the money that is due us. Won't you please send us your check in the next mail. Sincerely yours, (2)

(1 Minute at 90)

291. Dear Mr. James: You must have a good reason for not having paid anything on your account since October. We are sure of/that. However, don't you think it only fair to tell us that reason?

If we knew the facts, we are confident that we could work out//some arrangement that would relieve your mind and satisfy us too.

Could you send us a part payment with your letter? Whether you///enclose a payment or not, however, at least tell us what is wrong. Let us help you if we can.

Don't wait; do it now. Sincerely yours, (3)

(1 Minute at 100)

292. Gentlemen: Our credit manager has just suggested that we turn your delinquent account over to our lawyers. He showed me copies of/three letters that have been mailed to you since April 5.

I do not wish to authorize such action without personally discussing this matter//with you.

I am inclined to believe that you have some good reason for not writing to us. I will, therefore, hold this correspondence for ten///days to give you an opportunity to send us your check.

You must realize that this matter is most important to you. Very sincerely yours, (4)

(1 Minute at 110)

293. Dear Mr. James: The ten days that I promised to wait before taking legal action on your account have passed, and I have not heard from you. I am, therefore,/authorizing our credit manager to turn the matter over to our lawyers.

I do not like to do this, because neither of us will profit by this//action. We shall have to pay a collection fee and your credit standing will suffer.

All this seems so unnecessary. There is still time to prevent///litigation. You have only to send us your check in the enclosed envelope. When we receive it, your account will once more be in good standing. Sincerely yours, (5) (450)

Reading and Writing Practice

294.

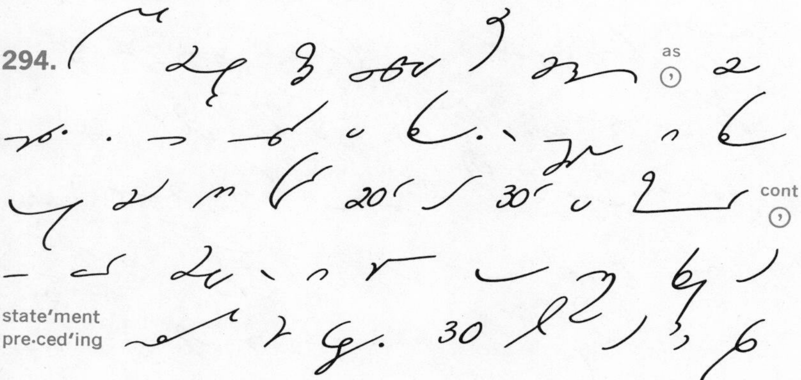

nc ; intro ,

if ,

nc ;

(152)

295.

Transcribe:
No. 3616
$1.50

ap ,

intro ,

intro ,

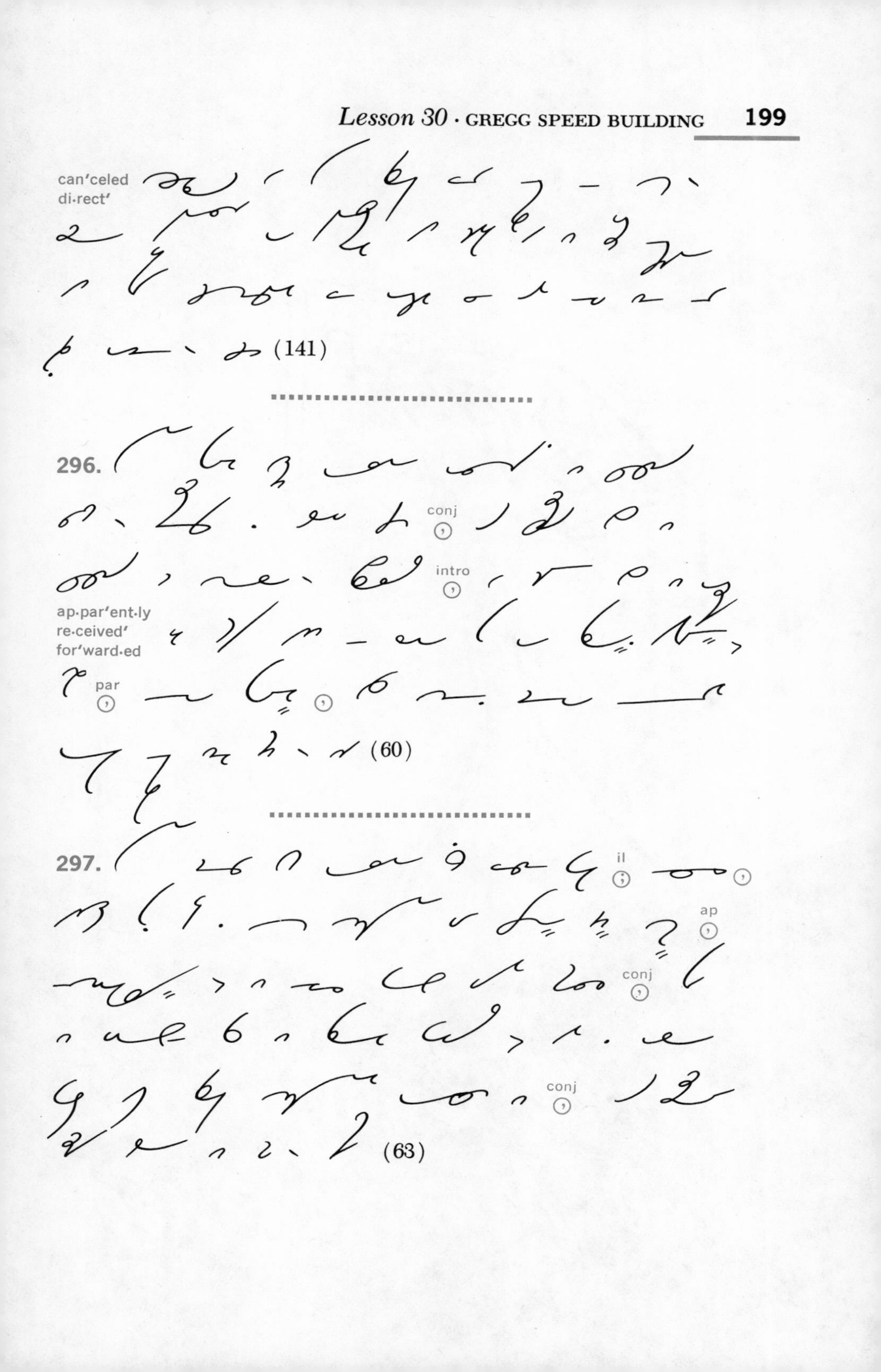

can'celed
di·rect'

(141)

296.

conj

intro

ap·par'ent·ly
re·ceived'
for'ward·ed

par

(60)

297.

il

ap

conj

conj

(63)

CHAPTER

7

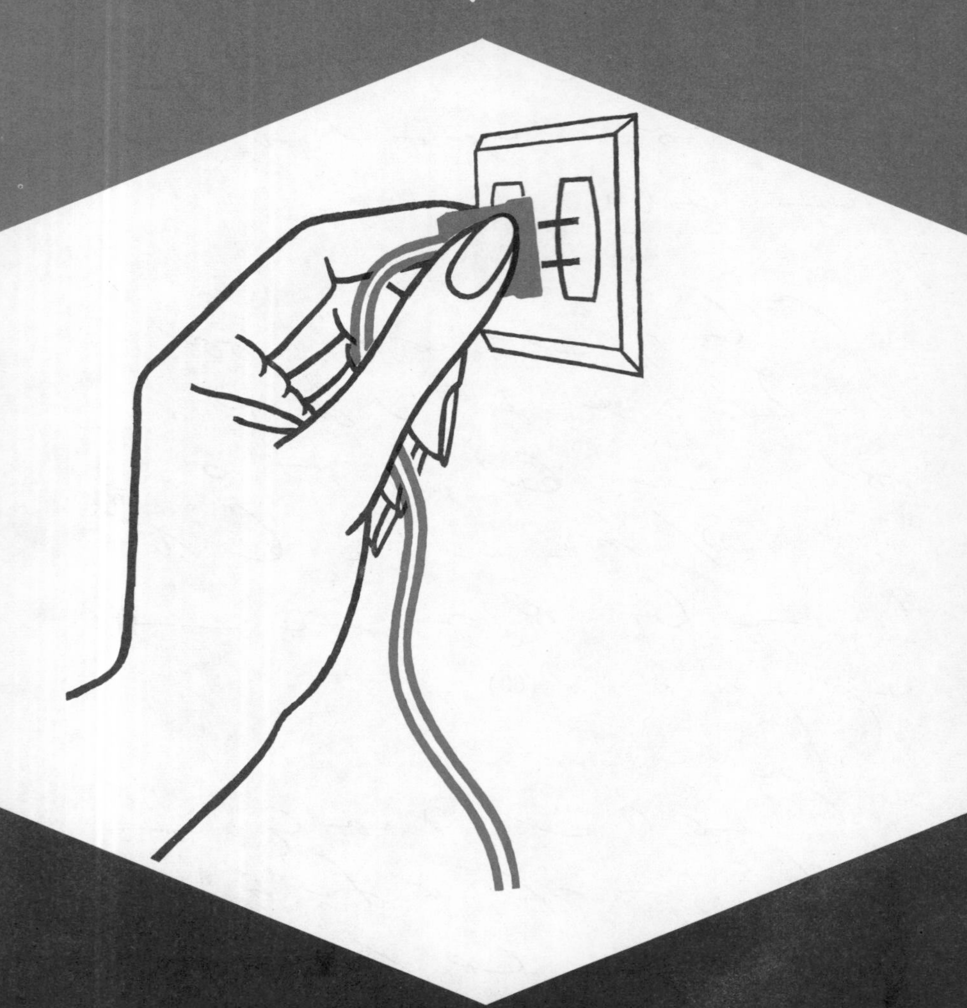

Home Equipment and Maintenance

Developing Shorthand Writing Power

298. OUTLINE CONSTRUCTION

Word ending -ion. The word ending *-ion* is expressed by *oo-n* after *n;* by *n* in other cases.

Expressed by OO-N

a

Expressed by N

b

a. Union, onion, companion, dominion, reunion.
b. Champion, million, billion, criterion, rebellion.

Word endings -ious, -eous. The word endings *-ious, -eous* are expressed by *us.*

a

b

a. Industry, industrious; envy, envious; injury, injurious; study, studious.
b. Serious, various, curious, obvious, previous, erroneous, courteous.

Building Transcription Skills

299. SIMILAR-WORDS DRILL

Confidently, confidentially

confidently Trustfully; with assurance.

He confidently expected to receive the promotion.

confidentially Secretly; privately.

John told me confidentially that he was resigning.

Reading and Writing Practice

300. Six Promises of a Good Citizen

(177)

LETTERS

301.

fig'ur·ing
life'time'

par

340

par

wom'en
drudg'er·y

cont

nc

conj

thor'ough·ly
e·lec'tri·cal·ly

intro

cr

(162)

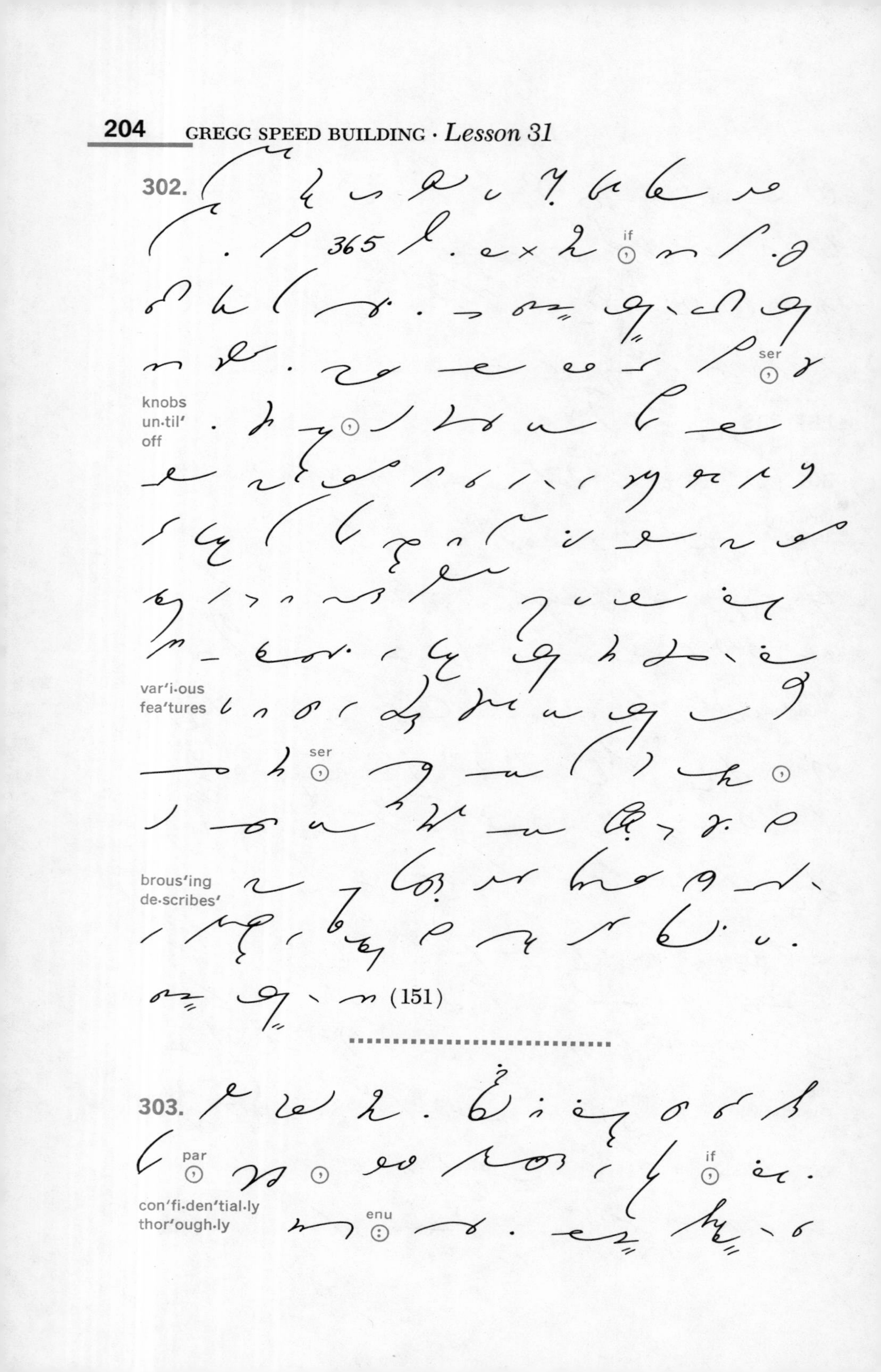

302.

365

if

ser

knobs
un·til′
off

var′i·ous
fea′tures

ser

brous′ing
de·scribes′

(151)

303.

par

if

con′fi·den′tial·ly
thor′ough·ly

enu

Transcribe:
3 cents
whole

nc

conj

if

(139)

304.

phys'i·cal
suf'fered
sim'i·lar

fur'ther·more'
fi·nanc'ing

intro

low'-cost'
hyphenated before noun

(79)

LESSON 32

Developing Shorthand Writing Power

305. RECALL DRILL — O

In this drill you will review the different combinations in which *o* is used.

O

a

Oi

b

Al-

c

Over-

d

-ort

e

a. Pour, ball, on, home, store, stole, show, shown.
b. Toy, toil, soil, boy, annoy, destroy, appointment.
c. Almost, alternate, alternative, already, Albany, also, alteration.
d. Over, overcome, overcrowd, overlook, overhead, overrule, overreach, overstay.
e. Sort, assort, port, support, reported, mortal, quart, quarter.

Building Transcription Skills

306. ACCURACY PRACTICE

The Accuracy Drills in this lesson also deal with groups of outlines that tend to look alike when they are written under the stress of rapid dictation. Practice the drills following the suggestions given on page 179.

Writing these outlines legibly will give you no problem if you will:

1. Keep the straight lines straight, the curves deep.
2. Make the *a* circle very large, the *e* circle tiny.
3. Watch your proportions carefully.

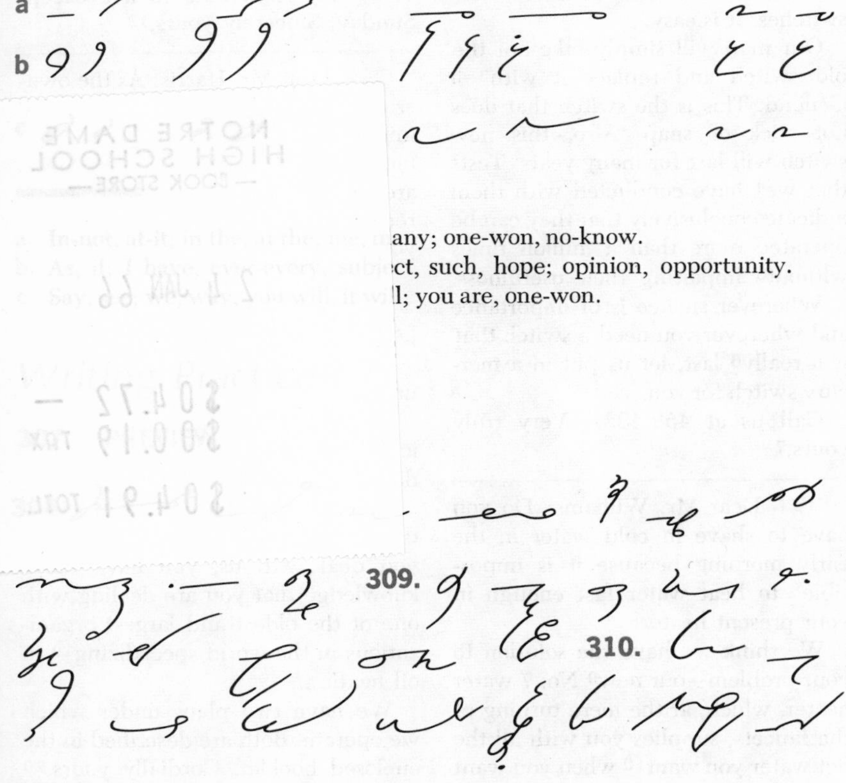

…any; one-won, no-know.

…ct, such, hope; opinion, opportunity.

…l; you are, one-won.

309.

310.

308. Few minutes, modern, one of our, mercury, switch, noisy, indicate, conclusively, a million, usefulness.

309. Shave, impossible, enough, solution, turning, faucets, next time, neighborhood, I am sure, except.

310. Burner, important, advantages, let us, prompt, oldest, specializing, both, described, enclosed.

LETTERS

308. Dear Mr. West: In just a few minutes you can add a modern touch to your home. That is all it will take for one[1] of our men to install a silent mercury switch. If you now have a noisy or worn-out switch, call us and let[2] us put in one of these new switches. It is easy.

Our man will simply take out the old switch and replace it with[3] a General. This is the switch that does not click or snap. Also, this new switch will last for many years. Tests that we[4] have conducted with them indicate conclusively that they can be operated more than a million times without[5] impairing their usefulness.

Wherever silence is of importance and wherever you need a switch that will really[6] last, let us put in a mercury switch for you.

Call us at 459-4321. Very truly yours,[7]

---

309. Dear Mr. Williams: Do you have to shave in cold water in the early morning because it is impossible[8] to heat water fast enough in your present heater?

We think we have the solution to your problem—our new[9] No. 7 water heater, which, at the mere turning of the faucets, supplies you with all the hot water you want[10] when you want it.

This new heater is on display in our local showroom at 415 Main Street. Why not ask our[11] representative to show you this unit the next time that you are in that neighborhood. I am sure you will never[12] regret your visit. The showroom is open every day from nine to five except Sunday. Sincerely yours,[13]

---

310. Dear Mr. Harris: As the owner of an oil burner, you realize how important it is for you to be protected[14] by a good service plan. Here are a few of the advantages that you receive when you let us take care of[15] your burner:

1. You save money.
2. You eliminate the necessity for heavy expenses for labor[16] and parts.
3. You increase the life of your unit.
4. You are assured of prompt service during twenty-four hours of[17] the day.

We have a service plan to meet the desires of every homeowner. When you deal with us, you have the[18] knowledge that you are dealing with one of the oldest and largest organizations in the world specializing[19] in oil heating.

We have two plans under which we operate. Both are described in the enclosed booklet. Cordially yours,[20] (400)

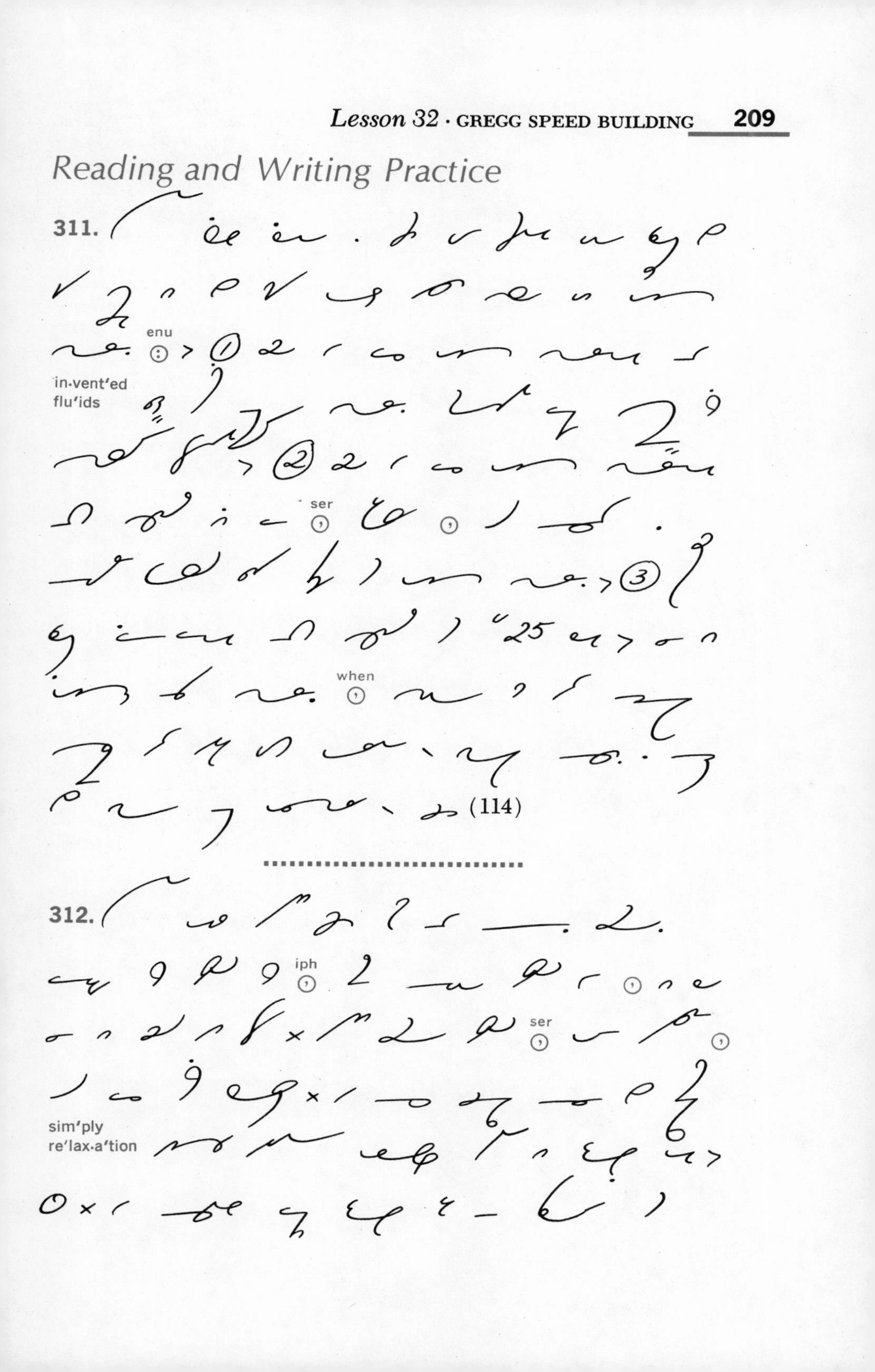

Reading and Writing Practice

311.

enu

in·vent'ed
flu'ids

ser

when

(114)

312.

iph

ser

sim'ply
re'lax·a'tion

right
un'in·ter·rupt'ed

and o

intro

par

Transcribe:
$39

(164)

313.

crumbs
floors

intro

sur'face
du'ra·bil'i·ty

ap

iq

(92)

Developing Shorthand Writing Power

314. WORD FAMILIES

-rer

a

-rt

b

a. Wearer, bearer, nearer, dearer, fairer, clearer.
b. Shirt, alert, flirt, concert, insert, reinsert.

315. FREQUENT NAMES

Last Names

a

Women's First Names

b

a. Graham, Griffin, Hamilton, Hanson, Harris.
b. Dorothy, Edith, Edna, Eleanor, Elizabeth, Esther.

Building Transcription Skills

316. BUSINESS VOCABULARY BUILDER

affirmative Positive; favorable.

storm windows Temporary windows placed over permanent windows to protect against the cold.

laundered Cleaned and ironed.

Writing Practice

317. PREVIEW

318. 319. 320. 321.

318. Affirmative, regarding, one of the most, economical, units, not only, instruments, post card.
319. Indicate, systems, desirable, condition, temperatures, determine, telephone.
320. Worn, afford, efficiently, why not, consumes, uniform, engineers, obligation, winter.
321. Fuel, as soon as, result, popular, inside, annoyance, consequently, approval, enjoyed.

LETTERS

318. Dear Mr. Hanson: Now is the time to take affirmative action regarding that old burner of yours. Don't wait[1] until it breaks down and leaves you without heat some cold night.

There is no time like the present to install a Griffin[2] Burner, one of the most economical and efficient units on the market today. By installing one[3] of our units, you will be making a fine investment. Not only will you be assured of a comfortable[4] winter, but you will save on your bills as well.

Regardless of the make of your present burner, your local Griffin[5] dealer will give it a complete test, using our special instruments, for just $5.

Get all the facts today.[6] All you have to do to get them is mail the enclosed card. It does not require any postage. Yours very truly,[7]

---

319. Dear Mr. Graham: Our records indicate that one of our heat-control systems was installed in your home a few years[8] ago. With the high cost of fuel, it is desirable to have your control system in first-class condition. This[9] will result in fuel savings and even temperatures.

We shall be glad to inspect your system at no cost to[10] you to determine whether repairs are needed. Telephone us at 629-1702. Sincerely yours,[11]

---

320. Dear Mr. Griffin: Is your oil burner old and worn? Will it cost you more to heat your house than you can afford?

Let us[12] check the burner for you and tell you whether it is operating efficiently. If it needs replacing, why[13] not consider an Adams Oil Burner, which will help keep your oil bills down. This burner consumes oil efficiently[14] and gives a uniform heat.

Our heating engineers are at your service at no expense or obligation to[15] you. If you act now, you will have no heating problems next winter.

Write or telephone us today. Sincerely yours,[16]

---

321. Dear Mr. Harris: Fuel costs are going up, but your costs will go down as soon as you have a set of our storm windows[17] installed. They keep cold air out and warm air in. The result is that you will be able to keep your house more[18] comfortable at less cost.

One of the features of our windows that has been very popular with our customers[19] is the device that enables them to place screens in windows from inside the house, thus saving many hours of[20] labor and annoyance.

We want you to understand fully the many advantages of our windows;[21] consequently, we shall be glad to install a complete set of these windows in your house on approval.

After you[22] have enjoyed the comfort of our windows, you will wonder why you did not install them long ago. Cordially yours,[23] (460)

Reading and Writing Practice

322.

wor'ry
weath'er

switch
com·plete'ly

cont

intro

Transcribe:
$200

if

if

conj

(166)

323.

pleas'ant
draw'er
wear

nc

wo

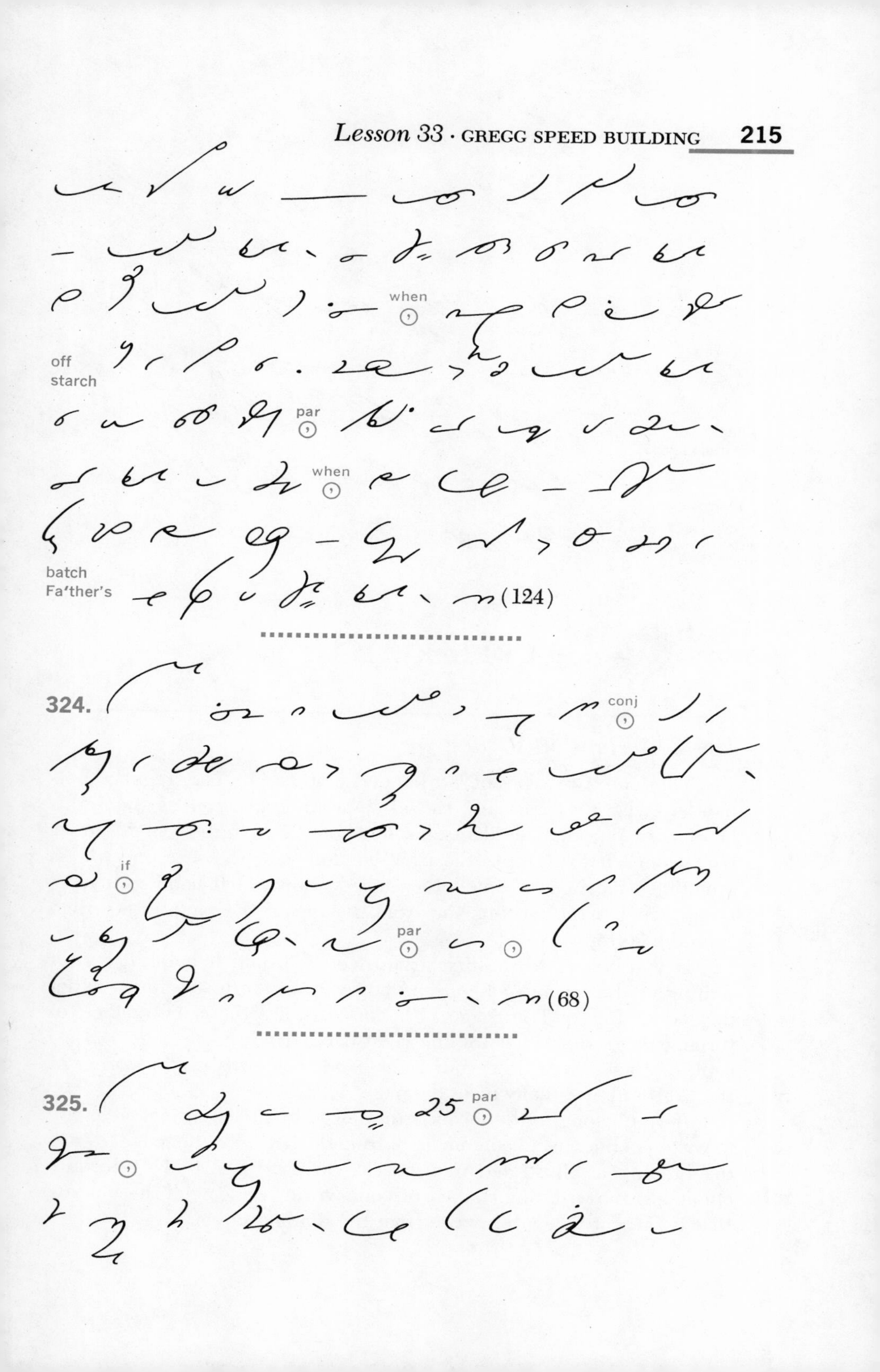

when

off
starch

par

when

batch
Fa'ther's

(124)

324.

conj

if

par

(68)

325.

25

par

In·te'ri·or

sat'is·fac'to·ry

if

(127)

SECRETARIAL TIP

The Left-Handed Writer

There are two types of left-handed writers. (1) The "regular" left-hander, who uses basically the same writing position as the right-hander, except that he slants his notebook from right to left rather than from left to right, as the right-hander does. (2) The one who is sometimes facetiously called the "upside down" left-hander; that is, he approaches the writing line from the top of the page rather than from the bottom.

If you belong to the first group, you will find it helpful to start writing at the second column and finish up in the first column, as indicated in Figure 1 on page 217. You may use the same method of turning pages described for the right-handed writer on page 188 except, of course, it will be your right hand that turns up the corner of the page and eventually turns the page.

If you belong to the second group of left-handers, it may help you to write (in the second column first) from the bottom of the page toward the binding as illustrated in Figure 2 on page 217. This procedure eliminates the irritating contact of your writing hand with the binding that is present when you write from the binding down.

Figure 1

Figure 2

LESSON 34

Developing Shorthand Writing Power

326. FREQUENT PHRASES

To Do

a

Omission of Words

b

a. To do, to do it, to do the, to do so, to do this, to do that, to do your.
b. One of our, every one of the, in the past, in the future, some of the, some of them, many of the.

327. GEOGRAPHICAL EXPRESSIONS

-son

a

States

b

Foreign Cities

c

a. Atchison, Dawson, Ferguson, Harrison, Hutchinson, Madison.
b. Alabama, Georgia, Kentucky, Missouri, North Carolina, South Carolina.
c. Portsmouth, Southampton, Inverness, Birmingham.

Building Transcription Skills

328. BUSINESS VOCABULARY BUILDER

landscaping The laying out of grounds or gardens.

insecticide Insect-killing chemical.

termites Bugs that are highly destructive to buildings, furniture, etc.

Writing Practice

329. PREVIEW

330.

331.

332.

333.

330. Grounds, I am sure, damage, landscaping, to serve, supervision, one of our, you will find.

331. Believed, science, experimentation, experience, instructors, newest, effective, consult.

332. Gardening, entertained, Lazy, chuckle, without, collection, contribute, profit.

333. Hundreds, already, helpful, recently, developed, fertilizer, sanitary, ingredients, postal.

LETTERS

330. Dear Mr. Dawson: The grounds about your home are of great importance to you. I am sure you will want to take the[1] best possible care of them. Perhaps this past winter has done damage to your grounds and you are considering some[2] landscaping work.

Our organization is ready to serve you. It has a staff of well-trained men who will carry[3] out the work under the supervision of one of our experts.

May I have an opportunity of discussing[4] the care of your grounds with you? I know you will find our discussion helpful and interesting. Cordially yours,[5]

---

331. Dear Mr. Pine: Our organization has always believed that the care of trees is a science.

It has taken[6] years of experimentation to develop the service that we render today. Our research and our field experience[7] have aided us in finding ways to kill pests and to help trees grow. Our instructors spend many hours each week[8] teaching our men the newest and most effective ways to take care of trees.

More people than ever are using our[9] service. If you have trees on your grounds, consult your phone book for our nearest agent or write us direct. Sincerely yours,[10]

---

332. Dear Friend: Would you like to know how you can make your gardening more fun and less work? Would you like to learn how you can[11] do this and be entertained at the same time?

If you would, get a copy of a new book entitled "Gardening[12] for Lazy People." This entertaining book gives you the facts about gardening in a style that will make you chuckle.[13] At the suggestion of your gardener, Harry H. McMann, we are sending you a copy of this new book[14] without charge.

In the back of the book you will find a collection of ideas on how our products contribute to[15] making your gardening more fun.

We hope that you enjoy and profit by this new book. Yours very sincerely,[16]

---

333. Dear Friend: Did you enjoy reading "Gardening for Lazy People"? Hundreds of persons have already told us that[17] the book has not only given them much helpful advice but that it has also provided them with many chuckles.[18]

Our Research Department has recently developed a new type of fertilizer that is clean and sanitary[19] and yet provides every one of the many different ingredients that plants need in order to[20] grow properly.

Your gardener, Harry H. McMann, has this new product in stock and will be glad to supply you[21] with as much as you need.

In the meantime, please tell us how you liked "Gardening for Lazy People." A postal card is all that is necessary. Cordially yours,[22] (440)

Reading and Writing Practice

334.

se·vere'
ex·pe'ri·enced

intro

par

rav'ag·es
in·sec'ti·cide

nc

wo

re·ceive'
sched'ule
past

when

(112)

335.

intro

dis·cuss'ion
ex·ter'mi·na'tor

ap

conj

re'in·spect'
prem'is·es
san'i·tar'y

Transcribe:
$5

if

par

(128)

336.

lawn
Dale's

conj

well built
no noun, no hyphen

if

if

25

(100)

337.

intro

enu

a·vail'a·ble
in·te'ri·or
ex·te'ri·or

in'di·vid'u·al'i·ty
guar'an·tee'

conj

(98)

Developing Shorthand Writing Power

338. WORD BEGINNINGS AND ENDINGS

Trans-

a

Dis-

b

Inter-

c

a. Transit, transportation, translate, transmit, transpose, transatlantic, transpire.
b. Disappeared, disturbed, district, desirable, dismayed, displaced.
c. Interrupt, interruption, interesting, international, interview, internal, interest.

Building Transcription Skills

339. BUSINESS VOCABULARY BUILDER

in transit On the way.

expedite To speed up.

completion Conclusion; ending.

Progressive Speed Builder (80-120)

The Progressive Speed Builder in this lesson runs from 80 words a minute to 120 words a minute. Does 120 words a minute sound fast to you? You won't find it fast if you practice the words and phrases in the preview.

Remember, try to get something down for every word; and under no circumstances should you stop writing!

340. PREVIEW

341.

342.

343.

344.

345.

341. Gentlemen, ordered, has not yet been, delivered, has been, transit, desperately.
342. To me, transportation, locate, meantime, first, you have been, inconvenienced, delay.
343. As soon as, second, started, turned, word, tomorrow, to see, correspondence.
344. Understand; Boston, Massachusetts; about this matter, disturbed, handled, reasonable, attention.
345. News, thus, success, disappeared, subjected, situation, beyond, we hope, in the future.

LETTERS

(1 Minute at 80)

341. Gentlemen: On August 20, I ordered one of your No. 16 beds, which is listed on page 18 of/your catalogue. As it is now September 16 and the bed has not yet been delivered, I am wondering//whether my order was lost or whether the bed has been shipped but delayed in transit.

We need the bed desperately;/// and unless you can ship it at once, I shall have to make arrangements to purchase it elsewhere. Sincerely yours, (1)

(1 Minute at 90)

342. Dear Mr. West: Your letter stating that you have not received the No. 16 bed we shipped you on September 3 has been/referred to me.

We have traced this order with the transportation company, but they cannot locate it. We are, therefore, sending//you a replacement shipment. This shipment should arrive by September 19. In the meantime, we will continue our efforts///to locate the first shipment.

I am sorry that you have been inconvenienced by this delay in delivery. Sincerely yours, (2)

(1 Minute at 100)

343. Mr. Pace: On September 16, Mr. E. H. West wrote us that he had not received the No. 16 bed that he ordered on August/20. As soon as I received his letter, I had a second bed shipped to him and started tracing the first shipment with the express company.//The missing shipment has not yet turned up, and I have had no word from the express company. As I am leaving on my vacation tomorrow,///please follow up this matter to see whether you can locate the missing bed.

All the correspondence on the matter is attached. J. B. White (3)

(1 Minute at 110)

344. Gentlemen: On September 3, we shipped one of our beds to Mr. E. H. West, 416 Beacon Street, Boston, Massachusetts. I understand that Mr./White, of our company, called you about this matter and asked you to trace the shipment. We have not yet had any word from you about the missing shipment.//We are disturbed about the way this entire matter has been handled. We have had shipments delayed in transit before, but the shipments have always///turned up in a reasonable time.

As we promised to let our customer know the cause of the delay, won't you please give this matter your attention. Sincerely yours, (4)

(1 Minute at 120)

345. Dear Mr. West: I have delayed writing to you in the hope that I would soon have news about the original shipment we made to you on September 3. The express/company has been trying to locate the shipment, but thus far they have met with no success. Apparently the bed has just disappeared.

By this time you have no doubt received//the second shipment we made to you on September 16. We are sincerely sorry for the inconvenience to which you have been subjected, but we know that you///will understand that this was a situation that was beyond our control.

We hope that we may have many opportunities to serve you in the future. Sincerely yours, (5) (500)

Reading and Writing Practice

346.

per'ma·nent
pave'ment

if

e·quip′ment
neigh′bor·hood

as

451–3165 if

par

re′al·ize
in′con·ven′ience
ex′pe·dite

(166)

347.

as

ap

20

intro

iph

par

intro

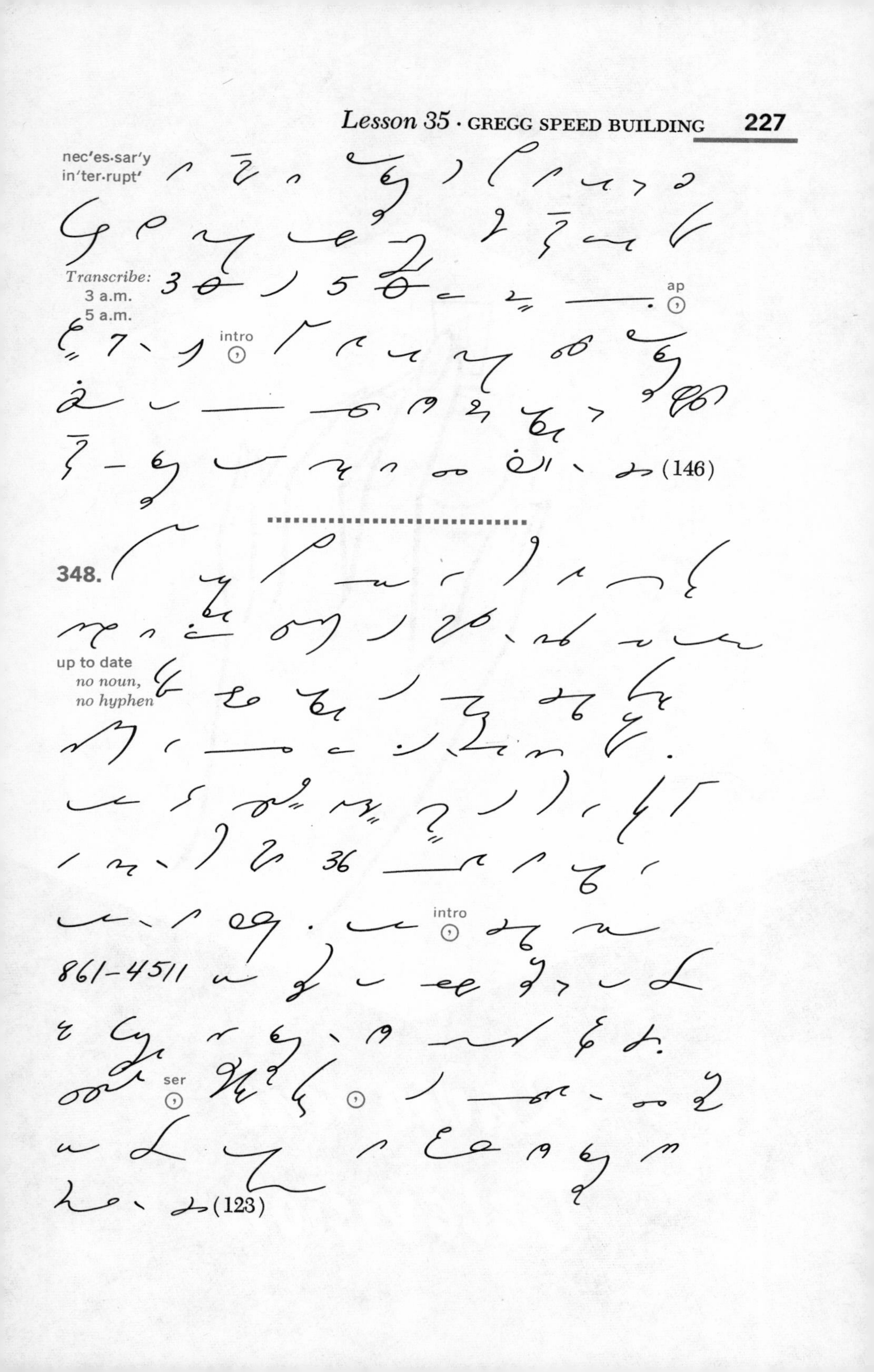

nec'es·sar'y
in'ter·rupt'

Transcribe:
3 a.m.
5 a.m.

ap

intro

(146)

348.

up to date
no noun,
no hyphen

36

intro

861-4511

ser

(123)

CHAPTER 8

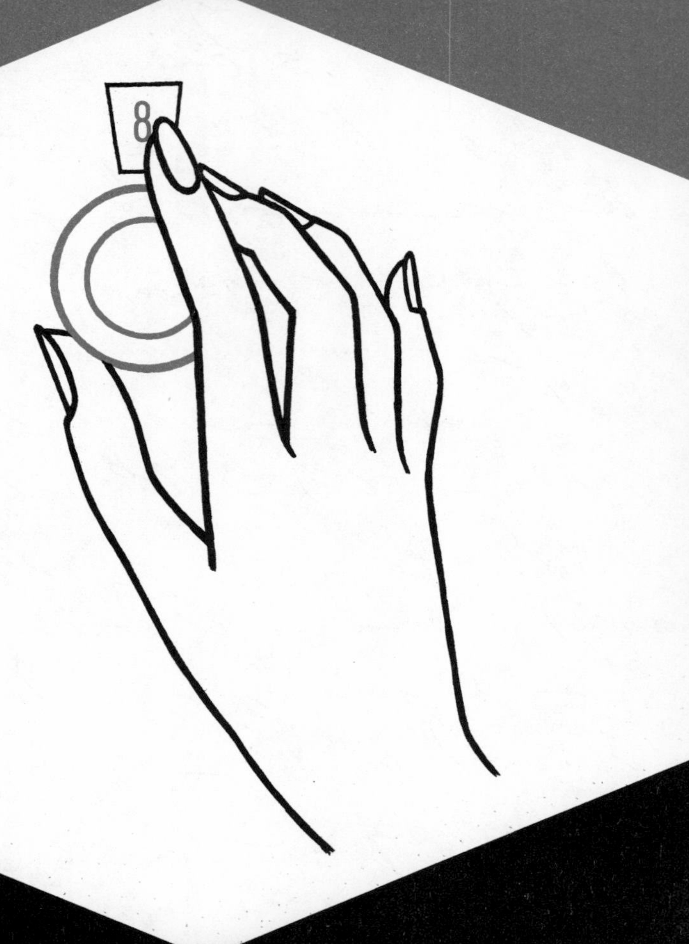

Radio and Television

Developing Shorthand Writing Power

349. OUTLINE CONSTRUCTION

Word endings -vity, -city. In the interests of facility, the vowel is omitted in the endings *-vity, -city*.

Activity, brevity, captivity, gravity, capacity, electricity.

Omission of short i and e. In order to obtain outlines that are easy to read, short *i* and *e* are omitted between:

P and N, T, D

a

B and N, T, D

b

a. Open, happen, dispense, appetite, perpetual, repetition, competition, rapid.
b. Robin, exhibit, habit, inhabit, prohibit, rabbit, rabid.

Building Transcription Skills

350. SIMILAR-WORDS DRILL

Lead, led

lead *(verb)* To guide or conduct; to follow the path or course of.

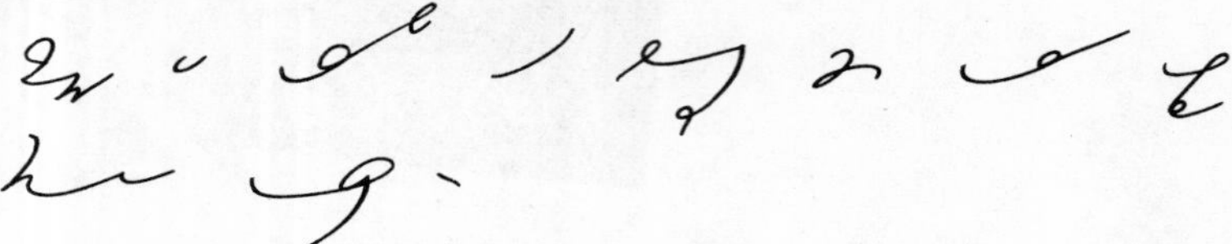

He will lead us in song at the party.
As a result of radio and television, we can lead richer, fuller lives.

led The past tense of *lead.*

He led us in singing at the party.
John led a rich, full life.

Note: A very common error that stenographers make is to spell both the present and the past tense of *lead* alike, perhaps because both the present and the past tense of *read* are spelled alike. Don't you make this mistake! The past tense of *lead* is spelled *l-e-d.*

Reading and Writing Practice

351. Modern Miracles

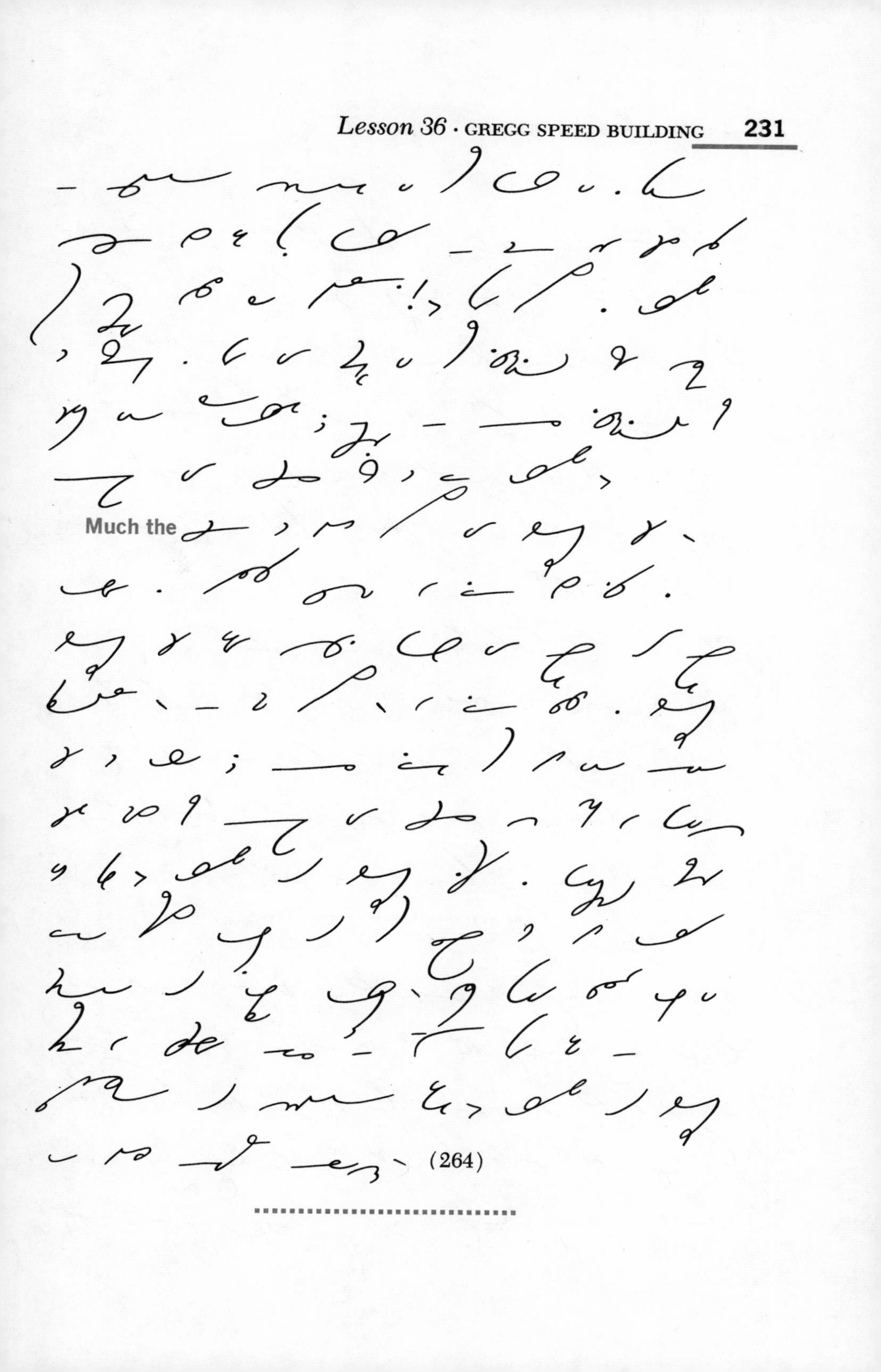

Much the

(264)

LETTERS

352.

ap

par

Transcribe: 7 p.m.

ef·fect'
led
lis'ten

bc

intr

wheth'er
tran'script

par

par

(114)

353.

bc

ap

iq

ex·am′ple
whole

intro

ser

as′pect
post·pon′ing
un·til′

17

if

par

5

(148)

354.

ap

iph

scripts
ad·van′tag·es

13

as

a′re·a
in·struc′tor

(135)

LESSON 37

Developing Shorthand Writing Power

355. RECALL DRILL — E

In this drill you will review the different uses of the alphabetic stroke *e*.

E

a

-ly

b

-ingly

c

Y-

d

a. Kneel, meal, steal, feel, real, deal.
b. Fairly, greatly, neatly, only, humanly, deadly, simply.
c. Willingly, unwillingly, unfailingly, sparingly, amazingly, knowingly.
d. Yacht, yawn, young, younger, youngster, youthful, youthfulness.

Building Transcription Skills

356. ACCURACY PRACTICE

The drills in this lesson are designed to help you join circles to straight lines correctly. Follow the practice suggestions given on page 179.

In practicing these groups:

1. Keep the straight lines straight.
2. Close each circle.
3. Make the *a* circles large; the *e* circles tiny.

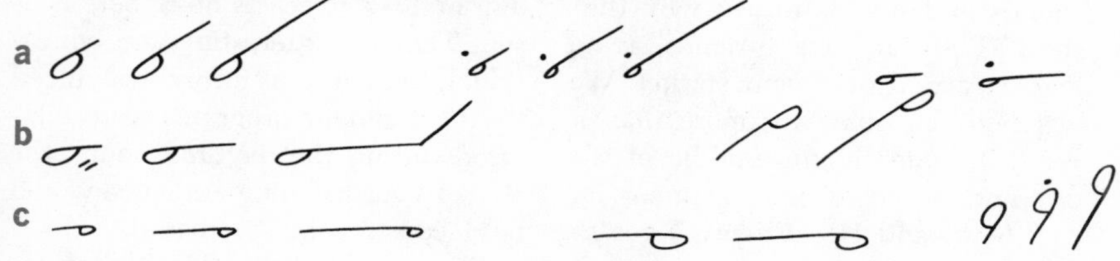

a. Ate, add, added; heat, heed, heeded; when, him.
b. Ann, I am, amend; day, today.
c. Knee, me, many; may, memoranda; I shall, hatch, age.

Writing Practice

357. PREVIEW

358. Behalf, myself, provided, entertainment, forward, won't, happened, television.
359. Comments, viewers, telecast, sponsored, chemical, sustaining, program, we hope that, refreshing.
360. Enlisted, diversion, educational, similar, televised, listening, audience, congratulate, appreciative.
361. Suggestion, unfortunately, province, advertiser, designates, accordingly, theater.

LETTERS

358. Gentlemen: I am writing this letter on behalf of a number of my friends and myself to ask why the[1] show "Betty and Her Friends" is no longer carried over your station. We watched this show for more than a year. It came[2] in the middle of the day and provided entertainment for us. "Betty and Her Friends" was so refreshing and[3] alive that we looked forward to it each day. It was our favorite program.

Won't you please tell us what happened to[4] the show and whether we can expect to see it on television again in the near future. Yours sincerely,[5]

---

359. Dear Mrs. Lawrence: We are always glad to receive comments from our viewers about the shows that are telecast[6] over our channel.

"Betty and Her Friends" was sponsored by the American Chemical Company. They canceled[7] the show on January 2. Unfortunately, our time for sustaining features is limited, and there[8] was no spot into which we could fit the program.

We hope that some other sponsor will take over "Betty and Her[9] Friends" and that once again you will be able to enjoy the refreshing humor of the show. Cordially yours,[10]

---

360. Gentlemen: Here at Fort Smith both the enlisted men and the officers depend largely on television for[11] entertainment and diversion.

One of the programs that gives us a great deal of pleasure is the Saturday night[12] telecasts of Robert Nelson. They are interesting and educational; and I am firmly convinced that[13] if similar programs were televised during the daytime hours, the size of your listening audience would be[14] considerably increased.

Please congratulate Mr. Nelson for us on his entertaining program and assure[15] him that he always has a very appreciative audience at Fort Smith. Very cordially yours,[16]

---

361. Dear Mr. Miller: We appreciate your interest in our show "The Star Theater of the Air" and your suggestion[17] that we make it available over the station that serves Springfield.

Unfortunately, it is not within[18] our province to decide where a given show will be telecast. When an advertiser buys time on a network[19] program, he designates the particular areas where he wishes his message heard and he is charged accordingly.[20]

Up to the present time the sponsor of "The Star Theater of the Air" has not included Springfield in the[21] areas in which he is interested.

The number of areas in which this program is being telecast[22] is increasing, and perhaps in the future the Springfield area will also be included. Very cordially yours,[23] (460)

Reading and Writing Practice

362.

mod'el
Col'or
per·form'ance

ser intro

ri'val
de·scrip'tion

nonr

Transcribe:
$169

916-7272

it's
whole

intro

(142)

363.

KDKK

com·mer'cial
car'ried

(112)

if

364.

8-page

4-col'or

hyphenated before noun

and o

nc

wo

cam·paign'

ef·fec'tive

lo'cal

(138)

Developing Shorthand Writing Power

365. WORD FAMILIES

-ser

a

-duct

b

a. Sponsor, announcer, freezer, razor, bracer, dispenser, tracer.
b. Conduct, product, induct, deduct, abduct, by-product.

366. FREQUENT NAMES

Last Names

a

Men's First Names

b

a. Henderson, Hoffman, Hughes, Hunter, Jackson, Johnson, Johnston.
b. Felix, Francis, Frederick, George, Gilbert, Godfrey.

Building Transcription Skills

367. BUSINESS VOCABULARY BUILDER

marine Having to do with the sea or ocean.

service clubs Organizations such as the Kiwanis Club, the Rotary Club, etc., that serve their communities.

"snow" Light and dark spots on a television screen that result from the same causes that produce static in radio.

Writing Practice

368. PREVIEW

369.

370.

371.

372.

369. Sponsorship, efforts, directed, betterment, community, appropriation, broadcast, daily, announcements, activities, cordially, intended, facilities, we hope you will find, helpful.
370. Studied, budget, fiscal, allotments, submit, further.
371. American, schedule, director, publicity, arrangements.
372. Purchased, report, records, occasions, picture, few minutes, amount, perform, satisfactorily, request, new.

LETTERS

369. Gentlemen: We are pleased to announce that we have undertaken sponsorship of a new 15-minute program[1] over WJOY that we feel will be of service to all organizations whose efforts are directed[2] to the betterment of the community and that do not have an advertising appropriation.

This program[3] is entitled "The Parade of Events" and is broadcast daily Monday through Friday from 10:00

to 10:15[4] each morning. The program consists of announcements from churches, service clubs, and other civic organizations[5] whose activities are non-profit making. We cordially invite you to make full use of our program.

This[6] program is intended as a public service on the part of our station; and, of course, there will be no charge to[7] you for the use of the station's facilities.

We hope you will find this service helpful. Yours very truly,[8]

---

370. Mr Jackson: I have studied the advertising budget that you prepared for the next fiscal year. I am in[9] agreement with all the allotments you have made except the amount indicated for radio and television[10] advertising.

Before we submit the budget to the Finance Committee, I suggest that we discuss[11] the matter further.

Will Friday at eleven o'clock in my office be convenient for you? George H. Hoffman[12]

---

371. Gentlemen: We shall be pleased to discuss with you the final plans for a new radio series entitled "Great[13] American Heroes." May I schedule a meeting in our office for May 10 at 10 a.m.?

Our program[14] director, Mr. Hughes, and I will be prepared to offer some definite dates for fall scheduling. Our Publicity[15] Department has agreed to send a representative to our meeting. There should be no reason why we cannot[16] complete the arrangements for this series.

Please let me hear from you if this date is convenient. Cordially yours,[17]

---

372. Gentlemen: About a month ago, I purchased one of your television sets and had you install it in my[18] home. I am sorry to report that we have had nothing but trouble with it.

Your records will indicate that your[19] serviceman has been here six times. On each visit he has made some adjustment and on two occasions installed new[20] parts. In spite of his efforts we still cannot get a clear picture. Every station to which we turn comes in with[21] so much "snow" that it is impossible to sit and watch a program for more than a few minutes.

I feel that our[22] set is a "lemon" and that no amount of adjustment will make it perform satisfactorily. May I request,[23] therefore, that you have your man call for the set and that you replace it with a new one. Sincerely yours,[24] (480)

Reading and Writing Practice

373.

iq

10 KRKR

spon'sor
par·tic'i·pants

as

iq

ap

nonr

track
wheth'er

iq

(121)

374.

intro

bc

intro

ex·am'ple
fur'nac·es
lev'el

nonr

ser

chim'neys
med'i·cal

THE HYLE-McCANN COMPANY

San Diego, California | Terre Haute, Indiana | Council Bluffs, Iowa | Baltimore, Maryland

1700 WABASH AVENUE, TERRE HAUTE, INDIANA

December 23, 19--

The New York Insurance Company
221 Broadway
New York, New York 10028

ATTENTION: Mr. Parsons

Gentlemen:

This is just a note to tell you how glad we are that we took your advice a few years ago and purchased business-interruption insurance.

As you know, on May 16 of last year our store was burned to the ground. We could easily have been bankrupted as a result of the fire, which caused considerable damage. Thanks to our policy with your organization, however, everything turned out all right.

Of course, we obtained temporary quarters quickly. However, we suffered operating losses of more than $50,000. In addition, we had extra expenses amounting to $30,000 for fixtures and other items. We recovered this $80,000 because we had invested in your business-interruption insurance.

While I am president of our company, we will never be without business-interruption insurance.

Cordially yours,

Harold G. Green

Harold G. Green
President

HGG:MH

Average-Length Letter
Semiblocked Style, with Attention Line
Standard Punctuation

intro

wrecks
worth'while'

(187)

375.

intro

vo·ca'tion
cho'sen

ap

du'ties
an·nounc'er

(110)

Developing Shorthand Writing Power

376. FREQUENT PHRASES

To

a

Say

b

a. To spend, to sell, to supply, to surrender, to select, to spare, to spell.
b. To say, I would say, glad to say, I can say, I cannot say, would not say.

377. GEOGRAPHICAL EXPRESSIONS

New-

a

States

b

Foreign Cities and Countries

c

a. New York, New Orleans, New London, New Bedford, New Britain, Newark.
b. Arizona, Louisiana, Montana, Minnesota, North Dakota, South Dakota.
c. Glasgow, Wales, Ireland, Belfast, Dublin.

Building Transcription Skills

378. BUSINESS VOCABULARY BUILDER

warrant To justify; to merit.

dotes Is foolishly fond of.

earmarked Set aside for a specific purpose.

Writing Practice

379. PREVIEW

380. [shorthand] **381.** [shorthand] **382.** [shorthand] **383.** [shorthand]

380. Years ago, benefit, listeners, brushing, shorthand, nine o'clock, distributed, request, used, course.
381. Sponsoring, mechanical, as a result, warrant, judgment, medium, contract, in the future.
382. Promised, possibility, itself, directly, prospects, profit, to visit.
383. Family, cowboy, presentation, continue.

LETTERS

380. Gentlemen: About two years ago your television station had a program that was conducted for the[1] benefit of those listeners who were interested in brushing up on their shorthand and building up their shorthand[2] speed. The program was conducted by a New Orleans shorthand teacher, and it was telecast twice a week between[3] eight and nine o'clock in the evening. If I remember correctly, your station distributed a booklet free[4] upon request. Are you conducting a similar program now, or do you have any plans for one in the[5] future?

I am interested in such a program

because I find it necessary to use shorthand again[6] after not having used it in years. I know I would benefit from a television brush-up course. Cordially yours,[7]

---

381. Gentlemen: As you know, for the past six months we have been sponsoring a 15-minute program once a week on[8] your station advertising our new line of mechanical pencils. While our sales of these pencils have increased slightly[9] as a result of the program, we do not feel that the increase has been large enough to warrant our[10] continuing this type of advertising during the coming year. It is the judgment of our Advertising Department[11] that the radio is not the most satisfactory advertising medium for the promotion of[12] a product such as ours.

It is with regret, therefore, that we are giving up our program at the conclusion of[13] our present contract.

If we should decide to resume radio advertising in the future, we shall certainly[14] give first consideration to your station; we have nothing but praise for your fine service. Cordially yours,[15]

---

382. Dear Mr. Green: As I promised you when you were in my office on June 15, I discussed with our advertising[16] manager the possibility of using television to advertise our products.

It is his feeling[17] that television does not lend itself to advertising products like ours, which are sold directly to schools.[18] He feels that a great portion of the people we would reach would not be prospects for our products and that we shall profit[19] more from a direct-mail advertising campaign.

Thank you for taking the time to visit me. Cordially yours,[20]

---

383. Gentlemen: This is just a note to tell you how much my family and I enjoy your program, "History in[21] the Making." It is so interesting that even my eleven-year-old son prefers it to the cowboy features on[22] which he dotes. We enjoyed your Friday night presentation so much that I felt I had to write you about it.

I[23] hope that the sponsor will continue to offer this excellent program for many years to come. Sincerely yours,[24] (480)

Reading and Writing Practice

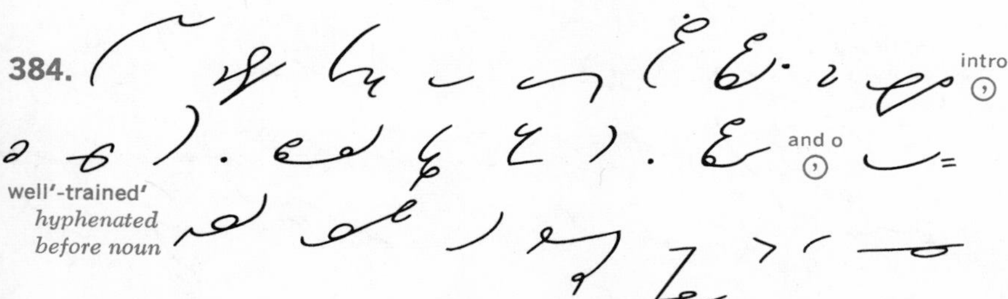

iph

intro

nc

be·gin'ning
rec'om·mend'

if

(172)

385.

Transcribe:
95 per cent

il

ad'ver·tis·ing
col'umns

nc

wo

intro

be·lieve′
mer′chan·dise

and o

intro

intro

(178)

386.

fam′i·lies
ad′ver·tis′ers

as

enu

if

915-6111

(124)

LESSON 40

Developing Shorthand Writing Power

387. WORD BEGINNINGS AND ENDINGS

Sub-

a

Per-, Pur-

b

-ification

c

a. Submitting, substantial, subnormal, subside, suburb, suburban, subway.
b. Performer, person, pertain, permission, permit, purchase, pursue.
c. Qualifications, notification, specifications, modification, classification, ratification.

Building Transcription Skills

388. BUSINESS VOCABULARY BUILDER

honorarium A token fee.

role A part.

stature Status gained by achievement or accomplishment.

Progressive Speed Builder (80-120)

389. PREVIEW

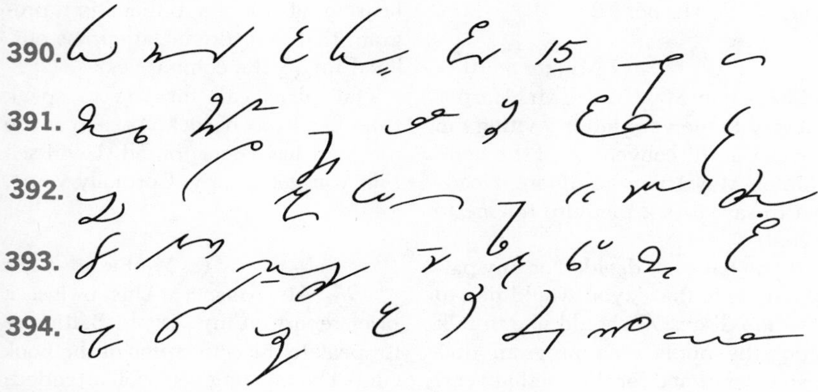

390. Board, suggested, speaker, Baltimore, expect, 1,500, message, of course.
391. As you will see, if you do not, invitation, return, office, explain, publication.
392. Referred, to me, topic, program, enjoy, things, store, final.
393. Particular, discuss, qualified, interest, to speak, six o'clock, as soon as, has been.
394. Report, attended, received, opportunity, several, very much, worthwhile, honorarium.

LETTERS

(1 Minute at 80)

390. Dear Mr. Harper: At a meeting of the board of directors of the Book Club, it was suggested that we invite/Mr. Charles Smith of your organization to be the speaker at our convention on May 16 in Baltimore.//We expect more than 1,500 of our members to attend, and I know they would enjoy Mr. Smith's message.///

We shall, of course, be glad to pay Mr. Smith's expenses. May we count on him to be with us? Cordially yours, (1)

(1 Minute at 90)

391. Mr. Smith: As you will see by the attached letter, you have been invited to speak to the convention of the Book Club in/Baltimore on May 16. If you do not have any other plans for that date, I suggest that you accept this invitation.//You can fly to Baltimore in the morning and return in the evening, so that you will lose only one day from the office.///

This will be a fine chance for you to explain the publication program that we have outlined for the coming year. H. R. Harper (2)

(1 Minute at 100)

392. Dear Mr. Casey: Mr. Harper referred to me your letter inviting me to speak at the convention of the Book Club on May 16/in Baltimore. Needless to say, it is a pleasure for me to accept.

If you have not decided on any particular topic that//you would like to have me discuss, I should like to talk about the publication program that we have outlined for the coming year. I think your///members would enjoy hearing about the things that we have in store for them.

When your final program is ready, please send me a copy. Yours truly, (3)

(1 Minute at 110)

393. Dear Mr. Smith: The board of directors was pleased to learn that you could be with us at the convention of the Book Club on May 16 in Baltimore.

We/have no particular topic in mind for you to discuss. We felt that you would be the one best qualified to decide the topic that would be of greatest//interest to our members. I agree that the members would enjoy hearing about the publication program that your organization has outlined for///the coming year.

Our plans call for you to speak from five to six o'clock. As soon as the program has been printed, I will see that you get a copy. Cordially yours, (4)

(1 Minute at 120)

394. Mr. Harper: This is just a brief report on my visit to Baltimore to speak to the convention of the Book Club. The meeting was well attended; there were more than/1,500 members present.

As you suggested, I talked about our publication program for the coming year, and the talk was very well received. After the talk,//I had an opportunity to see several of the officers of the Book Club, and all of them felt that the publication program that we have outlined was very///much worthwhile.

I am submitting my expense report to the president. I am not, however, accepting the honorarium that he has offered. Charles Smith (5) (500)

Reading and Writing Practice

395.

enu

re·spon'si·ble
hir'ing
ac'tors

when

conj

conj

cr

(113)

396.

stat'ure
war'rant

intro

when

per·form'er
to'ward

intro

com·mer'cial
cho'sen

cont

par

(129)

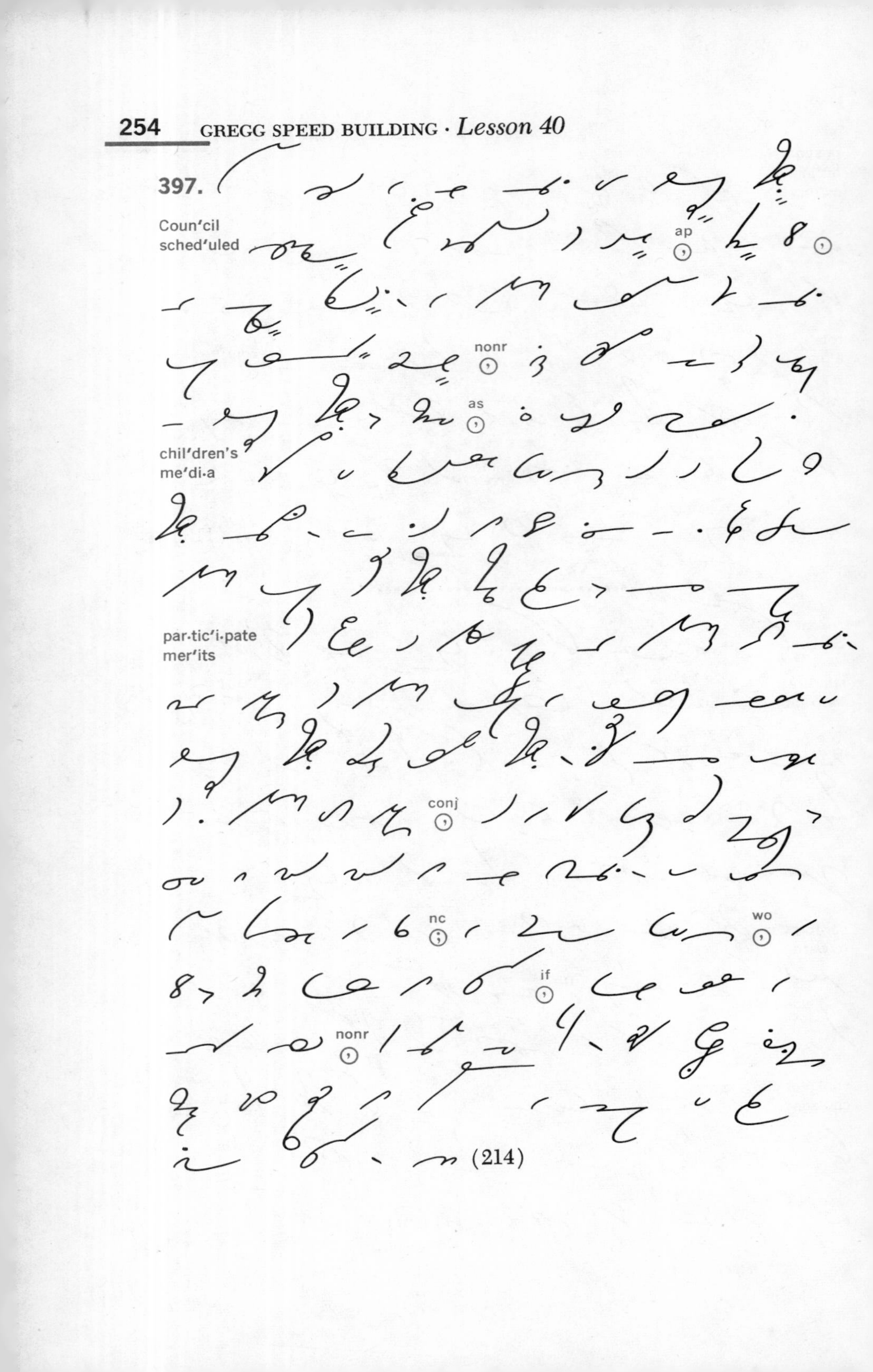

397.

Coun'cil
sched'uled

ap
nonr
as

chil'dren's
me'di·a

par·tic'i·pate
mer'its

conj
nc
wo
if
nonr

(214)

PART THREE

Schools and Education
Communications
Clothing
Paper and Printing

DEVISING SHORTCUTS

Some students have the erroneous impression that all they have to do to increase their shorthand speed is to learn a great many shortcuts. However, shortcuts are not the answer to shorthand speed. Shortcuts can be of value to you only if the words represented by the shortcuts occur regularly in your dictation. If they do not, the shortcuts will be more of a hindrance than a help in the development of your shorthand speed. Why? If the words do not occur frequently, you will not have an opportunity to use the shortcuts often enough to be able to write them automatically. The moment that a shortcut causes you to hesitate for even a fraction of a second, it is valueless; you will do far better to write the expression in full.

While you are developing your shorthand speed in school, you will be well advised to stay away from shortcuts almost entirely and write everything in accordance with the word-building principles of Gregg Shorthand. Time enough to think of shortcuts when you are on the job.

Even on the job, you should think carefully about any shortcut that you adopt. Before you adopt it, decide whether the shortcut meets the following essential requirements.

1. Is the full outline so long or difficult to execute that you cannot write it in full rapidly? Consider this question carefully, because there are relatively few outlines in Gregg Shorthand that cannot be written rapidly according to the word-building principles of the system.

2. Does the word come up in your dictation again and again to justify the additional burden that learning the shortcut imposes on your mind?

3. Is the shortcut distinctive enough to cause you no difficulty when you transcribe?

If the answer to these three questions is "yes," then the adoption of the shortcut may be worthwhile.

As a rule, it is best to use only shortcuts that you are able to devise at leisure and after some thought.

There is one situation, however, in which you would be justified in forming a new shortcut while the dictation is going on—that is, when a particular expression, the outline for which is a lengthly one, is used several times and you have good reason to believe that it will be used many more times in your dictation.

For example, a stenographer was taking dictation in which she was constantly meeting the expression one-class service. The first three times she wrote the expression in full; but when it occurred the fourth time, she phrased one-class and placed an s underneath to represent the word service. It came with such frequency, however, that she finally cut the outline to oo-k-intersected s. In this case the expression occurred so often that the stenographer found it desirable to shorten the shortcut!

After the dictation, the stenographer took the precaution of making a note of the shortcuts she used for one-class service so that if she had to transcribe her notes some days later, when memory was of little help, she would be able to read the shortcuts.

On page 258 you will find an illustration of shortcuts devised during dictation.

Although shortcuts have their limited place in taking dictation, you will be wise to follow the advice of an experienced shorthand reporter who said, "When in doubt, write it out!"

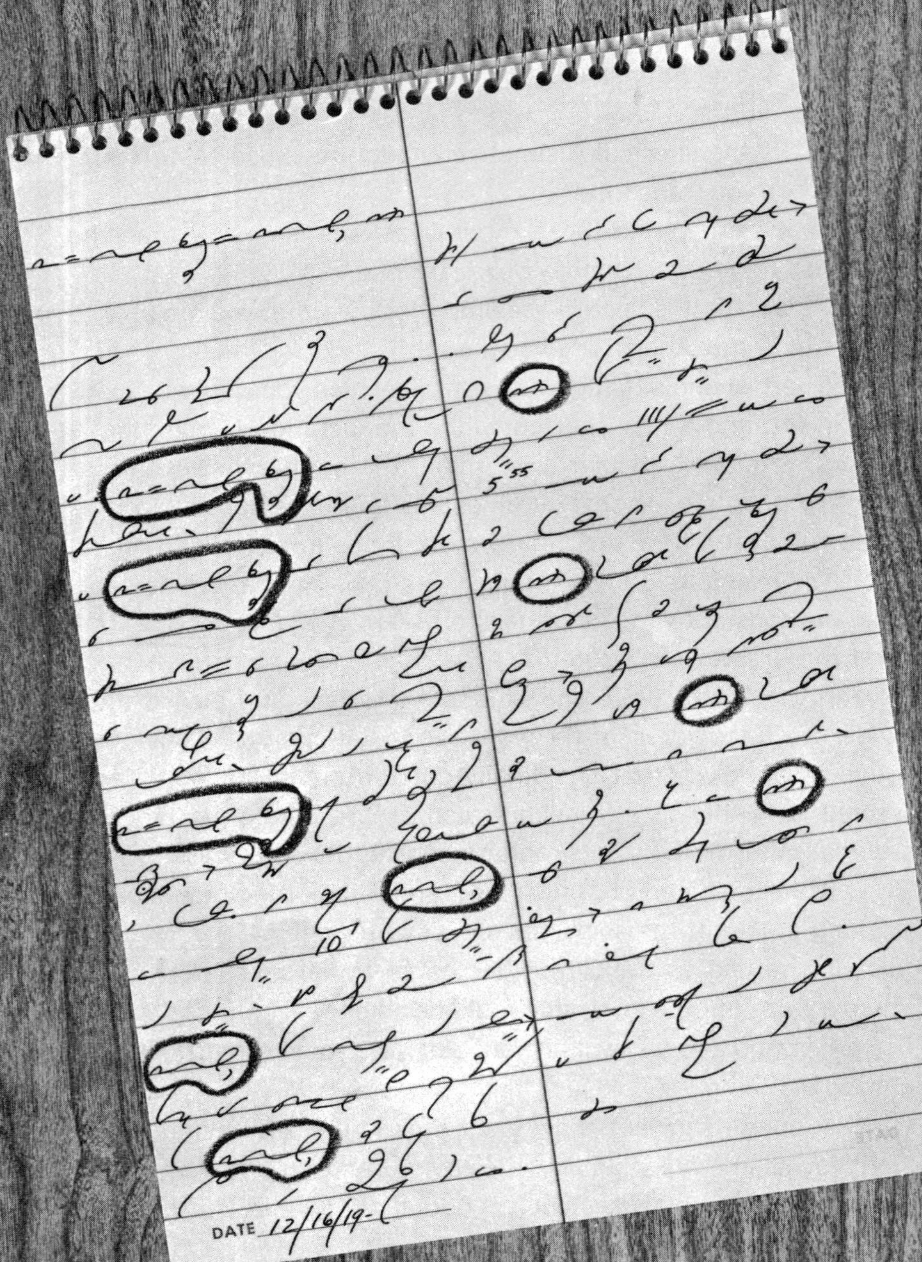

Illustration of Shortcuts Devised During Dictation

CHAPTER 9

Schools and Education

LESSON 41

Developing Shorthand Writing Power

398. OUTLINE CONSTRUCTION

Omission of short e between p and k. The omission of short *e* between *p* and *k* in words of more than one syllable results in outlines that are both fluent and legible.

Respect, expect, prospect, suspect, speculate, picture, picnic.

Omission of short e in -fect, -ject. The omission of short *e* in the combinations *-fect, -ject* enables us to obtain outlines that are easy to write and to read.

-fect

a

-ject

b

a. Perfect, affect, effect, effective, infect, defect, confection.
b. Project, inject, injection, eject, dejected, adjective, conjecture.

Building Transcription Skills

399. SIMILAR-WORDS DRILL

Adopt, adapt

adopt To take as one's own; to accept.

Many schools will adopt our new textbook.
He will adopt the boy from the orphanage.

adapt To fit; to adjust; to make suitable (usually followed by *to*).

He must be able to adapt himself to changing conditions.
Perhaps you can adapt these suggestions to your own selling situation.

Reading and Writing Practice

400. An Educated Person

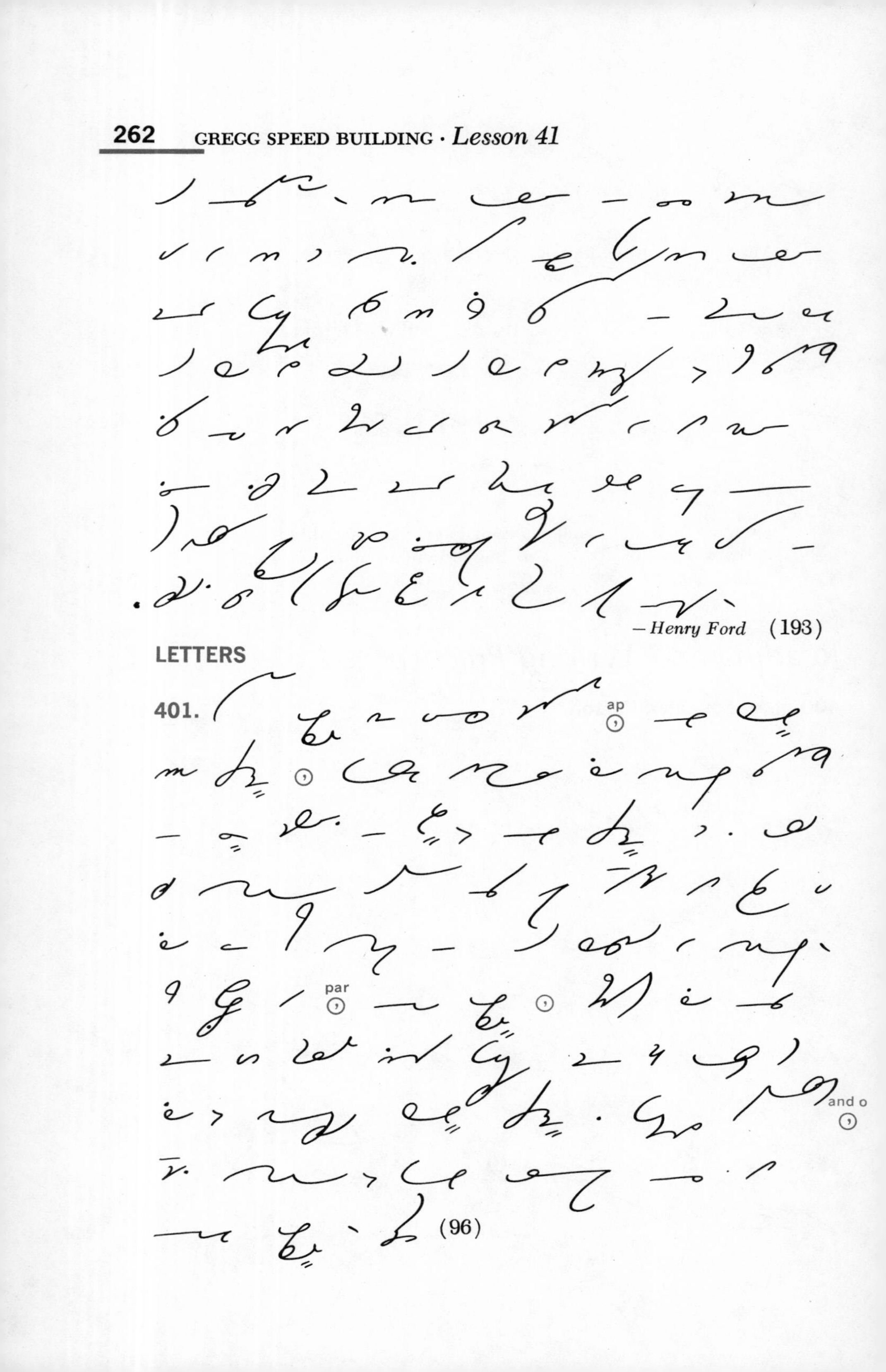

—*Henry Ford* (193)

LETTERS

401. ap and o par (96)

402.

ap

conj

brief'ly
a·dapt'ing

intro

daugh'ter
sights

conj

as

(141)

403.

sec'ond·ar'y
Bi·ol'o·gy
al·read'y

ap

iq

if ⊙

con·cise′
o·pin′ions

conj ⊙

(129)

404.

Transcribe:
25 cents
son's

25

25

in′ter·rupts′
de·scrip′tion

intro ⊙

(100)

LESSON 42

Developing Shorthand Writing Power

405. RECALL DRILL — T, D

In this drill you will review the different uses of the alphabetic strokes *t* and *d*.

Trans-

a

Past Tense

b

De-, Dĭ-

c

-ward, -hood

d

a. Transport, transfer, transmit, transform, transatlantic, transcontinental.
b. Packed, backed, relaxed, tried, distributed, stimulated, initialed.
c. Depart, delay, depression, depend, deport, delivered, direct, direction.
d. Forward, backward, onward, outward, neighborhood, childhood, motherhood.

Building Transcription Skills

406. ACCURACY PRACTICE

In this lesson you will study the correct joining of circles in the body of a word.

a. Writ, read; rate, raid; late, laid.
b. Take, tag; deck, dig; man, name.
c. Rack, lake; care, gale; pave, beef.

Writing Practice

407. PREVIEW

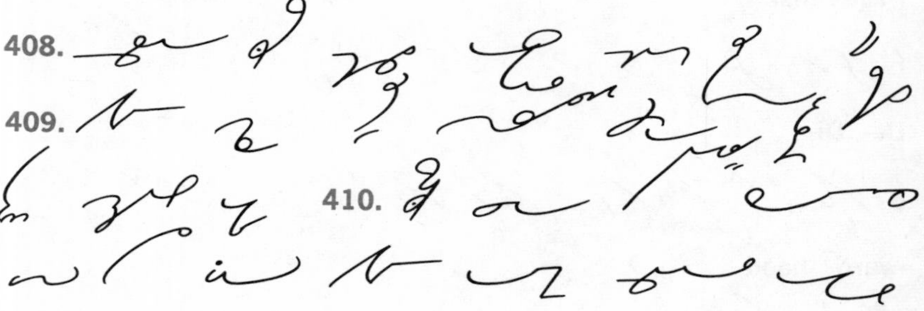

408. Material, aviation, unfortunately, library, instruction, we shall be glad, further.
409. Department, questionnaire, several thousand, graduates, faculty, specific, everyday, business world, consideration, report.
410. Association, annual, Detroit, alumni, occurred, to me, hold, department, luncheon, naturally, will you please.

LETTERS

408. Dear Mr. Keys: We are pleased to be of service to you in providing material that will be helpful in[1] your aviation program. Unfortunately, we cannot supply copies of this material for all your[2] students: but we are sending a set for you and another for your reference library. We have made many[3] of our training films available to schools offering instruction in aviation. If you would care to have[4] any of these films, we shall be glad to arrange to get them for you.

If we can be of any further service[5] to you in connection with your courses in aviation, it will be a pleasure to help you. Cordially yours,[6]

---

409. Dear Mr. Rice: The Placement Department of our college is planning to send a questionnaire to several thousand[7] of our graduates who are now teaching. It is our belief that this questionnaire can supply us with information[8] that will be useful to our students and faculty.

We are asking your help in formulating this[9] questionnaire. Are there any specific questions that you would like to have included, questions that will help your present[10] students meet the everyday problems of the business world?

Your questions will be given full attention and[11] consideration. We shall send a copy of the final report to you. Thank you for your help. Cordially yours,[12]

---

410. Dear Mrs. Beck: As you know, the National Teachers Association will hold its annual convention in[13] Detroit, Michigan, from March 28 to 30. This convention will be attended by our alumni[14] from all parts of the United States. It occurred to me that this would be a good time for the alumni to hold a[15] little get-together; and, with that in mind, I am writing you this note.

Mr. Smith, the head of the Business[16] Department, is arranging a luncheon at the College Inn on March 30, to which all alumni are invited.[17] Naturally, before any final plans for this luncheon can be completed, we shall have to know about[18] how many can be present. Will you please indicate on the attached card whether you will be there. Cordially yours,[19] (380)

Reading and Writing Practice

411.

di·rec'tor
vo·ca'tion·al
guid'ance

180

intro

20

intro

Transcribe:
10 cents

55400

(126)

412.

ser

an'swers
cit'i-zen

enu

intro

Transcribe:
$1
25 per cent

par

il

25,

(124)

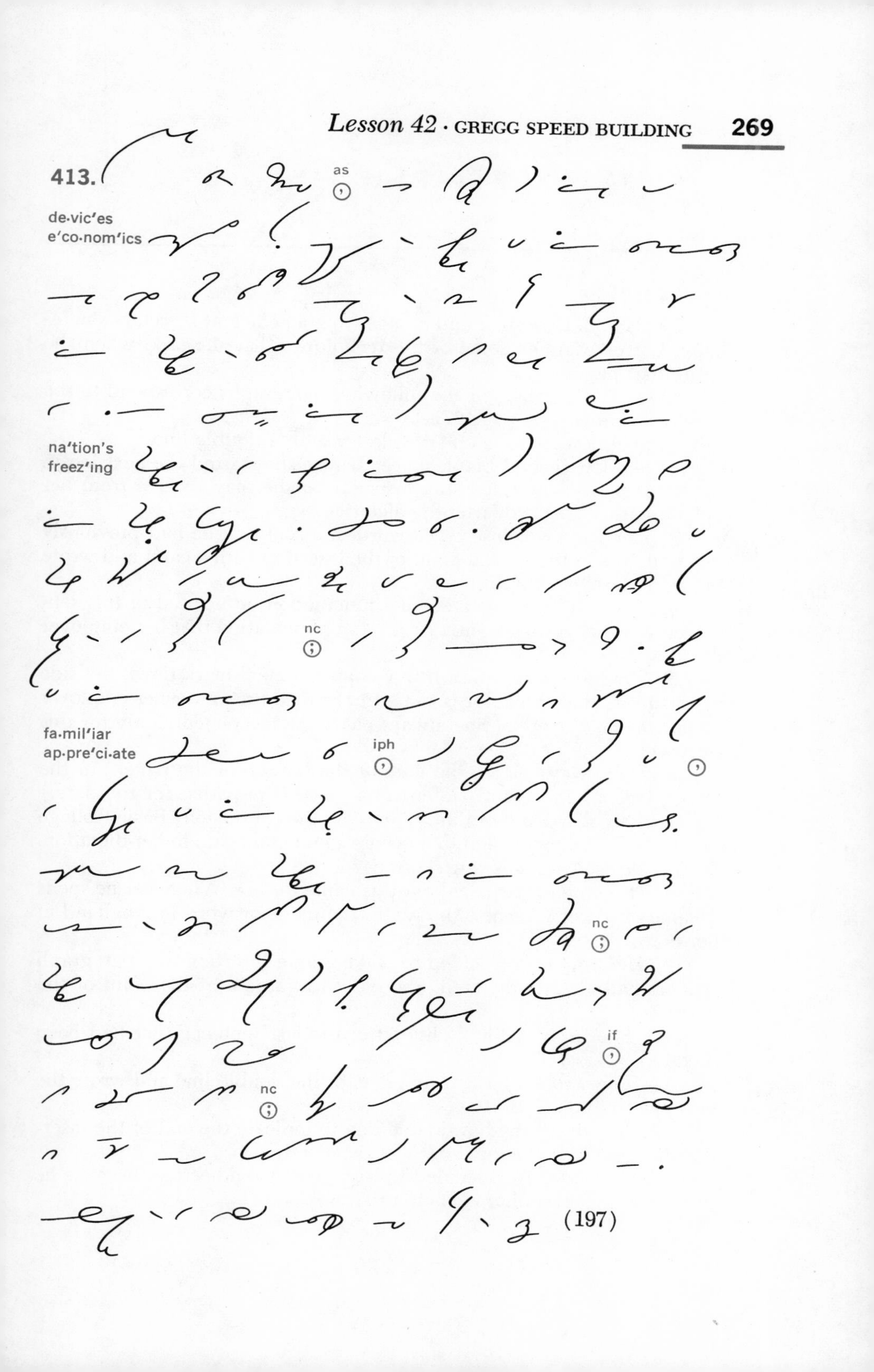

413.

as

de·vic′es
e′co·nom′ics

na′tion′s
freez′ing

nc

fa·mil′iar
ap·pre′ci·ate

iph

nc

if

nc

(197)

SECRETARIAL TIP

Page From a Secretary's Notebook

On page 271 you will find a page from an efficient secretary's notebook. Let us examine some of the techniques that she used when she wrote that page.

Note: The numbers of the following paragraphs correspond to the encircled numbers on page 271.

1. She indicated the end of a letter with a double line.

2. She left several blank spaces before she started the next letter. In these spaces she writes any instructions she may receive from her dictator either during or after the dictation.

3. Her employer inserted a word in a sentence he had previously dictated. She indicated the point of the insertion with a caret and wrote the word directly above it.

4. Her employer dictated the punctuation he wanted in this sentence. She always inserts, in a circle, any punctuation that her employer dictates.

5. She indicated with a heavy colored pencil mark down the side of this letter that the letter is to be transcribed first, after her employer completes his dictation. She always has a colored pencil handy for this purpose.

6. She always places the date at the bottom of the page. (In the Gregg Official Shorthand Notebook a place is provided for the date.)

7. This shorthand outline represents the expression "Basic College Accounting," an expression that occurs again and again in her dictation. She has devised a timesaving shortcut for it.

8. Her employer spelled out this name for her. Whenever he spells a name or a word for her, she writes the name or word in longhand in her notes.

9. Her employer decided to make a long insertion in a paragraph that he had already dictated. She placed a large *a* at the point of the insertion.

10. She drew a double line after the last sentence that had been dictated.

11. She wrote a large *a* underneath the double line and wrote the new material to be inserted.

12. She drew another double line to indicate the end of the insertion and continued taking the rest of the dictation.

13. Her employer decided to transpose two adjectives because he felt the sentence would read better that way.

A page from a secretary's notebook. The encircled numbers correspond to the numbered explanations on page 270.

LESSON 43

Developing Shorthand Writing Power

414. WORD FAMILIES

-sity, -city

a

-ically

b

a. Varsity, scarcity, capacity, publicity, simplicity, veracity.
b. Physically, technically, medically, radically, chemically.

415. FREQUENT NAMES

Last Names

a

Women's First Names

b

a. Kerr, King, Klein, Larsen, Levy, Lynch.
b. Flora, Florence, Georgiana, Gertrude, Harriet, Henrietta.

Building Transcription Skills

416. BUSINESS VOCABULARY BUILDER

on open account On credit.

matriculation Enrollment.

hazard Risk.

Writing Practice

417. PREVIEW

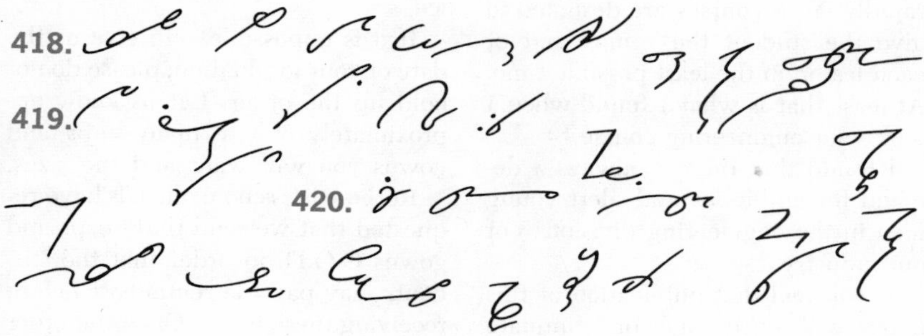

418. Radio, daily, audience, programs, designed, enough, to publish, announcement.
419. To know, helpful, studying, devote, ahead, engineering, demand, ambitious, encourage, stimulate.
420. Whether, how many, gowns, information, impossible, graduation, let us know, approximately, in the past, officials, C.O.D., items.

LETTERS

418. Dear Mr. Lynch: Radio has become an important part of our daily lives. You and your friends are part of[1] a vast radio audience. Because of the size of this audience, most radio programs are planned to appeal[2] to the general public. Every season, however, we offer a series of programs just for students.[3] This program is called "The School of the Air."

As this program is designed for students, we are eager to bring it to[4] the attention of as many boys and girls as possible. With this thought in mind, we ask whether you would be good[5] enough to publish the enclosed carefully worded announcement in your school paper.

If you can do this and will[6] send us a copy of the paper in which the story appears, we shall appreciate it very much. Yours truly,[7]

---

419. Gentlemen: You will be interested to know that I took your correspondence course in engineering and found[8] it most helpful.

By studying in my spare time, I gained many advantages. I found that I could apply much[9] of what I was learning from your lessons to my work.

The student who knows what he wants and is willing to devote[10] the necessary time to study can get ahead rapidly. Your courses are designed to give the student the[11] most out of each lesson in the least possible time. At least that is what I found when I took your engineering course.[12]

I found that there is always a demand for ambitious and alert young men in the engineering division[13] of our industry.

If you feel that publication of this letter will encourage or stimulate young men to[14] study in their spare time, I shall be happy to have you use it in any way that you think best. Cordially yours,[15]

---

420. Dear Mr. Klein: We are writing to ask whether you can tell us how many caps and gowns you will need this June. We should like[16] to have this information now so that we may give you the best possible service.

If it is impossible[17] to give us the date of your graduation, please do not hold up the order. Let us know approximately[18] how many caps and gowns you will want and the sizes.

In the past, school officials have requested that we send the[19] caps and gowns C.O.D. in order that the students may pay the rental cost before receiving these items. On[20] the other hand, if you would prefer to have us send these items on open account, we will do so. Sincerely yours,[21] (420)

Reading and Writing Practice

421.

ac·cept'

A·cad'e·my

out'-of-state'
hyphenated before noun

nc

intro

par

bc

intro

(105)

422.

traf'fic
Route

and o

intro

de·cid'ed
war'rant

enu 20 ser 25

passed
haz'ard

if

(161)

423.

sched'ule
var'si·ty

par

bc

par

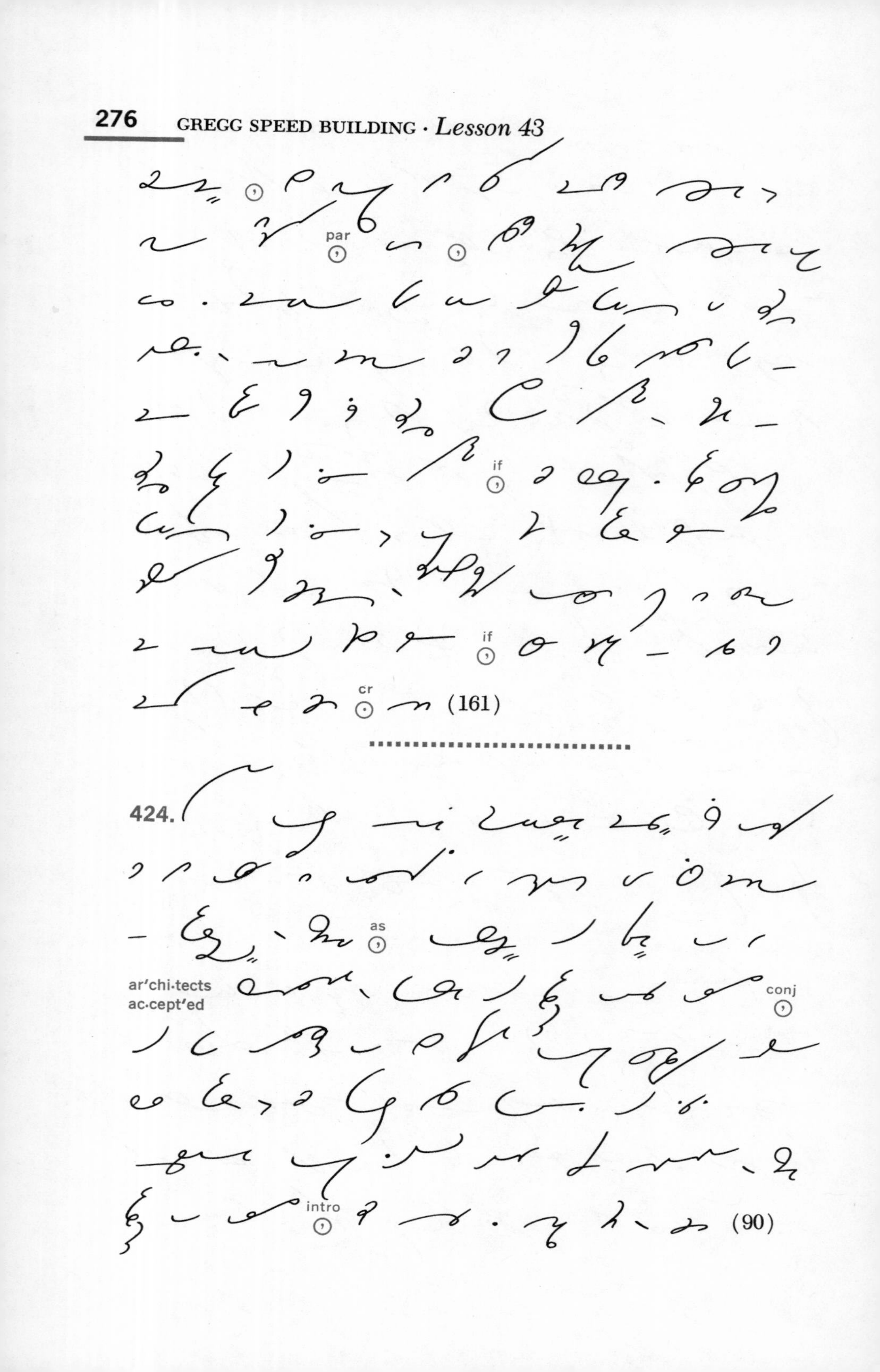

par

if

if

cr

(161)

424.

as

ar′chi·tects
ac·cept′ed

conj

intro

(90)

Developing Shorthand Writing Power

425. FREQUENT PHRASES

In Order

a

As You

b

a. In order, in order to see, in order to say, in order to be, in order to have, in order to be able.

b. As you know, as you may, as you are, as you did, as you say, as you will, as you can.

426. GEOGRAPHICAL EXPRESSIONS

-ville

a

States

b

Foreign Cities

c

a. Asheville, Nashville, Knoxville, Danville, Brownsville, Jacksonville, Evansville.

b. Colorado, Maine, Nebraska, Ohio, Tennessee, Washington, West Virginia.
c. Bordeaux, Marseilles, Cherbourg, Madrid, Lisbon, Brussels.

Building Transcription Skills

427. BUSINESS VOCABULARY BUILDER

foresight Act of looking ahead.

monograph A written discussion of a particular subject.

exorbitant Excessive; too much.

Writing Practice

428. PREVIEW

429.

430.

431.

429. Perhaps, employer, advancement, prepared, promotions, foresight, themselves, if you want, accounting, yourself, return, businessmen.
430. To become, unusual, developments, Washington, increasingly, government, education, outline, special.
431. Parcel, monograph, fortunate, assistance, grateful, distributed.

LETTERS

429. Dear Mr. Green: Perhaps your employer thinks highly of you personally. When an opportunity for[1] advancement comes along, however, will he give it to you or to the other fellow? You can be sure that it will[2] be the other fellow if he is better prepared. Today, more than ever, promotions are being given to[3] well-trained people who have had the foresight to prepare themselves to handle bigger jobs.

If you want to hold an[4] executive's position, you must understand accounting and you must know how your product is sold to the public.[5] How can you prepare yourself for advancement to an executive's position with your present firm?

Return the enclosed[6] card, which requires no postage. When we receive it, we will send you our free booklet, "Opportunities in Business.[7]" It will tell you about the training we have been giving to businessmen since 1910. Yours truly,[8]

---

430. Dear Mr. Bailey: You are invited to become a charter subscriber to Education News, an[9] unusual service prepared especially for school executives.

The service is available to you at[10] a time when developments in Washington are becoming increasingly important in educational[11] circles. There are 90 Government agencies in Washington whose activities affect every school and[12] teacher.

The purpose of Education News is to take all the happenings in Washington applying to[13] education and boil them down into one easily read booklet.

I am enclosing a brief outline of the other[14] features that Education News has to offer. When you have examined the outline, I am sure that you will wish to[15] take advantage of a special offer of a full year's subscription for only $9. Sincerely yours,[16]

---

431. Dear Mr. Cummings: We are sending you by parcel post our new, carefully planned educational monograph[17] entitled "The Air Age." It contains four parts.

In preparing this material, we were fortunate in obtaining[18] the advice and assistance of Dr. Peter Franklin, who is an expert in this field. We are grateful to[19] him for his many fine suggestions and ideas.

This unit will be distributed without charge through departments[20] of education. If you would like to have this material for use in your school system, let us know how many[21] monographs you need. We will then try to meet your requirements if it is at all possible. Sincerely,[22] (440)

Reading and Writing Practice

432.

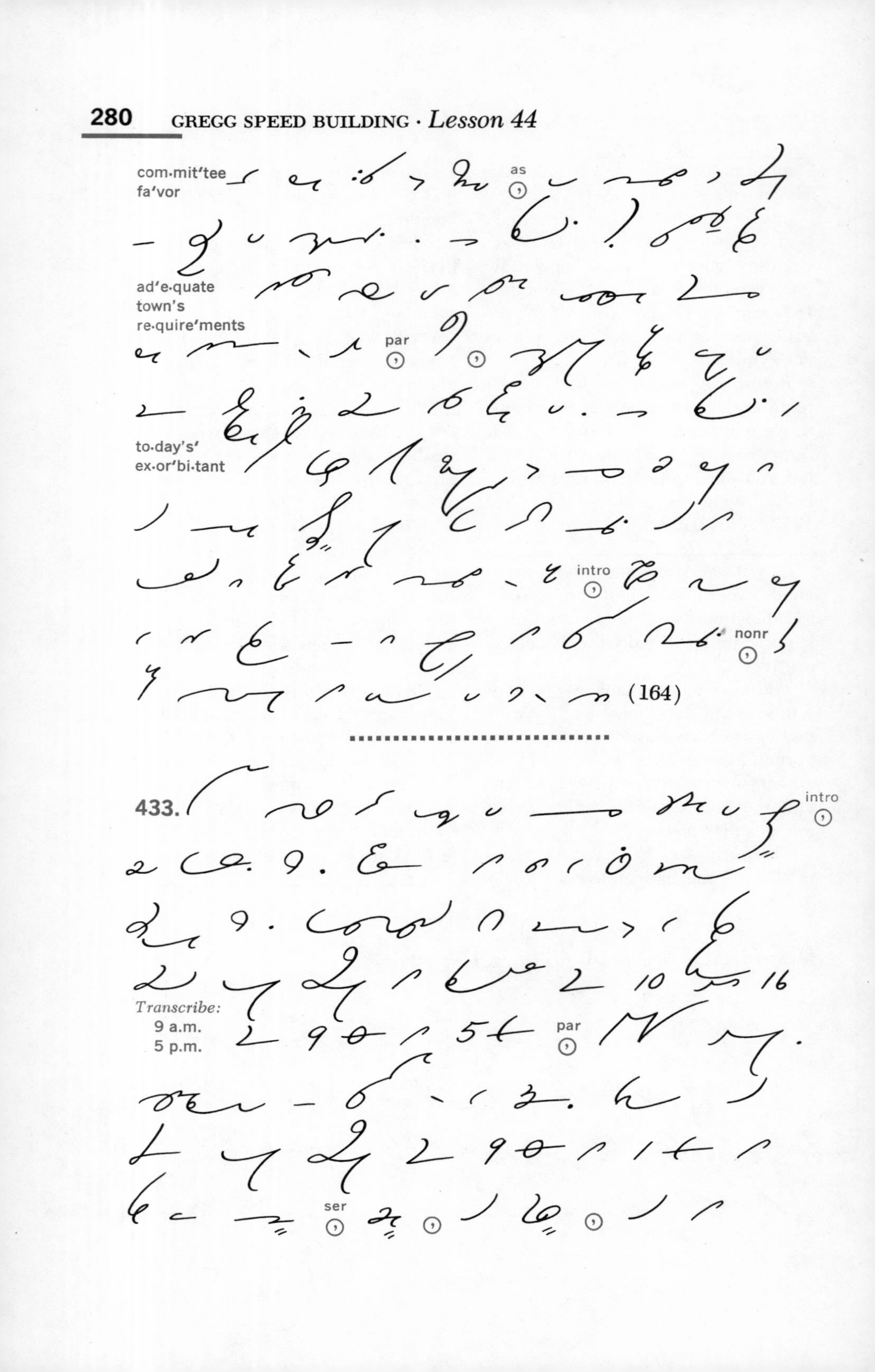

com·mit′tee
fa′vor

as

ad′e·quate
town's
re·quire′ments

par

to·day's′
ex·or′bi·tant

intro

nonr

(164)

433.

intro

Transcribe:
9 a.m.
5 p.m.

par

10 16

ser

STEPHEN SAMPSON & SONS

HUMBLE BUILDING 1216 MAIN STREET HOUSTON, TEXAS 77000

April 27, 19--

Mrs. Charles R. Gray
3131 Western Parkway
Houston, Texas 77009

Dear Mrs. Gray:

I must make a confession. When I came here last fall to take over the Houston branch of Stephen Sampson & Sons, I was sure that it would be easy to sell a great deal of furniture in a short time. The sight of the homes here in Houston must have caused me to be overoptimistic.

In anticipation of the sales that I expected, I bought large quantities of fine furniture. In spite of the quality of the furniture and the appeal of our low prices, however, sales fell far below my expectations. Now I have a warehouse full of merchandise that must be moved. What's more, there are new shipments on the way from several manufacturers.

The time for action has come. On Saturday, May 6, you will see in all the Houston papers an announcement of stock-disposal sales. Prices will be low. In many cases, our furniture will be offered at cost and even less. Of course, we expect a great response. Because of this, I feel that you and a few other preferred customers should have the opportunity to shop in comfort before public announcement is made of the sale.

Therefore, please consider this a personal invitation for you to shop at your convenience on May 3, 4, or 5. When you come, please give the enclosed card to one of our salesmen. He will then take you to the floor on which the sale will be held.

Very truly yours,

STEPHEN SAMPSON & SONS

Martin A. Foster

Martin A. Foster
Manager

MAF:CS
Enclosure

Long Letter
Indented Style
Standard Punctuation

ap

if

chil'dren

(145)

434.

as

crit'i·cal
for'tu·nate

intro

af·fect'
for'mer·ly
book'keep'ing

ser

intro

intro

if

(142)

LESSON 45

Developing Shorthand Writing Power

435. WORD BEGINNINGS AND ENDINGS

Super-

a

-ure

b

-ings

c

a. Supervision, supervise, supervisor, superior, superhuman, superlative, supersede.
b. Natural, picture, lecture, feature, future, miniature.
c. Meetings, greetings, readings, evenings, mornings, sayings.

Building Transcription Skills

436. BUSINESS VOCABULARY BUILDER

compiling Collecting literary material into one volume or source.

seminar A group of students engaged in research.

dismally Dreadfully; sadly.

Progressive Speed Builder (90-125)

The letters in this Progressive Speed Builder begin at 90 words a minute and run to 125 words a minute—or only 5 words a minute more than you wrote in the previous Progressive Speed Builder. Those five words may be brief forms or phrases and therefore should cause you no difficulty. You can do it!

437. PREVIEW

438. Girls, senior, include, supervision, to bring, materials, at this time, let us know, earliest.
439. Request, together, in the past, supplied, one of our, meetings, review, compiling.
440. Students, anyone, criticized, board, perfectly, familiar, recommending.
441. Working, another, week or two, understand, enclosed, highly.
442. Many thanks, promptly, hesitation, exception, immediately.

LETTERS

(1 Minute at 90)

438. Dear Mr. Nelson: Would you please mail me a list of the girls in the senior class who will complete their training in June.

Also,/would you include a list of the teachers under your supervision. We wish to bring our mailing list up to date before sending//out our college catalogues and other materials.

When you list the addresses, please give us the home addresses. If you///do not have the lists ready at this time, please let us know the earliest date on which you think you can send them. Very sincerely yours, (1)

(1 Minute at 100)

439. Mr. Jones: We have just received a request from Baker College for a list of the girls in our senior class who will complete their work in June./Baker College also asks for a list of our teachers and their home addresses.

In the past, we have supplied these lists to a number of//colleges. I remember, however, that you raised a question at one of our meetings whether we should review our policy on supplying these///lists.

We are now compiling these lists, and they should be ready soon. When they are ready, shall I send copies to Baker College? Harry Nelson (2)

(1 Minute at 110)

440. Mr. Nelson: I am glad you brought up the matter of supplying mailing lists of our students. Last year we supplied the list to anyone asking for/it, and this policy was criticized by several members of the Board of Education.

This year please refer to me all such requests, and I will decide// each case on its merits.

It will be perfectly all right to send the lists to Baker College. I am familiar with the work that they do there, and I///would have no hesitation in recommending the school highly to any student who is interested in the type of training that they offer. Frank H. Jones (3)

(1 Minute at 120)

441. Dear Mr. Decker: We shall be happy to supply you with the names and home addresses of our students who will complete their work in June. We are now working on this list,/but it will be another week or two before the lists will be available.

As we are naturally interested in the use that is made of these lists, we should//appreciate it if you would send us copies of any material that you mail to our students. I am sure that you will understand our reason for this request.

The///list of our teachers, together with their home addresses, is enclosed.

You will be interested to know that we think highly of the work your school is doing. Cordially yours, (4)

(1 Minute at 125)

442. Dear Mr. Nelson: Many thanks for your kindness in sending us the lists so promptly. Thank you also for your comment that you have no hesitation in recommending our school/to any of your girls who are interested in the type of training that we offer. I may say that we have had the pleasure of enrolling many of your //girls in the past, and almost without exception they have done well.

We shall, of course, be glad to send you copies of all materials that we send to your students. On the first mailing,///we plan to send a copy of our latest catalogue.

If you will let us have your bill for preparing these lists, we will send you a check immediately. Sincerely yours, (5) (545)

When you can't say anything nice about another person, you will be wise to follow the example of Calvin Coolidge, who said, "I have never been hurt by anything I didn't say."

Reading and Writing Practice

443.

isq

per·suade'
self'-im·prove'ment

if

iq

e·ven'tu·al·ly
sem'i·nar'

if

ap

15

bc

if

nc

(166)

444.

sur'vey
two'-thirds'

nc

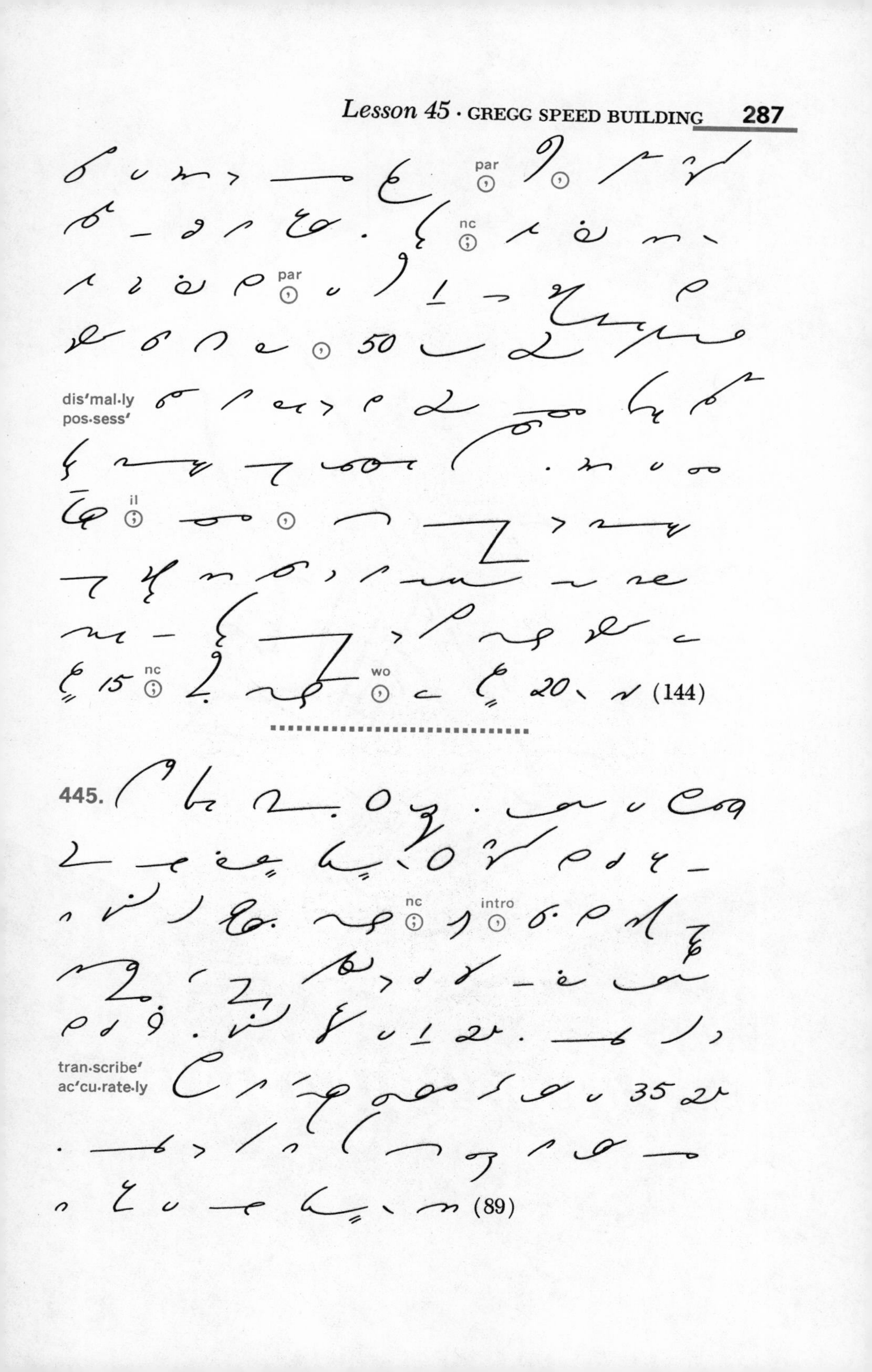

dis'mal·ly
pos·sess'

(144)

445.

tran·scribe'
ac'cu·rate·ly

(89)

CHAPTER

10

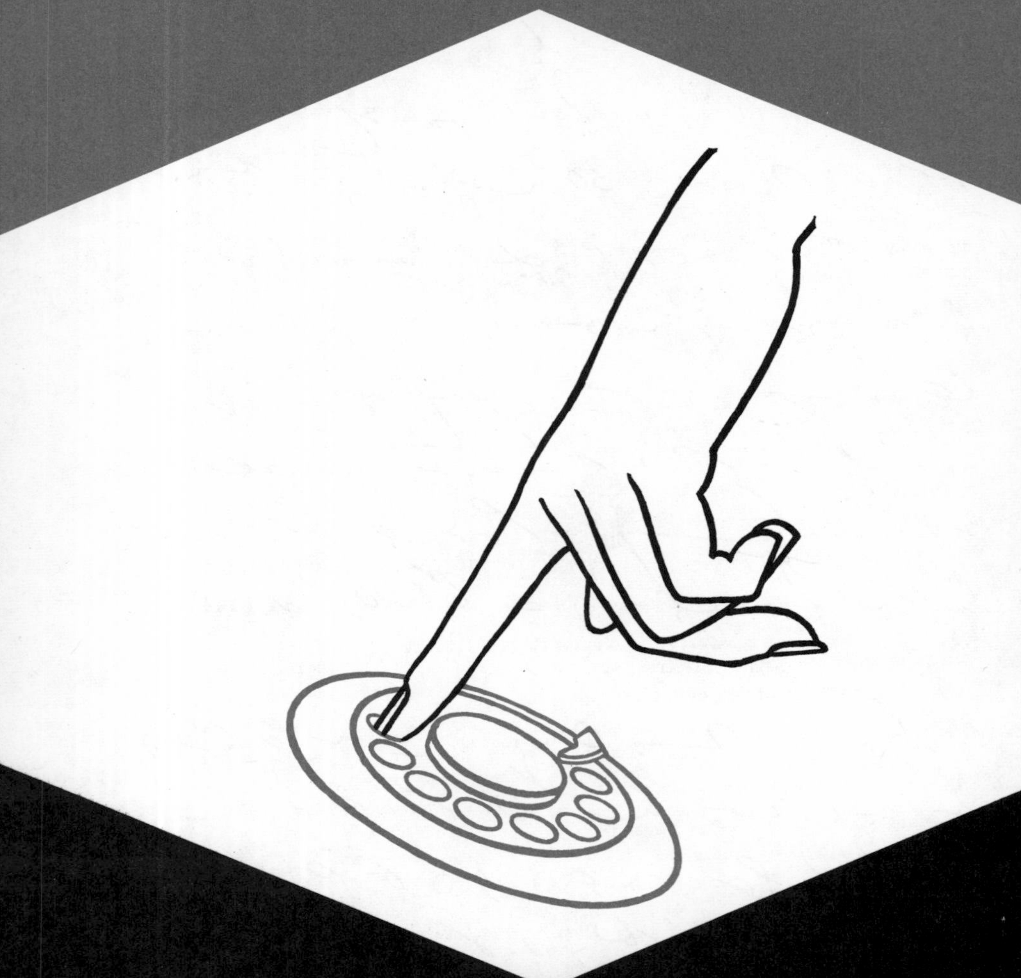

Communications

Developing Shorthand Writing Power

446. OUTLINE CONSTRUCTION

Word endings -tract, -trict, -truct. The vowel is omitted in the word endings *-tract, -trict, -truct.*

-tract

a

-trict, -truct

b

a. Tract, attract, distract, detract, extract, contract.
b. Strict, restrict, district, construct, instruct.

Building Transcription Skills

447. SIMILAR-WORDS DRILL

Expand, expend

expand Enlarge; spread out.

We plan to expand these services to other communities soon.

expend To use up; to spend.

Your executives will no longer have to expend time and energy visiting members of the staff in other parts of the building.

Reading and Writing Practice

448. Tandem on the Tightrope

He seized

I couldn't

"That was

—*F. G. Boyce* (382)

LETTERS

449.

scope
di·rec'to·ry
lo'cal·ized

conj

ap

af·fects'
num'bers
Con·nect'i·cut

ser

411

par

il 555-1212

nc intro

par 555-1212

par

intro ap

iq

if

(226)

450.

when

oth'er·wise'
ex·pend'
vis'it·ing

intro

cus'tom·ers'

intro

(134)

Morale in the individual is his zest for living and working—or lack of it. The person with high morale believes in himself, in his future, and in others. He thinks his work is worth doing and that he is doing a good job at it. High morale helps him to take minor irritations in stride, to work under pressure when necessary without blowing up, to get along with people who want to take more than they give. High morale makes a person unbeatable.—Laird and Laird

Developing Shorthand Writing Power

451. RECALL DRILL — M

In this drill you will review the different uses of the alphabetic stroke *m*.

-ment

a

Im-

b

Em-

c

-ingham

d

Million

e

a. Element, supplement, monument, compliment.
b. Impressed, impair, impart, impending, imperfect, impersonal.
c. Embarrass, embezzle, emblem, embrace, emphasis, emphatic.
d. Framingham, Buckingham, Nottingham, Cunningham, Birmingham.
e. 3 million, $3 million, 3 million pounds, several million dollars, a million.

Building Transcription Skills

452. ACCURACY PRACTICE

In this drill you will practice the joining of circles outside angles.

a

b

c

a. Rash, rich, latch; rain, lean, lame.
b. Cane, came, gain, game; nail, near.
c. Pain, been; fan, van; pick, fact; map, maybe.

Writing Practice

453. PREVIEW

454.

455.

456.

457.

454. Inform, statement, account, inaccurate, omitted, including, enclosed.
455. Introduce, dial, improvement, expansion.
456. Destroyed, $3,000,000, thereafter, modern, boulevard, one of the, convert, notify, adequate, continue.
457. Greetings, Christmas, rapidly, facilities, promptly, avoid, any time.

LETTERS

454. Dear Mr. Baker: I am sorry to inform you that the final statement we recently sent you on your account[1] for telephone service is inaccurate.

Through an error, the charges for toll calls were omitted when this[2] bill was prepared. A corrected bill including these charges is enclosed.

We regret that it was not possible[3] to include these items on your original bill and hope that this omission has not caused you any inconvenience.[4] In case there is anything about the enclosed bill that is not altogether clear, we shall be glad to[5] discuss the matter with you.

If we can be of service to you in the future, please call us. Very truly yours,[6]

---

455. Dear Mr. Jones: We are arranging to introduce dial service in your village late this fall.

Dial service for you[7] and our other customers in your area is part of the telephone company's improvement and expansion[8] program.

We are happy to bring you the convenience of dial service. If you have any questions about[9] this new service, please do not hesitate to get in touch with us. We shall be glad to help you. Sincerely yours,[10]

---

456. Dear Mr. Wills: Last January, as you no doubt will recall, fire destroyed the telephone building on Fourth and[11] Main Streets and caused more than $3,000,000 worth of damage.

Soon thereafter we erected a temporary[12] building to serve our customers while we were erecting a new, modern building on Foster Boulevard. That building[13] is now ready.

One of the first things we wish to do is convert the telephones we service to the dial system.[14] In the next ten days our serviceman will install a dial telephone in your home. We ask, however, that you[15] do not operate the dials until we notify you; we do not yet have adequate facilities in our[16] central office for their use. Until further notice, continue to place your calls as you always have. Yours sincerely,[17]

---

457. Dear Customer: If you plan to send holiday greetings to your loved ones by long distance telephone, you will avoid[18] the rush if you call before Christmas Eve or after Christmas Day. In that way your call will go through rapidly.[19]

Even though all our facilities will be available, it will be impossible to avoid delays on[20] Christmas. More calls are made on that day than it is possible to handle promptly.

You will avoid delays and still[21] take advantage of our reduced rates if you call any time on Sunday, December 23, or on any weekday[22] evening after six.

Thousands of telephone people will be on the job Christmas Day, and they will be ready[23] to give you the best possible service. All of them join us in wishing you a Merry Christmas. Cordially yours,[24] (480)

Reading and Writing Practice

458. ap iq

de·vel'op·ment
us'ing
des'ig·na'tions

intro

125

par

ap

ap·pre'ci·ate
de·stroy'ing

iq

(182)

459.

sale
ad

ser

iph

il

directory
buying

conj

intro

(141)

460.

when

competitor
agency
local

when

(104)

SECRETARIAL TIP

Your Office Typewriter

In your transcription course you no doubt do most of, if not all, your typing on one machine. Consequently, by this time, you are probably thoroughly familiar with its touch, its service mechanisms, and any special characters it may have. This is fine, because the more you are at home with your typewriter, the more rapidly will you be able to transcribe.

It is possible, of course, that when you report for that first job upon graduation you will find the same make and model typewriter on your secretarial desk as the one on which you now do your transcribing. If that is the case, you are lucky indeed, because you will have no problem adjusting to your new machine.

There are many fine and well-known brands of typewriters that are on the market today; therefore, the chances are strong that on that secretarial desk you will find a machine that is different from the one you used at school. If your present machine is a standard typewriter, in your office you may find an electric. If your present machine is an electric, you may find a standard. In addition, on your office machine you may find that:

Some of the service mechanisms, such as the tabulator and the backspacer, are located at different points from those on your school machine.

The number 1 is located on the top row of the keyboard; the lower case *l* is used only for that letter and not for the figure 1.

There are keys for special characters, such as the plus sign, the equals mark, and the division sign.

Of course, after you have typed on your office machine for some time, you will become as familiar with it as you are with your present machine.

But until you become adjusted to it, your production rate may suffer. You can shorten the period of adjustment, however, by making an effort, while you are still in school, to become familiar with as many makes and models of typewriters as possible.

In the various offices of your school there are probably several different makes of machines, and you may be able to obtain permission to examine them and even type on them. If you can arrange to visit a business office or two in your city, you are sure to find several models in use that you can study.

Remember, the sooner you adjust to the working conditions that prevail in your employer's office, the sooner will you become a productive worker—and your office typewriter is an important piece of equipment to which you will have to adjust!

IBM
R O Y A L

LESSON 48

Developing Shorthand Writing Power

461. WORD FAMILIES

-way

a

-rous

b

a. Parkway, byway, highway, passageway, driveway, causeway, halfway.
b. Prosperous, dangerous, numerous, generous, vigorous, humorous.

462. FREQUENT NAMES

Last Names

a

Men's First Names

b

a. Martin, McCarthy, McDonald, McKenzie.
b. Harold, Herbert, Howard, Hugh, Hugo, Isaac, Jacob.

Building Transcription Skills

463. BUSINESS VOCABULARY BUILDER

toll charge The extra charge above the local rate for long distance calls.

milestone A significant point in any course.

conversion Changeover.

Writing Practice

464. PREVIEW

465. 466. 467.

465. Years ago, won't, everything, except, community, 15 per cent, generally, we want, consumer.
466. In the past, grown, 20,000,000, circuits, productive, capacity, continue, extend, let us know.
467. Auburn, one of our, appointment, England, Scotland, Wales, comfortable, touch, to celebrate, milestone, to supply.

LETTERS

465. Dear Mr. Martin: There may still be a few things that you can buy for only a little more than you paid for them twenty-five years ago,[1] but they are mighty few.

The dollar that bought 100 cents' worth back in 1939 won't buy[2] that much today. Higher prices for almost everything you buy have cut that dollar nearly in half—except[3] when it buys telephone service.

The telephone gives you greater value today than ever before. Compared with[4] 1939, customers in the average community today can call twice as many places[5] without a toll charge.

Yet your telephone service fee has increased far less than most things you buy. Its increase[6] averages only 15 per cent since 1939 compared with an 89 per cent rise in[7] prices generally.

We want to assure you that in the days to come we will continue our policy to[8] provide the finest telephone service at the lowest possible price to the consumer. Yours sincerely,[9]

---

466. Dear Mr. Hughes: In the past ten years our telephone system has grown rapidly. Millions of people who never[10] had telephones now have them, because we have added nearly 20,000,000 new telephones in those ten years.

Business[11] and industry are better able to serve the country because there are now more than three times as many[12] long distance circuits.

Most important of all is the value of good telephone service to the productive capacity[13] of the country. Nothing is more important to our defense than quick, rapid communication.

We shall[14] continue to do all in our power to improve and extend our service in the future. If there are any ways[15] in which you think we can improve our service to you, it is our hope that you will let us know. Yours sincerely,[16]

---

467. Dear Friend: On June 10 in Auburn, New York, one of our men finished a routine telephone installation and went[17] on to his next appointment. That was telephone number 6,000,000, or about as many telephones[18] as are in England, Scotland, Wales, and Ireland combined.

That telephone is now making the life of a family more[19] comfortable, more pleasant. It is being used for shopping and errands and keeping in touch with friends.

We did not[20] stop to celebrate this milestone. Our men continued installing the cables and other equipment necessary[21] to supply today's telephone needs and to make our service better than ever.

In the days to come, we will[22] continue to improve our service; and we shall appreciate any suggestions you can give us. Yours sincerely,[23] (460)

Reading and Writing Practice

468.

In'ward
mod'ern
con·ver'sion

and o

par

tel'e·phone
in·vest'ed
sub·stan'tial

ser

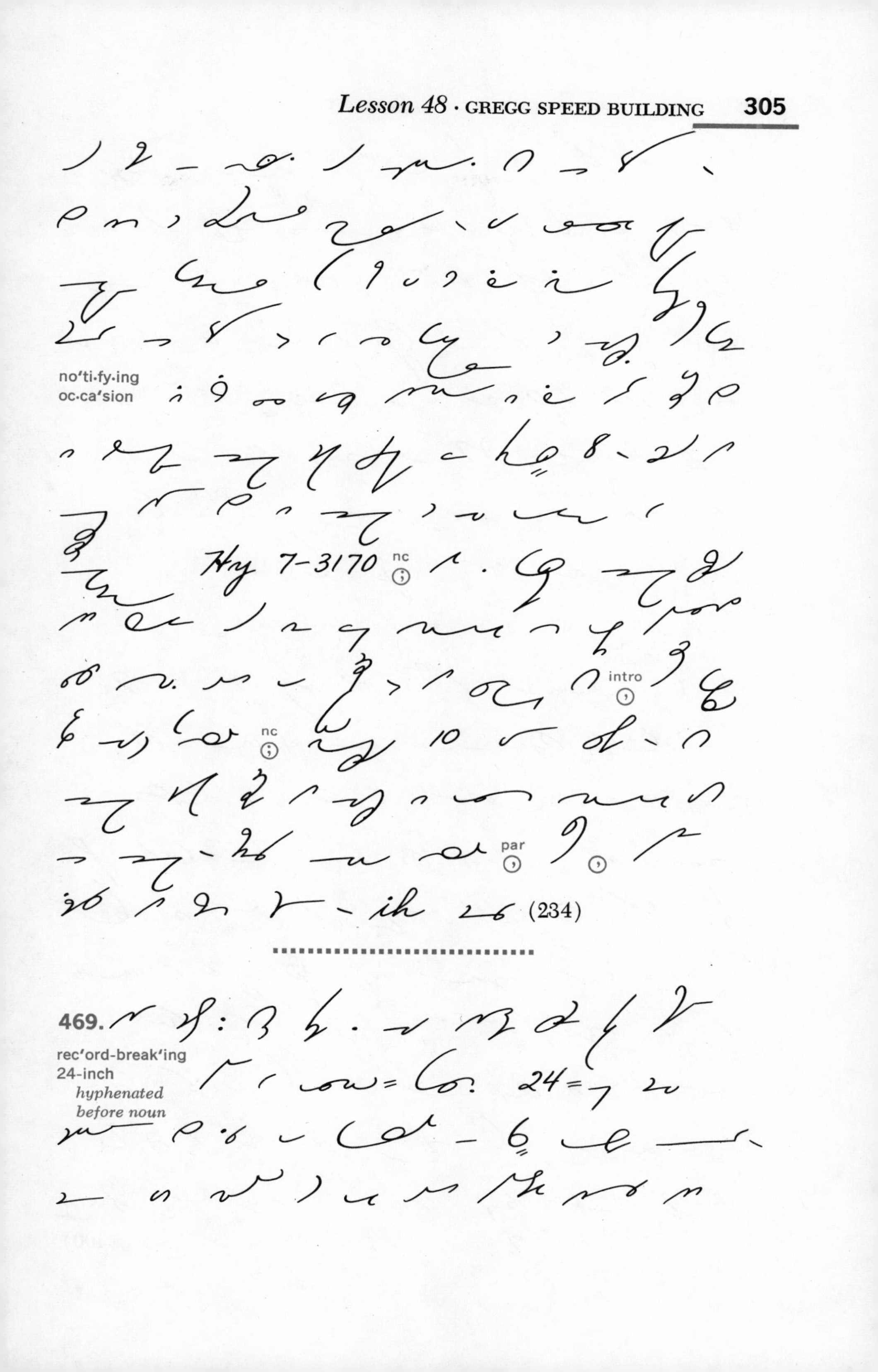

no'ti·fy·ing
oc·ca'sion

Hy 7-3170 nc ; intro , nc ; 10 par , , (234)

469.

rec'ord-break'ing
24-inch
hyphenated before noun

24=

intro

ap·pre'ci·a'tion
im·me'di·ate·ly

intro

nc

wo

as

and o

(131)

470.

sight
plan'ning

nonr

suit'a·ble
con·struc'tion

intro

(100)

LESSON 49

Developing Shorthand Writing Power

471. FREQUENT PHRASES

Words Omitted

a

Several

b

a. Will you please, one of the most, one or two, two or three, less and less, one of the best.

b. Several months, several months ago, several days ago, several times, several minutes.

472. GEOGRAPHICAL EXPRESSIONS

-wood

a

States

b

Foreign Cities

c

a. Elwood City, Greenwood, Maplewood, Oakwood, Ridgewood.

b. Connecticut, Idaho, Maryland, Nevada, Oklahoma, Texas, Wisconsin.

c. Berlin, Hamburg, Leipzig, Nuremburg, Munich.

Building Transcription Skills

473. BUSINESS VOCABULARY BUILDER

party line A single telephone circuit that serves two or more subscribers.

whereabouts Location.

conserve To save.

Writing Practice

474. PREVIEW

475. 476. 477. 478.

475. We have not been able, requested, weeks ago, we shall be able, growth, it has been, demand, engineers, required, almost, $800,000,000, we have not yet been able, entirety.
476. To know, continue, usual, greatest, underneath, already, bargain.
477. I am sure, introducing, neighborhood, short, described, advantage, further.
478. Considerably, overdue, attention, word, in addition, reason, we want.

LETTERS

475. Dear Mr. Bond: We regret that we have not been able to install the telephone that you requested some weeks[1] ago. It is our hope, however, that we shall be able to take care of this matter soon.

As you know, the growth[2] of your section of the city has been so rapid in the last five years that it has been a great task for us to[3] be able to supply the demand for telephone service.

Our engineers have planned and

worked as never before.[4] Meeting this demand for telephones has required the biggest expansion program undertaken by any[5] industry. We have invested almost $800,000,000 in new equipment, and we have not yet been able[6] to service the area in its entirety.

We appreciate your patience and understanding in this matter. Yours sincerely,[7]

---

476. Dear Customer: You will be glad to know that your telephone will be converted to dial operation at[8] 11 p.m. on August 9. Until that time please continue to call as usual —by lifting your[9] receiver and giving the number to the operator.

The enclosed folder explains how to use the dial[10] telephone. It also contains a list of the central offices that you will dial directly. To obtain the[11] greatest benefit from this dialing service, please follow the instructions in the folder.

When the dial system goes[12] into operation, party line numbers will be changed. If you have a party line, please remove the top number[13] plate on your telephone. Your new dial telephone number has already been placed underneath it by our[14] serviceman.

Your telephone service has always been a bargain. It will be a bigger bargain in the future. Yours truly,[15]

---

477. Dear Miss West: I am sure that you will be interested in the new service that we are introducing on a[16] trial basis. This service will be available to all subscribers in your neighborhood.

We call this service the[17] "Message Service"; it makes it possible for you to have your telephone answered by the operator, who will[18] take, as well as give, short messages.

This new service is described in the enclosed booklet. You will no doubt have[19] occasion to use the service to good advantage.

If you would like further information, call us. Yours sincerely,[20]

---

478. Dear Mr. Scott: As you know, your telephone bill is now considerably overdue. We recently called your[21] attention to this fact by mail, but we have received no word from you as to when you will pay the bill. In addition,[22] we have tried several times to reach you by telephone.

If there is any reason why you cannot pay the[23] bill, please let us know. We want to co-operate with you in arranging for the payment of your account. Yours truly,[24] (480)

Reading and Writing Practice

479. [shorthand] 26 [shorthand]

[shorthand] when [shorthand]

where'a·bouts'
con'fi·den'tial

intro

for'ward'ing
self'-ad·dressed'

and o

(103)

480.

intro

two'-way'
hyphenated before noun

un·nec'es·sar'y
ex·pense'

if

enu

cont

a're·a
pos'si·bil'i·ty

(199)

481.

one'-week'
hyphenated before noun

13

pro·ce'dure
de·scribed'

(141)

Developing Shorthand Writing Power

482. WORD BEGINNINGS AND ENDINGS

-ful

a

-sume

b

Im-, Em-

c

a. Grateful, wonderful, thoughtful, harmful, helpful, fearful, beautiful.
b. Consume, consumed, consumer, resume, resumed, presuming.
c. Impression, impress, imply, employ, employees, employment.

Building Transcription Skills

483. BUSINESS VOCABULARY BUILDER

accommodate To take care of.

preceding Coming before (do not confuse *preceding* with *proceeding,* which means "going ahead").

Progressive Speed Builder (90-125)

484. PREVIEW

485.

485. Tour, Chicago, to spend, double, funds, minimum, special, floor.
486. Thank you for your, pleasure, accommodate, crowded, we cannot, promise.
487. Reminder, eleven o'clock, elevator, various, questions, luncheon, anything, without.
488. Courtesies, grateful, delicious, especially, patience, remember, wonderful.
489. Acted, seemed, mentioned, encourage, not only, sources, attaching.

LETTERS

(1 Minute at 90)

485. Gentlemen: On Friday, April 20, I am planning to take my class of twenty girls on a tour of the telephone/building in Chicago. We plan to arrive in Chicago on Thursday, April 19, and to spend the night at your hotel. We should//like to have ten double rooms for the girls and one single room for me. As our funds are rather limited, we should like to have///rooms at your minimum rate.

It would be a special convenience for me if you could accommodate all the girls on one floor. Sincerely yours, (1)

(1 Minute at 100)

486. Dear Miss Lane: Thank you for your letter asking us to reserve ten double rooms and one single room on April 19 for you and the twenty/ girls that you are planning to take on a tour of the telephone building in Chicago. It will be a pleasure to accommodate you.

We//can give you the double rooms at $9 a day and the single room at $6.50 a day. All the hotels in Chicago///will be crowded during the week of April 14; therefore, we cannot promise you that all the rooms will be on the same floor. Sincerely yours, (2)

(1 Minute at 110)

487. Dear Miss Lane: This is just a reminder that we are expecting you and your class of twenty girls at eleven o'clock Friday, April 20. When you/arrive at our building, take the elevator to the second floor and ask for Mr. Green, who will be your guide. He has planned a tour of the various//departments of our organization that I know will be of interest to your students. I hope the girls will feel free to ask him any questions that occur///to them.

After the tour, you are to be our guests for luncheon.

If anything should happen to change your plans, please let us know without delay. Sincerely yours, (3)

(1 Minute at 120)

488. Dear Mr. Green: I cannot thank you enough for the many courtesies you extended to my girls and to me. We are also very grateful to you for the delicious/luncheon that was served to us in your dining room.

I especially appreciated your fine explanation of the work of the various departments of the//telephone company and the patience with which you answered the many questions that the girls asked. I am sure that the girls will long remember their visit.

Several girls///said that your organization seems to be a wonderful place to work, and I should not be surprised if you receive applications from a number of them. Sincerely yours, (4)

(1 Minute at 125)

489. Mr. Gray: On Friday, April 20, I acted as guide for a class of twenty girls from the East High School in Springfield. The girls and the teacher seemed to enjoy the trip, and I/think they left with a very good impression of our organization. In fact, the teacher, in her letter to me, mentioned that we might expect to receive applications for//positions from several of the girls.

I believe that we should encourage more schools to bring their students to visit our building. Not only will these visits give us an opportunity/// to promote public relations, but they may also offer us new sources of supply for office help.

I am attaching the bill for the lunches. William H. Green. (5) (545)

Reading and Writing Practice

490.

intro

ser

if

tel′e·phon·ing
av′er·ag·es

20

70

ser

gro′cer·ies
chat′ting
al′ways

intro

intro

de·pend′a·ble
con·tin′u·ing

par

if

(215)

491.

18

ap

pre·ced′ing
in·ter′nal

intro

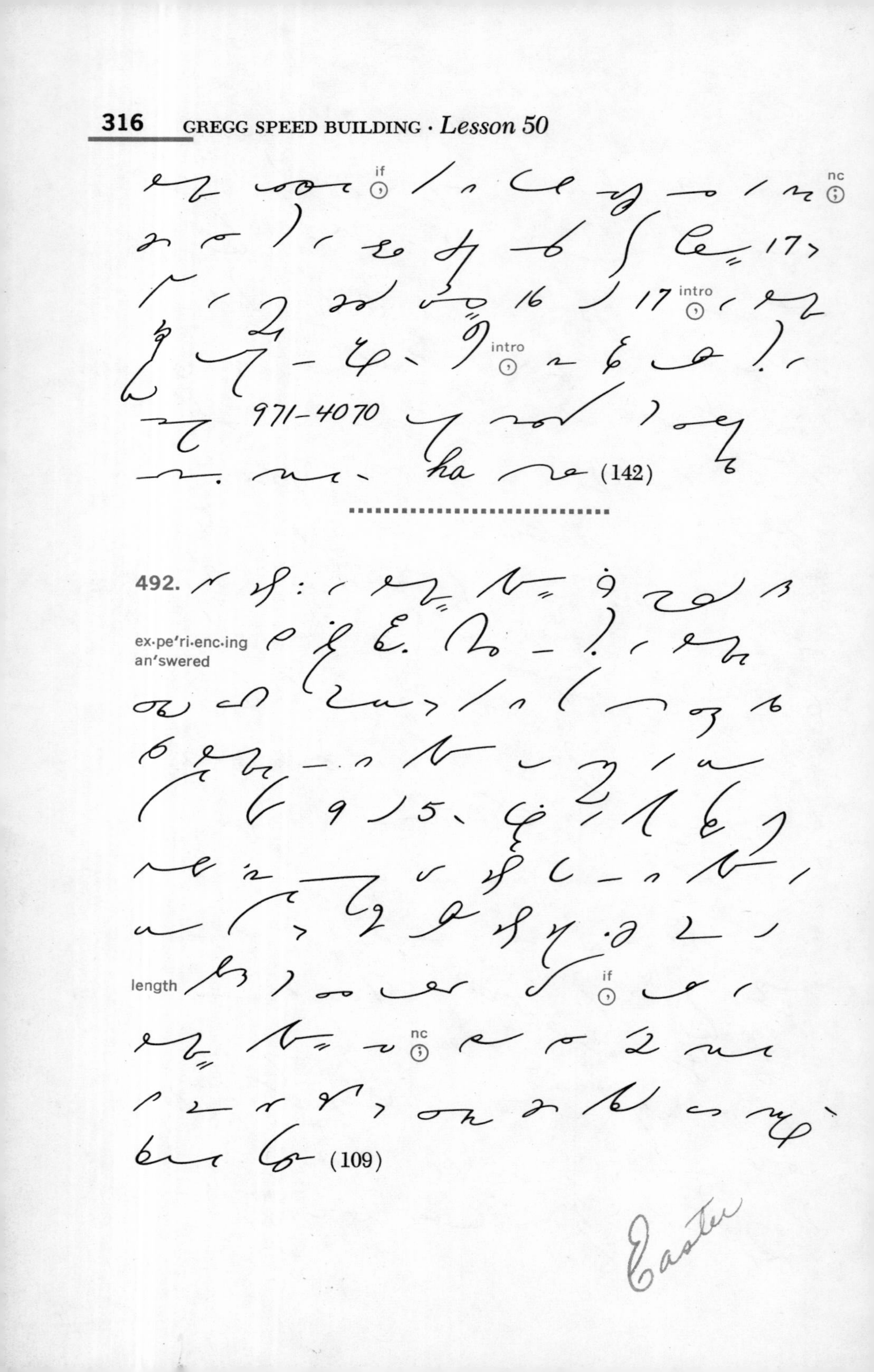

if nc

intro

intro

971-4070

(142)

492.

ex·pe′ri·enc·ing
an′swered

length

if

nc

(109)

CHAPTER

11

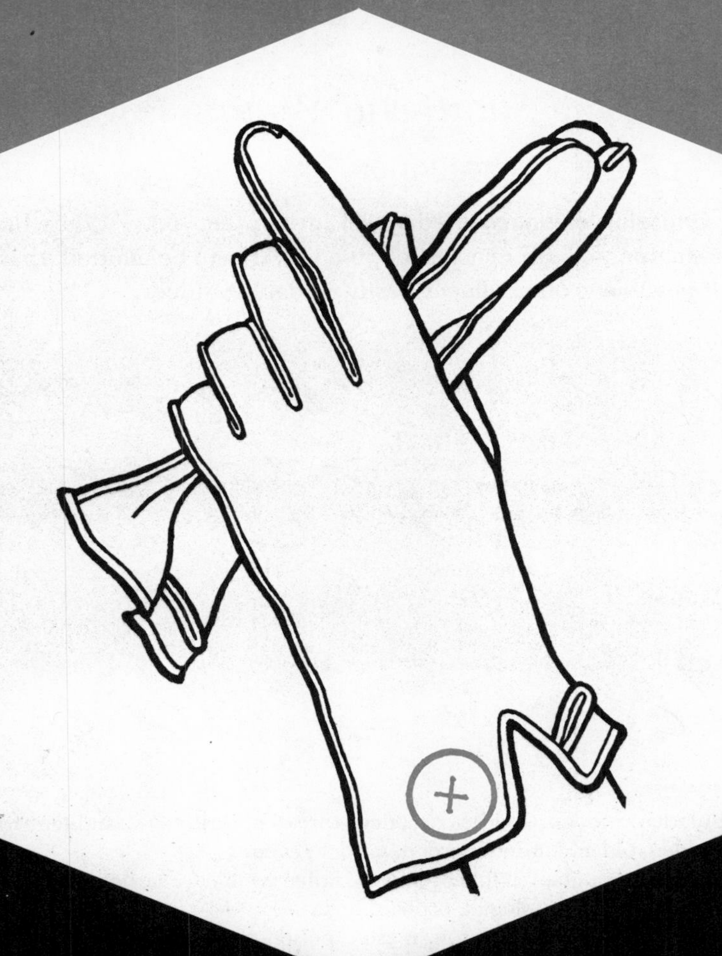

Clothing

LESSON 51

Developing Shorthand Writing Power

493. OUTLINE CONSTRUCTION

Omission of unaccented vowel in -en, -an, -on. When the endings *-en, -an, -on* are unaccented, the vowel may be omitted, thus making it possible to obtain fluent, easily readable outlines.

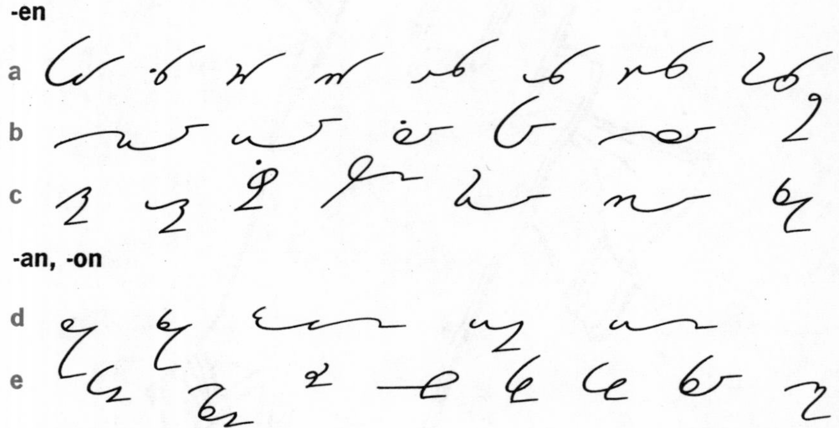

a. Broaden, hidden, sudden, wooden, threaten, written, straighten, frighten.
b. Golden, olden, harden, burden, garden, even.
c. Toughen, roughen, hyphen, darken, fallen, woolen, sharpen.
d. Urban, suburban, slogan, orphan, organ.
e. Person, comparison, season, mason, poison, prison, pardon, coupon.

Building Transcription Skills

494. SIMILAR-WORDS DRILL

Collar, color

collar (pronounced *kŏl′ẽr*) Something worn about the neck; the part of a shirt or coat that goes about the neck.

The shirt had a soft collar.

color (pronounced *kŭl'ẽr*) A hue.

The color of his shirt was white.

Reading and Writing Practice

495. The Biggest Job on Earth

It is true

Even more

—*Ludwell Denny* (321)

In meeting the public, your best approach is a polite, interested manner; and your best technique is to smile. A smile has an amazing effect, even over the phone.

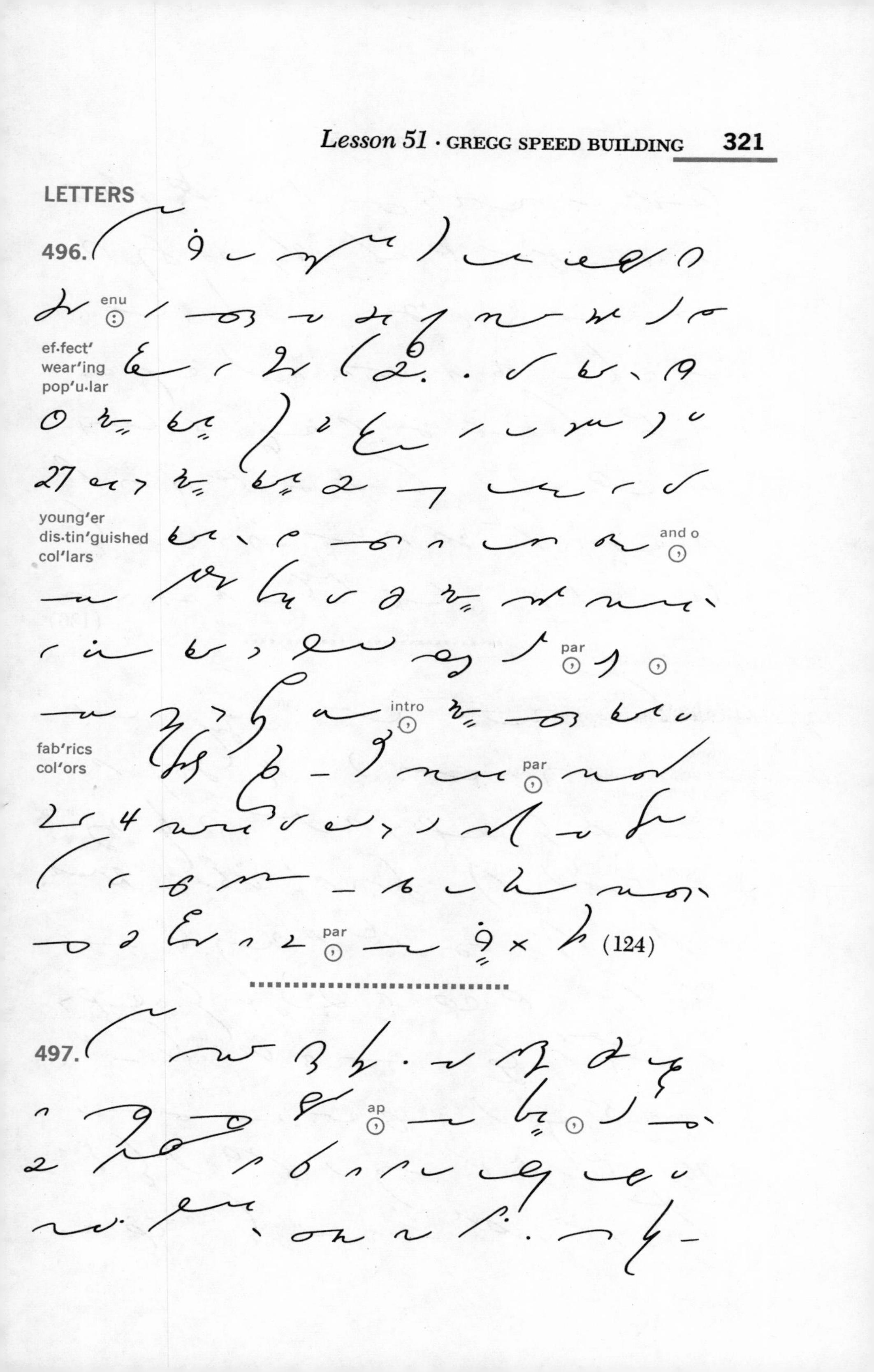

LETTERS

496.

enu

ef·fect′
wear′ing
pop′u·lar

young′er
dis·tin′guished
col′lars

and o

par

intro

fab′rics
col′ors

par

par

(124)

497.

ap

nc
wo
par
bc
if
when

(136)

498.

and o

well′-known′ *hyphenated before noun*

intro

intro

keen

a·rise′

iph

Transcribe: $7,500

intro

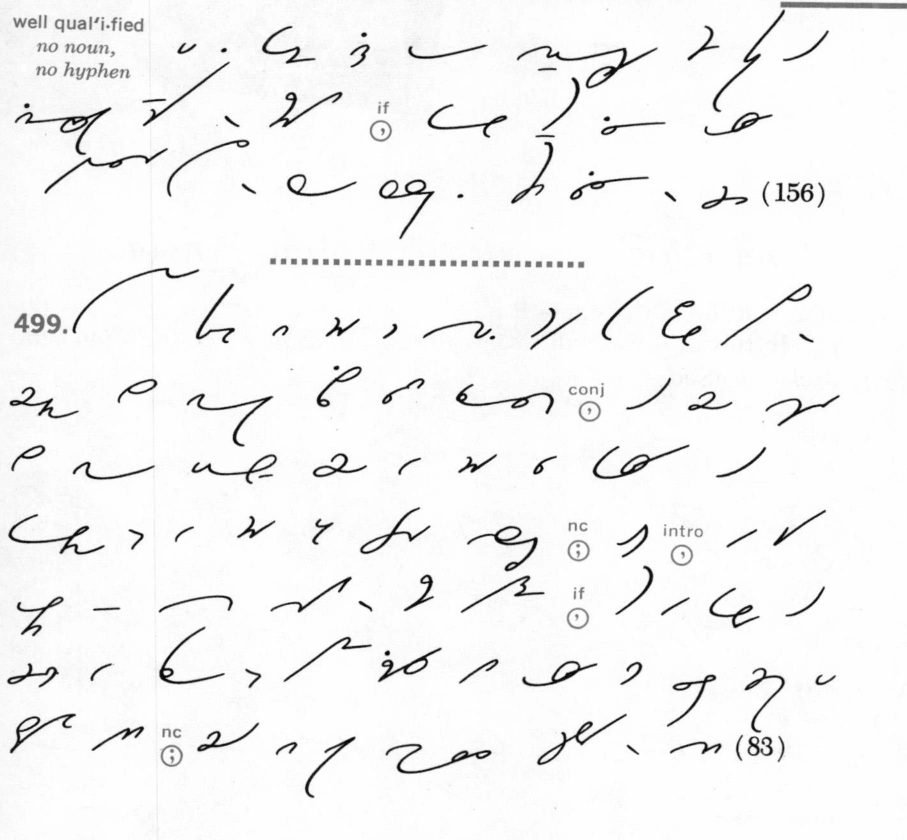

The secretary doesn't divulge confidential information about her employer's activities, for she knows that this can lead to complications. She doesn't run down her boss when she's in a bad mood or when things aren't going just the way they should, for this only reflects on her own integrity. She doesn't take advantage of her boss by keeping late hours or overstaying her lunch hour, for these are forms of disloyalty and show a lack of responsibility.—Ray Josephs, Author and Public Relations Consultant

Developing Shorthand Writing Power

500. RECALL DRILL — R

In this drill you will review the situations in which the alphabetic stroke *r* is used.

Re-

a

-er, -or

b

-rity

c

a. Represent, receipt, repay, receive, reorganize, reorder, react.
b. Greater, purchaser, director, reader, letter, writer, speaker.
c. Sincerity, similarity, prosperity, maturity, minority, majority.

Building Transcription Skills

501. ACCURACY PRACTICE

In this Accuracy Practice you will practice a number of the fluent, graceful blends of Gregg Shorthand.

a

b

c

a. Acre, glad; clear, great; dark, milk.
b. Present, please; brain, below; free, flee, value.
c. Company, can be; confer, confident, convey; govern, can have.

Writing Practice

502. PREVIEW

503.

504.

505.

506.

507.

503. Intrepid, nothing, induce, altogether, strangely, assumed, exercise, imagination, committing, browsing, feelings.
504. Will you please, fur, examine, renovate, appreciate, dispose.
505. Overcoat, to come, purchaser, excellent, $100.
506. Thank you for your order, delivery, at the time, payment.
507. Exceptionally, stockings, continue.

LETTERS

503. Dear Mr. Green: We know men who are intrepid; they are afraid of nothing. They would climb an alp or swim the deepest[1] river—but nothing could induce them to go browsing in a clothing store. For some reason salesmen scare them.

We[2] cannot altogether blame them. The man who says "I'm just looking" is apt to get looked at rather strangely in some[3] stores. For it is commonly assumed that every man who goes into a clothing store wants to buy something[4] immediately.

Maybe he does and maybe he doesn't. He[5] might like to exercise his imagination. He might like to get a few ideas without committing himself. He might like to do a little comparison[6] shopping.

Here at Smith's we encourage browsing. When you come into one of our stores, a salesman comes up to you and[7] says, "May I help you?" If you want to browse, just say so. You won't hurt his feelings. You will be on your own. Yours truly,[8]

---

504. Gentlemen: Will you please have your driver call at my home for my fur coat, which I wish to put in storage for the[9] summer.

Perhaps one of your men can examine the coat and determine the repairs necessary to renovate[10] it. Before you proceed with the work, however, please let me know what work will have to be done and the cost.

As I[11] am leaving for the summer on May 15 for a hard-earned vacation, I should appreciate it if you[12] would let me hear from you before that date. I should like to dispose of this matter before I leave. Sincerely yours,[13]

---

505. Dear Mr. Day: It pays to buy a good overcoat. It pays to select a style that will be in good taste for years[14] to come.

Our overcoats represent a long-term investment for the purchaser.

On our floor today you will find[15] excellent buys ranging from $50 to $100. Come in and make your selection. Cordially yours,[16]

---

506. Dear Miss Packard: Thank you for your order for a new coat on which we are to hold delivery until November[17] 2. The coat will be delivered to you on that day.

At the time of delivery you may pay for the[18] coat in cash or charge it, making full payment within 60 days.

We hope we may serve you often. Yours sincerely,[19]

---

507. Dear Miss Carroll: We were greatly pleased to receive your letter of May 19 telling us about the exceptionally[20] fine service you had from a pair of our stockings.

We have been making stockings from the finest materials[21] for more than thirty years. Before a pair of stockings is released, it is examined many times.

We hope that[22] through the years you will continue to use our stockings with equally satisfactory results. Cordially yours,[23] (460)

Reading and Writing Practice

508.

rea′son·a·bly
de·spite′

conj

intro

Transcribe:
f.o.b.

ap

when

(128)

509.

of·fi′cial
ac·ces′so·ries

nonr

as

boys′
e·quipped′

nc

intro

ser

pleased
cour′te·ous
un·hur′ried

and o

(121)

510.

men's cloth'ing

conj

il

when

nc

ex·ces'sive

when

(100)

511.

conj

(84)

Developing Shorthand Writing Power

512. WORD FAMILIES

-coming

a

Coat

b

a. Coming, becoming, welcoming, overcoming, incoming, unbecoming.
b. Coat, coatings, topcoat, overcoat, raincoat, turncoat.

513. FREQUENT NAMES

Last Names

a

Women's First Names

b

a. Miller, Mitchell, Moore, Morgan.
b. Hortense, Ida, Irene, Jean, Jeannette, Josephine, Judith, Julia.

Building Transcription Skills

514. BUSINESS VOCABULARY BUILDER

pouch A bag.

trivial Small; minor.

tradition Something handed down from the past.

Writing Practice

515. PREVIEW

516.

517.

518.

519.

516. Wearer, interested, Broadway, season, assembled, comprehensive, found, outside, beauty, collection.
517. Quarter, century, decided, establish, handsomely, successfully, during the year, England, United States.
518. Prepared, career, leisure, profitable, opportunities, women, excitement, enclosed, informative.
519. Celebrate, anniversary, volume, compliments.

LETTERS

516. Dear Mrs. Moore: As a wearer of Smith shoes you will be interested in what is happening in our Broadway[1] store.

For this summer season we have assembled the most comprehensive stock of shoe styles to be found in any[2] store in New York City.

Like all Smith shoes, these models are styled for beauty and comfort.

Please accept this letter[3] as your personal invitation to come and see our wonderful collection. Mr. Farmer, the manager,[4] and his staff of well-trained, courteous salesmen are ready to help you make your personal selections. Cordially yours,[5]

517. Dear Mr. Miller: Over a quarter of a century ago our raincoat experts decided to do something[6] about the weather. They helped us to establish this policy: Raincoats must be handsomely styled so that the[7] owner will be proud to wear them in any kind of weather. Our experts successfully produced that type of raincoat,[8] and today thousands of men buy their raincoats from us.

At any time during the year you will find attractive[9] raincoats on our racks. Some are made in England; others, in the best tailor shops in the United States.

If you need[10] a raincoat, by all means stop in to see us soon. Our prices are more reasonable than ever. Cordially yours,[11]

---

518. Dear Friend: We recently prepared a new edition of our interesting booklet entitled "A Career in[12] Dress Designing." Copies have just been received from the printer, and I believe you will be interested in having[13] one to read at your leisure. You will find it profitable reading.

The booklet tells you about dress designing[14] and the opportunities it affords women who want to get ahead. It shows, in addition, how it is[15] possible to enjoy the excitement of originating your own dresses while you are taking the course.

The enclosed[16] postal card requires no postage. If you will mail it at once, your copy of this interesting, informative[17] booklet will be sent to you immediately. This creates no obligation on your part. Cordially yours,[18]

---

519. Dear Mrs. Hill: On January 15 we shall celebrate the twenty-fifth anniversary of the[19] opening of our Main Street store. In honor of the occasion, we have prepared a special volume entitled "Fine[20] Furs," which not only outlines the growth of our organization but also gives an account of the fur industry[21] in general. Because you have been a good customer of ours for many years, we are sending you a copy[22] of this book with our compliments. We are confident that you will find in it much helpful information about[23] furs, as well as many facts about our organization and its employees that will interest you. Yours truly,[24] (480)

Reading and Writing Practice

520.

stretched
day's

conj

pouch
cig'a·rettes'

ser ⊙ isq ⊙ iq ⊙ conj ⊙

and o ⊙ nc ⊙

Smith's
zip'pers

ser ⊙ par ⊙ par ⊙

intro ⊙ (165)

521.

cus'tom·ers'
wom'en

isq ⊙ iq ⊙

ar·rives'
an'a·lyze
col'or

intro ⊙

GRISTMEYER BROTHERS, Inc. *In the Great Southwest*
TULSA, OKLAHOMA

November 29, 19--

Mr. Perry R. Strong, President
Harrison Manufacturing Company
4125 North Fifth Avenue
Denver, Colorado 80200

Dear Mr. Strong:

Subject: Employees' Handbooks

I am sending you today by express all the material that we have available on how to prepare an employees' handbook.

You will be interested, I am sure, in our experience in helping the Martin Miller Company prepare its latest handbook. When we were called in, that company already had a handbook; but it was out of date. The organization had grown considerably since that handbook was prepared; consequently, the handbook had to be completely rewritten. The new handbook was ready at the end of last year. It benefited by many lessons that had been learned during the work on the first

While working with Martin Mil
three points are important in

1. It should not be a
should and should n

2. It should take adva
satisfaction with w
The handbook should
ing that feeling of

3. It should set down
that they are impor
give them informati
organization and ad

In the first edition of the h
the history of the company.
plished by the time the seco
publication. Consequently,
history of the company was o

Mr. Perry R. Strong 2 November 29, 19--

These are just a few thoughts that come to me at this time. I am sure that the Martin Miller Company would be glad to send you a copy of their new handbook. I believe that you may find many suggestions in it that you would be able to use when you prepare your handbook.

Needless to say, we are at your service. If you think that a visit with one of our men would be helpful, please call us. We will be glad to arrange an appointment.

Cordially yours,

R. L. Kane

R. L. Kane, Vice-President

RLK:IRT

P. S. I have just learned that Fred Hopkins, the member of our staff who worked with Martin Miller Company, will be in Denver all next week. Would you like to meet him and talk with him?

Two-Page Letter Blocked Style, with Subject Line and Postscript Standard Punctuation

nc

nc

intro

racks
pur'chased

intro par isq

iq (156)

522.

as·sem'bling
a·vail'a·ble
ad·vance'

intro

ap 31

ap 5 (73)

LESSON 54

Developing Shorthand Writing Power

523. FREQUENT PHRASES

To

a

Contractions

b

a. To make, to know, to me, to us, to be, to form, to see, to value.
b. We couldn't, I couldn't, I don't, you don't, he shouldn't, he didn't, they aren't.

524. GEOGRAPHICAL EXPRESSIONS

-boro, -borough

a

States

b

Foreign Cities

c

a. Attleboro, Goldsboro, Jonesboro, Hillsboro, Marlborough.
b. Arkansas, Illinois, Massachusetts, New Hampshire, Oregon, Utah, Wyoming.
c. Naples, Rome, Sicily, Budapest. Vienna, Prague.

Building Transcription Skills

525. BUSINESS VOCABULARY BUILDER

conceded Admitted to be true.

inappropriate Out of place.

refurbish To brighten or freshen up.

Writing Practice

526. PREVIEW

527. 528. 529. 530.

527. Informed, Minneapolis, thank you for, established, identification, suggestions.
528. Clothes, partnership, enviable, reputation, located, neighborhood.
529. Announcement, conduct, service, altered, wife.
530. Correctness, self-respecting, relaxes, gradually, conceded, toward, formality, why not.

LETTERS

527. Dear Mr. Taylor: I have just been informed by the manager of our Minneapolis clothing store that you[1] have opened a charge account with us.

Thank you for giving us the opportunity to serve you. I hope the[2] confidence established between you and our store will be a source of pleasure and convenience to you.

Should you wish[3] to shop at any of our other stores, your credit card will serve as an identification.

Feel free to write[4] me, Mr. Taylor, if you have any suggestions for improving our service or merchandise. Sincerely yours,[5]

528. Dear Mr. Casey: As a man who has always been interested in fine clothes, you will be interested in[6] learning that I am going into partnership with a man who has had an enviable reputation as[7] a tailor in a New York clothing store for more than twenty years.

In my opinion and in the opinion of[8] thousands of men of this city, Frank Harris knows more about men's clothes than any other tailor in the clothing[9] business.

Mr. Harris and I have opened a shop called "Harris and Allan." It will be located on the corner[10] of Fifth Avenue and 12th Street. We will make the finest men's clothes at prices ranging from $60[11] to $100. Come in to see our merchandise the next time you are in the neighborhood. Cordially yours,[12]

---

529. Dear Mr. French: In our announcement of the opening of our new store, "Harris and Allan," we failed to make two[13] points clear:

1. Our major line of men's clothes will range in price from $60 to $100. However, we[14] shall also carry fine men's suits that sell for as little as $40.

2. We shall also conduct a complete[15] tailoring service, through which you may have suits pressed, repaired, and altered at reasonable prices.

We invite[16] you to take advantage of this service. Clothes will be called for and delivered at no extra cost.

Make it a point[17] to come in to visit us soon, and bring your wife along. I know that she will like our low prices. Yours sincerely,[18]

---

530. Dear Mr. Smith: We are often asked to comment on the correctness of wearing brown shoes.

There was a time when only black[19] shoes were correct for wear in the city. No self-respecting man would have been found on the city streets in a pair[20] of brown shoes. Custom relaxes gradually. Had we been writing this thirty years ago, we would have stated[21] that brown shoes might be worn with a brown suit and with nothing else.

Today it is generally conceded that brown[22] shoes may be worn correctly with the lighter shades of gray.

Whether the trend is toward formality or away from[23] it, we predict that 1975 will see one thing unchanged: The Jonesboro Clothing Store will still be the place[24] to come for good clothes—and for good shoes to go with them.

Why not drop in soon to see our latest styles. Cordially yours, [25] (500)

Reading and Writing Practice

531.

enu

worn
cam'pus·es

when

if

Stu'dent's
Ad·vi'sor

conj

intro

(159)

532.

intro

par

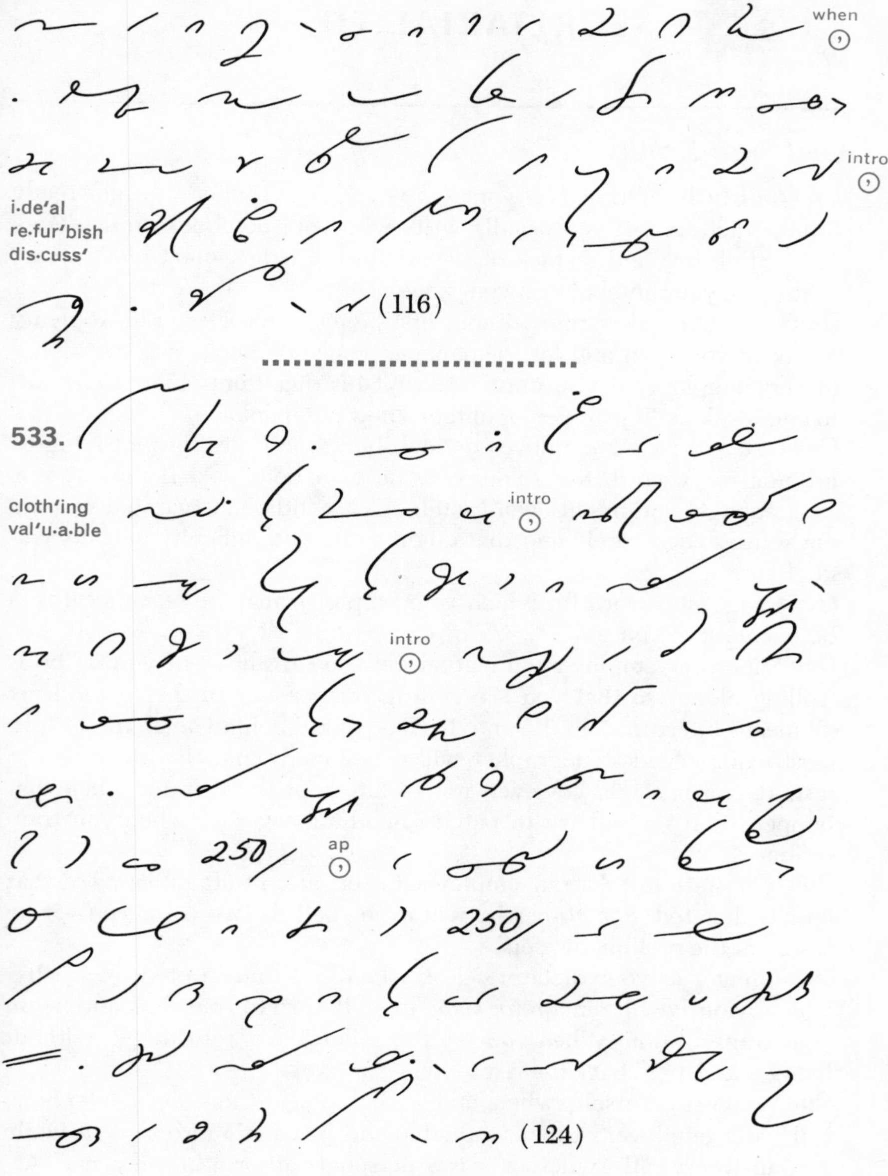

Get your day off to a good start by wishing everyone a cheery "Good morning."

SECRETARIAL TIP

Dictation Don'ts

Don't disturb anything on your employer's desk when you get ready to take dictation. If you usually write with your notebook on the ledge of his desk but find a stack of papers on the ledge, don't move them; write with your notebook on your knee.

Don't report for dictation without first being sure that you have plenty of ink in your pen and lots of paper in your notebook. It is disturbing to your employer if you must interrupt his dictation while you return to your desk to fill your pen or obtain a new notebook.

Don't stare at your employer or look bored as he is concentrating or groping for a word. Keep your eyes on your notebook. If the pause is long enough, you might even "patch up" an outline or two that you did not write so accurately and that might cause you difficulty in transcribing later.

Don't suggest a word for which your employer may be reaching unless he encourages you to.

Don't let your employer's dictation get too far ahead of you. If he is "rolling along" so that you are getting further and further behind, by all means interrupt him. It is no disgrace to fall behind; even the fastest, most experienced stenographer will occasionally find the dictation too fast. It is a mistake, however, not to interrupt the dictator when that happens and instead try to patch something together when you transcribe.

Don't hesitate to ask your employer to repeat an unfamiliar word that he has dictated. Sometimes he will even spell the word for you—if he is sure of the spelling himself!

Don't linger at your dictator's desk when he is interrupted by a caller who obviously will remain for some time. Return to your desk and begin your transcription. When you see the caller leave, return and, without being asked, read back the last sentence or two.

Don't excuse yourself, when taking dictation, to answer a telephone call; your employer's time is valuable and he can't afford to wait while you answer a call—whether it is a personal call or a business call. Arrange to have someone answer your phone while you are taking dictation and take messages for you.

WORLD

LESSON 55

Developing Shorthand Writing Power

534. WORD BEGINNINGS AND ENDINGS

-ual

a

-ly

b

-ult

c

a. Annual, gradual, actual, perpetual, schedule.
b. Carefully, weekly, substantially, constantly, consequently, completely, nearly.
c. Result, consult, insult, consultant, resultant, insulted, adult.

Building Transcription Skills

535. BUSINESS VOCABULARY BUILDER

insertion Each appearance of an advertisement, as in a newspaper.

stationary Not changing, fixed. (Do not confuse *stationary* with *stationery,* which means such items as paper, pencils, erasers, etc.)

interim Coming in between, meanwhile.

Progressive Speed Builder (100-130)

You didn't have difficulty writing 125 words a minute for one minute in the previous Speed Builder, did you? Do you think you can squeeze into one minute just five words more? The last letter in this Progressive Speed Builder is counted at 130 words a minute. If you can get something down for every word in the 130 words a minute letter, you are making progress indeed!

536. PREVIEW

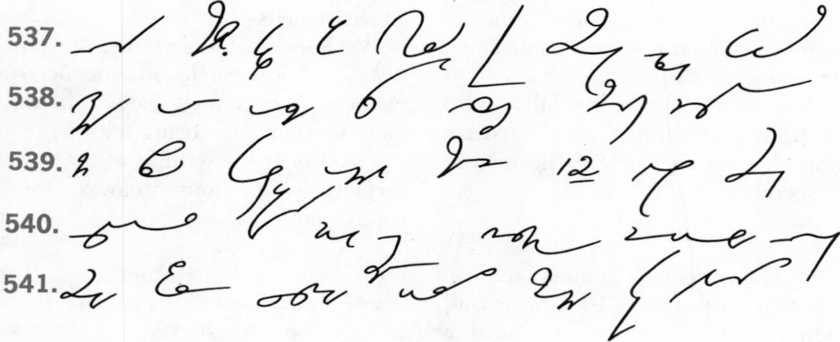

537. Enclosed, advertising, position, opinion, different, judgment, available, insertion, promptly.
538. Thank you for your order, run, request, items, carefully, effective, schedule.
539. Issue, appeared, believe, results, afternoon, 1,200, tribute, very much.
540. Naturally, obtained, source, investment, unusual, smallest, encourage.
541. First, experiment, announced, already, as a result, budget, discontinue.

LETTERS

(1 Minute at 100)

537. Gentlemen: Enclosed is copy for 5 inches of advertising that we should like to have you run in the April 10 issue of your paper./This is to appear in a top position on your page of personal items. If in your opinion this advertisement could be placed to//advantage in a different position, please feel free to use your judgment in the matter.

I do not at the moment have a schedule///of rates available; therefore, would you please send me a bill for this insertion. I will see that it is paid promptly. Very cordially yours, (1)

(1 Minute at 110)

538. Dear Mr. Trees: Thank you for your order for the advertisement that you asked us to run in the April 10 issue of our newspaper. As you request,/we shall place it in a top position on our page of personal items. After considering the matter carefully, we have decided that that would//be the most effective position for it.

A schedule of our rates is enclosed. The rates decrease as the number of issues in which you run your///advertising increases.

We are not enclosing a bill for this insertion at this time. You will receive your bill on the first of the month. Sincerely yours, (2)

(1 Minute at 120)

539. Gentlemen: You may remember that, in the April 10 issue of your newspaper, our company placed a small 5-inch advertisement. It appeared in a top position/on your page of personal items.

We believe that you will be interested in the results that we obtained from that small advertisement. During the//afternoon of April 10, we received more than 200 orders by mail. By the end of the week, the advertisement had brought in more than 1,200 orders, ranging from $5///to $10 each. This is a fine tribute to the power of advertising in your newspaper. We are very much pleased with these wonderful results. Sincerely yours, (3)

(1 Minute at 125)

540. Dear Mr. Trees: We were naturally very pleased to receive the report on the results that you obtained from your advertisement in the April 10 issue of our newspaper./ It is a source of pleasure to us to learn that you received so fine a return from such a small investment.

It may surprise you to learn that returns like these are not unusual// for our advertisers. New advertisers are often amazed at the results that they obtain from even the smallest advertisement.

We hope that the results of your first///advertisement in our newspaper will encourage you to place more of your advertising with us.

Thank you for writing us; we appreciate your thoughtfulness. Sincerely yours, (4)

(1 Minute at 130)

541. Mr. Farley: I am sure that you will be interested in our first experience as advertisers in the Tribune. As an experiment, we placed a small advertisement/in the April 10 issue, in which we announced two of our new products. We have already received more than 1,500 orders as a result of that advertisement, and orders are still//coming in. I believe that this is the greatest return we have ever received from an advertisement of that type.

I believe that it would be wise to revise our advertising///budget and make provision for at least a weekly advertisement in the Tribune. If necessary, we could discontinue some of our present advertising. Henry J. Trees (5) (585)

Reading and Writing Practice

542.

in′ter·im
its
ware′house′

cont

and o

ab·sorbed′
con′se·quent·ly

nc
intro

sta′tion·ar′y
sug·ges′tions

par

par

(148)

543.

as

1930

an′nu·al
cloth′ing

iph

50,

as

pri'or
an·nounce'ment
mer'chan·dise

nonr

par

(121)

544.

weath'er
cit'y's

intro

cont

ser

un·bear'a·ble
bank's
car'ried

when

ser

e'qual·ly
guard'ed

par

par nc intro bc

(174)

545.

cloth
un·hes′i·tat′ing·ly

intro iph intro

ob·tain′a·ble
tai′lor·ing

par

(132)

CHAPTER 12

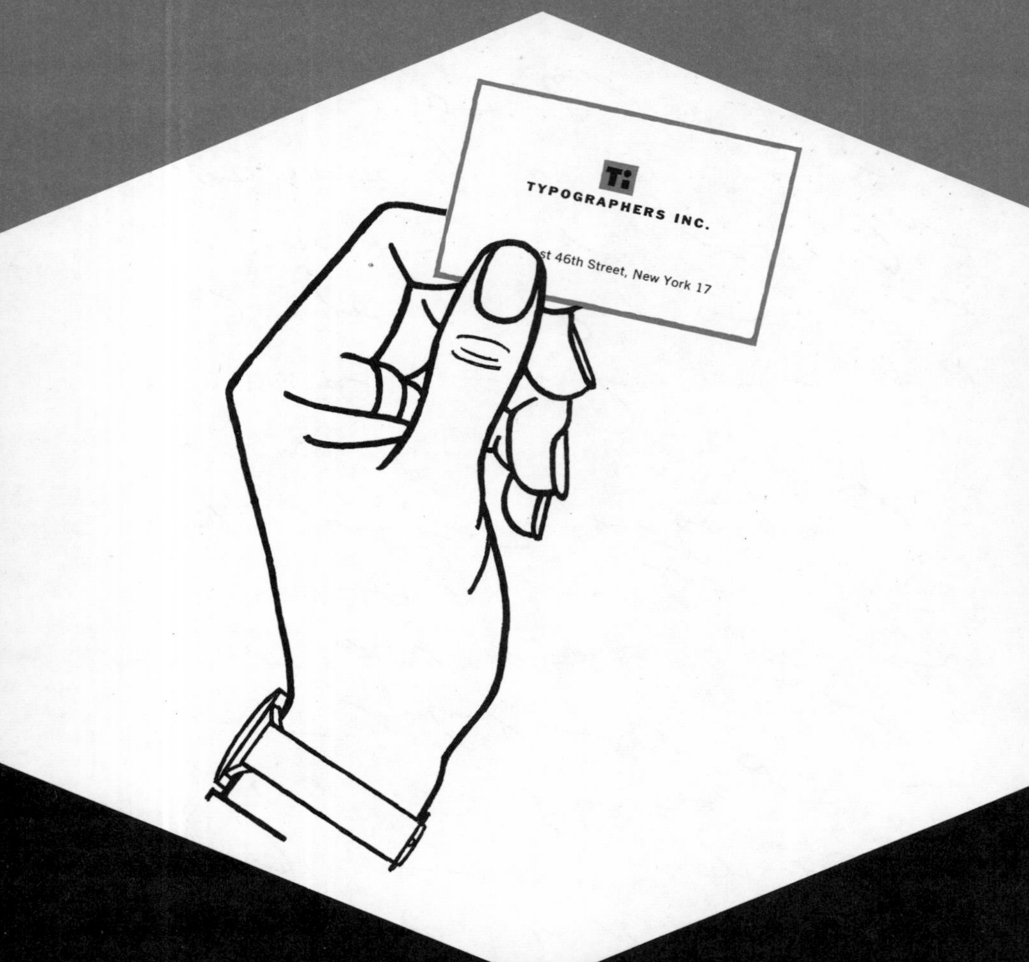

Paper and Printing

Developing Shorthand Writing Power

546. OUTLINE CONSTRUCTION

Omission of vowel in -vent, -vention. The vowel is omitted in the combinations *-vent, -vention.*

a
b

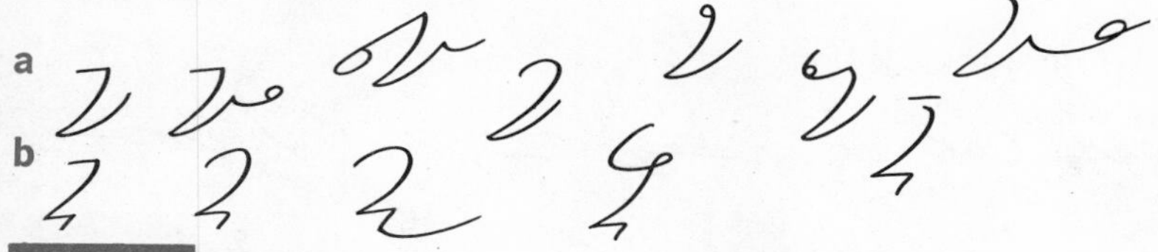

a. Invent, inventory, adventure, convent, event, servant, ventilate.
b. Invention, convention, conventional, prevention, intervention.

Omission of vowel in -sive. The vowel is omitted in the ending *-sive.*

Extensive, defensive, expensive, expansive, comprehensive, impulsive, decisive, evasive, excessive.

Building Transcription Skills

547. SIMILAR-WORDS DRILL

Device, devise

device (*noun*) Something that has been created or invented; a scheme.

He has a device for closing the garage door automatically.

devise (*verb*) To invent; to make up.

The Chinese were the first to try to devise a kind of movable type.

Reading and Writing Practice

548. Printing

This block

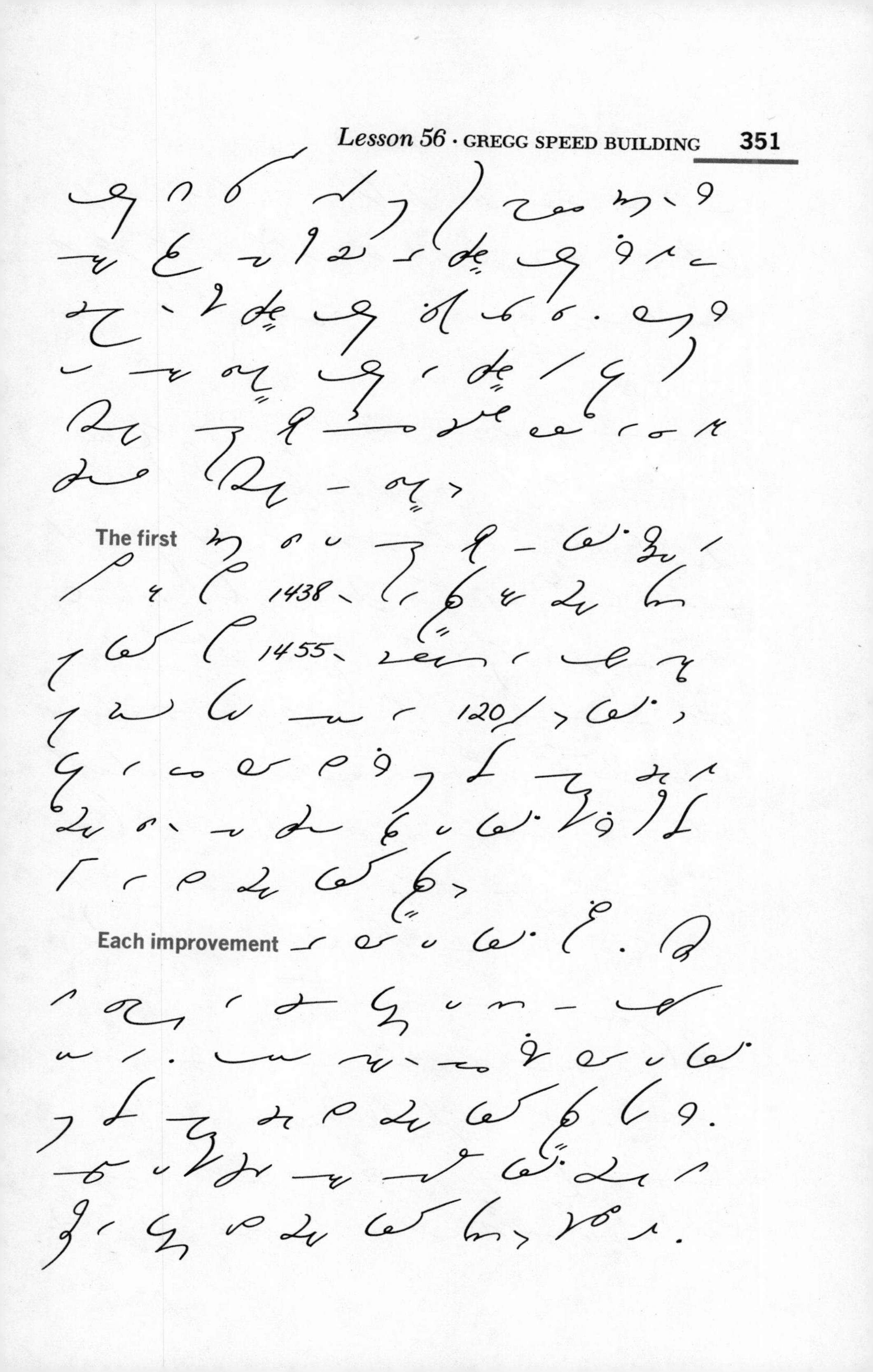

The first

1438

1455

120

Each improvement

(398)

LETTERS

549.

Transcribe:
October 16
No. 16

par

sched'ule
pre'vi·ous

intro

conj

ac'tu·al·ly
con'tra·ry
ar·range'ment

intro

(139)

550.

em·bar'rassed
un·for'tu·nate·ly

intro

high′-grade′ *hyphenated before noun*

iph

first′-class′ *hyphenated before noun*

conj

chem′i·cals
ma′jor

intro

(141)

551.

as

e·quip′ment
ex·ten′sive·ly
ru′ined

nc

wo

intro

par

du′ly
cred′it·ed

(124)

Developing Shorthand Writing Power

552. RECALL DRILL — L

In this lesson you will review the situations in which the alphabetic stroke for *l* is used.

Well-

a

-lity

b

-lty

c

a. Welfare, welcome, welcomed, farewell, well-known.
b. Ability, inability, stability, reliability, formality, utility.
c. Penalty, faculty, novelty, loyalty, royalty.

Building Transcription Skills

553. ACCURACY PRACTICE

The subject of your practice in this drill is the letter *o*. Remember to keep the *o* hook deep and narrow.

a

b

c

a. Of, ocean, was, hope, object; row, low; toe, dough, ditto.
b. No, mow, memorandum; what, order, audit; show, jaw.
c. So, sore, fall; or, all; of course, of the, ordinary, autumn.

Writing Practice

554. PREVIEW

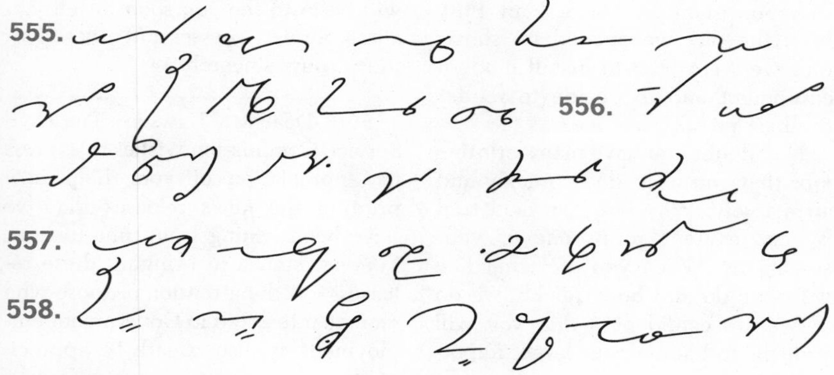

555. Reorganized, years ago, glad to say, volume, greater, constantly, we have been able, during the past, up-to-the-minute, accuracy.
556. Interested, already, modern, attractively, entrusting, confident, few minutes, facilities.
557. Location, enlarged, equipment, aware, patient, schedule, presses.
558. Civil, Commission, appreciation, Government, urgently, employment, constructive.

LETTERS

555. Dear Mr. Brown: As you may know, Jones & Company reorganized two years ago. We are glad to say that things[1] have been going well with us since that time.

Our present volume of business is ten times greater than it was two[2] years ago. We have five times as many accounts as we had then, and the number is constantly growing. We have[3] made many new friends, and we have been able to welcome many old customers back into the fold.

During the past[4] year we have

doubled our space and installed many new, up-to-the-minute presses that produce more and better work.[5]

Why not let us take care of your printing orders? You will be pleased with our speed and accuracy. Yours sincerely,[6]

---

556. Dear Mr. Hatfield: Even though our business is only four weeks old, you will be interested to know that we[7] already have a large volume of work on hand. The fact that our plant has been kept busy from the day we opened it[8] shows that we were wise to install modern equipment and to decide to render the best possible service.

No[9] doubt you have many printing jobs that you want done quickly and attractively. Why not give us a trial by entrusting[10] to us one of your small jobs. When you see what fine work we do and how quickly we do it, we are confident[11] that you will want us to handle your large, important jobs, too.

Will you let me know on the enclosed card when you will[12] have a few minutes to spare. I should like to tell you personally about our facilities. Sincerely yours,[13]

---

557. Dear Mr. Mead: On April 10 the Brown Printing Company will move to its new location at 162[14] South Street. We have enlarged our facilities and installed equipment that is up to the minute in every[15] respect. Needless to say, you are invited to visit us at our new address at any time.

We are aware[16] that in the past year or two some of our deliveries were slow in arriving. You have been very patient[17] with us. From now on we will be able to complete your printing work on schedule.

Our representative, Mr.[18] Brown, will be in to see you soon to tell you about our new presses and other facilities. Yours sincerely,[19]

---

558. Dear Mr. Lawson: The Civil Service Commission wishes to express its appreciation of your help in[20] printing the news releases that we have been issuing from time to time. Your assistance in bringing these releases[21] to the attention of those who may be interested in Government employment is also greatly[22] appreciated.

The co-operation of the press is particularly valuable because the Government[23] urgently needs capable persons for various positions. Never before have there been so many[24] employment opportunities for constructive and interesting positions with the Government. Yours sincerely,[25] (500)

Reading and Writing Practice

559.

ed′i·tor
cus′tom·ers
re·lieve′

ser

par

par

conj

415-3156

(129)

560.

pri′ma·ry
re·lieve′

cont

dis·pos′al
mod′ern

well′-kept′
hyphenated before noun

ser

1902-246

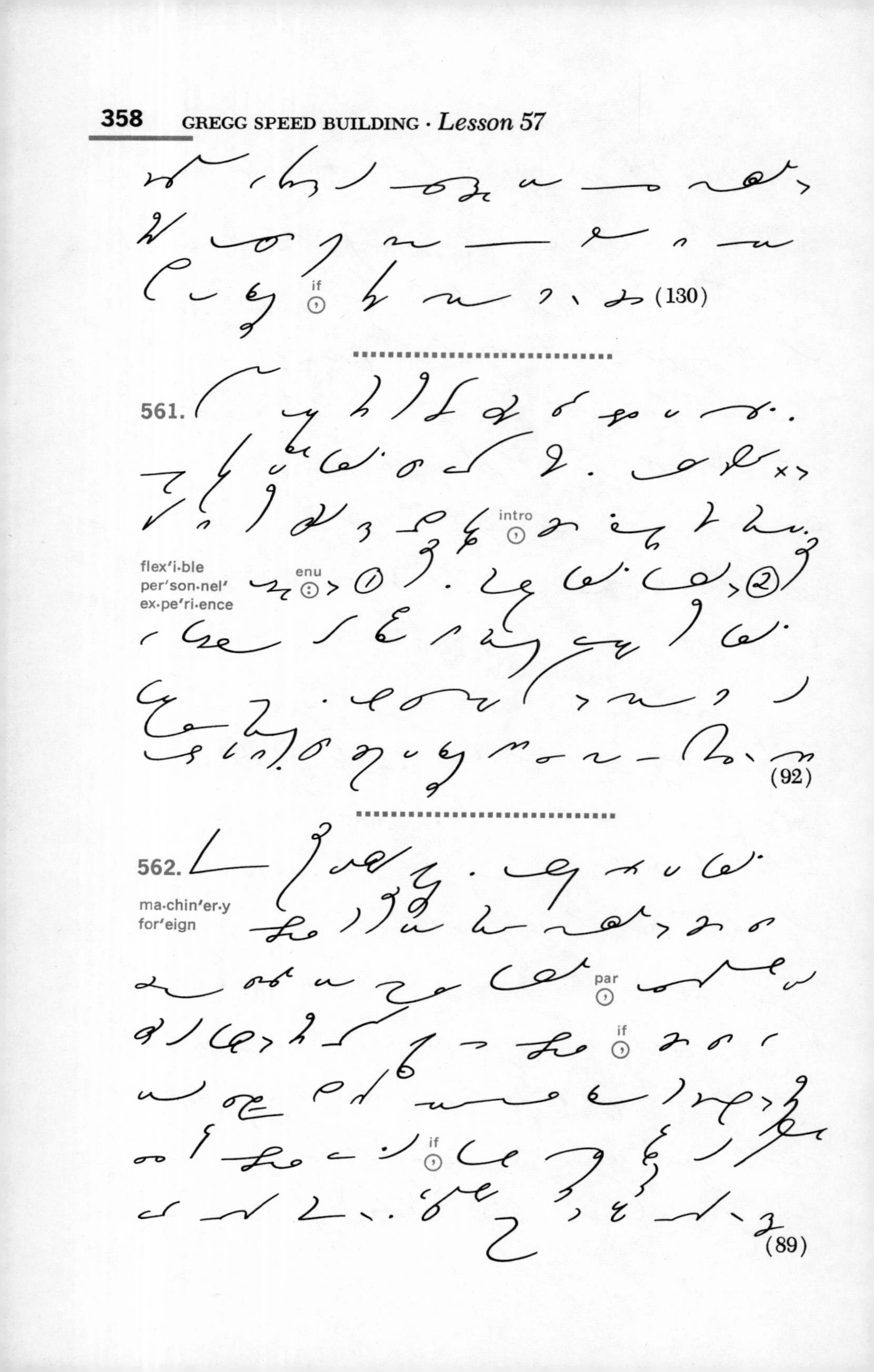

if (130)

561.

intro

flex'i·ble
per'son·nel'
ex·pe'ri·ence

enu

(92)

562.

ma·chin'er·y
for'eign

par

if

if

(89)

Developing Shorthand Writing Power

563. WORD FAMILIES

Ind-

-pression

a. Industry, indistinct, indispensable, indirect, indicate, indisposed, indiscreet.
b. Impression, depression, expression, compression, oppression.

564. FREQUENT NAMES

Last Names

Men's First Names

Women's First Names

a. Morris, Morrison, Morse, Munroe, Murray.
b. John, Jonathan, Joseph, Julian, Lawrence, Leonard, Louis.
c. Laura, Lillian, Louise, Lucy, Margaret.

Building Transcription Skills

565. BUSINESS VOCABULARY BUILDER

managerial Pertaining to the running or management of a business.

solely Alone; only.

Writing Practice

566. PREVIEW

567.

568.

569.

567. Elbow, we shall be glad, without, representatives, average, naturally, acquired, judgment, results, each dollar.

568. Expansion, California, Washington, qualifications, he should be able, managerial, potential.

569. Building, reception, solely, successful, executives, used, if you wish, designers, one of the, things, ordinary.

LETTERS

567. Dear Mr. Morris: Would you like to have a printing expert at your elbow when you plan your next advertising[1] campaign? You can have one for the asking. We shall be glad to supply him without obligation to you. Our[2] representatives are experienced men who have spent years helping our customers get the most for the money they[3] spend on printing.

Our representatives average more than twenty-five years in the printing business. During that[4] time they have naturally acquired a balanced judgment and valuable understanding of the way to obtain[5] the best results from each dollar spent on printing.

When you start to plan your next campaign, call us. Cordially yours,[6]

568. Dear Mr. Monroe: Because of the expansion of our printing business, we are in the market for an experienced[7] salesman to represent us in the states of California, Washington, Oregon, and Nevada. The man[8] we should like to have should possess, among other things, the following qualifications:

1. He should be able[9] to get along well with executives of leading organizations.

2. He should know how to sell services[10] as well as printing.

3. He should possess managerial potential.

If you know of any young man who you[11] think meets our rigid requirements, won't you please have him get in touch with me as soon as possible. Cordially yours,[12]

---

569. Dear Mr. Murray: Your callers form an impression of your organization from your building, your reception room,[13] or your sales office. Readers of your business letters form their impression solely from your business stationery.[14] The design of your letterhead, the information it contains, and the quality of paper and printing are[15] therefore of vital importance.

That is why so many successful business concerns insist that their letterheads[16] be printed on Mead Paper. That is also why so many executives have sent for our kit of sample[17] letterheads and have used to advantage the suggestions given in it.

If you would like to have one of these kits, all[18] you have to do is ask for it. If you wish, enclose a copy of your present letterhead; our designers[19] will be glad to show you how your letterhead can be improved so that it will make the best impression.

One of the things we think[20] you will like is the fact that Mead Papers cost only a little more than ordinary papers. Cordially yours,[21] (420)

Reading and Writing Practice

570.

let'ter·head'
es·pe'cial·ly

well'-word'ed *hyphenated before noun*

conj

nc

conj

par

(160)

571.

re·cep'tion·ist
pleas'ant

and o

par

wel'come
at'mos·phere

intro

conj

par

nc

(136)

572.

im·pres′sion
greet′ing

conj

a·piece′
sam′ple
suf·fi′cient

if

(92)

573.

past
sta′tion·er′y
sat′is·fac′to·ry

intro

(87)

Developing Shorthand Writing Power

574. FREQUENT PHRASES

Words Omitted

a

In Addition

b

a. Some of our, many of the, one of the, in the future, about the matter, in the world, on the question, on the subject.
b. In addition, in addition to the, in addition to these, in addition to those, in addition to that, in addition to them.

575. GEOGRAPHICAL EXPRESSIONS

St.

a

States

b

a. St. Paul, St. Charles, St. John, St. Augustine, St. Lawrence.
b. Delaware, Indiana, Michigan, New Jersey, Pennsylvania, Vermont.

Building Transcription Skills

576. BUSINESS VOCABULARY BUILDER

enhance To advance; to make greater.

craftsmen Persons who are skilled in some trade or art.

expedite To speed up.

Writing Practice

577. PREVIEW

578.

579.

580.

578. Contribution, competition, appetite, $300,000,000, Vermont, enhance, publish.
579. Produced, craftsmen, material, occasion, performance, turning.
580. Conversation, accordance, similar, understanding, approximately, 48,000, druggists, prospects, anxious, distributed, P.S.

LETTERS

578. Dear Mr. Abby: In homes all over the country, books are making a vital contribution to better living.[1] In spite of competition from other fields, this large appetite for books of all kinds has built an industry[2] that does $300,000,000 worth of business.

For more than fifty years Vermont Papers have played an important[3] part in this expansion. They have helped make books more readable and more attractive.

Vermont Papers enhance the appeal[4] of books and make them attractive to the customer in many ways.

If you are interested in increasing[5] the sale of your books, we can help you do it. Try Vermont Paper in the next book you publish. Cordially yours,[6]

---

579. Dear Mr. McMann: As I am sure you know, there are many different degrees of quality in printing. Fine[7] quality printing is produced by craftsmen who take pride in the work they produce.

The cost of a printed piece of[8] material is only a fraction of its value to the buyer. Such material stands or falls on how[9] it looks and what it says. It represents you; it represents your company.

Those who have placed their printing with us[10] have never had occasion to regret their action. We have a record of performance of which we are very[11] proud. Day after day, year after year, our men have been turning out work that is well done and reasonably priced.

May[12] we have an opportunity to show you what we can do the next time you have a printing job. Sincerely yours,[13]

---

580. Dear Mr. Fleming: This will confirm our telephone conversation of April 15.

In accordance with our[14] agreement, we are sending you by truck today 50,000 booklets similar to the one enclosed. It is[15] our understanding that you will mail copies of these booklets to approximately 48,000 druggists[16] on your list. This list, we understand, has been recently revised so that the 48,000 names represent[17] true prospects for our products.

Also, please send 200 of the booklets, in one package, to our St. Paul[18] office. Use the attached label for this purpose.

We are very anxious to have these booklets distributed; therefore,[19] anything you can do to expedite the mailing will be appreciated. Yours sincerely,

P. S. Our[20] check for $600 to cover the cost of the mailing is enclosed. Thank you for your fine co-operation.[21] (420)

Reading and Writing Practice

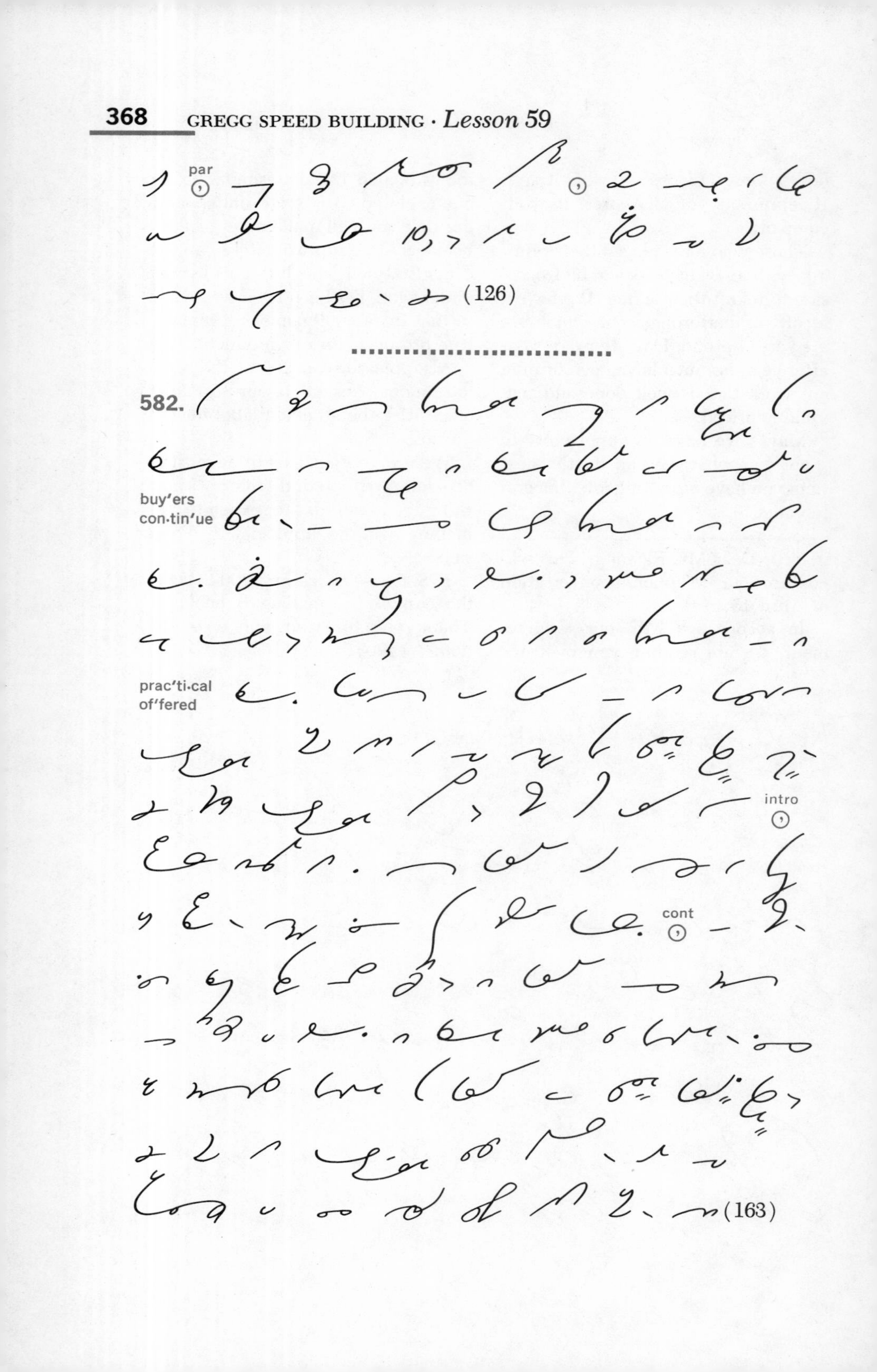

par

(126)

582.

buy'ers
con·tin'ue

prac'ti·cal
of'fered

intro

cont

(163)

583.

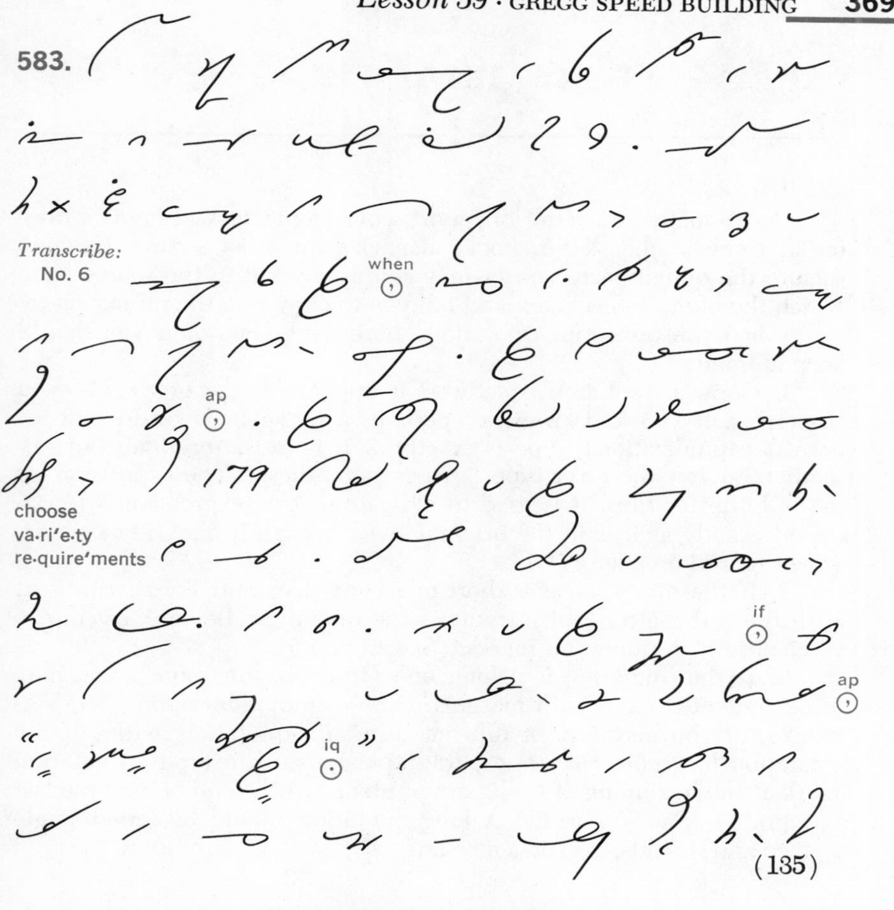

No person can hope to work at top efficiency at his job unless he takes care of his health. You will be an efficient worker if you:

1. *Get ample sleep each night.*
2. *Follow a well-balanced diet.*
3. *Get some exercise each day.*
4. *Reserve some time in your week for relaxation and enjoyment.*

SECRETARIAL TIP

Typing Quotations

Occasionally in a letter or report, your employer will insert a quotation from another letter, book, magazine, or other source. He may dictate the quotation to you or may simply mark it in the source from which the quotation is taken and tell you to copy it in the proper place.

When you transcribe quotations, here are a few points you should keep in mind:

1. Copy a quotation exactly as it appears in the original – even the errors. If you find an error (perhaps a misspelled word or an incorrect capitalization), type it exactly as it is in the original; but immediately after the error type (*sic*) in parentheses. The expression *sic* is the Latin for *thus*. It is used to indicate that an expression is reproduced exactly as it is in the original, even though it may be incorrect. (See Figure 1 on page 371.)

2. If the quotation is a short one (less than four lines), run it in with the text matter that introduces the quotation. Be sure, of course, to enclose it in quotation marks. (See Figure 1.)

3. If the quotation is a long one (four lines or more), you may either indent it from both margins *without* quotation marks (see Figure 2), or you may type it full measure *with* quotation marks. If the quotation has more than one paragraph, be sure to type a quotation mark at the beginning of each paragraph and at the end of only the last paragraph. (See Figure 3.) A long quotation should be typed single spaced and should begin on a new line.

Punctuation Reminders

A short quotation is introduced by a comma; a long quotation, by a colon.

Commas and periods are always placed inside quotation marks; colons and semicolons, always outside.

Question marks are placed inside or outside the quotation mark, depending on the sense of the sentence.

A quotation within a quotation should be enclosed in single quotes – the apostrophe mark on your typewriter. (See Figure 3.)

There will also be times when your employer will dictate a quotation, the exact wording of which he is not sure. It will be your job, as secretary, to obtain the exact wording of the quotation from some reference source.

Figure 1

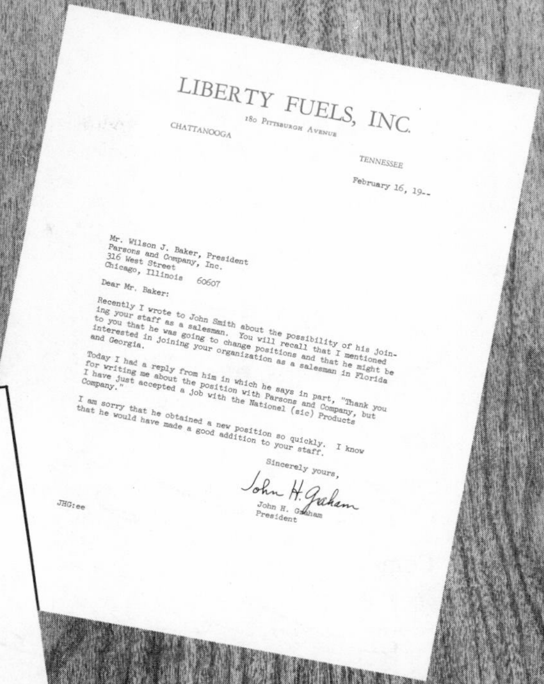

LIBERTY FUELS, INC.
180 Pittsburgh Avenue
CHATTANOOGA TENNESSEE

February 16, 19--

Mr. Wilson J. Baker, President
Parsons and Company, Inc.
316 West Street
Chicago, Illinois 60607

Dear Mr. Baker:

Recently I wrote to John Smith about the possibility of his joining your staff as a salesman. You will recall that I mentioned to you that he was going to change positions and that he might be interested in joining your organization as a salesman in Florida and Georgia.

Today I had a reply from him in which he says in part, "Thank you for writing me about the position with Parsons and Company, but I have just accepted a job with the Nationel (sic) Products Company."

I am sorry that he obtained a new position so quickly. I know that he would have made a good addition to your staff.

Sincerely yours,

John H. Graham

John H. Graham
President

JHG:ee

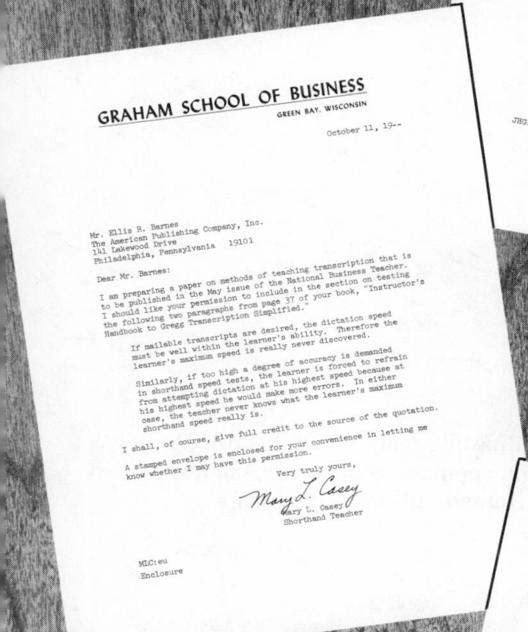

Figure 2

GRAHAM SCHOOL OF BUSINESS
GREEN BAY, WISCONSIN

October 11, 19--

Mr. Ellis R. Barnes
The American Publishing Company, Inc.
141 Lakewood Drive
Philadelphia, Pennsylvania 19101

Dear Mr. Barnes:

I am preparing a paper on methods of teaching transcription that is to be published in the May issue of the National Business Teacher. I should like your permission to include in the section on testing the following two paragraphs from page 37 of your book, "Instructor's Handbook to Gregg Transcription Simplified."

> If mailable transcripts are desired, the dictation speed must be well within the learner's ability. Therefore the learner's maximum speed is really never discovered.
>
> Similarly, if too high a degree of accuracy is demanded in shorthand speed tests, the learner is forced to refrain from attempting dictation at his highest speed because at his highest speed he would make more errors. In either case, the teacher never knows what the learner's maximum shorthand speed really is.

I shall, of course, give full credit to the source of the quotation.

A stamped envelope is enclosed for your convenience in letting me know whether I may have this permission.

Very truly yours,

Mary L. Casey

Mary L. Casey
Shorthand Teacher

MLC:eu
Enclosure

Figure 3

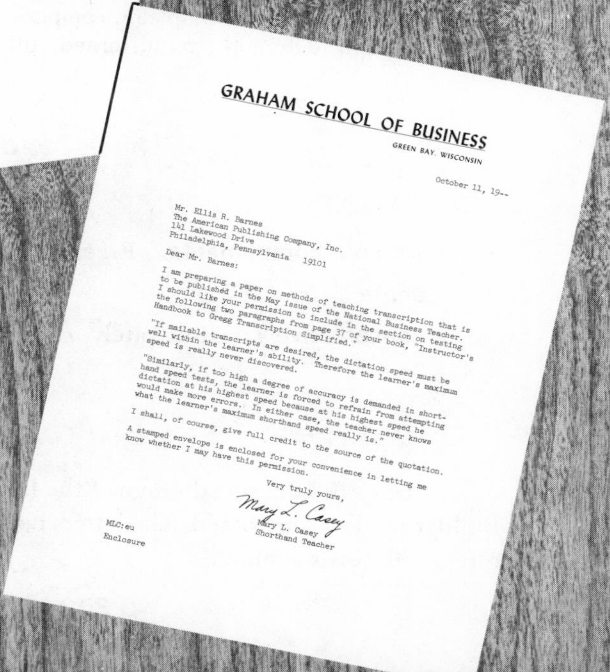

GRAHAM SCHOOL OF BUSINESS
GREEN BAY, WISCONSIN

October 11, 19--

Mr. Ellis R. Barnes
The American Publishing Company, Inc.
141 Lakewood Drive
Philadelphia, Pennsylvania 19101

Dear Mr. Barnes:

I am preparing a paper on methods of teaching transcription that is to be published in the May issue of the National Business Teacher. I should like your permission to include in the section on testing the following two paragraphs from page 37 of your book, "Instructor's Handbook to Gregg Transcription Simplified."

"If mailable transcripts are desired, the dictation speed must be well within the learner's ability. Therefore the learner's maximum speed is really never discovered.

"Similarly, if too high a degree of accuracy is demanded in shorthand speed tests, the learner is forced to refrain from attempting dictation at his highest speed because at his highest speed he would make more errors. In either case, the teacher never knows what the learner's maximum shorthand speed really is."

I shall, of course, give full credit to the source of the quotation.

A stamped envelope is enclosed for your convenience in letting me know whether I may have this permission.

Very truly yours,

Mary L. Casey

Mary L. Casey
Shorthand Teacher

MLC:eu
Enclosure

Developing Shorthand Writing Power

584. WORD BEGINNINGS AND ENDINGS

-ily

a

Com-

b

-tern, etc.

c

a. Steadily, easily, readily, family, hastily, temporarily, heartily, heavily.
b. Completed, comment, complaint, compare, comparable, compromise.
c. Turn, return, determine, term, turned, attorney, modern.

Building Transcription Skills

585. BUSINESS VOCABULARY BUILDER

with our compliments Free.

acute Crucial.

conservatively Moderately; cautiously.

Progressive Speed Builder (100-130)

Once again, the speed range of the letters in this Progressive Speed Builder has been increased. The letters begin at 100 words a minute and run to 130 words a minute.

586. PREVIEW

587. Glad to know, revision, months ago, unable, steadily, users, very much.
588. Thank you for your, some time ago, anxious, edition, recover, assume, judging, you have done.
589. Finished, very well, during the past, production, will be glad, consider, I hope that.
590. Confident, we shall be able, 30,000, particularly, reorganization, improved, indicated.
591. Town, explained, Chicago, immediately, quickly, notifying, promotion.

LETTERS

(1 Minute at 100)

587. Dear Mr. Warner: You will be glad to know that I have finally completed the revision of my book, "Money and Banking." I had hoped/ to complete the job months ago, but on May 10 I became ill and was unable to work on it steadily for about a month.

In revising//the book, I have tried to follow all the suggestions that I have received from the present users of the book.

I am sending the manuscript/// to you today by express. After you have read the manuscript, I should like very much to have your opinion of it. Very sincerely yours, (1)

(1 Minute at 110)

588. Dear Mr. Clay: Thank you for your letter with the good news that you have completed revision of your book, "Money and Banking." As I wrote you some time/ago, we are very anxious to have this revision because the sales of the present edition are not what they should be. I believe that with a new edition//we will soon recover the ground that we have lost.

The manuscript has not yet arrived. I assume that it will reach us either today or tomorrow.///As soon as I receive it, I will read it. Judging by the work you have done in the past, I am sure that this revision will be a fine one. Sincerely yours, (2)

(1 Minute at 120)

589. Mr. Lloyd: Mr. Clay has finally finished the revision of his book, "Money and Banking." The manuscript arrived Friday, and I read it over the weekend.

Mr./Clay has done very well; and I am confident that, with this revision, we shall be able to recover the ground that we lost during the past year with the first edition.//

Before we place the manuscript into production, I wish that you would read it and let me have your frank opinion. If you feel that any changes should be made, I am/// sure that Mr. Clay will be glad to consider them.

I hope that you can spare the time to read the manuscript, as I should like to start production soon. James H. Wilson (3)

(1 Minute at 125)

590. Mr. Wilson: After reading Mr. Clay's revision of his book, "Money and Banking," I, too, am confident that we shall be able to recover the ground that we lost during/the past year with the first edition. If we do not sell at least 30,000 copies in the first year, I shall be very much surprised.

I particularly like his//reorganization of the material in the book and his treatment of branch banking. I did find a few things that in my opinion could easily be improved. I indicated ///them right on the manuscript.

Should I return the manuscript to Mr. Clay, or would it be better to ask him to come in to discuss my suggested changes? John H. Lloyd (4)

(1 Minute at 130)

591. Mr. Wilson: Mr. Clay was in town yesterday and came in to discuss my suggested changes in his book, "Money and Banking." He had hoped to see you while he was here, but I/ explained to him that you were in Chicago.

We spent about an hour discussing my suggested changes, and he agreed to them all. In fact, after our meeting he sat in your office and//made all the changes immediately.

The manuscript is now complete and ready for production. I believe that it will be finished quickly. If all goes well, we may even///have copies by September 1.

I am notifying the Advertising Department that the revision is ready and suggesting that they give some thought to promotion. John H. Lloyd (5) (585)

Reading and Writing Practice

592.

com'pli·ments
in·form'a·tive
ac·quaint'

ap
iq
and o

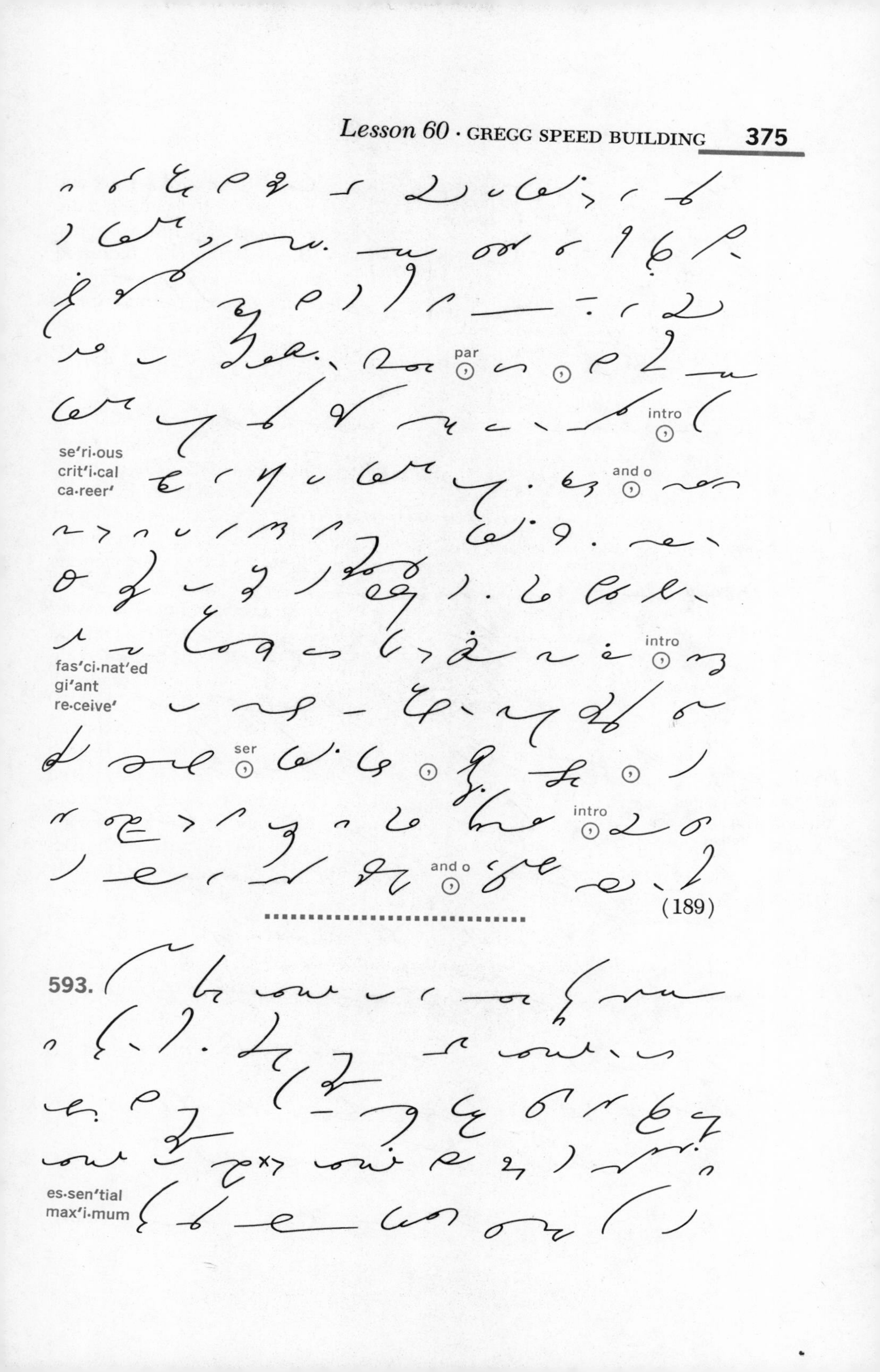

par

intro

se'ri·ous
crit'i·cal
ca·reer'

and o

intro

fas'ci·nat'ed
gi'ant
re·ceive'

ser

intro

and o

(189)

593.

es·sen'tial
max'i·mum

nonr

(126)

594.

ap

sep'a·rate
De·signs'

iq

a·dapt'ed
ap·pear'ance
lo'cal

when

a·gree'a·bly
com'pa·ra·ble
sta'tion·er'y

intro

350

(142)

PART FOUR

Travel and Transportation
Publishing
Automobiles
Real Estate

ON-THE-JOB IMPROVEMENT OF SPELLING AND VOCABULARY

No one ever knows the spelling and meaning of every word; the English language is too vast and too eccentric. During your study of shorthand and transcription, your teachers and your textbooks have done all they can to help you to improve your spelling and to enlarge your vocabulary. Soon you will be working in an office, and you must be responsible for continuing the improvement of your spelling and vocabulary.

Just as there are two main problems in the improvement of your spelling and vocabulary, so there are two directions in which to pursue this improvement. The one problem, the biggest problem, is the general improvement of your spelling and vocabulary, improvement that every literate person should continue to work at all his life. The other problem, more urgent but much easier, is the improvement of your spelling and vocabulary for the specific job you may have. This is urgent and important, because your success as a secretary will depend rather heavily on your ability to understand and to spell the words that are dictated in the course of the day's work. If you are not familiar with a word, it is seldom possible to spell it. In your own transcription work you have undoubtedly made some serious errors because you simply did not know the meaning of a word.

Fortunately for the secretary, each type of business has its own characteristic vocabulary; and each dictator within the business has his own characteristic vocabulary and phraseology. This greatly simplifies the problem of the new secretary. It is not necessary to know and to be able to spell every word in the language; it is necessary to know and to be able to spell only the relatively small vocabulary used in the office where you work.

There is a right way and a wrong way to do this. The wrong way, of course, is to wait until you make a mistake on each word and have to rewrite the letter. In this wrong way you will eventually learn all the necessary words. There is a much better way, however.

Usually you have a few days' notice before you report to work on a new job. If so, try to obtain any printed matter or price lists or catalogues issued by the company for which you are going to work. Study these carefully for new words. Look the new words up in the dictionary. Learn the meaning and the spelling. Make lists of the most difficult ones so that you will have them conveniently available when you start work.

Once you begin work, ask permission to read some of the correspondence from the files (on your own time, of course), and compile lists of words from the correspondence. When you notice that any word or phrase occurs very frequently, devise and learn a shorthand shortcut for it; but be very sparing with the shortcuts. You should be able to hold down the list of worthwhile shortcuts to ten or twelve. If you devise too many shortcuts, you will find them to be more of a hindrance than a help.

Finally, after working on this plan for a week or two, you may find that there are a few words whose spelling or meaning still bothers you. Make a list of these few words on a filing card and keep them on your desk as you transcribe. Thus you can check the spelling of any one of these doubtful words in a second by glancing at the card.

The improvement of your general ability in spelling and vocabulary is a more difficult task. It involves much reading and a constant awareness of the necessity for remembering the spelling and meaning of words that you meet in your reading.

Whether you are attempting to improve your general ability or your ability to spell and recognize the words peculiar to your job, always remember that your best friend and most patient helper is a good English dictionary.

CHAPTER

13

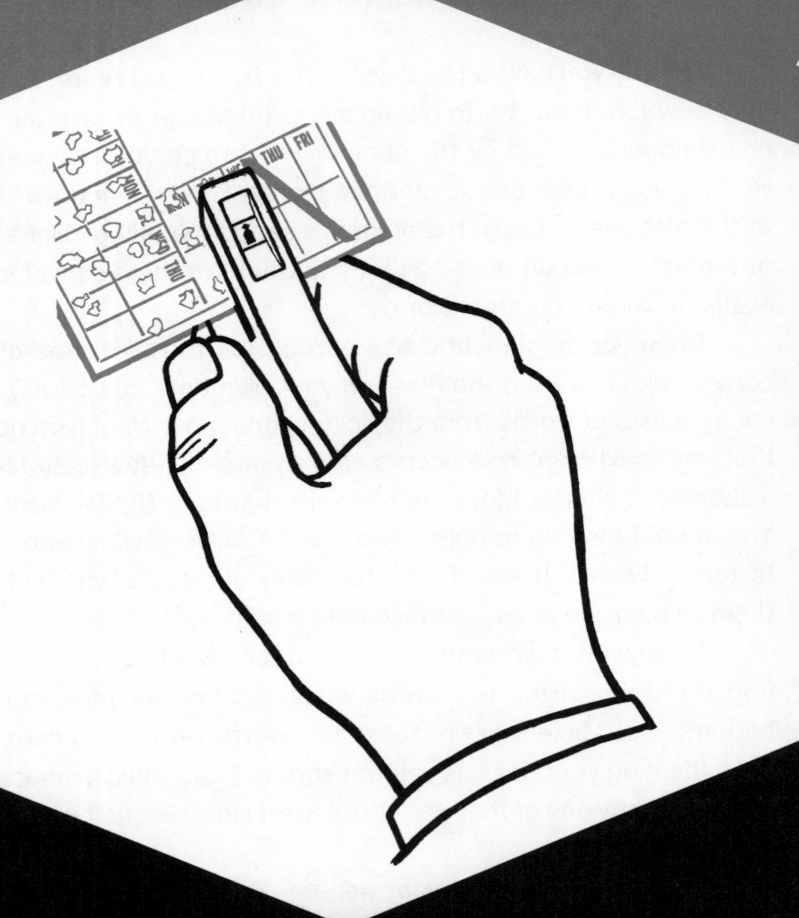

Travel and Transportation

Developing Shorthand Writing Power

595. OUTLINE CONSTRUCTION

Double consonants. It is unnecessary to repeat the double consonant sound in compound words like "bookkeeper."

Bookkeeping, neckcloth, roommate, headdress, storeroom, nighttime, earring.

Ness after words ending in n or m. The word ending *-ness* is joined to *n* or *m* with a jog.

a. Dimness, slimness, calmness, firmness, meanness.
b. Suddenness, openness, plainness, thinness, sternness.

Building Transcription Skills

596. SIMILAR-WORDS DRILL

Plane, plain

plane An airplane; an aircraft.

The plane landed at the airport at 4:15.

plain (*noun*) Level land; a broad strip of flat land.

He crossed the plain on horseback.

plain Clear; obvious.

It was plain that he had no intention of paying the charge.

Reading and Writing Practice

597. Travel, the Educator

Travel has

With the

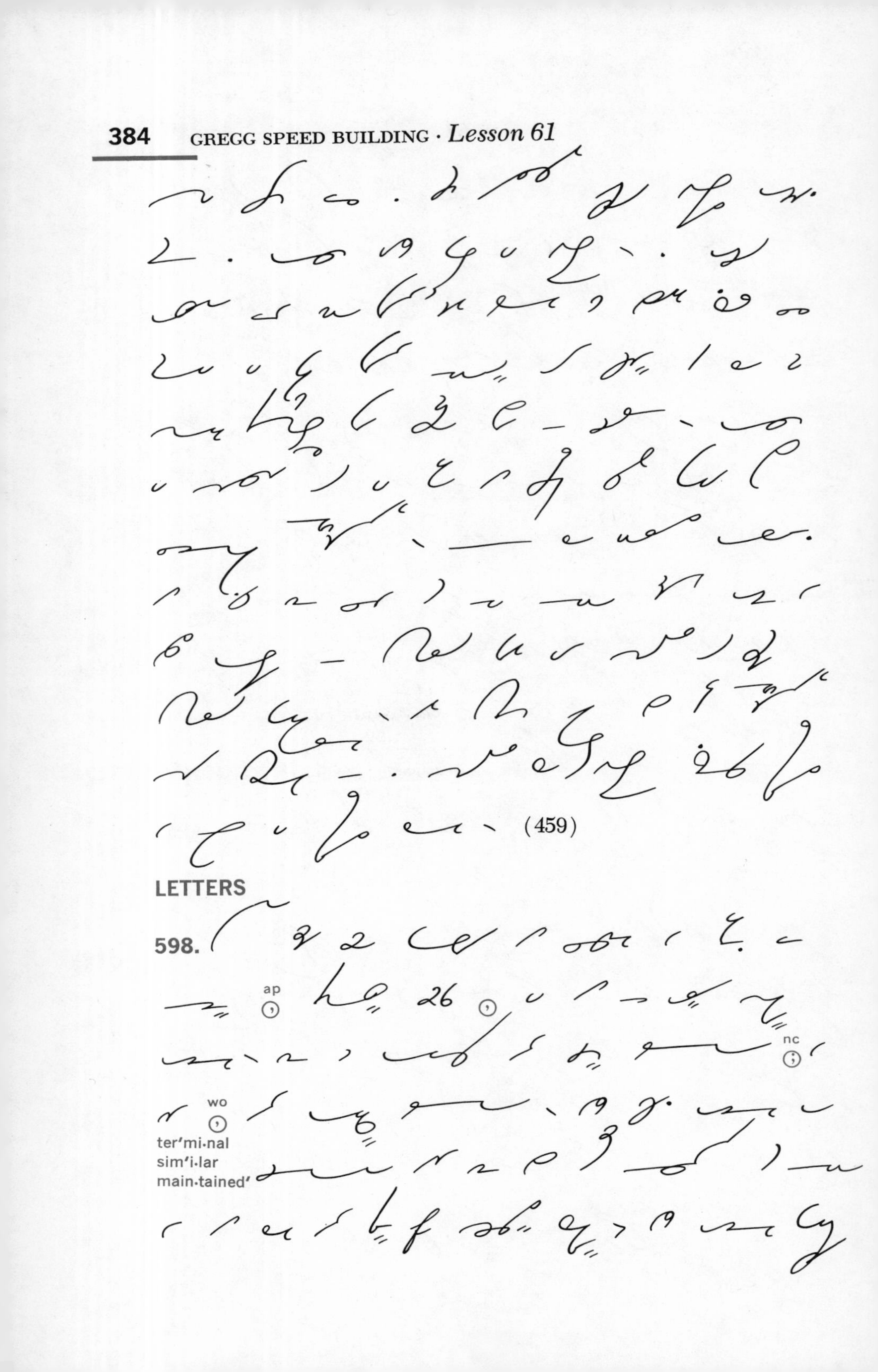

(459)

LETTERS

598.

ap

nc

wo

ter'mi·nal
sim'i·lar
main·tained'

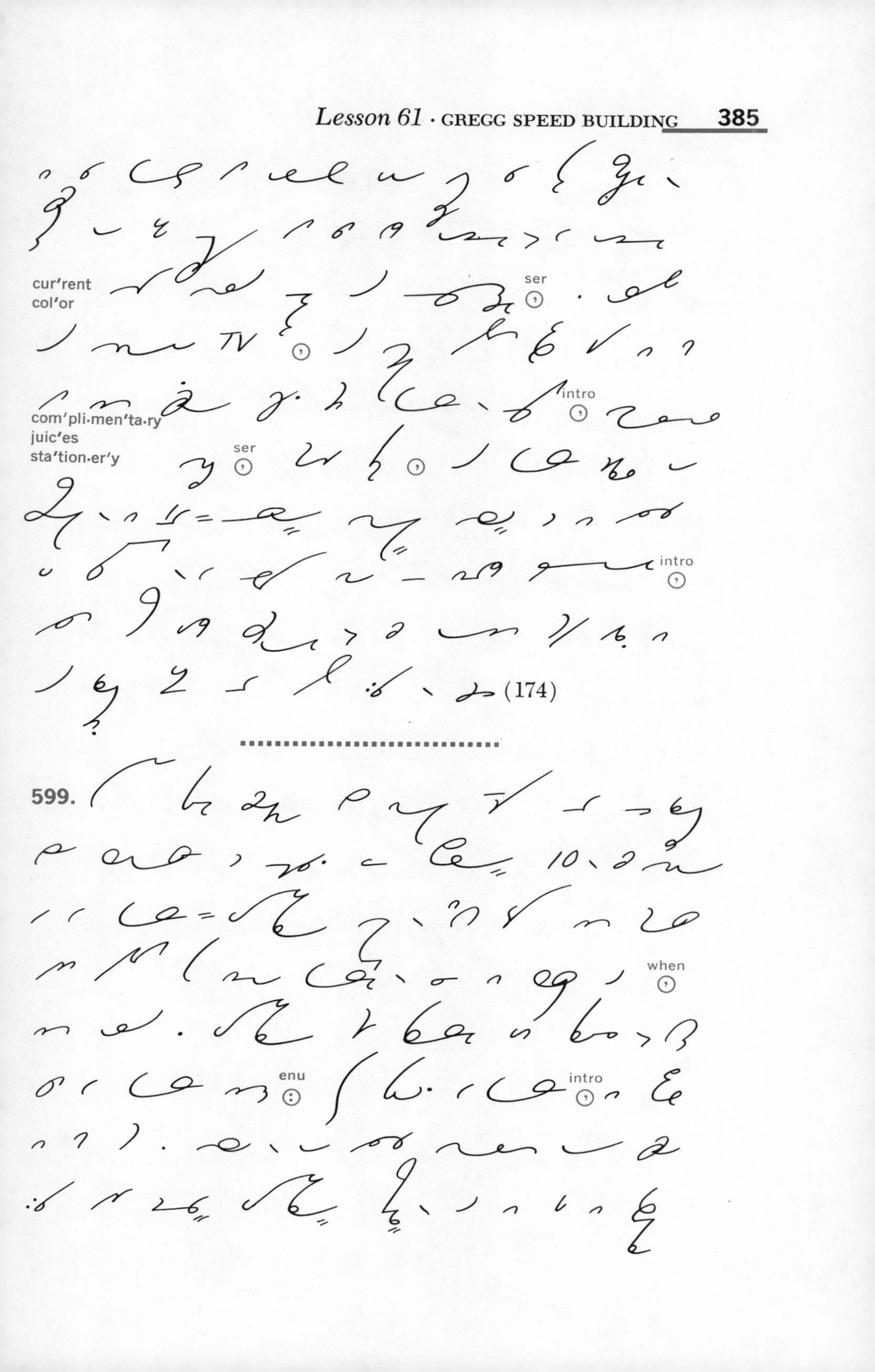

cur'rent
col'or

ser

TV

intro

com'pli·men'ta·ry
juic'es
sta'tion·er'y

ser

intro

(174)

599.

10

when

enu

intro

re·ceipt'
driv'er's
li'cense

intro

cr

(140)

600.

grat'i·fy·ing
as·sur'ance

27

15

af·fect'ing
Flight
stew'ard·ess

par

(98)

LESSON 62

Developing Shorthand Writing Power

601. RECALL DRILL — TEN BLEND

In this drill you will review the various combinations represented by the *ten* blend.

a. Tend, tentative, tenant, attend, tension, attention, retention, intention.
b. Dentist, deny, denote, wooden, hidden, sudden, identify, evidence.
c. Contain, maintain, retain, pertain, captain, obtain.
d. Wilmington, Kensington, Huntington, Lexington, Washington.

Building Transcription Skills

602. ACCURACY PRACTICE

In this drill you will practice the various joinings of the *oo* hook. Keep the *oo* hook *deep* and *narrow*.

a. You-your, world, you can; Yours truly, you would, other; wood, woman.
b. Shoe, chew; one, whom; you want, you are, you will.
c. New, none, numb; nut, mood.
d. Cool, gull; us, you have; rubber, group, up.

Writing Practice

603. PREVIEW

604.

605.

606.

604. Europe, if you wish, London, pleasant, examine, schedule, one-way, assistance.
605. Scarcely, professional, itself, comfortable, leisure, practical, in addition, 300 pounds, demonstration.
606. Announce, newest, addition, flyer, Newark, Los Angeles, altitude, enclosed, Chicago, Kansas City, Denver, necessary.

LETTERS

604. Dear Mr. Case: Have you been thinking of a trip to Europe? If you have, why wait? Reserve a seat on one of our[1] jet planes. Within hours of the time when you step aboard our plane, you will be in Ireland, Paris, or Rome.[2] If you wish, you can fly to London and then on to

Paris for the price of a London ticket alone. You fly[3] at ten miles a minute, and the trip is smooth and pleasant.

If you will examine the enclosed schedule, you will see[4] that we have sixteen flights a week to Europe. What is more, the rates are lower than ever. You can now obtain a[5] special 30-day round-trip fare that costs only one-third more than a regular one-way ticket.

If you would like[6] to have assistance in planning your trip to Europe, by all means get in touch with us. Planning trips to all parts of[7] Europe is only one of the many services that we offer without charge to our customers. Sincerely yours,[8]

---

605. Dear Mr. Scott: Scarcely a week passes that we do not receive a letter from a business or professional[9] man that reads like this:

"My Johnson plane is paying for itself. It makes my days more productive and my traveling[10] more comfortable. What is more, it adds many hours to my leisure time."

A surprising number of these men are[11] over forty. That fact pleases us. We designed our latest model as a professional plane that anyone[12] can learn to fly quickly, easily, and safely.

This new model is very practical, too. Four people may fly[13] in it in complete comfort. In addition, it will carry over 300 pounds of luggage.

See your Johnson[14] dealer today for a demonstration flight in the new model. He will also arrange free flying lessons for you. Sincerely yours,[15]

---

606. Dear Mr. Smith: We are happy to announce the newest addition to our flight schedule, the American Flyer.[16] This flight leaves Newark, New Jersey, daily at 6 p.m. and arrives at Los Angeles, California, at[17] 8:30 p.m.

Remember, when you fly in our planes, you fly at a comfortable altitude. More[18] important, you fly on a line backed by forty years of experience.

We suggest that you retain the enclosed[19] folder, which tells all about our New York-to-Los Angeles schedules. It also lists the service available[20] to Chicago, Kansas City, Denver, and many other important centers in the United States.

Call us[21] the next time you must make a long trip. The number is 916-3201. We shall be happy to make[22] all the necessary arrangements for you. Sincerely yours, (451)

Reading and Writing Practice

607.

intro

and o

nc

wo

(85)

608.

ser

av′er·age
length
ar·riv′al

21

10

sur·pris′ing
sur′vey
Eu′rope

4

par

2

(106)

609.

i·tin′er·ar′y
be·gin′ning

ap

15

as

Interoffice Memorandum

TO	F. J. Marvin	FROM	A. R. Smith
LOCATION	Personnel Department	LOCATION	Foreign Department
SUBJECT	Job Replacement	DATE	May 20, 19--

My secretary, Miss Helen A. Hicks, has just informed me that she is to be married on June 15. She plans to leave on June 1.

If it is possible, I should like to get someone to fill the vacancy immediately, so that Miss Hicks can help in the training of the new girl.

As you know, most of my correspondence is with customers in South and Central America. Consequently, it would be a great help to me if you could find a girl who has some degree of proficiency in Spanish.

I shall be in Cleveland on May 21 and 22, but I shall be back on the morning of May 23. I shall, therefore, be able to interview any girls you send me any time after May 22.

A. R. S.

ARS:HH

Interoffice Memorandum

one′-day′ *hyphenated before noun*

ser ser ser

par nc

round′-trip′ *hyphenated before noun*

if (105)

610. par (68)

611. if

au′tumn ac·tiv′i·ties

intro

nonr

(60)

LESSON 63

Developing Shorthand Writing Power

612. WORD FAMILIES

-minal

a [shorthand]

-line

b [shorthand]

a. Terminal, nominal, criminal.
b. Airline, underline, outline, streamline, headline.

613. FREQUENT NAMES

Last Names

a [shorthand]

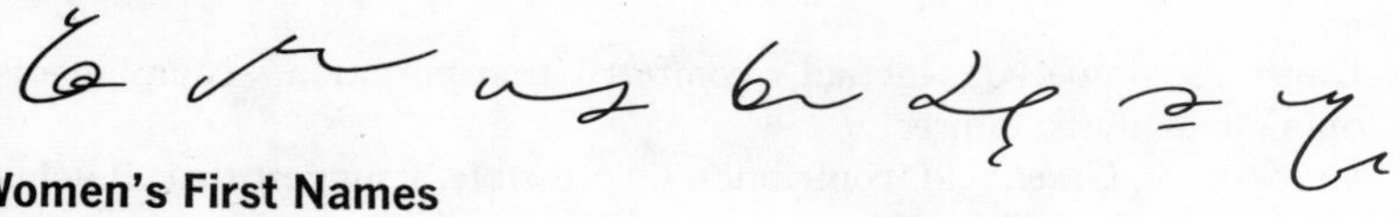

Women's First Names

b [shorthand]

a. O'Brien, O'Donnell, Olsen, Parker, Phillips, Quinn, Roberts.
b. Marian, Martha, Matilda, Mildred, Nora.

Building Transcription Skills

614. BUSINESS VOCABULARY BUILDER

accessible Easy to get to.

phase Aspect; side.

terminal Station; depot.

Writing Practice

615. PREVIEW

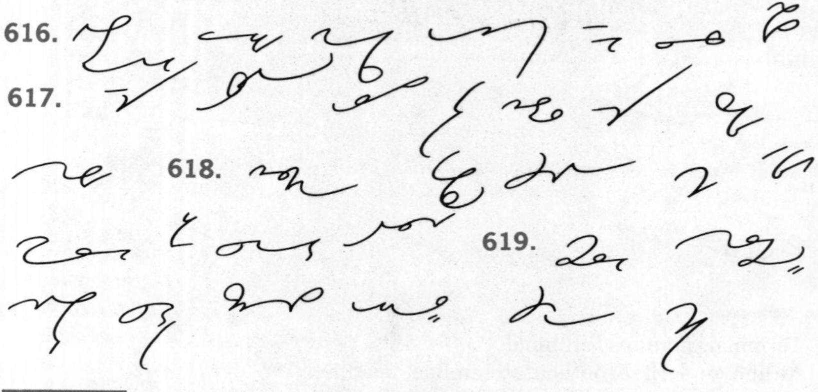

616. Travelers, almost, you will be able, luggage, entrance, immediately, we hope that.
617. Interested, entitled, readily, public, unnecessary, instead, airport, greatest.
618. Unusual, prepared, factual, comfort, transportation, compliments, opinion, analysis, indirect.
619. Conference, Greenfield, contribution, accessible, I suggest that, Raleigh, faculty, comfortable.

LETTERS

616. Dear Mr. Olsen: On June 6 we shall place in operation a new plane that you and other travelers have[1] helped to design. The new plane will travel at almost ten miles a minute.

You will find the new plane convenient in[2] many ways. For example, you will be able to carry your luggage onto the plane, if the luggage is fairly[3] light, and place it in the convenient racks at the entrance. When you leave, it is immediately available[4] to you.

We hope that you will have occasion to ride on our fine new plane in the near future. Sincerely yours,[5]

617. Dear Mr. Morris: As a businessman who flies a good deal, you will be interested in the enclosed folder[6] entitled "More About Air Travel." This folder will give you information that is not readily available[7] to the general public. It will also tell you about our new procedure that makes it unnecessary for[8] you to pick up your reservations in advance. Instead, you can pick them up at the ticket office when you arrive[9] at the airport. This is another move to assure you the greatest possible benefit and convenience[10] from your travel by air.

We hope that you will have many opportunities to use our airlines. Cordially yours,[11]

---

618. Dear Mr. Quinn: If you travel on business, I believe that you will be interested in an unusual[12] booklet we have just prepared. This booklet is unusual because it presents a factual study of the [13] time, cost, and comfort factors involved in air travel and also in other methods of transportation.

We shall[14] be pleased to send you a copy with our compliments if you will return the enclosed request card.

In our opinion,[15] the use of air travel by businessmen will continue to increase only if it offers definite[16] advantages to the traveler. Our booklet shows how in many cases air travel saves the businessman time and[17] money.

The booklet also gives a detailed analysis of direct and indirect travel costs. Cordially yours,[18]

---

619. Dear Mr. Nathan: I am delighted that you will be able to be with us for our conference in Greenfield, North[19] Carolina, on July 16. I know that you will enjoy your visit with us and that we shall profit by your[20] contribution to the conference.

I am sorry to say that Greenfield is not easily accessible. I[21] suggest that you fly to Raleigh, where I shall be glad to meet you. I will then drive you to Greenfield. I understand[22] that there are several flights each day from New York to Raleigh. If you prefer to come by train, you can take a sleeper[23] to Raleigh.

We are reserving for you the guest room in our faculty apartment building, where[24] I am sure you will be comfortable during your stay.

I shall look forward to hearing from you. Cordially yours,[25] (500)

Reading and Writing Practice

620.

iph

ques'tion·naire'
at·tempt'
flights

intro

if

phase
pleas′ant

if

par

if

nonr

(156)

621.

intro

1933

nonr

watched
fa·cil′i·ties

par

han′dling
re′cent·ly

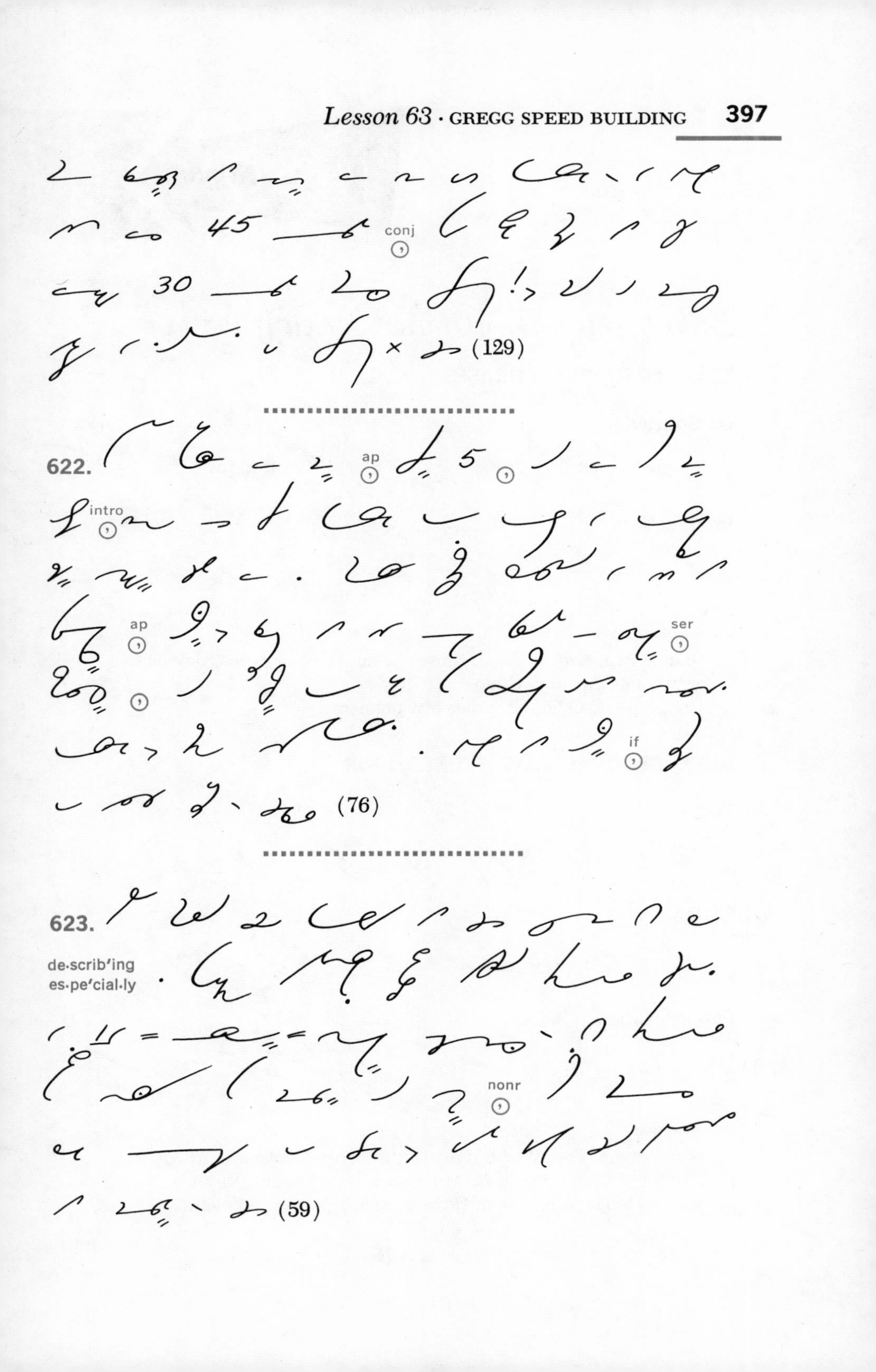

45 conj 30 (129)

622. ap 5 intro ap ser if (76)

623. nonr (59)

de·scrib′ing
es·pe′cial·ly

LESSON 64

Developing Shorthand Writing Power

624. FREQUENT PHRASES

Or Omitted

a 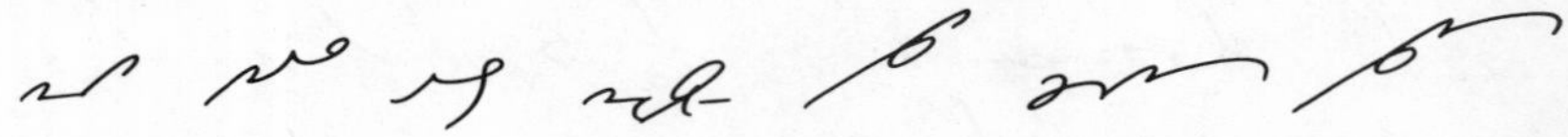

Intersection

b 

a. One or two, two or three, three or four, once or twice, day or two, week or two ago, day or two ago.
b. P.m., a.m., C.O.D., Chamber of Commerce.

625. GEOGRAPHICAL EXPRESSIONS

Fort

a 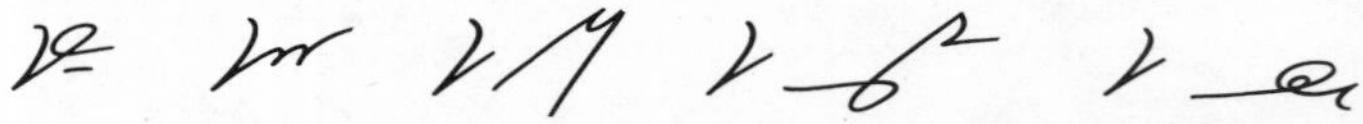

States

b 

Foreign Cities

c 

a. Fort Wayne, Fort Worth, Fort Dodge, Fort Madison, Fort Myers.
b. District of Columbia, Iowa, Minnesota, New Mexico, Virginia.
c. Mexico, Singapore, Tokyo, Havana, Santiago, Rio de Janeiro.

Building Transcription Skills

626. BUSINESS VOCABULARY BUILDER

resumption Act of starting again.

deficit Loss.

Writing Practice

627. PREVIEW

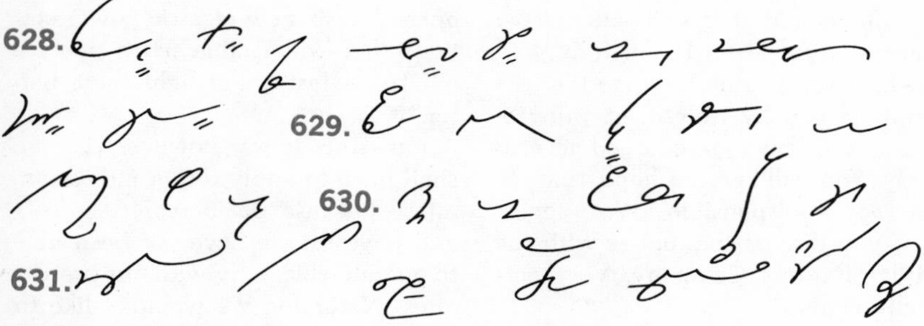

628. Billings, Chamber of Commerce, to join, Mexico City, resumption, some years ago, Fort Worth, Seattle.
629. Experienced, trunk, Boston, steamship, railroad, discovered, I hope, responsible.
630. Thank you for your, reason, explanation, obviously, situation.
631. Scheduled, to do this, equipment, electric power, naturally, understand, deficit.

LETTERS

628. Dear Mr. Billings: The Chamber of Commerce invites you and your friends to join us in a special trip to Mexico[1] City from October 3 to October 31. This is a resumption of a practice that we started[2] some years ago but discontinued in 1960. We already have reservations[3] from people from the following cities: Los Angeles, San Francisco, Fort Worth, and Seattle.

This is an[4] inexpensive tour that affords the travelers an opportunity of going to Mexico under the guidance[5] of a staff that is well trained. The party will travel in special coaches that are air-conditioned.

If possible,[6] we should like to know

by next Monday whether you or any of your friends are interested in this trip. Yours truly,[7]

---

629. Dear Mr. Pace: I was sorry to learn that you have experienced some difficulty with your trunk. As soon as[8] I received your letter, I wrote our agent in Boston. He tells me that, through an error on the part of the Miller[9] Express Company, your trunk was delivered to the Eastern Steamship Lines instead of to our railroad station.[10] By the time the error was discovered, it was too late to have the trunk put aboard your train.

Our agent then shipped[11] the trunk to you by freight, at your request, and you were charged accordingly. You will agree, I hope, that we are not[12] responsible. We suggest that you discuss the matter with the Miller Express Company. Very cordially yours,[13]

---

630. Gentlemen: Thank you for your letter of November 10, explaining the reason for the freight charges on my trunk.[14] From your explanation, it is quite clear that you are not responsible. I shall discuss the matter with the Miller[15] Express Company, as they are obviously responsible for the situation. Very cordially yours,[16]

---

631. Dear Mr. Jones: Thank you for your letter suggesting that we add another train to those scheduled between White Plains[17] and New York. It is not possible for us to do this immediately, but we shall do it as soon as we have[18] the necessary equipment.

You may be interested in one of our recent improvements. We have opened[19] six new electric power stations that will enable us to operate our trains faster and light them better.[20]

I am sorry to say, however, that we shall have to apply for an increase in rates. Because of increased costs[21] and payrolls, we have not been able to operate efficiently with our present rates. Naturally, we would[22] like to maintain our rates as low as possible; but you will understand that we cannot continue to operate[23] on a deficit, as we have done during the past year.

Again, thank you for your suggestion. Sincerely yours,[24] (480)

Reading and Writing Practice

632.

if

conj

board'ing
des'ti·na'tion

intro

mod'els
more·o'ver

conj

intro

350

intro

32

(145)

633. 26 16

berth
Transcribe:
No. 167

12

167

4

9

par

Transcribe:
5:15 p.m.
9:30 a.m.

5:15

9:30

if

(102)

SECRETARIAL TIP

Always be extra careful:

When you transcribe names. A person's name is important to him. His pride is wounded when he receives correspondence on which his name is misspelled. He feels that he is not very important in the eyes of the writer who does not make an effort to spell his name correctly. When there is the slightest doubt in your mind about the correct spelling of the name of the person to whom your employer is writing, check it in the files or through some other source.

When you type dates. When your employer says he is going to do something on "Friday, April 10," be sure that Friday is the tenth and not the ninth or the eleventh.

When you type figures. If you should type "$5,000" instead of "$4,000," you have made only one typing error – but that error may cost your company $1,000 and you your job!

When you type a member of a pair of "similar words." You will look very foolish if you type that the "made answered the door." It is easy to make this type of error unless you are "on your toes."

When your employer says he is enclosing something. When your employer says, "I am enclosing a booklet," he does not mean that *he* is going to enclose it; he wants *you* to enclose it. Always place enclosures in the envelope before you submit letters for signature and indicate on the carbon that the enclosures were made.

When you cannot read an outline in your notes. If you cannot read an outline that obviously affects the sense of a sentence, don't "make a stab at it" and submit the letter for signature. If your guess is wrong and your employer discovers the error, you won't enhance your reputation in his eyes as an efficient stenographer or secretary. Your employer will want you to consult him when you can't read an outline. It is no disgrace *not* to be able to read an outline now and then. Even the most experienced shorthand reporter will occasionally be unable to read an outline that he wrote.

634.

its
ac·com′mo·da′tions
at′mos·phere

pri′va·cy
scen′er·y
Ca·na′di·an's

intro

(119)

635.

pleas′ant

intro

if

if

(95)

LESSON 65

Developing Shorthand Writing Power

636. WORD BEGINNINGS AND ENDINGS

-ward

a

Circum-

b

Under-

c

a. Upward, backward, onward, homeward, outward, likelihood.
b. Circumstance, circumstances, circumstantial, circumnavigate, circumvent, circumference.
c. Understand, understood, undergo, underpaid, undermine, underneath.

Building Transcription Skills

637. BUSINESS VOCABULARY BUILDER

Orient The countries of Asia.

tourist class The most inexpensive travel accommodations.

facilitate To make easy.

Progressive Speed Builder (110-135)

The Progressive Speed Builder in this lesson runs from 110 words a minute to 135 words a minute.

638. PREVIEW

639. We have had, why not, Orient, one of our, few minutes, short, as long, we shall be glad, afford.

640. Daughter, graduation, decided, ports, funds, tourist, let us know.

641. Choice, memorable, perfect, San Francisco, prepared, forwarding, accommodations.

642. Carefully, Pacific, definitely, $100, deposit, of course, passports, procedure.

643. Promptly, rapidly, disappoint, thank you for your, except, in time, Federal, building.

LETTERS

(1 Minute at 110)

639. Dear Mr. Ogden: Though you might not think so from the weather we have had during the past few weeks, summer is only six weeks away and you will/soon be making plans for your vacation.

Why not do something really different and relaxing this summer? Why not take a trip to the Orient on//one of our fine liners?

Devote a few minutes to reading the enclosed booklet, which gives all the details about the trips available and the cost of///each. We have trips that are as short as five weeks and trips that are as long as three months.

We shall be glad to help you plan a trip that you can afford. Sincerely yours, (1)

(1 Minute at 120)

640. Gentlemen: My daughter will complete her nurse's training on June 15, and I have promised to give her a boat trip to any part of the world as a graduation/present. She has decided that she would like to visit the Orient.

We are interested in a trip that will last about three months and that will touch as many//different ports in the Orient as possible.

Our funds, of course, are limited; therefore, we could not consider anything but tourist class.

Would you outline a suggested/// trip for us, indicating the ports that we would visit. Also, please let us know what the cost would be.

We shall be grateful for any help you can give us. Sincerely yours, (2)

(1 Minute at 125)

641. Dear Mr. Ogden: You have made a fine choice in your gift of a trip to the Orient for your daughter, who will complete her nurse's training in June. It will be a memorable/ experience for her and a relaxing vacation for you and your wife.

I believe we have the perfect trip for you. Our liner, "The Pacific," will leave San Francisco//on June 18 and return on September 18. It will stop at most of the important ports in the Orient.

We have prepared a special folder on this trip, and I am///forwarding a copy to you. It explains the types of accommodations that are available on "The Pacific " and the cost of each. Very cordially yours, (3)

(1 Minute at 130)

642. Gentlemen: We have carefully studied the folder that you sent us explaining the types of accommodations that are available on "The Pacific." This trip seems to be/ideal for my daughter; therefore, we have definitely decided to take it. I have checked on the folder the accommodations we should like to have, and I am enclosing my//check for $500 as a deposit.

As this is the first trip of this kind that any of us have taken, we shall, of course, need all the help you can give us in preparing/// for the trip. For example, we assume that we shall need passports. Just what is the procedure? Also, when will it be necessary for me to make final payment? Yours very truly, (4)

(1 Minute at 135)

643. Dear Mr. Ogden: I am glad that the trip we suggested pleases your daughter and that you decided so promptly to take it. Space on this trip is going very rapidly; and if you/ had delayed reaching a decision, we might have had to disappoint you.

Thank you for your deposit of $500. It will not be necessary to make your final payment until//June 10.

We will make all the necessary arrangements except in the matter of your passports. I suggest that you take immediate steps to obtain these, so that you will have them in///time for the trip.

It is a simple matter to obtain passports. Apply for them on the third floor of the Federal Building in San Francisco.

You will be hearing from us soon. Sincerely yours, (5) (620)

Reading and Writing Practice

644.

iq

ac·cept′
calm′ness

par

dis′ap·point′
oc·ca′sions

iq

(126)

645.

intro

iq

par

succ·cess′
like′li·hood
ca·pac′i·ty

bc

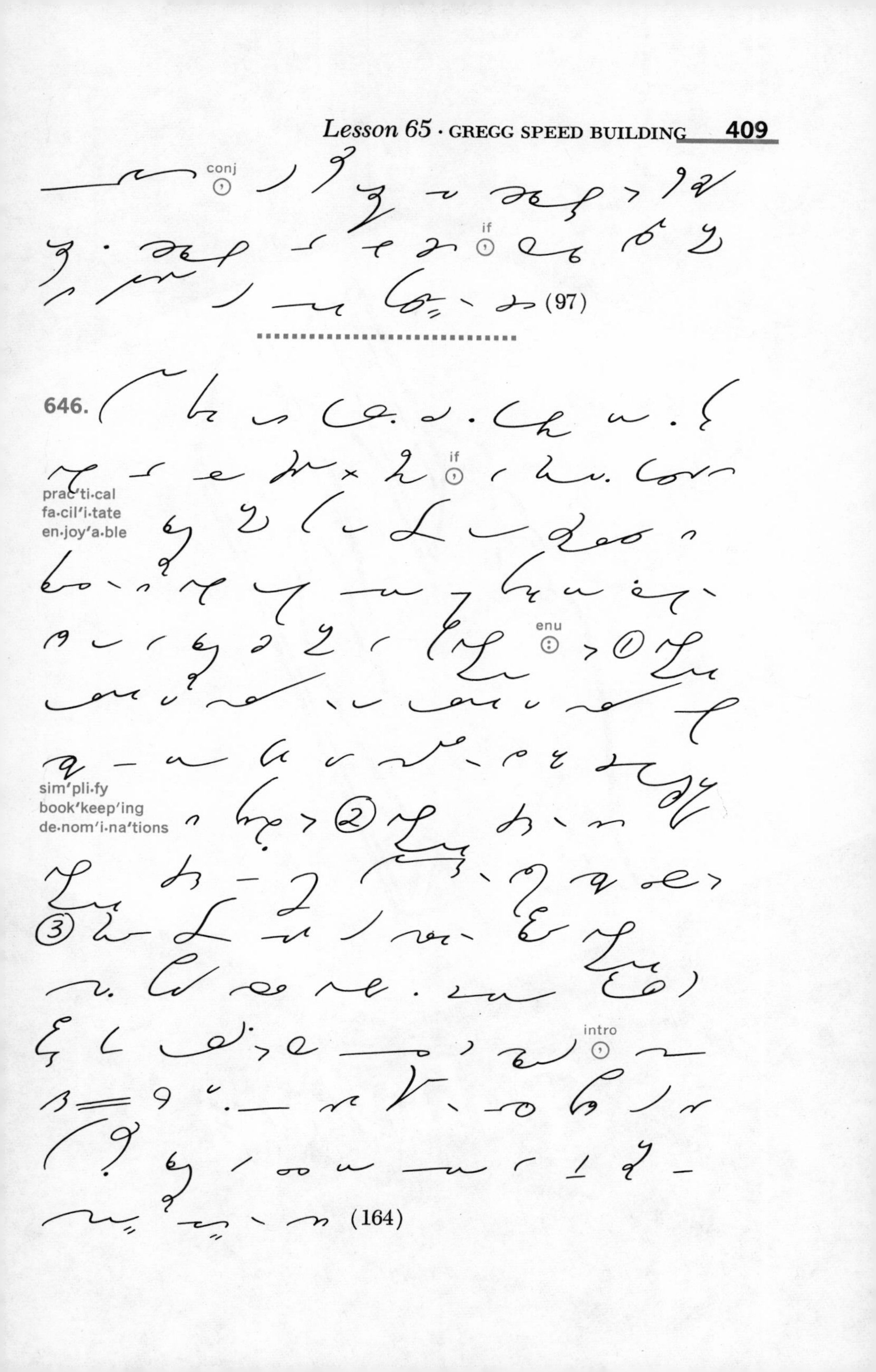

conj

if

(97)

646.

if

prac′ti·cal
fa·cil′i·tate
en·joy′a·ble

enu

sim′pli·fy
book′keep′ing
de·nom′i·na′tions

intro

(164)

CHAPTER 14

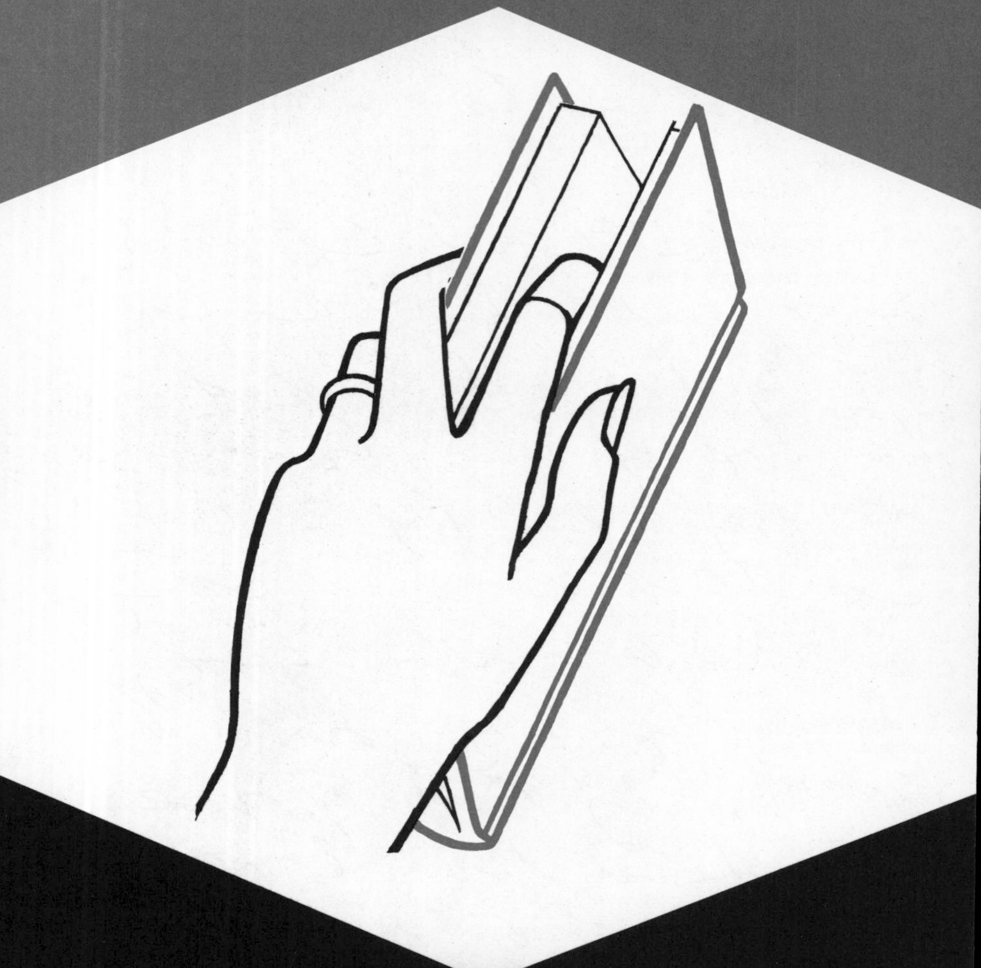

Publishing

Developing Shorthand Writing Power

647. OUTLINE CONSTRUCTION

Ū represented by oo hook. In many words a more facile outline is obtained by writing the *oo* hook for *ū*.

Reduce, introduce, produce, induce, subdue, educate, duty, deduce.

Word endings -uate, -uation, -uity. In writing the endings *-uate, -uation, -uity* we obtain more legible outlines by including the *e* in the diphthong.

-uate

a

-uation, -uity

b

a. Graduate, actuate, punctuate, perpetuate, fluctuate.
b. Graduation, insinuation, punctuation, continuity, ingenuity.

Building Transcription Skills

648. SIMILAR-WORDS DRILL

Raising, rising

raising Lifting (by someone or by something); moving upward.

We are raising our advertising rates in the near future.

rising Lifting itself or oneself; moving upward on its own accord.

Our costs have been rising steadily.

Reading and Writing Practice

649. You Can Do It

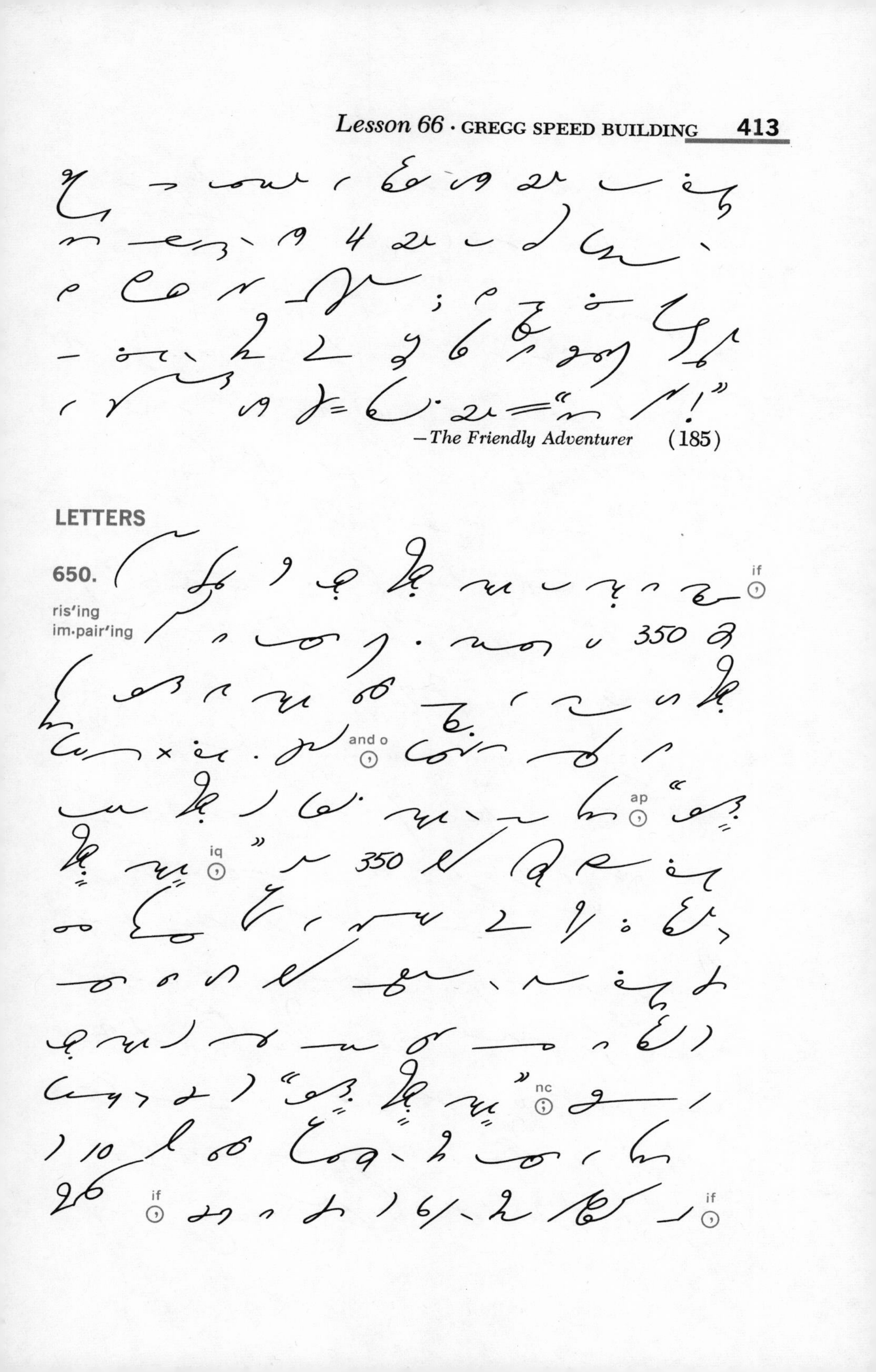

—*The Friendly Adventurer* (185)

LETTERS

650.

ris′ing
im·pair′ing

(163)

651.

choos'ing
grad'u·a'tion

par

sub·scrip'tions
self'-ad·dressed'

ap

and o

(79)

652.

full'-page'
hyphenated before noun

par

par

iph

ad·ver'tise·ment
to'tal
cop'ies

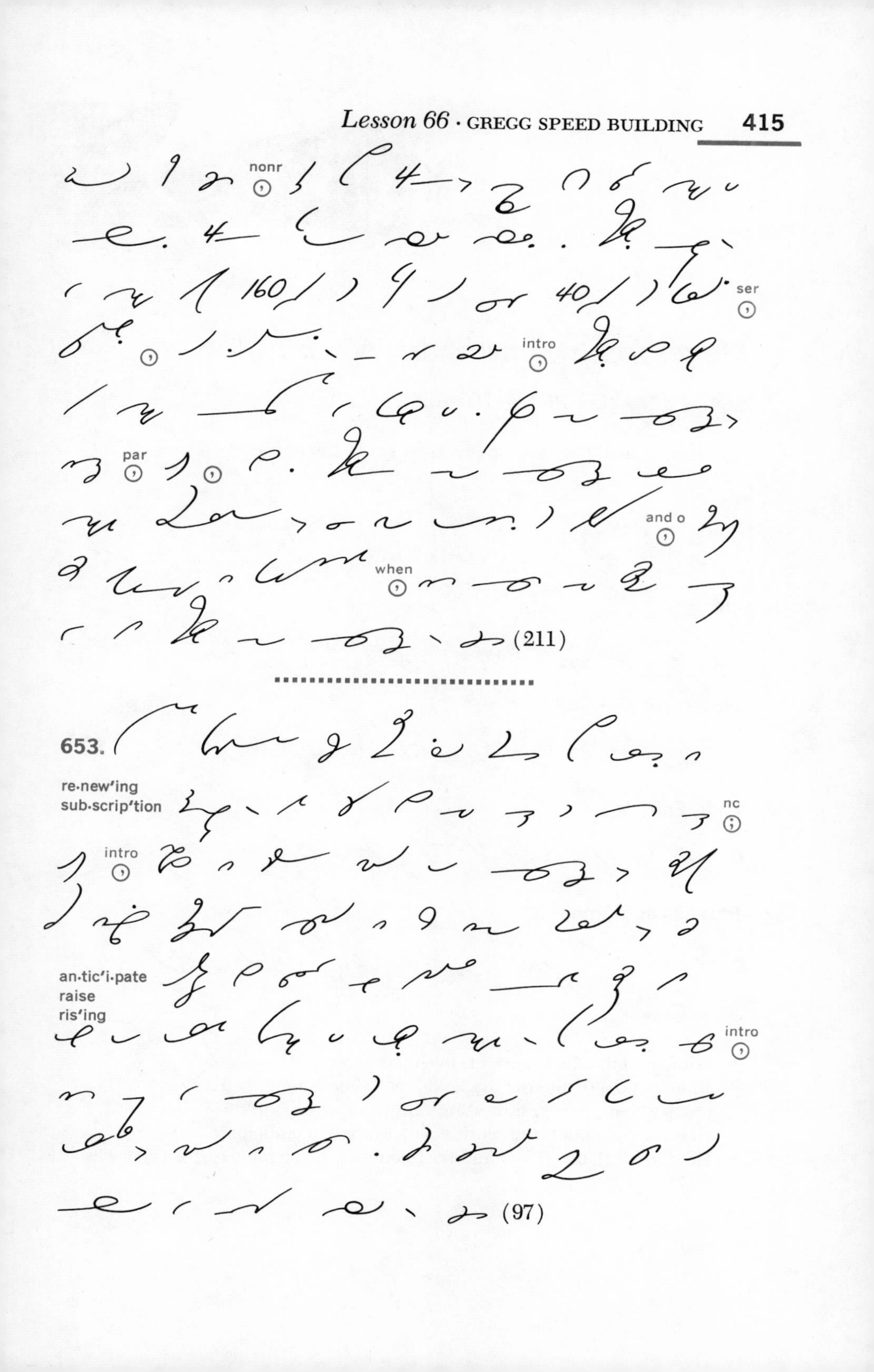

nonr

160 40 ser

intro

par

and o

when

(211)

653.

re·new′ing
sub·scrip′tion

nc

intro

an·tic′i·pate
raise
ris′ing

intro

(97)

FRI.

LESSON 67

Developing Shorthand Writing Power

654. RECALL DRILL — NT BLEND

In this drill you will review the uses of the *nt* blend.

-nt

a

-nd

b

Ind-, Int-

c

End-, Ent-, Ant-

d

Phrases and Amounts

e

a. Print, rental, client, current, event, different, sent.
b. Brand, ground, thousands, kindness, refined, binder, trend.
c. Independent, index, indicating, indicator, intact, into, intellect.
d. Enduringly, endurance, entitle, entrust, entry, anticipate.
e. He doesn't, I don't, I wouldn't, I couldn't, he shouldn't, it isn't, it wasn't, $400.

Building Transcription Skills

655. ACCURACY PRACTICE

In this drill you will practice the joining of the two forms of *s* to other alphabetic strokes of Gregg Shorthand. Remember to give the *s* a *deep* curve and to keep it *small.*

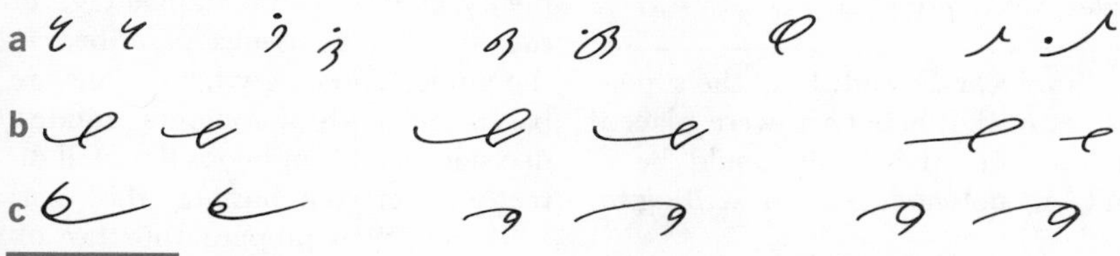

a. Also, was; whose, who is; uses, house; eyes; there is, hands.
b. Race, rest; last, least; mass, next.
c. Sail, sell; keys, guess; case, gas.

Writing Practice

656. PREVIEW

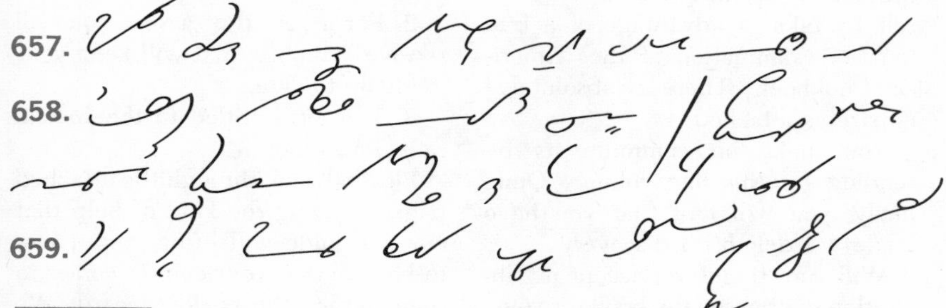

657. Up-to-date, various, music, description, quotation, authorities, many of these, enclosed.
658. Superlatives, dictionary, monotonous, American, judge, absolutely, strings, commitments, volume, discovery, yourself, postal, postage, required.
659. Forward, savings, up-to-the-minute, period, reports, entitled, to be sure, anticipate, demand.

LETTERS

657. Dear Mr. Brown: Enclosed you will find an up-to-date list of books that we have issued on various phases of[1] music. You will notice that for each book we have provided a brief description as well as a quotation or[2] two from authorities who have read the book.

As a music lover you will want many of these books in your music[3] library.

You may use the convenient form that is also enclosed to send us your order. Cordially yours,[4]

---

658. Dear Friend: If all the superlatives in the dictionary were placed end to end, the result would be a dull,[5] monotonous piece of writing to read.

Frankly, a description of the "American Cookbook" calls for the use of[6] a great many superlatives; but if I were to use them, you probably would not believe that this book on cooking[7] could be all that we claim it is.

Therefore, I am asking you to be judge and jury and decide for yourself by taking[8] advantage of a free ten-day examination of the "American Cookbook." There are absolutely[9] no strings attached.

You make no commitments by sending for this fine volume. Quite likely, you will find that you have made[10] a delightful discovery.

Will you, therefore, accept my invitation to examine the book for yourself[11] by sending in the enclosed postal card.

The card is ready for mailing; no postage is required. Sincerely yours,[12]

---

659. Dear Mr. Riley: The publication date of "Smith's Tax Guide" has been moved forward from January 1 to[13] November 1. We have advanced the date so that our friends will have plenty of time to take advantage of the new[14] tax savings described in the guide. These new tax savings are based on up-to-the-minute rulings, decisions, and[15] opinions that will directly affect your business this year.

To help you prepare your tax returns and take advantage[16] of the new savings now available, we have reserved a copy of our tax guide for you. As our special[17] customer you are entitled to have the new guide on the following plan:

1. On November 1 you will receive[18] the new guide, ready for instant reference on tax problems.

2. For a period of a year you will receive[19] reports that will keep your guide up to date.

3. You are entitled to the special rate of $3 a month.

Please[20] look through the attached pages showing the kind of help that our tax guide will bring you. Then, to be sure that your copy[21] comes in time, return the enclosed card. We anticipate a heavy demand for this tax guide. Cordially yours,[22] (440)

Reading and Writing Practice

660.

vol'ume
whole

cont

enu

des'per·ate·ly
ti'tles

intro

conj

intro

(163)

661.

intro

em·ploys'
nurse

and o

up'-to-the-min'ute
hyphenated before noun

il

ap

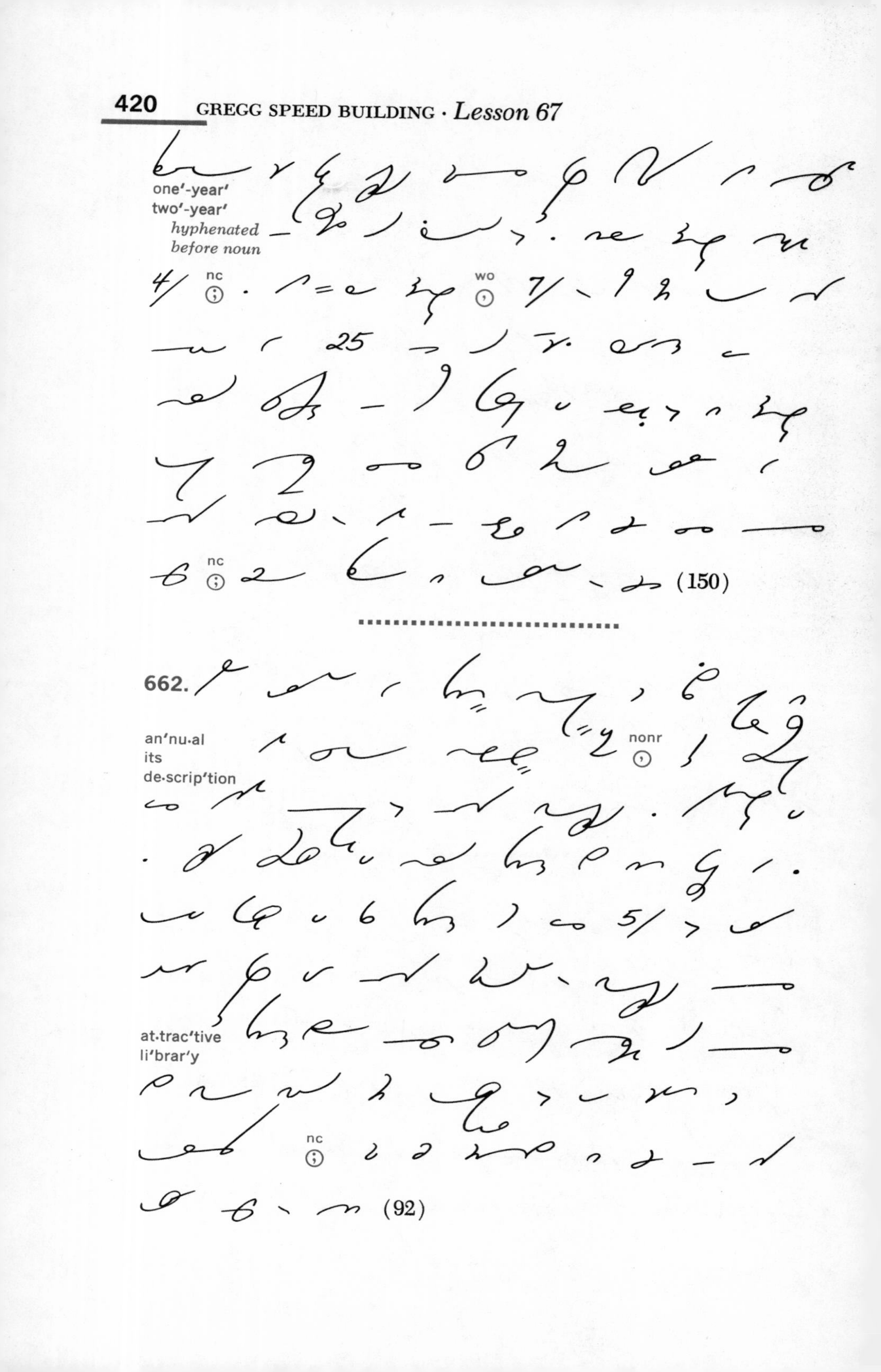

one'-year'
two'-year'
hyphenated before noun

nc
wo

25

nc

(150)

662.

an'nu·al
its
de·scrip'tion

nonr

5/

at·trac'tive
li'brar'y

nc

(92)

Developing Shorthand Writing Power

663. WORD FAMILIES

-mentary

a

-form

b

a. Elementary, supplementary, complimentary, rudimentary.
b. Form, transform, inform, perform, reform, conform, uniform.

664. FREQUENT NAMES

Last Names

a

Men's First Names

b

a. Robertson, Robinson, Rogers, Russell, Ryan, Schmidt, Schneider, Scott.
b. Norman, Nicholas, Oliver, Oscar, Owen, Patrick, Peter.

Building Transcription Skills

665. BUSINESS VOCABULARY BUILDER

patronage Business.

transform Change the shape or character of.

unequivocally Without doubt; sincerely.

Writing Practice

666. PREVIEW

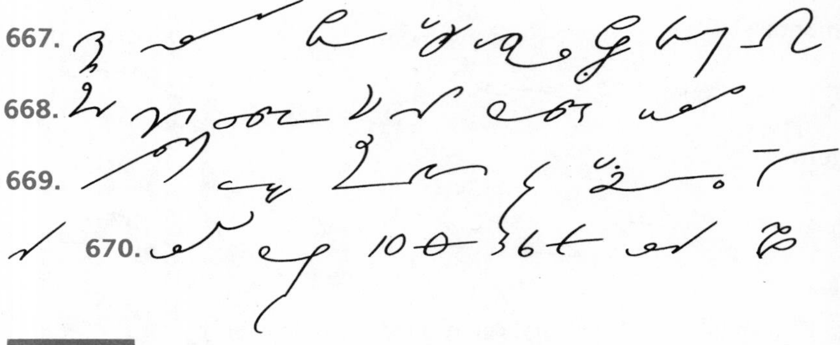

667. Thank you for your, credited, apology, oversight, occasionally, appreciate, patronage, endeavor.
668. Effect, confidential, announcement, further, continue, allowances, already.
669. Detective, almost, several months ago, publishes, overwhelmingly, entertainment, your order.
670. Rendered, eligible, 10 a.m., 6 p.m., renewed, we hope that.

LETTERS

667. Dear Mr. Schmidt: Thank you for your remittance of $2 for the book we shipped you on March 18. It has been1 credited to your account.

Will you please accept our apology for the $2 invoice that was enclosed2 with your March book. This invoice was sent through an oversight on our part; we received your remittance in payment of3 the February book some time before the March book was shipped. We regret the error, but we believe that you will4 understand that mistakes will occasionally happen.

We appreciate your patronage, Mr. Schmidt, and we5 assure you that we shall endeavor to give you the best possible service in the future. Sincerely yours,6

---

668. Mr. Baker: We are planning to increase our prices on a number of books, to take effect on August 1.[7] This information is confidential for the present, however, as no announcement will be made until we[8] revise our price list and have it printed.

After we increased our prices on February 1, we did not wish[9] to increase them any further; but binding and printing costs continue to rise. Consequently, another increase[10] is now necessary.

Also, since February 1 we have been quoting exchange allowances of only[11] 2 per cent of the list price. We have already made this 2 per cent exchange allowance to several important[12] customers in this territory.

I will send you more information on this matter in a few days. John Green[13]

---

669. Dear Mr. Ryan: Are you fond of detective stories? Almost every family has at least one member[14] who is; and the happiest detective-story fans are those who read the Post.

A survey made several months ago[15] by one of the leading research organizations in the world asked: "Which magazine publishes the best[16] mystery stories?" Mystery fans voted so overwhelmingly for the Post that it was almost a crime!

Of course,[17] each issue of the Post contains many other features that are of interest to the entire family.

Why[18] not have the Post delivered to your door each week. For only $5 a year you will receive hundreds of pages[19] of fine entertainment.

The enclosed envelope will bring your order and remittance to me. Sincerely yours,[20]

---

670. Dear Mr. Russell: As a newcomer to Greenfield you will be interested in the services rendered by[21] our library. Any person whose home or business is in Greenfield is eligible to use the library[22] without charge.

The library is open on Mondays and Wednesdays from 1 p.m. to 9 p.m.; on Tuesdays, Thursdays,[23] Fridays, and Saturdays from 10 a.m. to 6 p.m.

Books are issued for two weeks and may be renewed for[24] another two weeks.

We hope that you will make use of our library and will let us know whenever we can render[25] some special service. Remember that the library is here to serve your reading needs. Very cordially yours,[26] (520)

Reading and Writing Practice

671.

best'-sell'ing *hyphenated before noun*

if

if

au'to·mat'i·cal·ly
mere'ly

nc

if

isq

iq

month's
sub·scrip'tion

(137)

672.

if

fas'ci·na'tion
week's
Man's

iq

week's
un'e·quiv'o·cal·ly

if

IBM

conj (116)

673. intro enu ser 25, (80)

674. a·chieve' sten'cils (71)

Developing Shorthand Writing Power

675. FREQUENT PHRASES

Many

a

Some

b

a. Many things, many days, many times, many of them, too many.
b. Some time, some time ago, some years ago, some of the, some of our.

676. GEOGRAPHICAL EXPRESSIONS

-mont

a

States

b

Foreign Cities

c

a. Oakmont, Edgemont, Piedmont, Dumont.
b. Alaska, Florida, Kansas, Mississippi, New York, Rhode Island, New Jersey.
c. London, Bristol, Manchester, Plymouth, Edinburgh.

Building Transcription Skills

677. BUSINESS VOCABULARY BUILDER

transpiring Happening; occurring.

impartially Without favoring one side or another; with an open mind.

cogent Compelling; convincing.

Writing Practice

678. PREVIEW

679.

680.

681.

679. Easily, overlook, away, transpiring, regularly, pertinent, impartially, presented.
680. Cogent, succeed, among the, financial, $10,000, $20,000, successful, associations, few dollars, income.
681. Years ago, annual, inventions, creating, commerce, one of them, never.

LETTERS

679. Dear Mr. Edgemont: You are going to be very busy just before you leave on your well-earned vacation, and[1] you could easily overlook to arrange to have the Times mailed to you while you are away. To avoid finding[2] yourself without your favorite newspaper, why not make immediate use of the form that is enclosed.

So much[3] is transpiring in the world today that an important event may take place while you are on your vacation. With[4] the Times reaching you regularly, you will have all pertinent facts impartially presented to you at all[5] times.

Fill in the enclosed form, and mail it in the self-addressed envelope that is also enclosed. Cordially yours,[6]

680. Dear Mr. Cooper: One cogent reason why some men succeed faster than others is that they have more information on[7] which to base their decisions. You will find among the men who succeed, many who read the Financial Daily. For[8] example, there are on our lists several men who make from $10,000 to $20,000 a[9] year. It is quite likely that these men would be successful without the Financial Daily, but many of them declare[10] that it has helped them succeed.

The Financial Daily is more than a newspaper; it is the only business[11] paper served by all four big press associations.

You may have a trial subscription for three months for only[12] $6. Just send us a note with your name and address and enclose your check for $6.

Don't delay. A few dollars[13] spent for the Financial Daily now may mean a considerable increase in your income. Sincerely yours,[14]

681. Dear Mr. Brady: A few years ago an annual income of $5,000 was a reasonable[15] goal for a young man. Today, with increased taxes and higher living costs, a person needs $10,000 to[16] buy what $5,000 used to buy.

This increase in salary requirements is only one of many changes taking[17] place in America. New inventions, new industries, and new ways of doing business are creating new[18] opportunities for young men who want to increase their incomes.

The Commerce Journal tells you about these opportunities.[19] Because the Commerce Journal is issued every day, our readers are able to seize quickly new[20] opportunities to win advancement or earn more money. The Commerce Journal is a paper for those men who[21] will be the leaders of tomorrow. Will you be one of them?

Fill out the enclosed blank, and enter your order for[22] a trial subscription today. You will be making a move that you will never regret. Very cordially yours,[23] (460)

Reading and Writing Practice

682.

judg'ments
be·lieve'
wel'come

intro

week'-af'ter-week'
hyphenated before noun

three'-month' *hyphenated before noun*

intro ,

par , ,

intro ,

il ;

, 18 par , ,

3 intro ,

(180)

683. 13

ben'e·fit'ed al·read'y sub·scrib'er

par , ,

intro ,

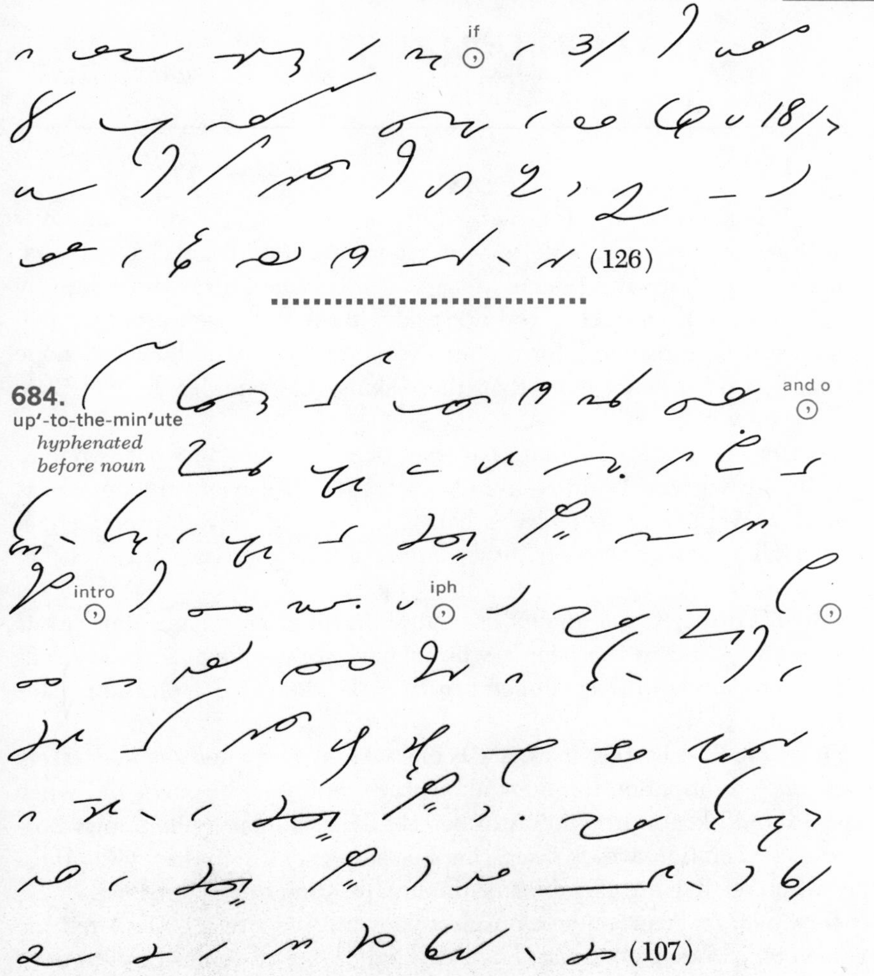

Many young people who have special talents or interest in drama, music, art, journalism, politics, and so on, have found that secretarial training works almost like magic in gaining entrance to these areas of work.—John Robert Gregg

SECRETARIAL TIP

Traits

When you apply for that all-important first job, your employer will expect you to be able to write shorthand rapidly, to have a command of spelling and punctuation, and to be able to transcribe rapidly and accurately. In fact, if you don't have these skills, you probably will not even be considered for the job. Your employer will, however, hope that you have much more than these skills. As examples, he will hope that you will be:

Tactful. Tact is a trait that enables a person to handle what is potentially a disagreeable situation in a way that will leave everyone happy. A stenographer or secretary is called upon every day to exercise tact in dealing with customers, other employees, executives, and even her own boss!

Loyal. Loyalty is the quality of being faithful to an organization, to its objectives, and to the people who manage it. The loyal secretary sells her company and does all she can to make the office a pleasant place in which to work.

Discreet. The discreet secretary is one who knows when she may safely disclose information to others about her employer's business and when she should keep information to herself. The secretary who knows how to use discretion avoids discussing her employer's activities with others —whether they are members of the organization or are outsiders.

Dependable. A prominent businessman said recently, "Once I tell my secretary to do something, I can depend on her to do it – and to do it right. I wish I could say this about all my employees; my job would be far simpler. That girl will go far in our organization." Will your employer be able to say the same about you?

Poised. Anyone can maintain poise when things are running smoothly. The real measure of a person's poise, however, is his conduct under trying and difficult situations, which arise all too frequently in the business office. The secretary who can remain calm when everything seems to go wrong is worth her weight in gold!

LESSON 70

Developing Shorthand Writing Power

685. WORD BEGINNINGS AND ENDINGS

Electric-, Electr-

a

Enter-, Entr-

b

-tial, -cial

c

a. Electrical, electrician, electricity, electric wire, electric fan, electric light.
b. Entering, entertain, entertainment, enterprise, entrance, entrances.
c. Special, essential, crucial, partial, impartial, credential, substantially, initially.

Building Transcription Skills

686. BUSINESS VOCABULARY BUILDER

avidly Eagerly; keenly.

indifferent Not easily interested or moved; neither good nor bad.

concept Idea.

Progressive Speed Builder (110-135)

The letters in this Progressive Speed Builder range in speed from 110 to 135 words a minute.

687. PREVIEW

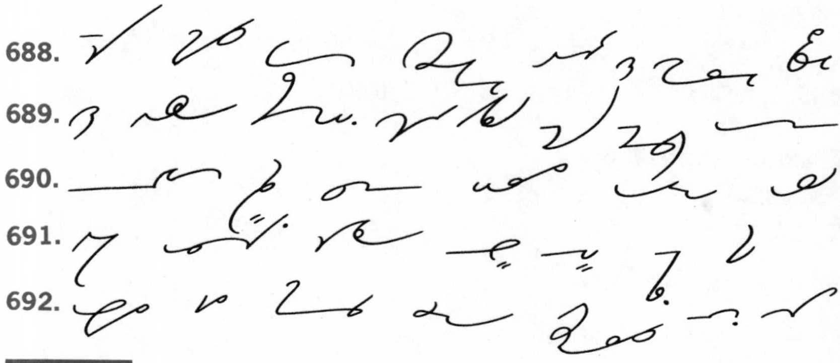

688. Interested, up to date, progress, developments, throughout the, yourself, compliments, expires.
689. Thank you for, trial, ever-growing, confident, depend, informed, informative, welcome.
690. Months ago, February, acknowledgment, already, longer, rather.
691. Trouble, regarding, stencil, Massachusetts, Missouri, enjoying, further.
692. Rapidly, shortly, up-to-the-minute, single, to facilitate, enclosing, continue.

LETTERS

(1 Minute at 110)

688. Dear Miss May: As you are a person who is interested in keeping up to date on current events, you will like our weekly magazine, Progress. Progress/will inform you of the latest developments throughout the world.

We should like you to see for yourself the type of reporting that Progress brings you. We are,//therefore, enclosing a copy of the January 12 issue. Please accept it with our compliments. If you are convinced that it is your type of magazine,///take advantage of our offer of 30 issues for only $4. You will have to act soon, as this offer expires in ten days. Sincerely yours, (1)

(1 Minute at 120)

689. Dear Miss May: Thank you for accepting our special offer of a trial subscription to Progress at the rate of $4 for 30 issues. Thank you, also, for your check./We are delighted to add your name to our ever-growing list of readers. We are confident that you will depend on Progress to keep informed on the events of the//world; you will look forward avidly to the arrival of each issue.

We are planning many new features during the coming year that will make Progress even more///interesting and informative. Watch for these features, and let us know how you like them.

Once again, welcome to our growing family of Progress readers. Sincerely yours, (2)

(1 Minute at 125)

690. Gentlemen: About two months ago I mailed you my check for a trial subscription of 30 issues of your magazine, Progress. I asked that my subscription begin with the/February 2 issue. It is now April 1, and I have not yet received any issues. Nor have I received an acknowledgment of my order, although my check has already//cleared through the bank. Would you be good enough to look into this matter immediately.

Please start my subscription with the April 15 issue, as the back issues will///no longer be of value or interest to me.

Also, please send the magazine to the address given in this letterhead rather than to my home. Very sincerely yours, (3)

(1 Minute at 130)

691. Dear Miss May: We are very sorry that you had to take the time and trouble to write your letter of April 1 regarding the delay in receiving your copies of Progress.

We/investigated the matter immediately and found that an error had been made in the stencil of your name and address. The clerk had typed your address as Springfield, Massachusetts,//instead of Springfield, Missouri. We have made a new stencil and, as you requested, will mail your copies to your business address rather than to your home address. Your subscription///will begin with the April 15 issue.

So that you may begin enjoying Progress without further delay, we are enclosing a copy of the April 8 issue. Sincerely yours, (4)

(1 Minute at 135)

692. Dear Miss May: Time passes rapidly. It seems only yesterday that we received your order for a trial subscription to Progress. Yet, your subscription will expire shortly — in one more month, /in fact.

We are sure that you have come to depend on Progress to bring you accurate, up-to-the-minute information on the events of the world. We are confident that you would not want// to miss a single issue. That is why we are taking this opportunity to remind you of the expiration date of your subscription and to facilitate your renewal so///that there will be no break in your subscription.

We are enclosing a card on which you need only check whether you would like your subscription to continue for one year or for two years. Sincerely yours, (5) (620)

Reading and Writing Practice

693. nonr

ac·cept'
com'pli·ments
guid'ance

if

15

99,

con'cept

12

5/

intro

(123)

694. ap

past
E·lec'tri·cal

par

bc

ser

and o ⓘ

self'-ad·dressed'
ar'ti·cles

up to date
no noun,
no hyphen

intro ⓘ

(152)

695.

its
sub·scrip'tion

long'-term'
hyphenated
before noun

conj ⓘ

nc ⓘ

(124)

CHAPTER 15

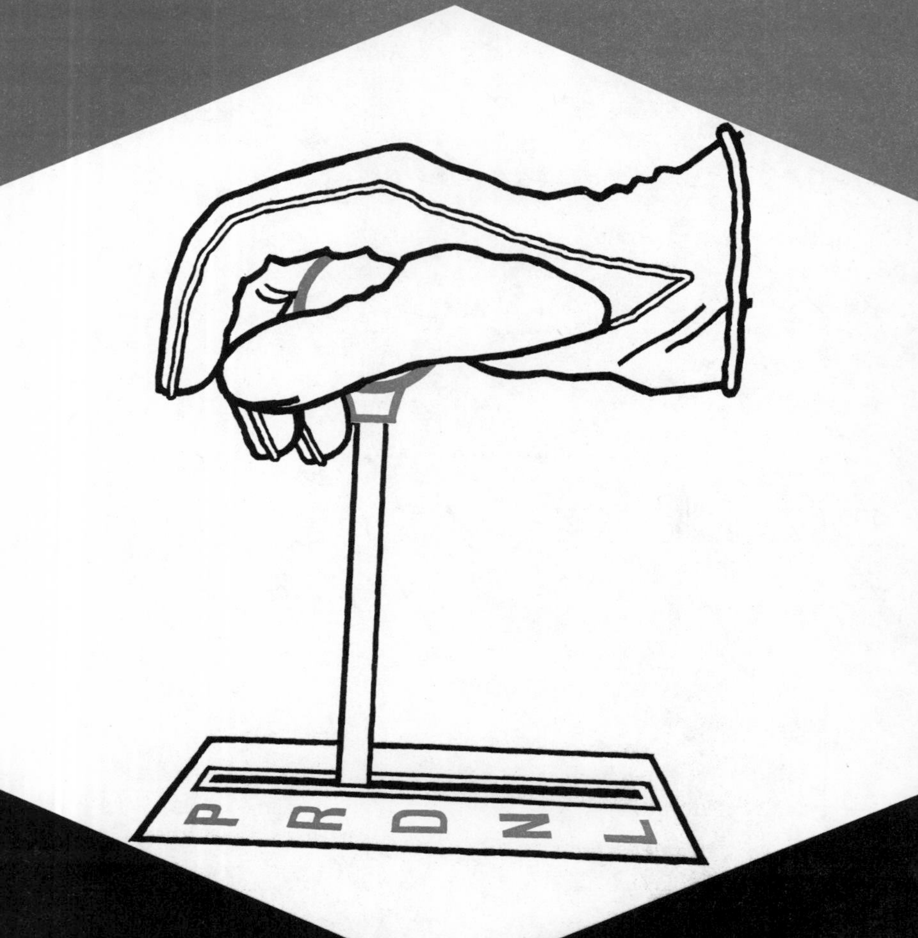

Automobiles

Developing Shorthand Writing Power

696. OUTLINE CONSTRUCTION

Unaccented diphthong u omitted before r and l. Omitting the diphthong *u* before *r* and *l* results in fluent outlines for many useful words.

a. Accurate, accuracy, vocabulary, ridiculous, popular.
b. Singular, inaugurate, stimulant, pendulum.

Building Transcription Skills

697. SIMILAR-WORDS DRILL

Excess, access

excess That which exceeds or goes beyond; more than the usual amount.

You must pay 20 cents a pound for all baggage in excess of 44 pounds.

access Approach; admission.

We have access to the reference room in the library on Mondays and Fridays.

Reading and Writing Practice

698. The Land of Inventions

"My own boyhood

When I first

(354)

LETTERS

699.

cor'dial
spa'cious

and o

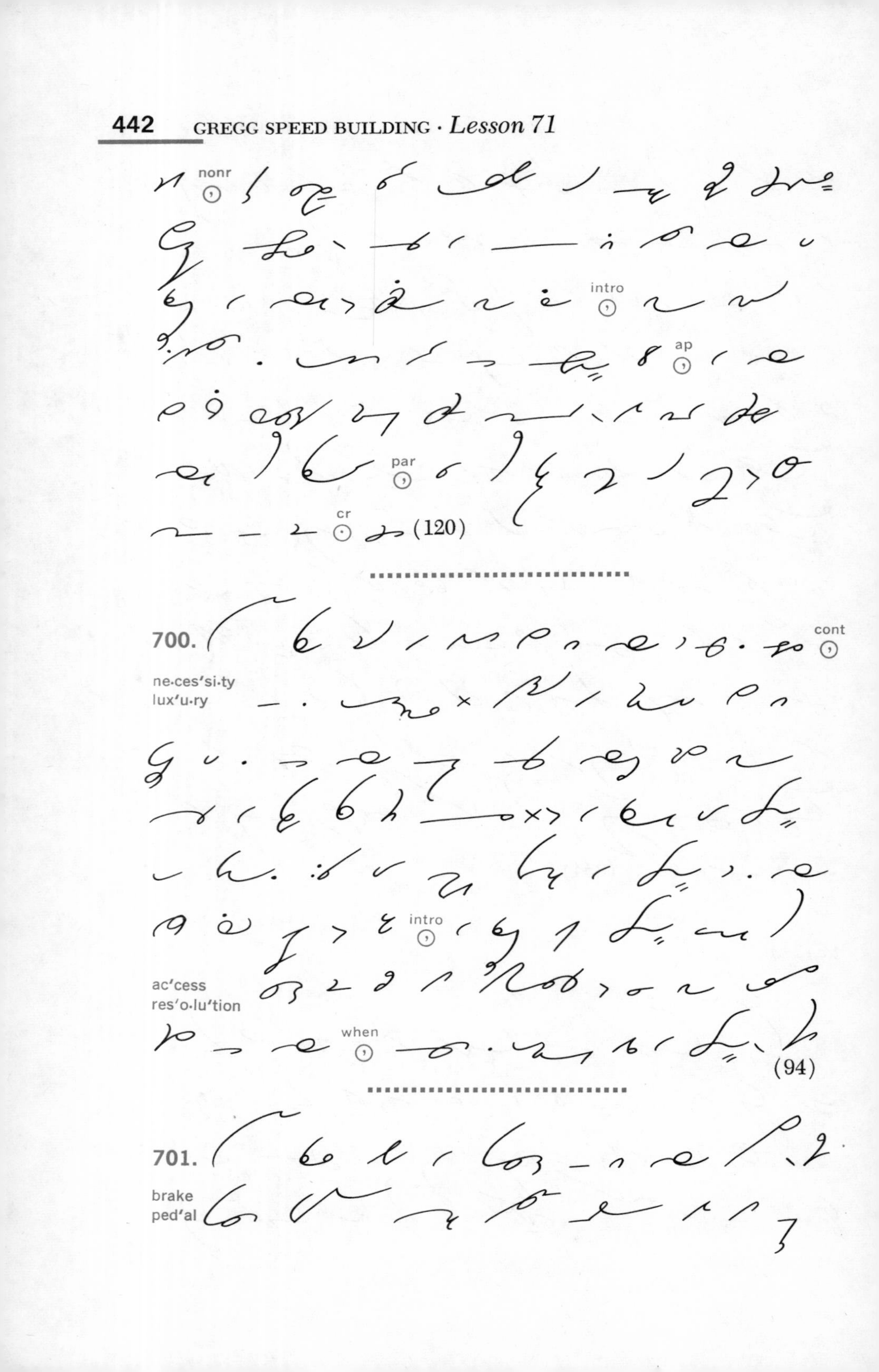

nonr

intro

ap

par

cr

(120)

700.

ne·ces′si·ty
lux′u·ry

cont

intro

ac′cess
res′o·lu′tion

when

(94)

701.

brake
ped′al

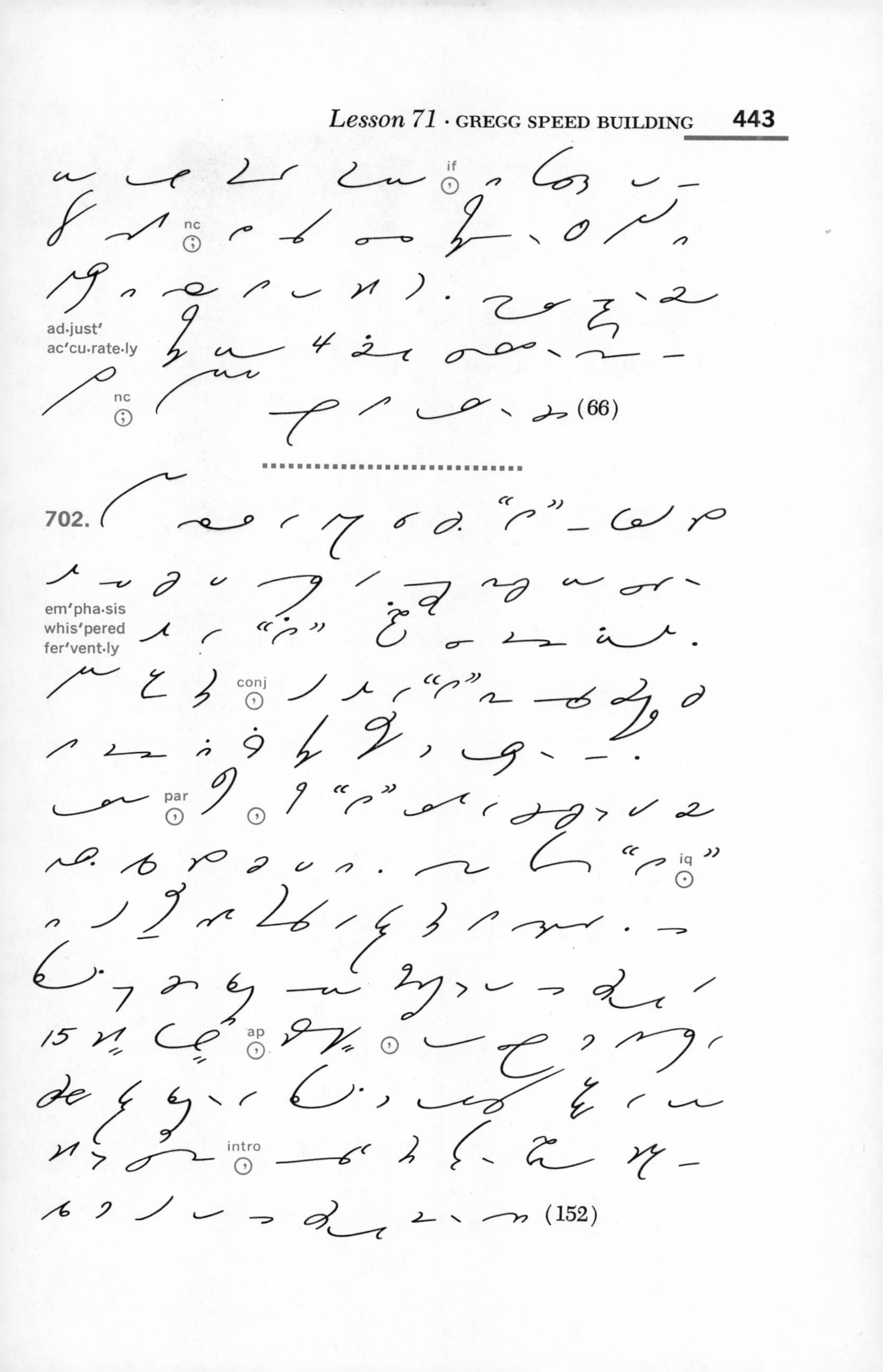

if

nc

ad·just'
ac'cu·rate·ly

nc

(66)

702.

em'pha·sis
whis'pered
fer'vent·ly

conj

par

iq

15

ap

intro

(152)

LESSON 72

Developing Shorthand Writing Power

703. RECALL DRILL — B

In this drill you will review the various uses of the alphabetic stroke *b*.

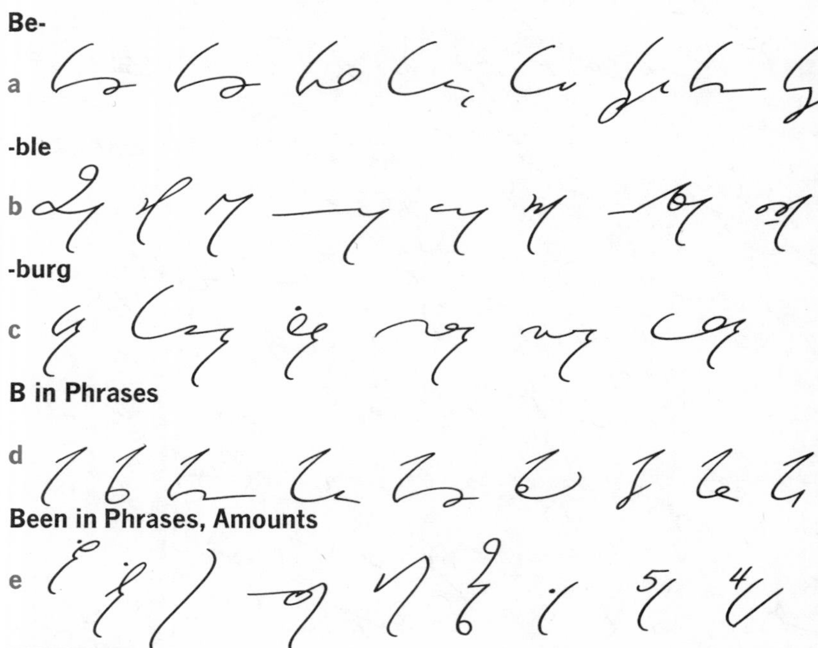

a. Begin, began, betray, belongings, below, besides, become, benefit.
b. Available, stable, trouble, memorable, honorable, suitable, undesirable, equitable.
c. Pittsburgh, Bloomsburg, Harrisburg, Greensburg, Warrensburg, Plattsburg.
d. To be, to be able, to become, to belong, to begin, to build, to beat, to bring, to brush.
e. Has been, it has been, have been, might have been, should have been, I have not been able, a billion, five billion, four billion dollars.

Building Transcription Skills

704. ACCURACY PRACTICE

In this drill you will practice additional joinings of the two forms of *s*.

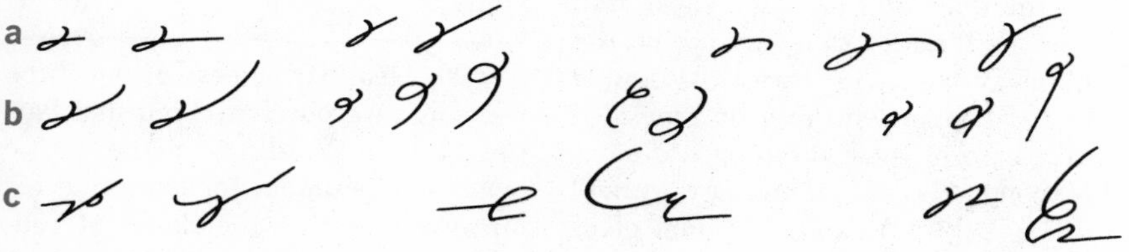

a. Seen, seem; set, said; seek, sag, sadden.
b. Sent, seemed; sees, safe, save; sip; face; session, sash, siege.
c. Institute, resident; mason, blossom; citizen, baptism.

Writing Practice

705. PREVIEW

706. 707. 708. 709.

706. Next time, highway, truth, any other, maintenance, why not, various, demonstrate.
707. Mileage, equipment, powerful, painstaking, craftsmen, superior, showrooms, hauling.
708. Years ago, experiment, determine, ourselves, substantiated, performance, dependability, wisest.

709. Announcement, terminated, termination, regarding, continue, embody, resulting.

LETTERS

706. Dear Mr. Jones: If you count the number of National Trucks that you see the next time you are on the highway, you will learn this[1] simple truth: People who rely on trucks to take care of their shipping use more National Trucks than any other[2] make. Why? Because National gives them lower operating and maintenance costs.

Why not see your National dealer[3] and let him show you the various models we make. Let him demonstrate for you the model that will best meet[4] your own needs.

Make it a point to see him. He will be happy to show you our complete line of trucks. Sincerely yours,[5]

---

707. Dear Mr. King: Are you interested in saving money on the maintenance of your company truck? Would you[6] like to get a full measure of trucking mileage from your equipment?

Of course you would. Then get a powerful new[7] Wilson Truck, built by the world's most painstaking truck craftsmen.

All over the country and on all kinds of work, Wilson[8] Trucks are recognized as superior in pulling power and in operating economy. Stop at[9] one of our showrooms now and see the proof. Check into the facts and figures that demonstrate the economy of[10] Wilson Trucks for your type of hauling.

Our showrooms are open every weekday from nine to five. Cordially yours,[11]

---

708. Dear Mr. Trees: About three years ago we purchased our first Parsons Truck. We did it in the nature of an[12] experiment to determine for ourselves whether the claims of your salesman would be substantiated by performance.[13]

We are happy to say that we are completely convinced of the economy and dependability[14] of the Parsons Truck. Every one of our old trucks has now been replaced with a Parsons, and we feel that this is[15] one of the wisest moves we have ever made.

We can recommend your trucks without reservation. Yours sincerely,[16]

---

709. Dear Mr. Grace: As an owner of a Nelson Truck, you have no doubt been interested in our announcement in[17] the local papers: "We have terminated our working agreement with the Nelson Truck Company." This termination[18] is to take place on June 3. The announcement may have brought some questions to your mind regarding the[19] servicing of the truck that you bought from us.

You may rest assured that we will continue to take care of your truck[20] whenever it needs attention. We have a sufficiently large supply of spare parts to last many years.

On July[21] 20 we plan to market

our own truck, which will embody improvements resulting from our twenty years'[22] experience. When our new truck is ready, you will receive complete information about it. Cordially yours,[23] (460)

Reading and Writing Practice

710.

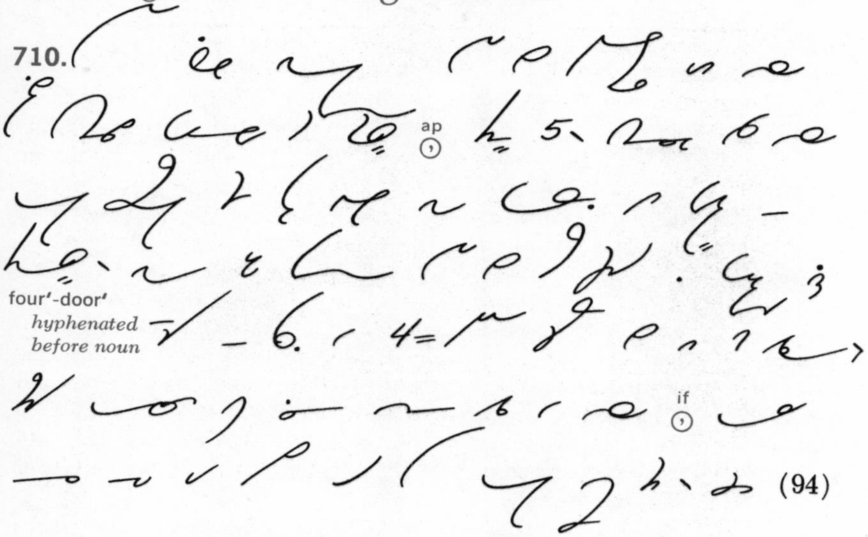

(94)

711.

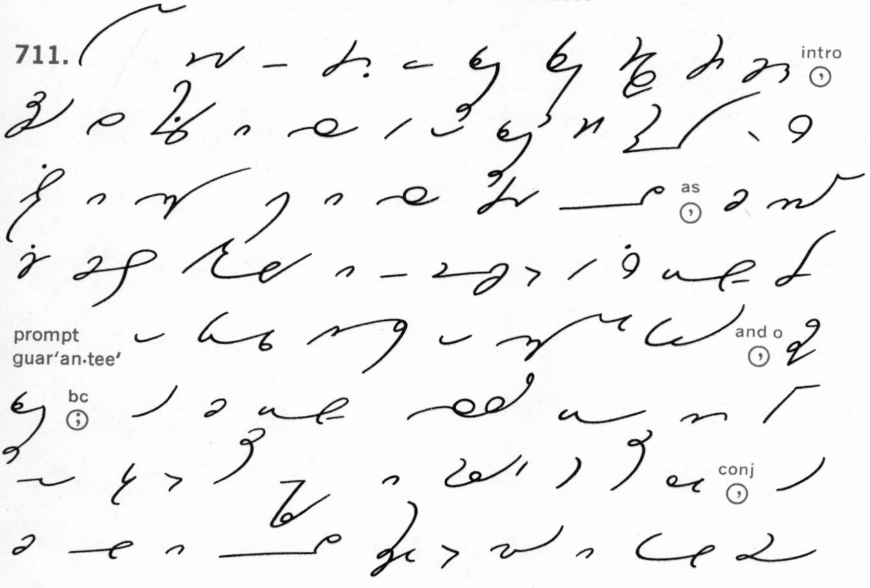

(98)

712.

au'to·mo·biles
mod'els

par

when

intro

bc

fur'ther
de·ci'sion

if

(133)

713.

its
fam'i·lies
fam'i·ly's

intro

up'-to-the-min'ute
hyphenated before noun

(58)

LESSON 73

Developing Shorthand Writing Power

714. WORD FAMILIES

-bility

a

Rea-

b

a. Durability, ability, inability, reliability, possibility, stability.
b. Reassure, reappear, reassert, reappraise, readmit, reapply.

715. FREQUENT NAMES

Last Names

a

Women's First Names

b

a. Shaw, Shea, Simpson, Snyder, Stevens, Stewart, Sullivan, Taylor.
b. Rosalie, Ruth, Sarah, Sophia, Susan, Sylvia, Victoria.

Building Transcription Skills

716. BUSINESS VOCABULARY BUILDER

minimize To keep to the smallest part possible.

durability The quality of lasting, of not wearing out.

reassuring Comforting; restoring confidence to.

Writing Practice

717. PREVIEW

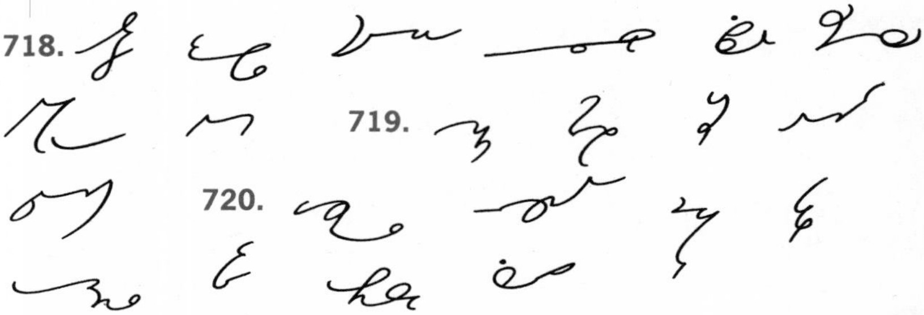

718. Anticipate, slippery, furthermore, minimize, hazards, safeguard, durability, traction.
719. Cautious, upkeep, official, throughout the, attractive.
720. Occasionally, encounter, snobbish, possession, luxury, support, reassurance, heartily.

LETTERS

718. Gentlemen: Alert businessmen anticipate emergencies. It is not surprising, therefore, that so many[1] business executives carry tire chains in their cars ready for use when roads are slippery.

Furthermore, alert executives[2] insist that the drivers of company cars and trucks use chains to minimize the hazards of winter[3] driving and to safeguard lives and shipments.

Taylor Tire Chains for cars, trucks, and busses offer the best value[4] in safety and durability. The special metal used in the chains adds extra miles of service. The unique[5] design of the chains gives better traction to keep vehicles moving safely on slippery roads.

In the interest[6] of safety, make sure that you have Taylor Tire Chains for every car and truck used in your business. Cordially yours,[7]

---

719. Dear Mr. Shaw: Every cautious man will ask himself the following questions before he buys a new car:

1.[8] Does it sell for a reasonable price?

2. Will it give good gasoline mileage?

3. Will the upkeep be low?

4.[9] Will the trade-in value always be high?

If you purchase a Dodge, the answer to all these questions is Yes.[10] Our car is the lowest-priced car in its field. Official tests show that it gives more miles on each gallon of gas than[11] any other car in its price field. The car is so well built that repair costs throughout the years are very small.[12] A Dodge keeps its value year after year, thus bringing attractive trade-in allowances.

We shall be glad[13] to have you visit us so that we may give you an opportunity to drive the new Dodge. You will then[14] be able to judge for yourself whether the Dodge is a car that you would be happy to own. Cordially yours,[15]

---

720. Dear Mr. Stevens: Occasionally we encounter a man who hesitates to buy a Johnson Car lest his[16] friends think him snobbish.

For such people we have reassuring news. The experience of Johnson owners indicates[17] that such fears are groundless. True, the world has long recognized the Johnson Car as a fine possession. Most people[18] understand, however, that quality is not a luxury.

The facts in support of the practicality[19] of our new car are so convincing that the mere recital of a few should be sufficient reassurance for[20] even the most hesitant buyer.

Take the matter of cost. There are eight other car manufacturers who have models[21] priced above the lowest priced Johnson. Thousands of motorists on the road actually paid more for their cars than[22] the man who owns the compact Johnson.

If you are ready for a new car, come in and place your order for a Johnson.[23] You will never make a more sensible purchase – and your friends and neighbors will heartily approve. Yours sincerely,[24] (480)

Reading and Writing Practice

721.

if

ap

iq

ser

traf'fic
prej'u·diced

intro par (131)

722.

rent'al
cap'i·tal

ser

enu

ser

theft
col·li'sion

par

intro

(111)

723.

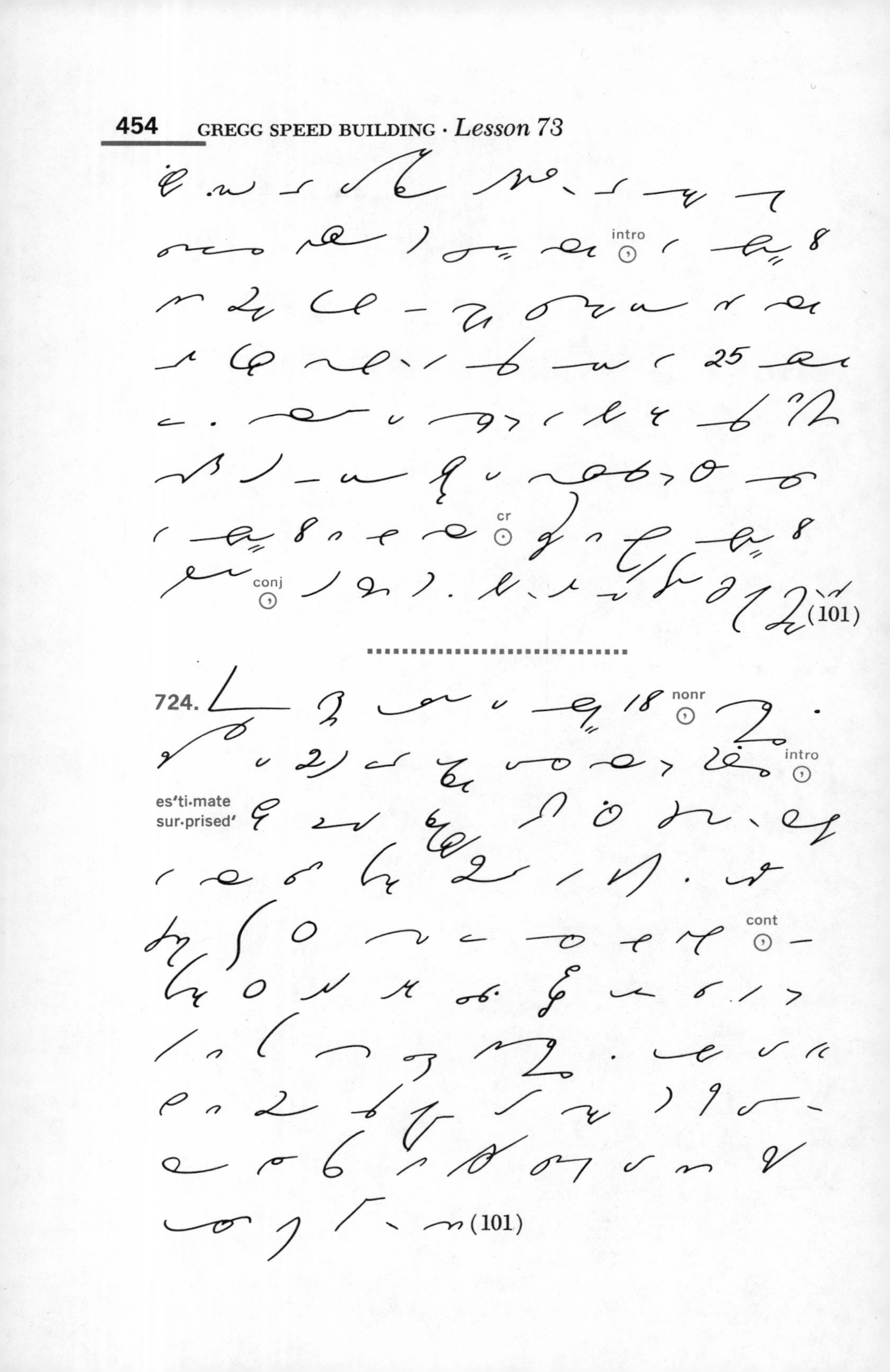

intro

25

cr

conj

(101)

724.

18

nonr

intro

es'ti·mate
sur·prised'

cont

(101)

LESSON 74

Developing Shorthand Writing Power

725. FREQUENT PHRASES

Word Modified in Phrases

a

A Omitted

b

a. Of course, as soon as, as soon as possible, to do, let us, to us, your order, I hope, we hope.
b. For a long time, for a few days, for a day or two, for a few moments, at a time.

726. GEOGRAPHICAL EXPRESSIONS

(United States Cities in Order of Population)

a

b

a. New York, Chicago, Los Angeles, Philadelphia, Detroit, Baltimore.
b. Houston, Cleveland, Washington, St. Louis, Milwaukee, San Francisco, Boston.

Building Transcription Skills

727. BUSINESS VOCABULARY BUILDER

convene To meet.

wholly Entirely.

maneuver To handle; to manage.

Writing Practice

728. PREVIEW

729.

730.

731.

732.

729. Board, automobile, convene, let us know, program, social.
730. Provided, prompt, expiration, recording, issuance, quotation.
731. Several days ago, few moments, membership, handbook, growth, motorists.
732. Weeks ago, renewal, has been, disabled, 10 per cent, accessories.

LETTERS

729. Dear Mr. Collins: The next regular meeting of the Board of Directors of the Automobile Club will convene[1] at the Hotel Smith in Chicago on June 7. We are sending you this notice well in advance so that[2] you and your staff can make plans to attend. Please let us know how many will attend from your office so that we may[3] make the proper hotel reservations.

There will be a long program of business, but we are making arrangements[4] for a number of social events, too. After all, all work and no play would make Jack a dull boy! Sincerely yours,[5]

730. Dear Member: Did you know that members of the Auto Club of St. Louis are provided with a fine automobile[6] insurance service?

Personal attention to all insurance problems and a prompt and friendly claim service[7] are available to you 24 hours a day.

If you will indicate the expiration date of your present[8] insurance on the enclosed card and mail it to us for recording, we will write you about the issuance of[9] a policy at that time.

For an immediate quotation, phone 316-8700. Yours sincerely,[10]

---

731. Dear Mr. West: Your membership in the Auto Club expired several days ago. It will take you only a[11] few moments to fill out and return the enclosed card renewing your membership. Why not do it now.

It is with[12] particular pride that we enclose your copy of our new handbook, which contains an outline of our many[13] services. We hope that you will find time to read about the constantly expanding benefits that you will derive[14] from membership in the Auto Club.

One of the main reasons for the growth of our organization is the fact[15] that our members have interested other motorists in the advantages of membership. Yours sincerely,[16]

---

732. Dear Mr. Parker: A few weeks ago we wrote you that on July 31 your membership in the Auto[17] Club would expire. If we do not receive your renewal on or before that date, you will have to pay an additional[18] fee of $5, or a total of $20, to renew your membership. This has been our[19] policy for a long time.

Even more important, after July 31 you will lose the following benefits:[20]

1. Free service when your car is disabled.
2. Access to our dependable Travel Department.
3. Our[21] special insurance policy.
4. The 10 per cent discount on gasoline and automobile accessories.[22]

If you have not already done so, please send your $15 now so that you may continue your membership[23] in good standing.

We are confident that it is not your intention to let your membership lapse. Cordially yours,[24] (480)

Reading and Writing Practice

733.

cur'rent·ly
thou'sands

iq

if

enu

col·li'sion
pur'chase

bc

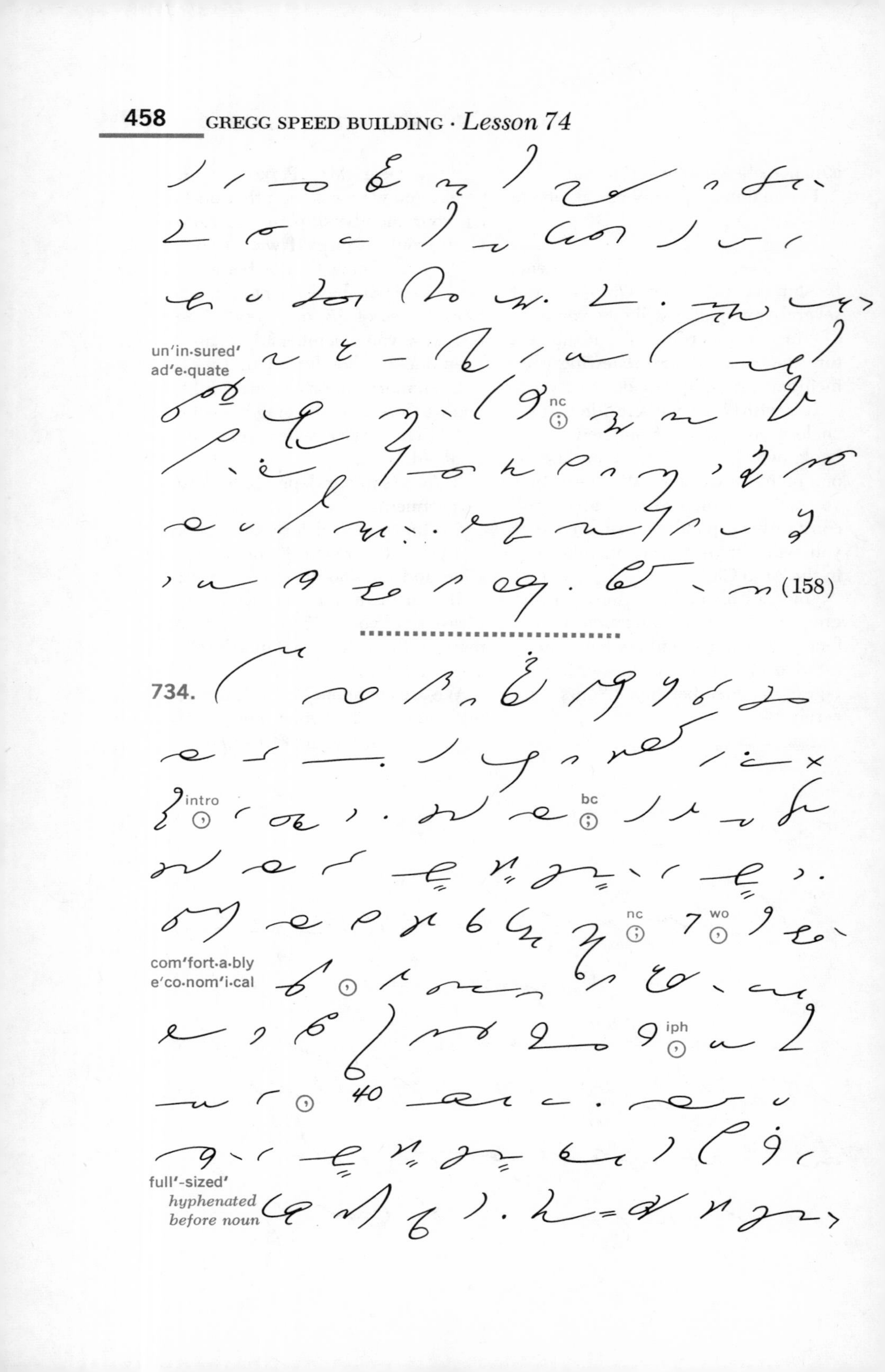

un′in·sured′
ad′e·quate

nc

(158)

734.

intro

bc

nc

wo

com′fort·a·bly
e′co·nom′i·cal

iph

40

full′-sized′
hyphenated before noun

intro

if

(159)

735.

par

rough'est

wheels

(107)

Letter of Application

One good way to obtain an interview for that first job, which is no doubt on your mind now that your stenographic training is almost complete, is to write an effective letter of application to the firms in which you think you might like to work. Here is an example of a letter that will certainly make a favorable impression on the reader and invite a personal interview.

273 North College Avenue
Salida, California 95368
May 23, 19--

Mr. Ralph King, Personnel Manager
Perkins-Nash Engineering Company
Salida, California 95368

Dear Mr. King:

Mr. Frank Kern, of the Kern Insurance Agency, has suggested that I apply for a position as stenographer in your company. Mr. Kern, a friend of my family's for many years, has talked with me on a number of occasions about my future; and he has recommended your company as one of the most desirable in Salida.

Here is a brief resume of my education and experience:

<u>Education</u>: Graduate of Salida High School, June, 19--

Subjects: Typewriting--55 words a minute on straight copy. Able to set up letters, reports, and various kinds of business forms.

Shorthand--120 words a minute. Can transcribe accurately at the rate of about 30 words a minute.

English--have made good grades in English throughout high school. Enjoy writing compositions.

Other subjects--Bookkeeping, filing, office machines, business law, secretarial practice.

<u>Experience</u>: One year as part-time salesclerk at Peggy's Dress Shop on Saturdays and Christmas holidays.

Two summers as typist and receptionist for the Salida Real Estate Agency.

<u>References</u>: Miss Agnes Miller, Business Teacher, Salida High School
Mr. Fred Trayton, Manager, Salida Real Estate Agency
Mr. Frank Kern, Kern Insurance Agency, 21 Main Street, Salida

May I have an opportunity to come in to talk with you? Since I am in school during the day and cannot be reached by phone until after four o'clock, perhaps you would prefer to write me. If you do wish to telephone after four o'clock, my number is 476-1042.

Sincerely yours,

Susan Davis

Susan Davis

LESSON 75

Developing Shorthand Writing Power

736. WORD BEGINNINGS AND ENDINGS

-self, -selves

a

Over-

b

-hood

c

a. Yourself, myself, himself, herself, itself, themselves, ourselves, yourselves.
b. Overcome, overdue, overcharged, oversupply, overestimate, oversee.
c. Neighborhood, childhood, parenthood, brotherhood, likelihood, sisterhood.

Building Transcription Skills

737. BUSINESS VOCABULARY BUILDER

accessories Such items in a car as radios, clocks, etc.

credentials Documents that certify that a person is entitled to certain rights and privileges.

Progressive Speed Builder (120-140)

The letters in this Progressive Speed Builder range from 120 to 140 words a minute. If you can take these letters from dictation and read them back, you need not fear the dictation of any dictator, even the most rapid.

Remember, don't stop writing!

738. PREVIEW

739.

740.

741.

742.

743.

739. Representative, to supply, sedan, perfect, requirements, disposal, quote, confident.
740. Area, familiar, has been, delivery, schedule, let us know.
741. Satisfied, latest, features, engineers, superintendent, in addition, accessories, specifications.
742. News, committee, tested, payment, treasurer's, promise, we do not.
743. I am sure, by this time, congratulations, vitally, consequently, difficulties, develop.

LETTERS

(1 Minute at 120)

739. Dear Mr. Pace: Our representative, Mr. Green, has written us that you are in the market for 20 cars, as you plan to supply all your salesmen with company/automobiles.

We believe that our business sedan would be perfect for your requirements, and we should like to place one at your disposal so that you may judge the car for//yourself.

We are writing Mr. Green to ask him to make the necessary arrangements if you decide to accept our offer. Mr. Green is in a position to/// quote prices to you and to answer your questions.

We are confident that once you have driven our business sedan you will be sold on its merits. Sincerely yours, (1)

(1 Minute at 125)

740. Dear Mr. Klein: As Mr Green has written you, we are in the market for 20 cars for our salesmen in this area. We plan to have all our men drive company cars rather/than their own. I am familiar with your business sedan; in fact, my son, who is also a salesman, has been driving one for more than five years. He is well satisfied with it//and plans to trade it in for a late model soon.

If we should place an order for a fleet of 20 cars, we should like to have delivery by June 15. Would it be possible///for you to meet this delivery schedule?

As we plan to reach a decision within the next week or ten days, please let me know as soon as possible. Sincerely yours, (2)

(1 Minute at 130)

741. Dear Mr. Pace: I am happy to learn that your son has been driving one of our business sedans for the past five years and that he is so well satisfied with it that he plans to trade /it in on our latest model. I know that he will be delighted with the new features that our engineers have built into it.

I talked to the home office about a delivery//schedule for the 20 cars, and the superintendent assures me that we can easily have the cars ready and in driving condition by June 15 if you place your order within///the next two weeks. In addition, we can have any special accessories installed if you will give us specifications on the date that you place your order. Sincerely yours, (3)

(1 Minute at 135)

742. Dear Mr. Klein: I have good news for you. The order is yours. The committee that was appointed to decide on the make of car we should purchase for our 20 salesmen carefully considered/the merits of five different makes. They tested the cars in every possible way; and, on the basis of their study, they decided on your business sedan. We do not plan to// have special accessories.

If you will bring the necessary papers to my office, I will sign them. Payment for the cars will be made through our treasurer's office upon their delivery.///

We rely on your promise to have the cars ready on June 15, the day on which our sales meeting ends. After the sales meeting I should like the men to drive away in the new cars. Yours truly, (4)

(1 Minute at 140)

743. Mr. Green: As I am sure you know by this time, we have received the order for 20 cars from Mr. Pace. All the credit for this order is yours. Congratulations on a fine job of selling./

The superintendent at the home office assures me that the cars will be ready for delivery on June 15. It is vitally important that we keep that promise. I am leaving//on a long business trip in a few days; consequently, I shall not be able to follow up on this matter personally. Would you, therefore, take it upon yourself to see that the cars are ready///on time.

I believe, too, that you should plan to be present when Mr. Pace's salesmen receive the cars.

If any difficulties develop on this order, be sure to call me. Harvey B. Klein (5) (650)

Reading and Writing Practice

744.

o'ver·charged' al'ways ser

traf'fic lone'ly

intro

conj

iq par

and o

cre·den'tials peace nonr

ser

20 = 26 365 (189)

745.

ser

par

trav'el·ing
un·u'su·al

60 ser 70

50

par

intro

nonr

de·scribed'
neigh'bor·hood

conj

(184)

CHAPTER 16

Real Estate

LESSON 76

Developing Shorthand Writing Power

746. OUTLINE CONSTRUCTION

Omission of vowel in -in. The vowel in the unaccented word ending *-in* is omitted because its omission gives us a better outline.

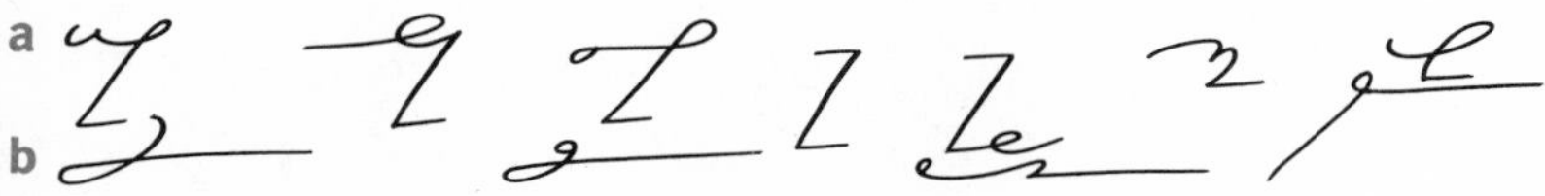

a. Origin, margin, imagine, engine, engineer, cousin, raisin.
b. Famine, examine, illumine, determine.

Word endings -ium, -eum, -dium. The word endings *-ium, -eum* are expressed by *em; -dium,* by the *dem* blend.

-ium, -eum

-dium

a. Uranium, chromium, premium, helium.
b. Auditorium, calcium, museum, gymnasium.
c. Radium, stadium, medium.

Building Transcription Skills

747. SIMILAR-WORDS DRILL

Prominent, permanent

prominent Noted; standing out.

He took piano lessons from a prominent musician.

permanent Not subject to change; lasting.

Before obtaining his present permanent position, he held a part-time job.

Reading and Writing Practice

748. Homes or Houses

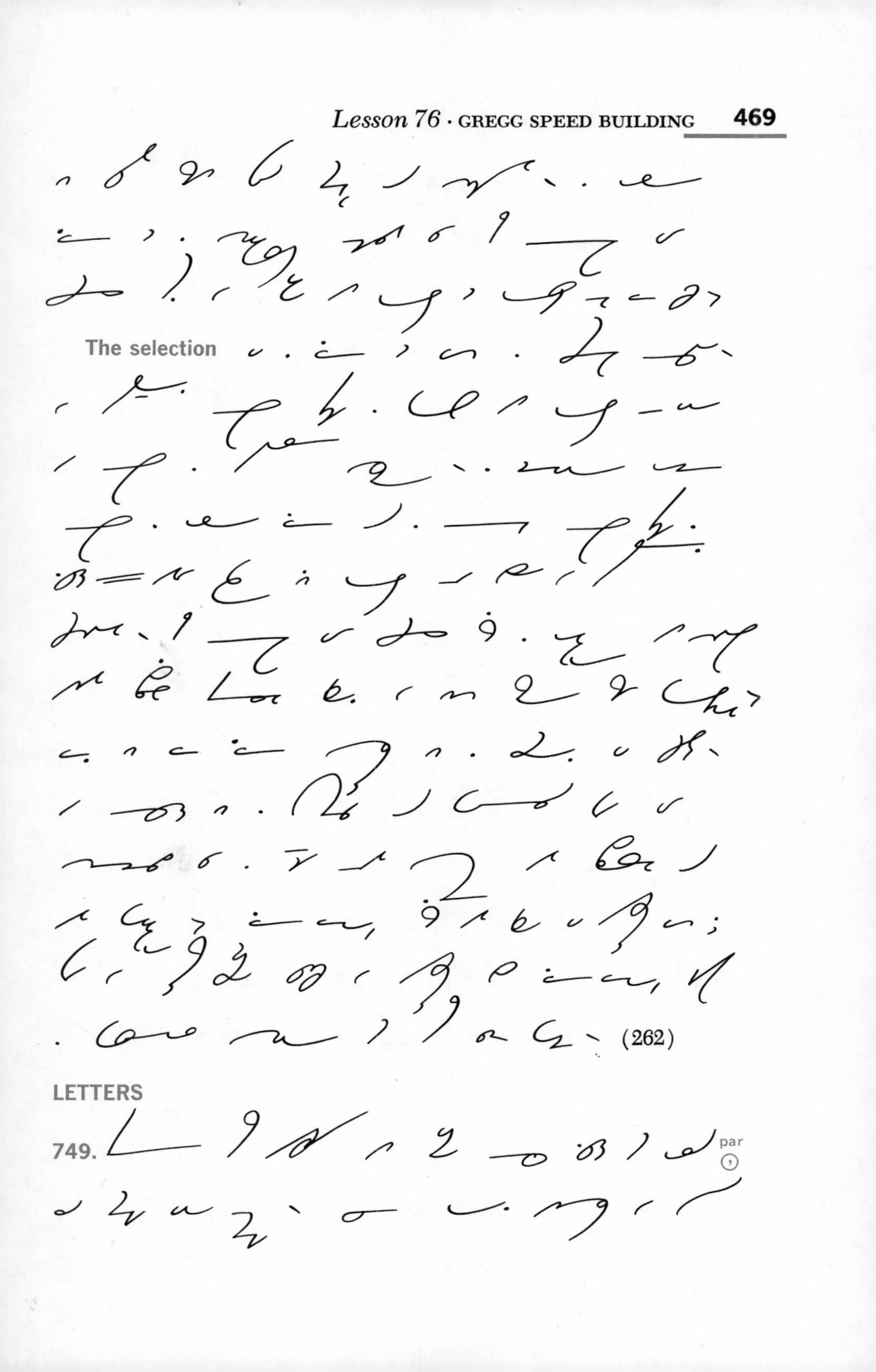

The selection

(262)

LETTERS

749.

par

two'-year' *hyphenated before noun*

if

op'tion mu·se'um

par

ser

Transcribe: $200 oc'cu·pan·cy

nc

wo

if

as

(163)

750.

prom'i·nent mu·si'cian

if

(83)

751.

isq

iq

iq

fac'tor
fam'i·ly's

intro

intro

ex·pe'ri·ence
fam'i·lies

intro

par

if

(163)

LESSON 77

Developing Shorthand Writing Power

752. RECALL DRILL — G

In this drill you will review the different uses of the alphabetic stroke *g*.

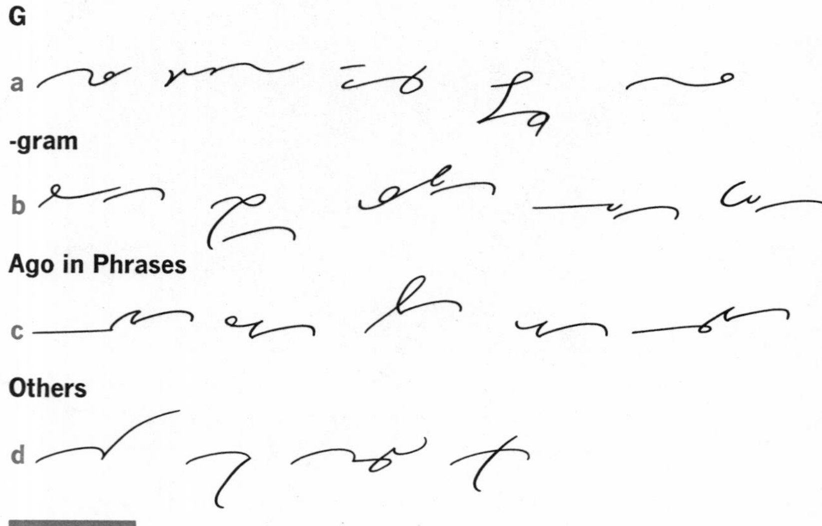

a. Greet, struggle, interrogate, navigation, gladly.
b. Telegram, cablegram, radiogram, monogram, program.
c. Months ago, years ago, days ago, hours ago, minutes ago.
d. Good time, good-by, good-natured, Great Britain.

Building Transcription Skills

753. ACCURACY PRACTICE

In this drill you will practice the joining of the diphthongs to the various alphabetic strokes of Gregg Shorthand.

a. Use, few, cute, continuation; how, now, loud.
b. Toy, oil, voice, loyal, soil, boil.
c. Tie, might, iron, pine, sign, dine, sight, silence.

Writing Practice

754. PREVIEW

755. Decided, recommend, reputation, construction, occupancy, meantime, inconvenience, as soon as possible, headway.
756. Has not been, experienced, materials, rectified, garage.
757. Specialists, Nebraska, $1,750,000, buyers, properties, represent, pertaining.

LETTERS

755. Gentlemen: As you know, last June 10 I decided to build a house, and I asked you to recommend a builder.[1] In view of the reputation of your real estate business, I felt that you were in a position to know who[2] would do the best job at the most reasonable price. You recommended the Brown Construction Company, and I[3] gave them the job.

When I signed the contract, I was promised that the house would be ready for occupancy by April[4] 20; and on the basis of that promise, I made arrangements to sell my present house by that time. The[5] Brown

Construction Company, however, did not meet the April 20 date; in fact, they now tell me that the[6] house will not be ready until July 1. In the meantime, my family and I have been living at a hotel[7] at considerable inconvenience and expense.

May I appeal to you to see what you can do to get[8] the house completed as soon as possible. I have been able to make no headway with the builder. Cordially yours,[9]

---

756. Dear Mr. Green: I am sorry that you have been inconvenienced by the fact that the Brown Construction Company[10] has not been able to meet its promise to have your house ready by April 20. I have talked to the [11] president, and he tells me that they experienced considerable trouble obtaining building materials;[12] but that situation has now been rectified.

He promises to place all available men on the job and[13] have them work overtime if necessary. He thinks that he will be able to have the house sufficiently finished[14] so that you and your family can move in about June 15. The garage will not be completed, and the[15] grounds will still need some work; however, these things can be done while you are living in the house.

I have personally visited[16] the house, and I am confident that you will be very happy with it when it is finished. Cordially yours,[17]

---

757. Dear Mr. Evans: Buying and selling farm land is our business. On our staff are 28 farm specialists, who[18] are located in 20 cities and towns of Nebraska and Iowa. These men have a combined sales record[19] of $1,750,000 since January 1. They are specially trained to give[20] down-to-earth advice in the selection and sale of a farm.

Our coverage makes it possible for us to bring[21] buyers from all parts of the country to see your property, often effecting a sale immediately. Therefore,[22] if you have a farm that you would like to sell, let us know; we can be of assistance to you.

We also offer[23] a wide selection of properties if you are interested in settling in another part of the country.[24] At the present time we have three farms in the heart of the corn belt that represent a wonderful investment.[25]

For anything pertaining to the purchase or sale of a farm, write us; we are at your service. Yours sincerely,[26] (520)

Reading and Writing Practice

758.

conj

per′ma·nent
es·pe′cial·ly

par

pref'er·a·bly
hour's
com·mut'ing

ac·com'mo·da'tions
tem'po·rar'y

conj

(155)

759.

ser

mind
neigh'bor·hood
shop'ping

par

enu

down'-to-earth'
hyphenated before noun

nc

wo

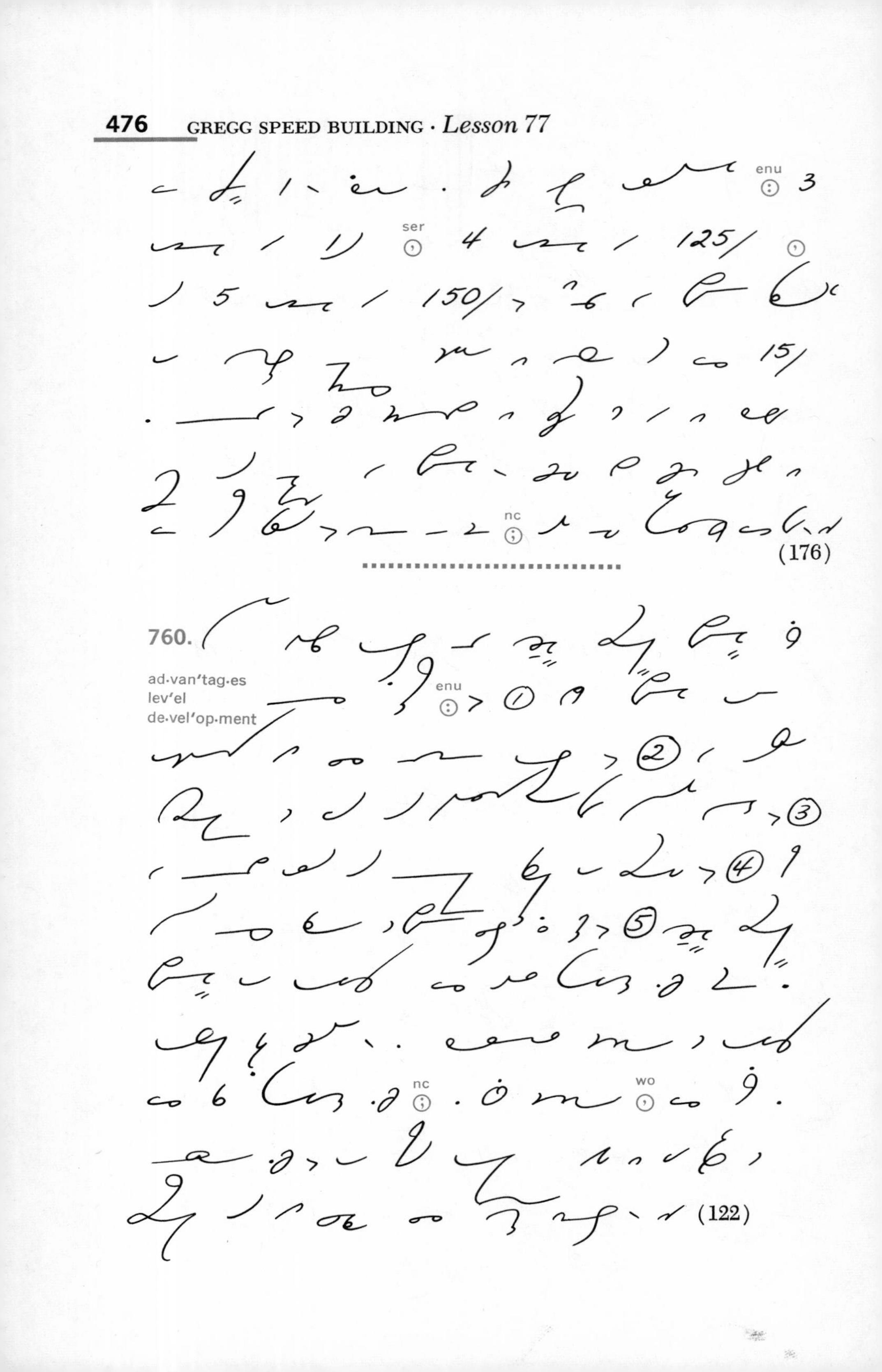

enu

ser

nc

(176)

760.

ad·van′tag·es
lev′el
de·vel′op·ment

enu

nc

wo

(122)

LESSON 78

Developing Shorthand Writing Power

761. WORD FAMILIES

-spect

a

-mination

b

a. Inspect, inspection, prospect, prospective, respect, respective, disrespect, aspect.
b. Determination, nomination, elimination, domination.

762. FREQUENT NAMES

Last Names

a

Men's First Names

b

a. Thomas, Walsh, Ward, Williams, Wood, Wright, Young.
b. Samuel, Stephen, Vincent, Walter, William.

Building Transcription Skills

763. BUSINESS VOCABULARY BUILDER

assigned Transferred title to property to another.

inclination A leaning toward.

heretofore Up to this time.

Writing Practice

764. PREVIEW

765. Has been, will you please, forwarded, mother-in-law.
766. Avenue, inspection, various, urge, layouts, someone, we shall be glad.
767. Spending, Chicago, furnished, highly, moderate, consequently, impossible, to make, journey.
768. Anniversary, first, understand, essential, family, effort, prospective, enabled, hesitate, whenever, assistance.

LETTERS

765. Gentlemen: You will be interested to know that Mrs. Watson's house on Market Street has been sold. The final[1] details of this transaction will be settled not later than January 31.

Will you please, therefore, make[2] out a statement of the rent account for this house. A copy need not be forwarded to Mrs. Williams, as she[3] has recently assigned her interest in this house to Mrs. Watson, her mother-in-law. Sincerely yours,[4]

---

766. Dear Mr. Turner: Floor plans for the new 24-story office building at 319 Fifth Avenue are[5] now ready for inspection. Floor space is available for offices of various sizes.

In the event[6] that you are considering changing your office location during the coming year, we urge you to inspect the[7] plans for the new building. Now is the time to make the special layouts required for the smooth operation of your[8] office.

There is someone in my office from 9 a.m. to 9 p.m. every day. If a representative[9] of your organization will call, we shall be glad to go over the building plans with him. Cordially yours,[10]

---

767. Dear Mr. Walsh: We are considering spending the months of February and March in Chicago if we can[11] find a small furnished house that will meet our needs. The Higgins Real Estate Company has sent me several prospects[12] that it highly recommends.

Would you be kind enough to examine these houses for me. I have received visiting[13] permits, which I am enclosing.

The rental that is asked is moderate – $40 a week. Consequently,[14] we do not expect too much in the way of furniture.

I realize that you are busy, but I am asking[15] you to do this because I find it impossible to make the journey to Chicago at this time. Cordially yours,[16]

---

768. Dear Mr. Ward: Today is our anniversary. Twenty years ago we opened the door of our real estate[17] office at First and Main Streets.

It is not difficult to understand that our profession is an interesting[18] and essential one. It helps to satisfy one of the strongest of man's desires – a plot of ground on which to build[19] a home for his family.

Realizing that a home is a major family investment, we have always made[20] every effort to provide each prospective homeowner with opportunities to obtain the home in[21] which he and his family would be happy. This policy has enabled us to make a host of friends during[22] our twenty years of operation.

We wish to thank you and the other homeowners whom we have served and to express[23] the hope that you will not hesitate to call on us whenever we can be of assistance. Yours sincerely,[24] (480)

Reading and Writing Practice

769.

ap·proached'
ac·quir'ing

when

par

worst
jus'ti·fied

nonr

intro

heed
re'al·ize

conj

rec'om·men·da'tions
coun'cil

nonr

(175)

770.

ap·pro'pri·ate
trus·tees'
fi·nan'cial

ap

debt
mort'gage

par

ser

bc

am'ply
re·pair'

intro

conj

dues
e·mer′gen·cies

nc

(194)

771.

con·sult′
suit′a·ble

conj

es·pe′cial·ly
heat′ing

ap

(89)

Developing Shorthand Writing Power

772. FREQUENT PHRASES

Able

a

Glad

b

a. You might be able, will be able, should be able, may be able, he will not be able, to be able.
b. We should be glad, I shall be glad, he will be glad, glad to hear, glad to have.

773. GEOGRAPHICAL EXPRESSIONS

(United States Cities in Order of Population—Concluded)

a

b

a. Dallas, New Orleans, Pittsburgh, San Antonio, San Diego, Seattle.
b. Buffalo, Cincinnati, Memphis, Denver, Atlanta, Minneapolis, Indianapolis.

Building Transcription Skills

774. BUSINESS VOCABULARY BUILDER

appraisal Estimate of value.

spacious Having plenty of room; large.

exterior The outside.

interior The inside.

Writing Practice

775. PREVIEW

776.

777.

778.

776. Appraisal, dwelling, engineers, exterior, interior, ordered, few days, confirms.
777. Minneapolis, Minnesota; suggested, Birmingham, possibilities, physical, $100.
778. Towns, hundreds, genuinely, thoroughly, we should be glad, appointment, necessary.

LETTERS

776. Dear Mrs. James: Let me take this opportunity to explain to you our delay in sending you an appraisal[1] of your dwelling. On February 2 one of the insurance company engineers and I went to[2] your house to make an appraisal. You were not at home, but we were able to make an appraisal by measuring[3] the exterior of the house and estimating the value of the interior.

I did not send this appraisal[4] to you immediately because it was much higher than you had estimated. I therefore ordered another[5] appraisal from another company and had hoped to receive it within a few days, That appraisal has[6] just arrived, and it confirms the first one.

In view of these facts I suggest that you increase your insurance to cover[7] the new value placed on your house. If you will call me, I will prepare a new policy for you. Cordially yours,[8]

777. Dear Mr. Clay: Our home

office in St. Paul has asked us to obtain for them certain information about the[9] property at 40 Central Avenue, Minneapolis, Minnesota. Mr. Brown, the manager,[10] suggested that you might assist us in this matter. You may recall that some years ago your organization[11] assisted us in a similar matter in Birmingham, Alabama. What we should like to have is a report[12] from a Minneapolis real estate firm on its opinion of the present market value and sales[13] possibilities of the property. We should also like to have its opinion of the physical condition of[14] the building and the approximate cost of any repairs that might be needed.

For similar reports we[15] have paid a fee of $100. We should be glad to pay the same fee for this report.

When the work is[16] completed, please send the report and bill to me at 312 North Street, Chicago 16, Illinois. Sincerely yours,[17]

---

778. Dear Mr. Wells: Are you interested in selling your home? If you are, why not let us handle the sale for you?[18] Here are a few good reasons why we are in a position to help you sell it at a good price:

1. We have four[19] offices in four of the largest towns in the county. Hundreds of people seeking to buy homes go to these[20] offices each week.
2. Your home will be shown only to those who are genuinely interested in purchasing[21] a house and who are able to pay the price you ask.
3. Our staff consists only of men who have had considerable[22] experience in selling homes in this county and who thoroughly understand the real estate field. These[23] men will be glad to inspect your house and tell you frankly the price that you may expect to receive for it should you[24] place it on the market. There is no charge for this service.

Our office is open from 8 a.m. to 10 p.m.[25] every day. We should be glad to have you visit us. No appointment is necessary. Yours sincerely,[26] (520)

Reading and Writing Practice

779.

as

par

ad'ver·tis'ing
com·mis'sion

bc

conj

intro

(139)

780.

intro

intro

(80)

781.

past

mod'el

ser

vis'i·tors

spa'cious

enu

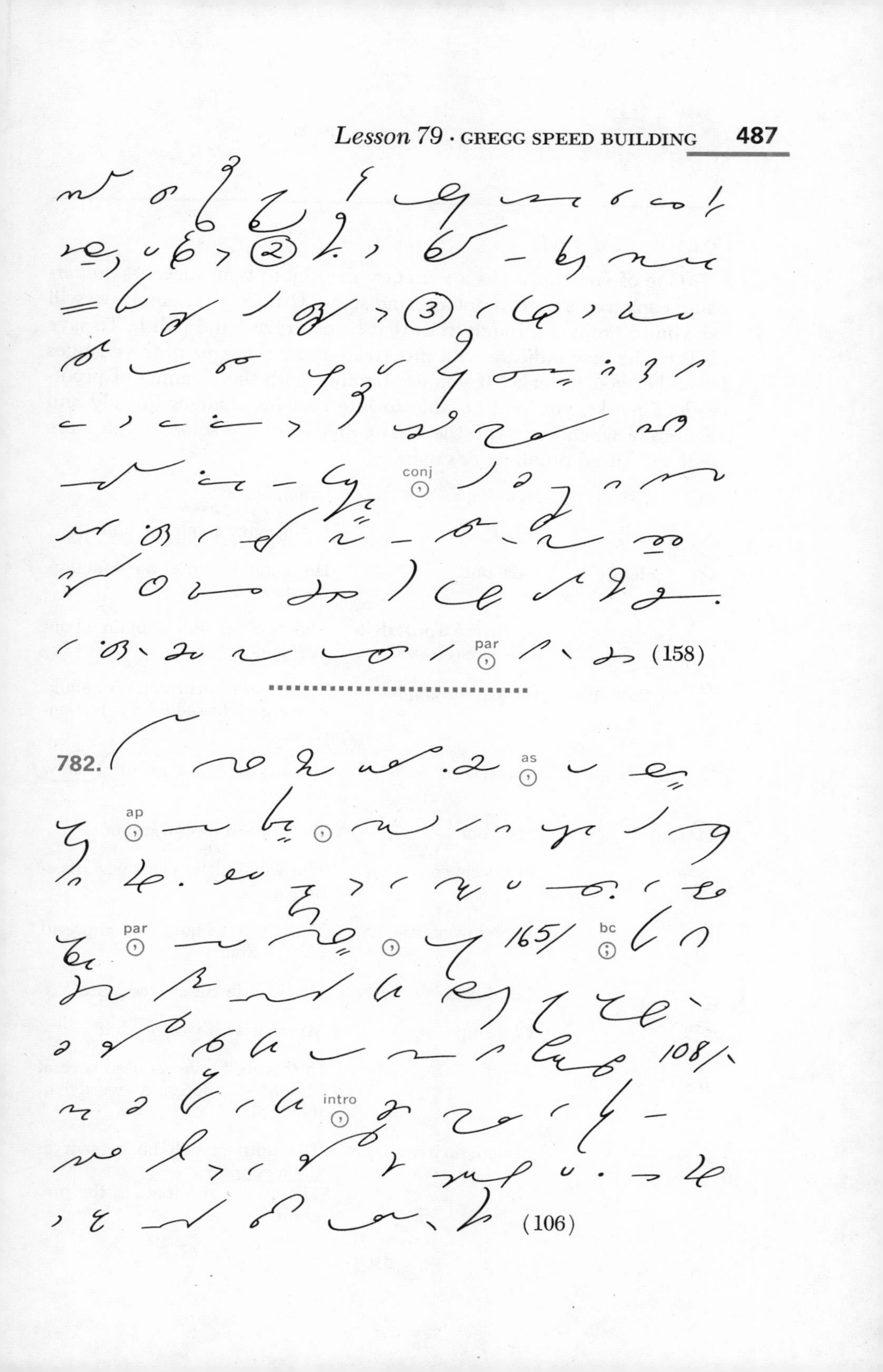

(2) (3) conj par (158)

782. as ap par bc intro (106)

SECRETARIAL TIP

Proofreader's Marks

One of your duties as a secretary may be to type speeches, advertising copy, reports, memoranda, and so on. Usually your employer will ask you to prepare a rough draft that he can revise and polish. To save his time, he may indicate with proofreader's marks some of the changes he wishes you to make. If you are familiar with the meaning of proofreader's marks, you will be able to interpret his changes quickly and accurately when you type the final copy. Here are some of the more frequently used proofreader's marks:

Mark	*Meaning*	*Example*
^ (caret)	Insert	I will, of course, make room for him.
(delete)	Take out	He cannot come ~~on Monday,~~ January 15.
..... (stet)	Retain the words that have been crossed out	The booklet will contain about ~~120~~ pages.
¶ (paragraph)	Insert paragraph	The order is incorrect. ¶ We should investigate to see who is responsible.
tr	Transpose	He was told to carefully follow all instructions.
○ sp	Spell out	The speech took (6) minutes.
#	Insert space	The value ofthe work was questioned.
lc	Type lower case	The United States is comprised of fifty States.
≡	Capitalize	He lived in the united states.
⁀	Close up	My visit was worth while.
//	Align	In this study we counted several hundred thousand words of material.
⁀	Run in; no paragraph	The authors will be present at the meeting. They will participate in the program.

HOW TO USE NOTES IN REVIEWING

Notes are virtaully indispensable in reviewing and preparing for examinations. An even more permanent value of notes is that they serve as a "memory Storehouse" for you; They are al ways available to refresh your thinking, your recall, your memory.

USING YOUR NOTES IN REVIEWING

Reviewing is a worth while process in learning. We tend to forget what we learn, and reviewing is an effective means of relearning. In addition through reviewing we often learn things that were not learned--or only partially learned--the first time.

Notes are an invaluable source of material for reviewing, whether they were made from reading a book, from a discussion, or from listening to a lecture.

Review your notes promptly. By reviewing notes promptly, you need less time to relearn and to fix previous learning. Also, notes can be "filled in," if need be, with pertinent bits of information, comments, facts, or ideas that were omitted when the notes were first made. reviewing promptly also givesyou an opportunity to change the content or organization of your notes while they are still fresh in mind.. For example, a point made in the latter part of a lecture may have significant bearing on a point made in the early part of the lecture.

Be sure that you organise your notes carefully. One effective system is to make your notesin outline form. Leave lots of space around yournotes so that you can make insertions latter if you have to.

A page of manuscript illustrating the use of proofreader's marks.

LESSON 80

Developing Shorthand Writing Power

783. WORD BEGINNINGS AND ENDINGS

-ship

a 

Mis-

b 

For-, Fore-

c 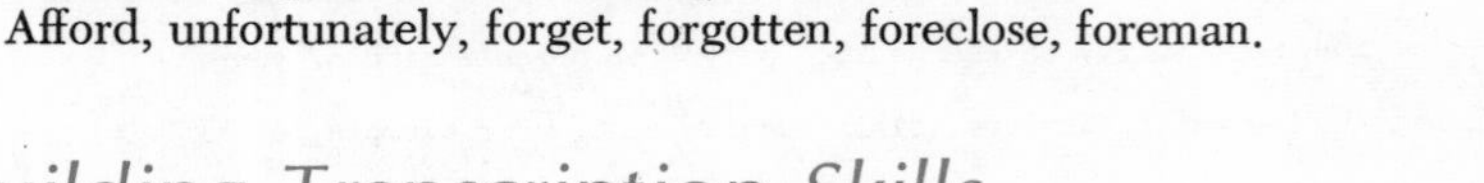

a. Relationship, authorship, ownership, partnership, leadership, township.
b. Mistake, misplace, mislead, misprint, misfortune.
c. Afford, unfortunately, forget, forgotten, foreclose, foreman.

Building Transcription Skills

784. BUSINESS VOCABULARY BUILDER

acceptance Approval; favorable reception.

incumbent Necessary.

Progressive Speed Builder (120-140)

785. PREVIEW

786. 

786. Possibility, summer, might have, children, available, anxious, to make, appreciate.
787. Occupies, directly, one of them, satisfactorily, $600, Saturday, five o'clock, to show.
788. Almost, request, away, apartment, young, college, acceptance, rental.
789. Perfectly, in the past, thoroughly, ordered, delivered, under these, I should be glad.
790. Thank you for, promptly, attends, weekends, incumbent, entitled, forward.

LETTERS

(1 Minute at 120)

786. Dear Mr. Gates: I am considering the possibility of renting a cottage on Lake Pleasant for the coming summer vacation. I understand from some friends/of mine that you have cottages to rent on Lake Pleasant and that you might have something that will meet our needs.

My family consists of my wife, two small children, and myself.//We should like to have a fairly large cottage with at least five rooms.

If you have any cottages available for the months of July, August, and September that would///meet our needs, please let me know.

As I am anxious to make final plans for our vacation, I should appreciate it if you would let me hear from you soon. Sincerely yours, (1)

(1 Minute at 125)

787. Dear Mr. Brown: As your friends have told you, I do have some cottages to rent on Lake Pleasant. I own five cottages, one of which my family occupies every summer./I rent all the others.

All the cottages are directly on the lake.

One of them, I think, will meet your requirements satisfactorily. It has four rooms, but one of them is// very large and can be divided into two rooms by a screen if necessary.

For the months of July, August, and September, the rental is $600.

I plan///to be at Lake Pleasant on Saturday, March 10, until five o'clock. If you would like to drive up on Saturday, I should be happy to show you the cottage. Sincerely yours, (2)

(1 Minute at 130)

788. Dear Mr. Gates: Thank you for showing my wife and me your cottages on Lake Pleasant.

We have almost decided to take the four-room cottage for the summer. There is one request we/should like to make, however.

As my family will be away for the summer, we shall not be using our apartment in the city. We have, therefore, decided to rent it to a//young man who is attending college in New York during the summer and who would like to have his family with him. His college term starts on June 15, and he would like to have our///apartment on that date.

Would it be possible for us to move into the cottage on June 15? If so, you may consider this letter our acceptance of the rental. Sincerely yours, (3)

(1 Minute at 135)

789. Dear Mr. Brown: It will be perfectly satisfactory to me to have you move into the cottage on June 15. However, it has been my practice in the past to use the period/from June 15 to July 1 to have the cottages thoroughly cleaned and to make any necessary repairs. If you wish to move into the cottage and take care of the cleaning//yourself, I shall be glad to let you have it for those two weeks for $50.

There is one other point. A canoe comes with the cottage. I have ordered a new one for the coming summer,///but it will not be delivered until July 1.

If you are willing to move into the cottage on June 15 under these conditions, I should be glad to have you do so. Sincerely yours, (4)

(1 Minute at 140)

790. Dear Mr. Gates: Thank you for writing me so promptly about the possibility of our moving into your cottage on June 15.

Since I wrote you, however, the young man who was going to/rent our apartment in the city has changed his plans and decided to leave his family at home while he attends college. He plans to visit his family on weekends. Therefore, it is no longer//incumbent upon us to leave our apartment on June 15. In addition, the prospect of cleaning up the cottage does not appeal to my wife, who feels that she, too, is entitled to///a vacation!

I am enclosing my check for $300. I understand that the remaining $300 is due when we move in.

We are looking forward to the summer. Sincerely yours, (5) (650)

Reading and Writing Practice

791.

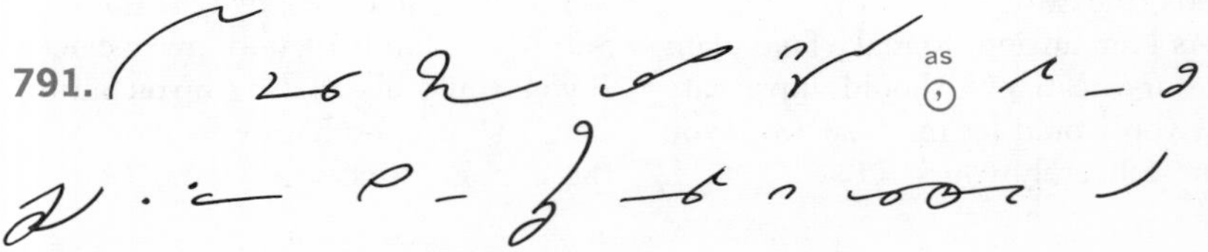

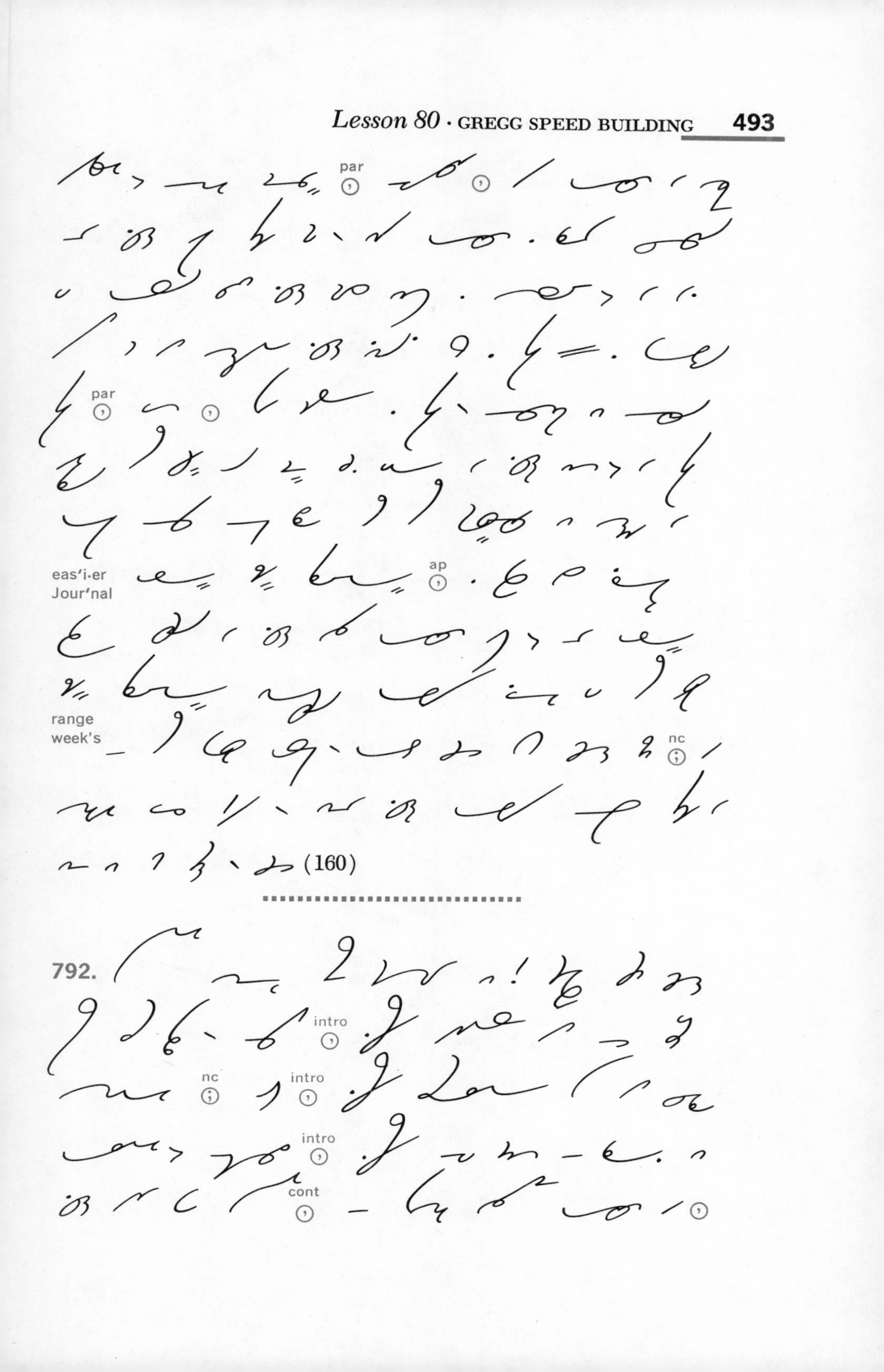

par

par

eas'i·er
Jour'nal

ap

range
week's

nc

(160)

792.

intro

nc

intro

intro

cont

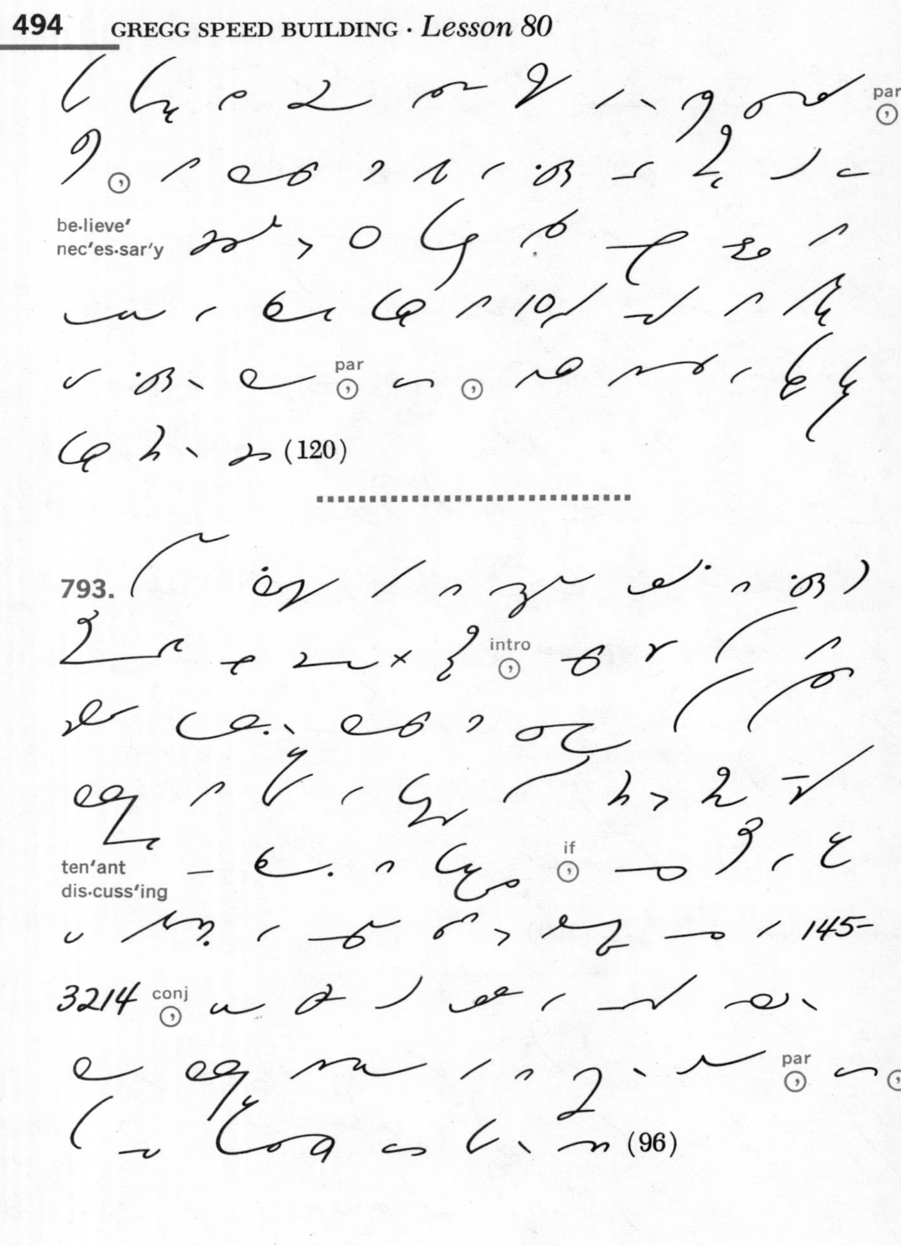
par
be·lieve'
nec'es·sar'y
par
(120)
793.
intro
ten'ant
dis·cuss'ing
if
145-
3214
conj
par
(96)

APPENDIX

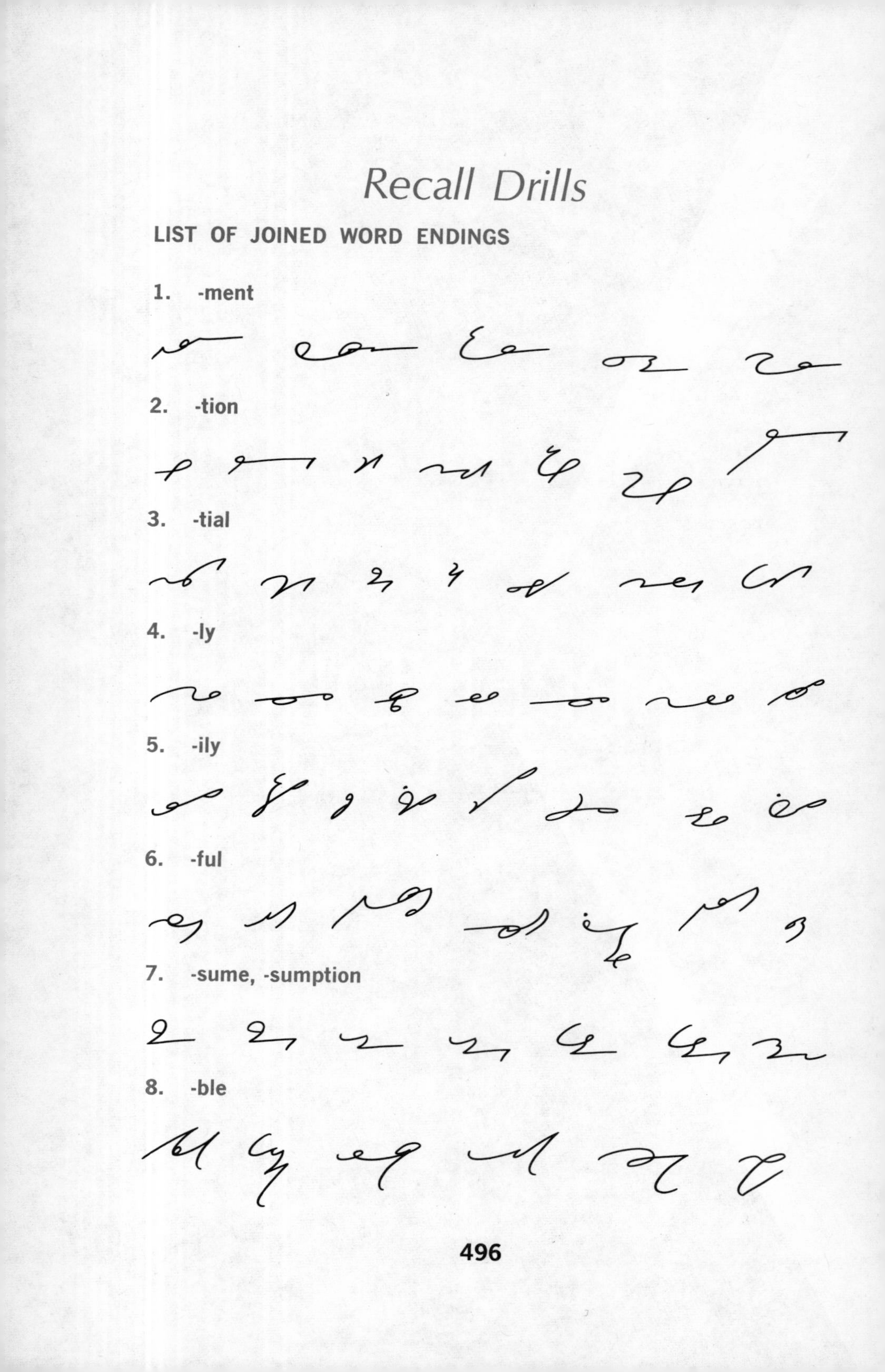

Recall Drills

LIST OF JOINED WORD ENDINGS

1. -ment

2. -tion

3. -tial

4. -ly

5. -ily

6. -ful

7. -sume, -sumption

8. -ble

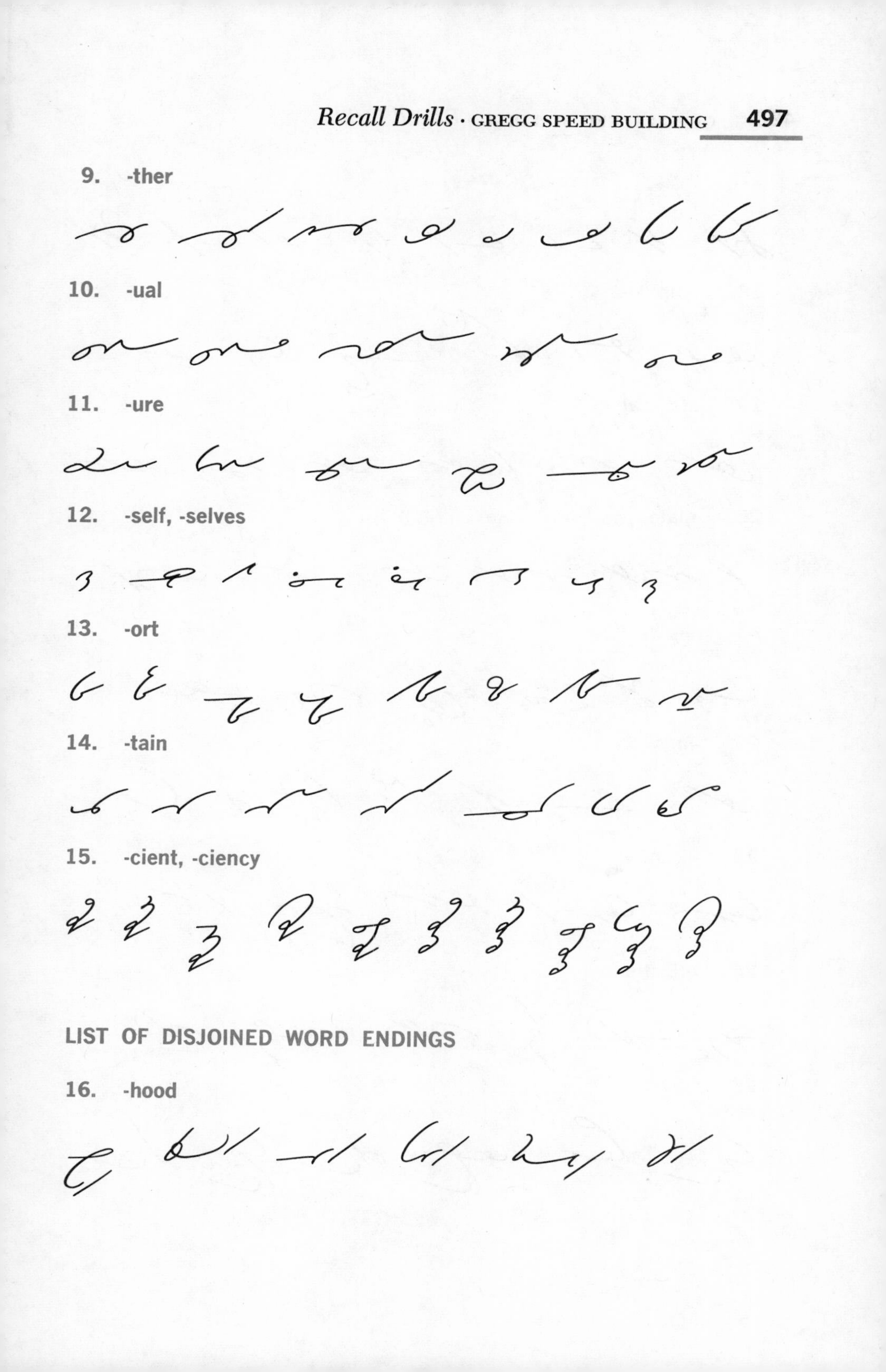

9. -ther

10. -ual

11. -ure

12. -self, -selves

13. -ort

14. -tain

15. -cient, -ciency

LIST OF DISJOINED WORD ENDINGS

16. -hood

17. -ward

18. -ship

19. -cle, -cal

20. -ulate

21. -ingly

22. -ings

23. -gram

24. -ification

25. -lity

26. -lty

27. -rity

LIST OF JOINED WORD BEGINNINGS

28. Per-, Pur-

29. Em-

30. Im-

31. In-

32. En-

33. Un-

34. Re-

35. Be-

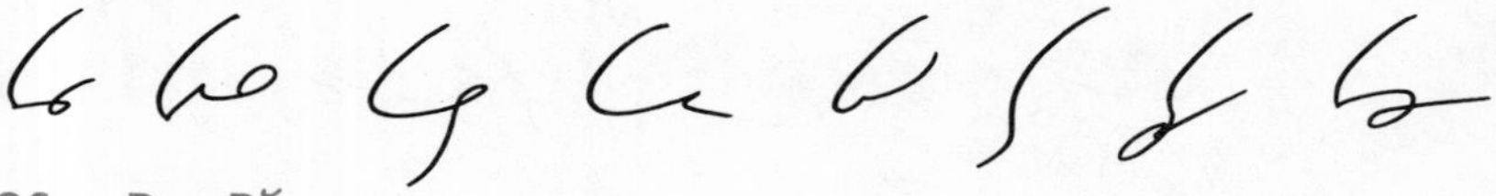

36. De-, Dĭ-

37. Dis-, Des-

38. Mis-

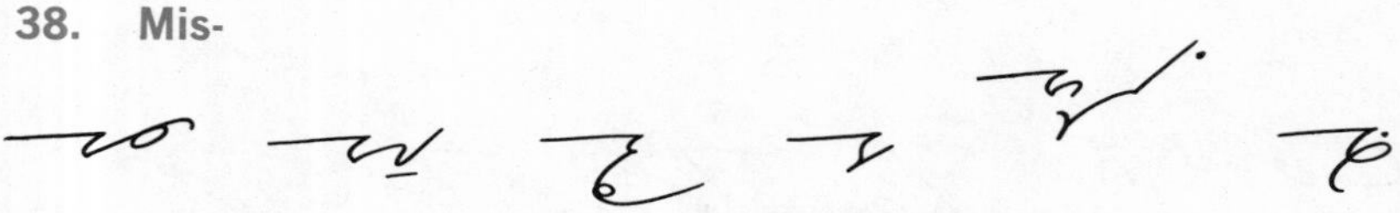

39. Ex-

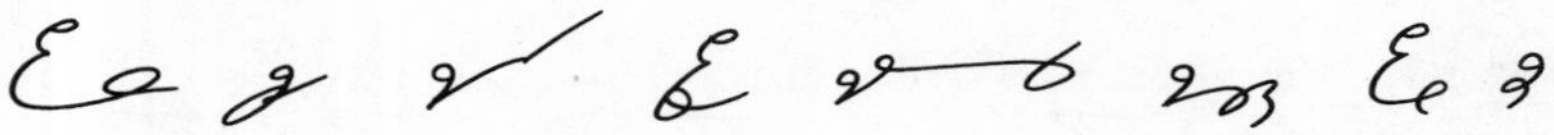

40. Com-

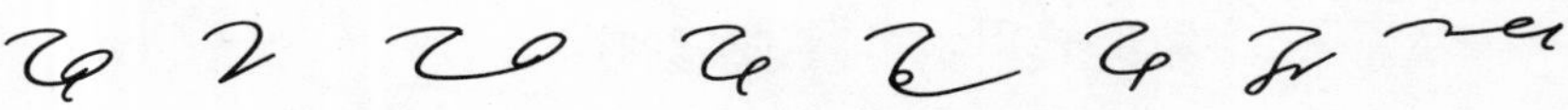

41. Con-

42. Sub-

43. Al-

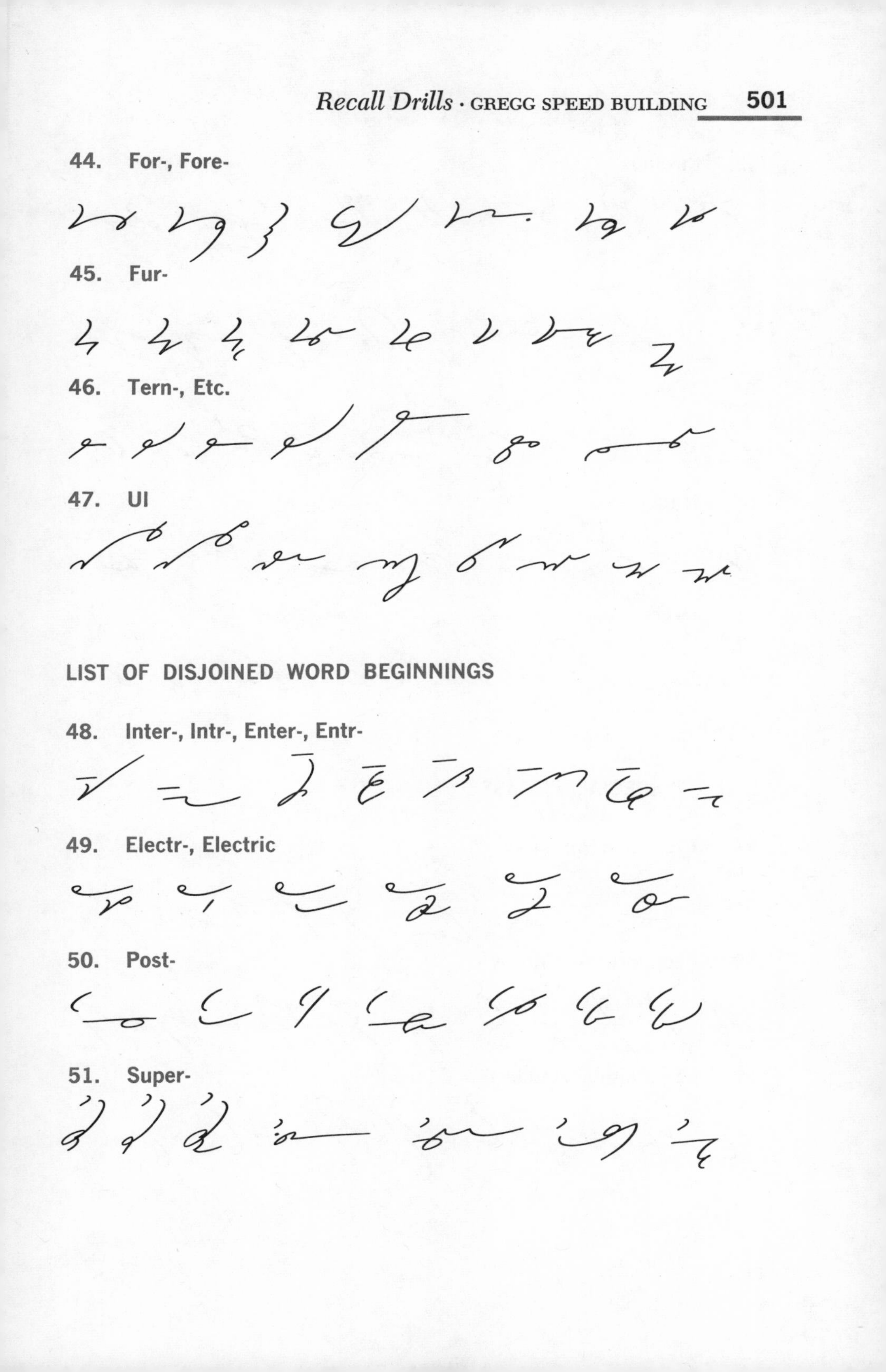

44. For-, Fore-

45. Fur-

46. Tern-, Etc.

47. Ul

LIST OF DISJOINED WORD BEGINNINGS

48. Inter-, Intr-, Enter-, Entr-

49. Electr-, Electric

50. Post-

51. Super-

52. Circum-

53. Self-

54. Trans-

55. Under-

56. Over-

LIST OF SPECIAL PHRASES

57. T for To in Phrases

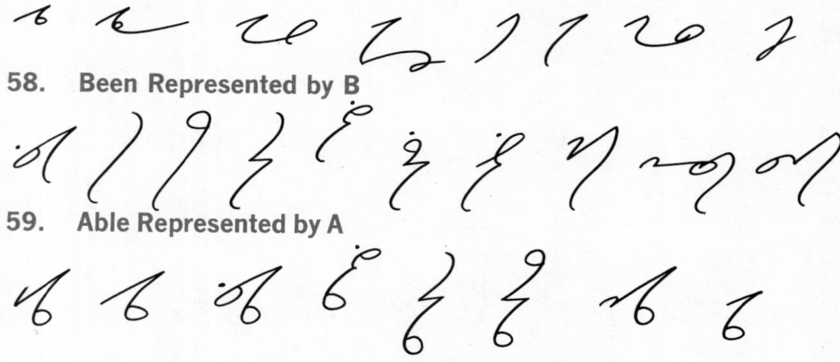

58. Been Represented by B

59. Able Represented by A

60. Want Preceded by Pronoun

61. Ago Represented by G

62. To Omitted in Phrases

63. The Omitted in Phrases

64. Of Omitted in Phrases

65. A Omitted in Phrases

66. Intersected Phrases

67. Special Phrases

Addresses to Be Used for Mailable Transcripts

(The numbers of the following names and addresses correspond to the numbers of the supplementary letters in the *Instructor's Handbook to Gregg Speed Building, Diamond Jubilee Series.)*

Chapter 1

1. Baker and Company, 416 Leonard Avenue, Phoenix, Arizona 85012
2. Mr. James C. Day, Ellis Book Company, Inc., 416 Wilson Avenue, Tucson, Arizona 85714
3. The National Jewelry Corporation, 315 Church Street, Little Rock, Arkansas 72201
4. The Arkansas Advertising Company, Inc., 424 Oxford Road, North Little Rock, Arkansas 72114
5. Mr Charles H. Mason, California Recording Company, 1980 Valencia Road, Berkeley, California 94700
6. Mr. J. C. Graham, The Baker Company, 361 Park Avenue, New York, New York 10016
7. Mr. James S. Fairfield, Fresno Real Estate Corporation, 318 Spring Street, Fresno, California 93700
8. Memorandum from Mr. J. J. Barnes to Mr. C. C. Green
9. Mr. John H. Smith, Andrews Jewelry Store, 450 North Hartwell Street, Long Beach, California 90805
10. Memorandum from John C. Gray to Mr. James Green

Chapter 2

11. Mr. Ralph J. Pryor, The Thomas Manufacturing Company, 416 Broad Street, Pueblo, Colorado 81009
12. Mr. Frank L. Davis, The West Side Insurance Agency, 316 Market Street, Denver, Colorado 80205
13. The Connecticut Insurance Company, 316 State Street, Bridgeport, Connecticut 06604
14. The Hartford Life Insurance Company, 416 Ridge Road, Hartford, Connecticut 06104
15. Mr. Charles J. Burke, 316 Indian Road, Greenwich, Connecticut 06830
16. Mr. Andrew J. Grace, The Baker School, 481 Harris Avenue, Dover, Delaware 19901
17. The Acme Insurance Company, 1800 Northern Avenue, Wilmington, Delaware 19807
18. Miss Jane C. Oxford, 607 River Street, Clearwater, Florida 33515
19. Mr. William C. Baker, 31 Prescott Avenue, Jacksonville, Florida 32201
20. Mr. Kenneth E. Gates, 198 Howard Avenue, Miami, Florida 33116

Chapter 3

21. Mr. Frank L. Jones, President, Wilson Products Company, 333 Houston Street, New York, New York 10077
22. First National Bank, 316 Parker Road, Macon, Georgia 31204

23. Mr. D. A. Smith, Brown Printing Company, 361 Peach Tree Road, Atlanta, Georgia 30310
24. Mr. Carl C. Mack, 31 Davis Avenue, Boise, Idaho 83701
25. Mr. James C. Clark, 316 Washington Avenue, Rockford, Illinois 61106
26. Miss Agnes A. Cooper, 500 Park Avenue, Chicago, Illinois 60612
27. Mr. Harvey L. Green, 461 South Street, East St. Louis, Illinois 60202
28. Mr. Harlan C. Casey, Casey and Jones, 188 Parsons Street, Rock Island, Illinois 61204
29. Mr. A. J. Riley, 1270 Amherst Street, Anderson, Indiana 46012
30. Miss Janet J. Fleming, 47 Scott Avenue, Ft. Wayne, Indiana 46805

Chapter 4

31. Mrs. Charles H. Brown, 316 West 18 Street, Terre Haute, Indiana 47802
32. Mrs. J. J. Graham, The Central Food Company, 418 Fulton Street, Des Moines, Iowa 50304
33. Mr. Paul J. Green, Green's Supermarket, 315 Garden Lane, Kansas City, Kansas 66109
34. Mr. Edward C. Jones, 43 Osage Street, Topeka, Kansas 66616
35. Mr. James L. Smith, Baker's Supermarket, 21 West Street, Wichita, Kansas 67205
36. Miss Alice C. Green, East High School, Louisville, Kentucky 40202
37. Mrs. Paul L. Bass, 615 Pine Street, Birmingham, Alabama 35206
38. Mrs. Stephen J. Baker, 610 De Soto Boulevard, Montgomery, Alabama 36107
39. Mr. C. C. Gray, 540 South Central Avenue, New Orleans, Louisiana 70110
40. Mr. Frederick J. West, American Products Company, Inc., 46 Mill Street, Bangor, Maine 04402

Chapter 5

41. Mr. Frederick J. Mills, 432 Country Road, Portland, Maine 04104
42. The American Typewriter Company, 24 Clinton Street, Baltimore, Maryland 21205
43. Mr. C. K. Adams, American Insurance Company, 808 Fanning Street, Hagerstown, Maryland 21740
44. Mr. J. J. Baker, David and Smith, Inc., 47 Florence Street, Boston, Massachusetts 02104
45. Mr. L. C. Green, The Ellis Publishing Company, 620 Franklin Street, Boston, Massachusetts 02111
46. Mr. William A. Duffy, Crane Motor Company, 98 Laurel Lane, Fall River, Massachusetts 02725
47. Mr. Eugene J. East, The National Rubber Company, 1361 State Street, Lynn, Massachusetts 01901
48. Mr. Ralph C. Davis, The Texas Air Conditioning Company, 61 East Alamo, Houston, Texas 77012
49. Mr. Louis A. Grace, Butler and Company, 380 Hillside Avenue, Lansing, Michigan 48903
50. Mr. Mathew L. West, Home Appliance Company, 38 Jackson Street, Muskegon, Michigan 49440

Chapter 6

51. Mr. Charles J. Palmer, Wilson Department Stores, Inc., 26 Wheeler Street, Roanoke, Virginia 24011
52. Miss Mary Gray, West Side High School, 415 Fifth Street, Richmond, Virginia 23205
53. Mr. David G. Green, 406 South State Street, Petersburg, Virginia 23801
54. Mr. Clifford L. Davis, 43 Mill Road, Burlington, Vermont 05403
55. Mr. Joseph C. Green, National Construction Company, Inc., 1366 Avenue J, Salt Lake City, Utah 84105
56. Memorandum from Mr. John R. Jones to Mr. Robert C. Baker
57. Mr. Roy C. West, 361 Stone Street, Ogden, Utah 84400
58. Memorandum from Mr. L. C. Gray to Mr. J. C. West
59. Mr. Wilson C. Brown, The Elwood Supply Company, 1588 Post Road, Waco, Texas 76700
60. The Jackson Department Store, 448 Parker Avenue, Lubbock, Texas 79412

Chapter 7

61. Mrs. Charles R. Gates, 336 Terrace Lane, Memphis, Tennessee 38108
62. Mrs. Henry J. Star, 1451 Post Road, Knoxville, Tennessee 37906
63. Mr. Edward C. Parks, 184 Granite Boulevard, Greenville, South Carolina 29604
64. Mr. C. C. Roy, 26 Southern Parkway, Charleston, South Carolina 29404
65. Mrs. Henry L. Chase, 1214 Fourth Avenue, Pittsburgh, Pennsylvania 15217
66. Mrs. Edgar C. Smith, 214 Gateway Road, Philadelphia, Pennsylvania 19106
67. Mrs. William C. Bond, 15 Garden Lane, Indiana, Pennsylvania 15701
68. Mrs. George A. Blair, 2400 Harper Avenue, Birmingham, Alabama 35210
69. The Stevens Construction Company, 100 Barton Street, St. Louis, Missouri 63105
70. Mr. Lawrence J. Macy, 115 Palmer Avenue, Helena, Montana 59601

Chapter 8

71. Mr. Frederick G. Davis, 161 West Street, Newark, New Jersey 07109
72. Mr. John R. Baker, Station WBBC, 215 Market Street, Newark, New Jersey 07160
73. Memorandum from Mr. J. J. Brown to Mr. C. J. Parker
74. The National Supply Company, 900 Greeley Avenue, Elizabeth, New Jersey 07201
75. Miss Mary C. Harper, 242 Locust Street, Shelbyville, Indiana 46176
76. Mr. James R. Casey, 426 Central Avenue, Winfield, Kansas 67156
77. Mr. William M. Star, American Products Company, Inc., 47 Church Road, Kansas City, Missouri 64107
78. Mr. Stephen P. Bell, New London Television Company, New London, Connecticut 06301
79. Memorandum from Mr. A. J. Barnes to Mr. C. C. Grace
80. Memorandum from Mr. C. C. Grace to Mr. A. J. Barnes

Chapter 9

81. Professor James L. Casey, University of Connecticut, Storrs, Connecticut 06268
82. Mr. Harry J. Richards, 146 Westminster, London WC 1, England
83. Miss Jane Kline, South Side High School, Des Moines, Iowa 50314
84. Mr. Elwood C. Pair, University of Tennessee, Knoxville, Tennessee 37906
85. Mr. Robert C. Gray, 1810 Continential Avenue, Superior, Wisconsin 54883
86. Mr. Eugene C. James, 432 Alamo Avenue, Houston, Texas 77016
87. Mr. Homer H. Pace, 111 Valley Road, Hutchinson, Kansas 67505
88. Mr. Gerald C. Gray, 643 Randolph Street, Nashville, Tennessee 37205
89. Mr. Frederick C. Crane, 80 North Clinton Street, Racine, Wisconsin 53405
90. Mr. Donald L. James, The American Insurance Company, 720 Weber Street, Harrisburg, Pennsylvania 17118

Chapter 10

91. Mr. Basil W. Smith, Wilson College, 614 Hartwell Avenue, Cincinnati, Ohio 45240
92. Mr. Kenneth C. Best, Editor, The Western Publishing Company, 211 Newton Street, Little Rock, Arkansas 72209
93. Memorandum from Mr. C. L. Smith to Mr. J. C. James
94. Mr. David L. Smith, Nelson, Graves and Company, 1400 Maine Street, Minneapolis, Minnesota 55407
95. Memorandum from James L. Green to the staff
96. Mr. Louis A. Green, The American Telephone Company, 240 South Wilson Avenue, Rochester, Minnesota 55907
97. The New Jersey Telephone Company, Ridgewood, New Jersey 07450
98. Mr. Richard C. Gray, Lynn & Carey, Inc., 15 Park Place, Trenton, New Jersey 08609
99. Mr. C. C. Smith, 31 Prescott Avenue, Omaha, Nebraska 68109
100. Memorandum from James R. Baker to the staff

Chapter 11

101. Mr. Harlan J. Macy, 198 Howard Avenue, Hyattsville, Maryland 20780
102. Memorandum from Mr. Harvey L. Thomas to Mr. C. C. Jones
103. Mr. Raymond G. East, National Products Company, 66 State Street, Chicago, Illinois 60612
104. Mrs. Mary C. Green, 861 Fifth Avenue, Tampa, Florida 33608
105. Mr. Sherman L. Davis, 312 West 67 Street, Harrison, New York 10528
106. Miss Helen C. Gates, 861 Central Avenue, Yonkers, New York 10708
107. Doctor Charles L. Gray, Dean, Wilson College, Chapel Hill, North Carolina 27514
108. Mrs. Mary C. Fenton, 473 Raleigh Street, Burlington, West Virginia 26710
109. Mr. Harry J. James, 180 East 76 Street, New York, New York 10046
110. The Clark Clothing Company, 316 Lakewood Drive, Elkhart, Indiana 46514

Chapter 12

111. American Paper Company, 80 South Park Place, Augusta, Maine 04302
112. The Philadelphia Book Company, 188 Market Street, Philadelphia, Pennsylvania 19106
113. Mr. Robert G. Clayton, Gray Publishing Company, 15 West Street, San Francisco, California 94108
114. Mr. John L. Barnes, The National Book Company, 321 Fourth Avenue, Mt. Vernon, New York 10553
115. Mr. Russell C. Bass, The Bell Publishing Company, 3615 Davis Avenue, Covington, Kentucky 41011
116. Memorandum from Mr. J. C. Smith to Mr. J. L. Green
117. Mr. Ellis C. Davis, Baker Publishing Company, 41 West 8 Street, New Orleans, Louisiana 70105
118. Mr. Chester J. Jeffrey, The Davis Book Company, Inc., 64 Washington Avenue, Lake Charles, Louisiana 70602
119. Mr. William J. Deems, 450 Brewer Street, Boston, Massachusetts 02105
120. Mr. John C. Klein, 710 Praline Street, Lake Charles, Louisiana 70604

Chapter 13

121. Mr. James R. West, The Davis Manufacturing Company, 81 Monroe Street, Chicago, Illinois 60604
122. Memorandum from Mr. J. C. Green to Mr. A. R. Jones
123. Memorandum from Mr. James R. Smith to the staff
124. Mr. William L. Evans, Parkside Paper Company, 450 Chestnut Street, Philadelphia, Pennsylvania 19104
125. Memorandum from Mr. A. R. Brown to Mr. C. J. Smith
126. Mr. Elmer C. Jones, Crane Manufacturing Company, 2600 Broad Street, Fairview, New Jersey 07022
127. Mr. J. C. Roy, The Baker Printing Company, 21 North Michigan Avenue, Chicago, Illinois 60604
128. Mr. J. C. Roy, The Baker Printing Company, 21 North Michigan Avenue, Chicago, Illinois 60604
129. Doctor Charles R. Brown, 321 Indian Field Road, Greenwich, Connecticut 06830
130. Mr. L. R. Walsh, Greenwich Travel Agency, 61 Putnam Avenue, Greenwich, Connecticut 06830

Chapter 14

131. Mr. Harry L. Green, Advertising Manager, Home Appliance Company, 385 Hillside Avenue, Hudson, New York 12534
132. Memorandum from Mr. J. H. Brown to Mr. Charles R. Hogan
133. Mr. Joseph C. Riley, 414 Graham Street, Mt. Vernon, Ohio 43050
134. Mrs. Elizabeth J. Smith, 416 East Main Street, Moline, Alabama 36604
135. Miss Nancy J. Baker, 550 Park Avenue, Boston, Massachusetts 02115
136. Mr. Hugh C. Kelly, 41 Davis Avenue, Lima, Ohio 45805
137. Mr. Wilson J. Case, President, Starlight Clothing Company, Inc., 52 Harding Place, Springfield, Illinois 62708
138. Mr. J. C. Duffy, 561 Western Avenue, Detroit, Michigan 48207

139. Mr. C. J. Smith, Editor, Electrical News, 421 Southern Boulevard, Dallas, Texas 75206
140. Mr. Harry L. Curtis, Vice President, American Products Company, 316 Davis Avenue, Dallas, Texas 75204

Chapter 15

141. Mr. James C. Black, 451 Pennsylvania Avenue, Washington, D. C. 20023
142. The Master "8" Agency, 531 Constitution Avenue, Washington, D. C. 20016
143. Mr. Harry H. Day, The Day Automobile Service, Inc., 631 Wheeler Street, Elizabeth, New Jersey 07201
144. Mr. Wilson J. Scott, 10 Norton Drive, Charleston, South Carolina 29401
145. Memorandum from Mr. J. C. Smith to Mr. A. C. Nelson
146. Memorandum from Mr. A. C. Nelson to Mr. J. C. Smith
147. Mr. Henry L. Harper, 370 South Park Place, Memphis, Tennessee 38104
148. Mrs. James A. Smith, 2600 Broad Street, Petersburg, Virginia 23801
149. Mr. C. C. Baker, 83 Jefferson Street, Niagara Falls, New York 14307
150. The New York Automobile Club, 366 Fifth Avenue, New York, New York 10038

Chapter 16

151. Mr. James R. Mann, 74 Worth Street, Waterbury, Connecticut 06701
152. Mr. J. L. Harris, The Westfield Real Estate Company, 104 Oak Lane, Westport, Connecticut 06880
153. Captain James R. Smith, 361 West End Avenue, Fort Lee, New Jersey 07024
154. Mr. Frederick C. Gray, 361 Shore Road, Wilkes Barre, Pennsylvania 18704
155. Mr. Harvey J. Riley, 186 Crane Road, Scarsdale, New York 10583
156. Mr. J. C. Davis, 316 Wilson Boulevard, Lincoln, Nebraska 68507
157. The Atlanta Real Estate Corporation, 36 Peach Tree Road, Atlanta, Georgia 30306
158. Mr. Joseph C. Blair, 51 Orchard Lane, Atlanta, Georgia 30301
159. Mrs. John C. Larry, 680 Clark Street, Orlando, Florida 32811
160. Mrs. Harvey L. Cummings, 361 Pine Street, Springfield, Illinois 62709

Index

The number next to each entry refers to the page in the text in which the entry appears.

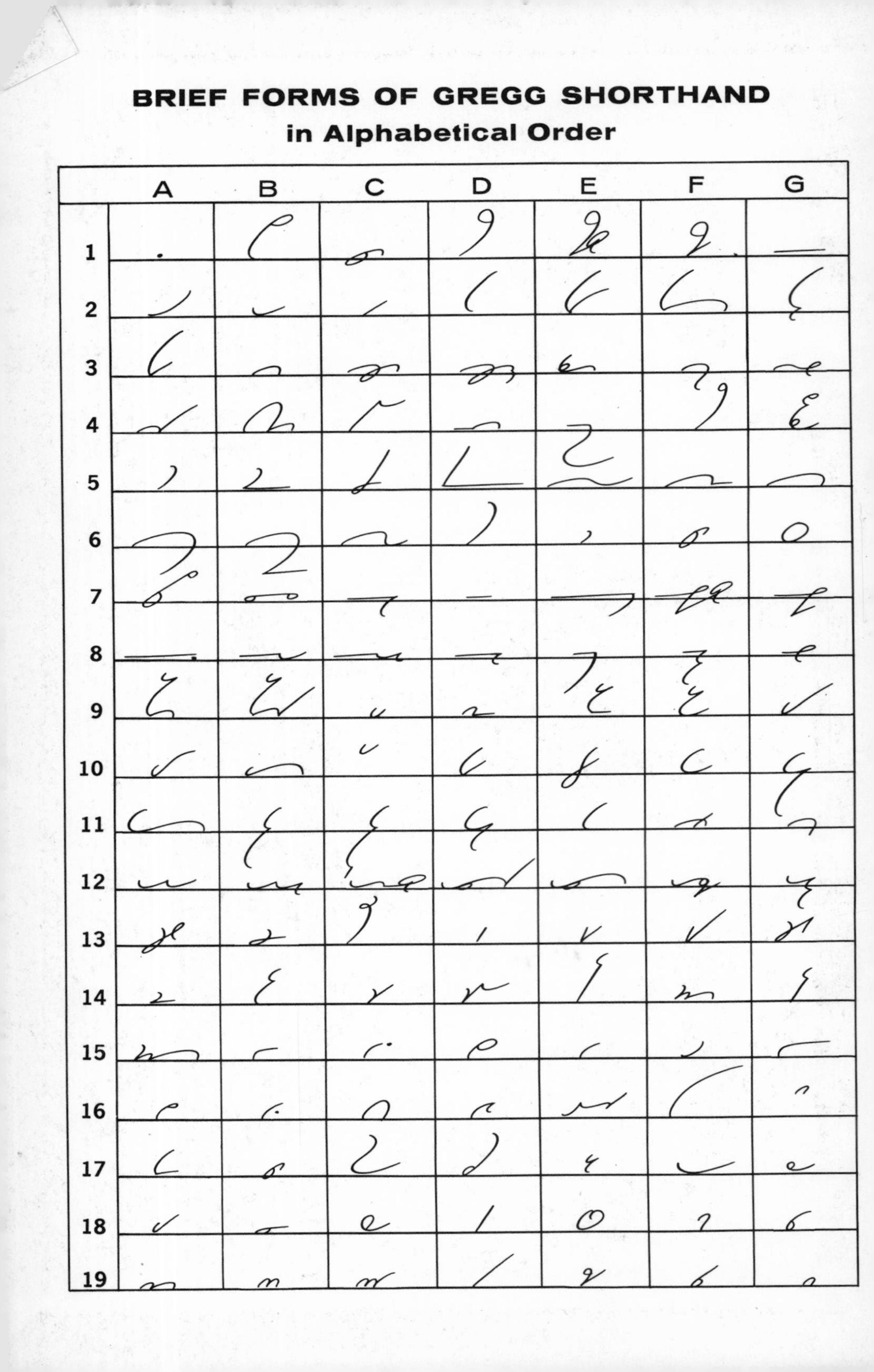

BRIEF FORMS OF GREGG SHORTHAND
in Alphabetical Order

	A	B	C	D	E	F	G
1							
2							
3							
4							
5							
6							
7							
8							
9							
10							
11							
12							
13							
14							
15							
16							
17							
18							
19							